Dimos Spatharas
**Emotions, persuasion, and public discourse in classical Athens**

# Trends in Classics –
# Supplementary Volumes

---

Edited by
Franco Montanari and Antonios Rengakos

Associate Editors
Stavros Frangoulidis · Fausto Montana · Lara Pagani
Serena Perrone · Evina Sistakou · Christos Tsagalis

Scientific Committee
Alberto Bernabé · Margarethe Billerbeck
Claude Calame · Jonas Grethlein · Philip R. Hardie
Stephen J. Harrison · Richard Hunter · Christina Kraus
Giuseppe Mastromarco · Gregory Nagy
Theodore D. Papanghelis · Giusto Picone
Tim Whitmarsh · Bernhard Zimmermann

# Volume 83

Dimos Spatharas

# Emotions, persuasion, and public discourse in classical Athens

---

Ancient Emotions II

DE GRUYTER

*Ancient Emotions*, edited by George Kazantzidis and Dimos Spatharas within the *Trends in Classics. Supplementary Volumes* series, investigates the history of emotions in classical antiquity, providing a home for interdisciplinary approaches to ancient emotions and exploring the interfaces between emotions and significant aspects of ancient literature and culture.

ISBN 978-3-11-076332-4
e-ISBN (PDF) 978-3-11-061817-4
e-ISBN (EPUB) 978-3-11-061842-6
ISSN 1868-4785

Library of Congress Control Number: 2019941260

**Bibliographic information published by the Deutsche Nationalbibliothek**
The Deutsche Nationalbibliothek lists this publication in the Deutsche Nationalbibliografie; detailed bibliographic data are available on the Internet at http://dnb.dnb.de.

© 2021 Walter de Gruyter GmbH, Berlin/Boston
This volume is text- and page-identical with the hardback published in 2019.
Editorial Office: Alessia Ferreccio and Katerina Zianna
Logo: Christopher Schneider, Laufen
Printing and binding: CPI books GmbH, Leck

www.degruyter.com

For Μαριλού and the 'boy'

# Preface

Although the importance of emotions for persuasion is salient in Western literature as early as Homer and although in recent years the history of emotions has become a sub-filed of Classics, the interfaces between persuasion and emotions have not as yet attracted the scholarly attention that they deserve. Modern commentaries fairly commonly employ the term 'appeal to emotion' (traditionally treated as a type of logical fallacy), but do not explain how audiences' sentiments can be the object of 'psychological manipulation'. 'Appeals to emotions' are not the equivalent of magic spells. Succinctly put, speakers cannot elicit emotional responses by virtue of the inherent causality of the words that they use. The use of the term 'appeal to emotion' reflects the culturally potent assumption that emotions are 'irrational', disruptive jolts rather than a cognitive phenomenon. Emotions can, of course, lead to irrational or inexpedient action and affect or distort our judgments, but in order to fully understand their uses in rhetoric, we need to familiarize ourselves with their 'rationality'. This book challenges the view that the rhetorical uses of emotions resist rational interpretation and proposes possible ways of exploring their role in persuasion. Yet, because the Greeks understood that persuasion (*peitho*, sometimes with a capital *P*) is not just a matter of words, my analysis addresses instances in which emotions intersect with non-verbal means of persuasion –especially the emotive potentialities of vision. As the prominence of direct, lustful gazes in modern advertisements indicates, non-verbal persuasion (and its emotive potentialities) is a phenomenon that permeates our modern cultures –albeit in culturally specific ways.

Quite naturally, this book is not an all-encompassing interpretation of emotions' implications for persuasion or rhetoric in antiquity. The literary material discussed here derives mostly from the fifth and fourth centuries BC. Although I treat a number of individual emotions, my goal is primarily to suggest methods of analysis which may facilitate our understanding of the literary, social, and cultural contexts in which persuasion is either theoretically discussed by ancient authorities or is practiced by public speakers in different settings. I also turn my attention to unsystematic, unscientific models of emotions, because these models reflect the different ways in which the ancient cultures or societies that attract our attention understood the interfaces between human sentiments and persuasion. Lastly, by focusing my attention to the uses of emotions in the public discourse of (especially) classical Athens, I emphasize possible ways in which the study of emotions can serve as a heuristic tool that enables us to look into potent cultural understandings and ideological assumptions.

Over the past years, I have accrued more intellectual or personal debts than I could possibly hope to repay. It is an honour to be able to acknowledge some of them here. My Glasgow PhD thesis on Gorgias was supervised by the late Douglas M. MacDowell. Although he would perhaps take issue with my reading of emotions and the book's 'psychological jargon', I have learned much from him on rhetoric and the orators. Costas Apostolakis, Loukia Athanassaki, Ewen Bowie, Douglas Cairns, Nick Fisher, Brenda Griffith-Williams, and Victoria Wohl read earlier versions of my work or earlier drafts of individual chapters and offered invaluable suggestions and criticism. They bear no responsibility for the remaining mistakes, obscurities, and shortcomings of this book, for which I alone must apologize. I am also indebted to the audiences of the seminars or conferences where I presented parts of this book. I also wish to thank warmly my colleagues in Crete, especially the members of the Division of Classics: my academic career in Crete can plausibly be described as a process of continuing education. I am also grateful to the anonymous readers for their useful suggestions and corrections. I also extend my warmest thanks to Eleni Mosiou for helping me compile the indices. Last but not least, I would like to thank the general editors of the series *Trends in Classics*, Professors F. Montanari and A. Rengakos, and George Kazantzidis, my co-editor in the sub-series *Ancient Emotions* (who also offered to comment on drafts of the Introduction), for their generous support.

D.S.

* * *

Chapter 4 is a revised version of a chapter that appeared as "Φθόνος ρητορική και lifestyle." In: *Ιδιωτικός βίος και δημόσιος λόγος στην ελληνική αρχαιότητα και στον Διαφωτισμό*, edd. L. Athanassaki, A. Nikolaidis, and D. Spatharas, 89–136, Crete University Press, Herakleion. My anaysis of Meidias' luxury (chapter 4, section 4) appeared as "The Mind's Theatre: Envy, Hybris and *Enargeia* in Demosthenes' *Against Meidias*." In: *The Theatre of Justice: Aspects of Performance in Greco-Roman Oratory and Rhetoric*, edd. S. Papaioannou, A. Serafim, B. Da Vela, 201–222, Brill: Leiden/Boston. A shorter version of chapter 5 appeared as "Self-praise and Envy: From Rhetoric to the Athenian Courts," *Arethusa* 44.2 (2011): 199–219.

# Contents

Preface —— VII

Introduction: Persuasion, rhetoric, and the theory of emotions —— 1
Preliminaries —— 1
*Peitho*, visuality, and emotions —— 3
Emotions, cognitions, and rhetorical argument —— 8
Outline of the book —— 21

| | |
|---|---|
| 1 | **Vision and emotions in Gorgias —— 24** |
| 1.1 | Preliminaries —— 24 |
| 1.2 | Vision and the generation of emotions in the *Encomium of Helen* —— 26 |
| 1.3 | Emotions, vision, and cognitive impairment —— 38 |
| 1.4 | The fabrication of likenesses: visual arts, speech, and emotions —— 43 |
| 1.5 | Helen's eyes, Gorgias' *epideixis*, and the poets —— 52 |
| | |
| 2 | **Vision and collective emotions in Thucydides: *eros*, *pothos*, and anger —— 57** |
| 2.1 | Introductory notes —— 57 |
| 2.2 | Pericles' lovers of the city —— 61 |
| 2.3 | Lovers of sights: *eros*, *pothos*, and vision —— 65 |
| 2.4 | Archidamus, vision, and anger —— 72 |
| 2.5 | Conclusions —— 78 |
| | |
| 3 | ***Enargeia*, emotions, and violence in forensic storytelling —— 80** |
| 3.1 | Forensic narratives: some preliminary observations —— 80 |
| 3.2 | Forensic narratives and Athenian courts —— 84 |
| 3.3 | *Enargeia*, verisimilitude, and emotions —— 89 |
| 3.4 | *Enargeia*, emotions, and stories about violence —— 94 |
| 3.5 | Conclusion —— 122 |
| | |
| 4 | **The ideological uses of 'legitimate envy' in classical Athens —— 123** |
| 4.1 | Introduction —— 123 |
| 4.2 | Equalities, inequalities, and the envy of the *hoi polloi* —— 129 |
| 4.3 | The democratization of envy: 'indignation' and democratic ideology —— 135 |

4.4    Meidias' lifestyle: spectacles of luxuriousness and legitimate envy —— 148

5     **Self-praise and envy in rhetoric and the Athenian courts —— 159**
5.1    Introduction —— 159
5.2    Self-praise and envy —— 160
5.3    Self-praise and envy avoidance strategies —— 166
5.4    Self-praise and cooperation in classical Athens —— 172
5.5    Conclusion —— 187

**Afterword —— 189**

**Bibliography —— 193**
**Index Rerum et Nominum —— 211**
**Index Auctorum Antiquorum et Locorum —— 215**

# Introduction: Persuasion, rhetoric, and the theory of emotions

## Preliminaries

In recent years, emotions have attracted significant scholarly attention in the field of Classics, even as, of course, emotions were always pivotal to the study of the literature, ethics, and cultures of antiquity. The burgeoning literature on the topic of ancient emotions indicates, among other things, that our understanding of Greek and Roman passions has been enhanced by interdisciplinary approaches. The conclusions of experimental and cognitive psychology, philosophy, and linguistics have been applied to the study of ancient emotions, thereby providing a better understanding of the cultures that attract our attention and their literary products. The prominence of emotions in ancient rhetorical theory and practice, the topics in which this book finds its focus, is obvious to any reader who takes the time to engage even in a cursory reading of the oratory or the rhetorical treatises of ancient times. The situation is no different in modern political communication and public speaking. Barack Obama's 2008 campaign, for example, invested in the most passionate aspects of hope, while the fear of terrorism shapes the political agenda, and, hence, the public discourse, in several modern countries.[1] At the same time, the place and appropriateness of emotions in the dispensation of justice, an issue that Aristotle treats in his *Rhetoric*, is fervently discussed by legal theorists and ethical philosophers.

Despite the importance of emotions for the art of persuasion, the topic remains under-explored.[2] A number of recent studies focus on the role of individual emotions in the Attic orators: 'social emotions', such as anger, pity, and envy, take pride of place in the relevant bibliography;[3] two recent studies explore systematically the forensic uses of a less obvious candidate, disgust, in Aeschines

---

[1] There is no definitive answer to the question of whether 'hope' is a member of the category emotion. For a discussion of the topic, see Cairns 2016, who also shows how hope and fear affected the public discourse about Scotland's independence. Fear and hope have also been pivotal to Greek politics during the ongoing debt-crisis. Ancient 'hope' (ἐλπίς and *spes*) is discussed in Kazantzidis/Spatharas 2018.
[2] But a recent volume (2016) edited by Sanders and Johncock includes contributions on persuasion and emotions in the orators and other literary genres.
[3] On envy, see Cairns 2003, Fisher 2003, and Sanders 2014; pity is discussed among others by Hall 1995; Konstan 2001; Tzanetou 2005; Sternberg 2005 and 2006; for a good discussion of anger in forensic oratory, see Rubinstein 2004; see also Allen 2000 and Harris 2017 (whose treatment,

https://doi.org/10.1515/9783110618174-001

and Demosthenes;[4] and an earlier paper focused on remorse and repentance (μεταμέλεια) in the Attic orators.[5]

In view of the importance of emotions for persuasion, *pathopoiia* figures predominantly in traditional scholarly discussions of individual orators and commentaries on their speeches. However, as I argue below, more systematic approaches to emotions have helped us explain in a more nuanced way their deployment in the extant speeches of the orators and their implications for pivotal aspects of the study of rhetoric, such as *hypocrisis* (*actio*), forensic storytelling, or the notion of *enargeia*.[6] Furthermore, because the orators seek to attain persuasion through verisimilitude, manipulation of emotions requires the construction of emotional scenarios centering on mainstream rather than peripheral ethical or social appraisals. For this reason, the uses of emotions in the orators serve as a heuristic tool that helps us understand with better hopes of accuracy the values privileged by the societies and the cultures that we study. This is particularly so, because, on account of the communicative qualities of emotions – including verbal and non-verbal means of signification–, the values that inform the appraisals that give rise to individual sentiments acquire notable salience.[7]

This book is about emotions and persuasion (especially visual *peitho*) in classical antiquity. The chapters that it comprises discuss verbal and non-verbal forms of persuasion and the points at which these types of persuasion intersect. The emotions to which I turn my attention are mainly *eros* (and *pothos*), envy, anger, and pity. The broader themes that I address are the intersections between visuality, emotions, and persuasion in folk and scientific models of understanding in the prose of classical antiquity, forensic narratives, *enargeia* and emotions, and the role of emotions –especially envy– in the sometimes difficult relationship between prominent individuals and the community.

---

however, does not take into account recent advancements in the study of emotions). Negative emotions in general are discussed by Sanders 2012. On anger and pity, discussed in chapter 3 of this book, see Rubinstein 2013.

4 Fisher 2017a and Spatharas 2017.

5 Fulkerson 2004.

6 On *hypocrisis*, see the recent volume by Papaioannou *et al.* 2017; see also Hall 1995 and Fantham 2002; on styles of delivery in connection with speakers' ethos, see Worman 2008: ch. 5; on performance and the orators, see Serafim 2017. Forensic storytelling is under-explored, but see Edwards 2004a–e; Spatharas 2009; and Kapparis 2017 on Apollodorus (further bibliography is provided in chapter 3 of this book); a forthcoming volume (coedited by M. Edwards and D. Spatharas) focuses on forensic narratives in Athenian courts. On *enargeia* and emotions, see Webb 1997 and 2009.

7 On the significance of social norms in the cognitions that give rise to emotions, see Konstan 2006: 22–24.

There is, of course, much more work to be done on emotions and persuasion. But if it is appropriate for an author to encourage specific modes of reading, I would suggest that this moderately sized contribution to the topic reflects my concern about methodological questions and possible answers that these questions may afford. I hope, however, that my emphasis on methodological aspects which, in my view, are central to the study of emotions in ancient oratory and rhetoric, will compensate for the *brevitas* and selectivity of my analysis. I also hope that my emphasis on theoretical and methodological questions will not elicit nauseating effects to readers who are impatient with theoretical approaches.

In the ensuing sections of this Introduction, I discuss theoretical issues indicating the main contours of my approach to emotions. I, therefore, focus on the relationship between non-verbal persuasion and emotions, the importance of cognitive approaches to emotions for the study of oratory and rhetoric, and the ways in which emotion studies can enhance our understanding of the social and ideological contexts in which the extant speeches were delivered. I also provide brief summaries of individual chapters, which may guide readers to their sense of which aspects of this book are more akin to their interests.

## *Peitho*, visuality, and emotions

First things first: In ancient Greek, *peitho* has a wider semantic range than 'rhetoric' and, therefore, Greek 'persuasion' encompasses phenomena for which rhetoric would be an inadequate, restrictive description. At the same time, however, any attempt to draw a clear-cut distinction between *peitho* and rhetoric and apply it to our evidence would be an exercise in conceptual clarity rather than a task that fits the cultural models of classical antiquity (see discussion below). But unlike rhetoric, roughly designating the systematic study of discursive means of persuasion, *peitho's* broader semantic field enlists different types of non-verbal means of persuasion which are normally excluded from systematic approaches to 'rhetoric' –with the possible exception of *hypocrisis*. Examples of non-verbal means of persuasion (or, for that matter, deception)[8] in Greek literature include, among other things, bribes,[9] gifts (as is commonly the case with male homoerotic communication), physical contact or gestures, perfumes, nudity –for example

---

**8** On the ambiguity of the relationship between *apate* and *peitho*, see Buxton 1982: 64.
**9** In some uses πειθώ is a metonymy for 'bribe', see *LSJ* s.v. A.II.2.

Helen's exposure of her breasts (in E. *Andr.* 627–30, Ar. *Lys.* 155–156)–, and displays of wealth.[10] Furthermore, as visual evidence shows, *peitho* sometimes appears as a personified entity (*Peitho*), especially in the frame of erotic narratives.[11]

These visual representations of the concept have their counterparts in ancient literature where, for example, erotic *peitho* is sometimes equated with an overpowering external force.[12] The blurring of the limits between *peitho* and necessity, compulsion, or violence in these uses is a typical aspect of *eros'* conceptualization as an external, overpowering force that overwhelms its targets. In addition, the notional identification of *peitho* with compulsion or violence in the frame of erotic communication also points to the wider problematization of *peitho's* role in political contexts, where *peitho's* power is sometimes explicitly or implicitly identified with violence. In a passage from Pindar's *Pythian* 4, for example, Medea is presented as the victim of magic and, through Jason's agency, of persuasion's lash (μάστιξ πειθοῦς, 216–219).[13] The oxymoronic identification of *peitho* with violence in this context contrasts with more typical normative uses of the concept, according to which *peitho* is a civilized and, hence, bloodless way of dealing with disputes, indeed a distinctive characteristic of humanness.[14]

The interfaces between vision, one of the most characteristic types of non-verbal persuasion, emotions, and persuasion are a recurring topic of investigation in this book. In chapters 1 and 2, I discuss the emotive power of vision in Gorgias and Thucydides; in chapter 3, the focal point is *enargeia* and emotions in forensic narratives about violence; and chapter 4 offers a general discussion of the ideological uses of (what I call) 'legitimate envy' in democratic Athens, but also explores the ways in which Demosthenes invests with salience Meidias' ex-

---

**10** For a detailed discussion of non-verbal means of persuasion, see Buxton 1982: 49–50.
**11** On *Peitho's* personification in art, see Smith 2011, esp. 55–60; Hurwit 1994; on the cult of *Peitho*, see Pirenne-Delforge 1991.
**12** On the metaphorical conceptualization of *eros* in Plato's *Phaedrus*, see Cairns 2013, including comparative material from earlier literature. The identification of *peitho* with divine will and violence plays a pivotal role in Gorgias' *Helen* that I discuss in chapter 1.
**13** Cp. also A. *Ag.* 385 and *Ch.* 726.
**14** On other instances of *peitho's* identification with violence (and deception), see Buxton 1982: 58–66 and Bobonich 1991: 366 n.6. On *peitho* as a non-violent, civilized means of settling disputes, cp. Lys. 2.19 (*peitho* distinguishes men from beasts); Arist. *E.E.* 1224a 39 (*peitho* is the opposite of *ananke* and *bia*). Cp. also S. *Ant.* 354f.; Isoc. 3. 6; 4. 48; 15. 254; Pl. *Cri.* 49e-51e; Xen. *Mem.*1.2.10. In Sophocles' *Philoctetes* (102–103), deceptive *peitho* and violence are presented as the only possible ways of retrieving the hero's bow.

cessive lifestyle, thereby constructing emotion scripts of 'indignation'. This section outlines methodological aspects pertaining to the interfaces between vision, emotions, and persuasion.

Quite naturally, students of ancient oratory and rhetoric usually lay stress on verbal means of persuasion, thereby engaging in analysis and classification of speakers' arguments. This logocentric approach to the surviving speeches has benefited in recent years from cognitive, appraisal-oriented approaches to emotions.[15] Indeed, Aristotle's *Rhetoric*, a treatise that has been tremendously influential in ancient and modern times, introduces what modern psychologists call cognitive approach to emotions or appraisal theory.[16] A pioneering scholar in the field of cognitive psychology, Richard Lazarus (2001: 40), has pointed out, that "[T]hose who favor a cognitive-mediational approach must also recognize that Aristotle's *Rhetoric* more than two thousand years ago applied this kind of approach to a number of emotions in terms that seem remarkably modern". Lazarus' point about psychologists' belated realization that cognitive approaches to emotions can be traced back to Aristotle also holds true in classicists' study of *pathopoiia*. As I argue below, commonsensical approaches to speech's *pathopoiia* commonly fail to explain *how* speakers' 'appeals to emotion' operate to achieve persuasion.[17] Notably, in his *Rhetoric* Aristotle deplores handbooks' treatment of passions (and, in the same context, *diabole* –indeed, not a *pathos* 1354a 16–17), because they fall short of an adequate explanation of how *pathe* enhance rational types of proofs –the real object of rhetoric.[18]

In spite of the fact that cognitive analysis, centering on verbally expressed emotion scripts, is particularly useful for the study of emotions, the emphasis that our sources place on the psychological impact of vision, one of the most distinct means of non-verbal persuasion in Greek culture has significant implications for the ways in which visuality is deployed in oratory. But the analysis of vision's role in persuasion transcends the limits of literary criticism. Because in many cases ancient cultural (and scientific) models of vision are different from their modern

---

**15** For discussion of the main contours of cognitive approaches to emotions, see Konstan 2006: 30–32.
**16** For a recent, book-length treatment of emotions in Aristotle's *Rhetoric*, see Dow 2015.
**17** Emotions are, of course, a complex phenomenon, involving the body and the mind, whose Cartesian understanding as a bipolar antithesis has had significant implications for the study of emotions in modern times.
**18** As Dow (2015: 111–116) shows convincingly, Aristotle's locution 'slander and pity, anger and similar passions of the soul' in book 1 refers, albeit elliptically, to handbooks' superficial discussion of these topics and, therefore, does not contradict his discussion and definitions of *pathe* in Book 2.

counterparts,[19] the investigation of vision's emotive aspects and of their bearing on ancient rhetorical theory is a task that requires cultural rather than just literary approaches.

As I argue below, an analysis that emphasizes the emotive potentialities of vision and their place in non-verbal persuasion is not incompatible with appraisal-oriented cognitive analysis. Quite the contrary, our task as historians of concepts is to ask if and to what extent cultural models of vision and, especially, their appropriations in the literary pieces that attract our attention intersect with cognitive approaches to emotions. My discussion is, therefore, complementary to a burgeoning bibliography exploring the function of visuality in rhetoric and oratory, but lays special emphasis on the *emotive* aspects of seeing.[20]

Ancient folk understandings and 'scientific' theories perceive vision as a haptic sense, a process that, in different models of explanation, requires different types of physical contact. The physicality of vision has important implications for the ways in which ancient sources associate emotions with vision. Although, as Douglas Cairns argues (2011), not all emotions fit cultural models of vision, it is important to note that the 'materiality' of vision, both in intromissive and extromissive models of explanation, is directly relevant to its perception as a sense that lays "one open to a variety of profound and often unwelcome physical changes" (Cairns 2011: 42). One of the most distinctive characteristics of vision's emotive power, a characteristic which is directly relevant to its physicalist perception, is the *immediacy* with which it arouses emotions. As the evidence that I discuss in chapter 1 indicates, the phenomenon is prominent in early Greek poetry and tragedy. Furthermore, because (especially in intromissive models) the beholder's eyes are perceived as a medium through which emotions are transmitted, vision models of emotion may be seen as an aspect of emotions' typical conceptualization as external, overpowering forces which reduce viewers to a state of passivity.

The interfaces between vision and emotion cultural models, emphasizing the importance of seeing for several aspects of specific emotions' phenomenology, especially erotic love and envy, are reflected in the prominence of vision in ancient conceptualizations of *peitho*. As Emma Stafford points out (2000: 111), non-

---

**19** On this topic, see Cairns 2011. For a general introduction to vision and visuality in antiquity, see Blundell *et al.* 2013 and Squire 2016 on the sense of sight.
**20** See, for example, the recent books by Serafim (2017) and Papaioannou *et al.* (2017) emphasizing performance and O'Connell's (2017) monograph on vision in the Attic orators. Ruth Webb's excellent study on *ekphrasis* (2009) explores the treatment of *enargeia* in ancient literary theory and rhetoric. See also Webb 2016: 205–219.

verbal, visual *peitho* blurs the limits between erotic persuasion and rhetoric – Gorgias' arguments in *Helen* offer a particularly notable example.[21] But if nonverbal, visual *peitho*, with its physical immediacy and psychotropic effects, may, by virtue of its emotive qualities, be taken as a metaphor for the seductiveness of rhetoric, what is the exact role of visuality in emotionally manipulative *rhetoric*, i.e. the art of words *par excellence*? And, what is more, is there sufficient room for appraisal-oriented analysis in cases where literature deploys the emotive qualities of the distinctively "material process" of vision?[22]

Although cultural models of vision and emotion are important for our appreciation of the sources that thematize them, it is equally important to stress that their employment in literature is so appropriated as to fit the wider scopes of individual authors. In chapters 1 and 2, I show how Gorgias and Thucydides employ folk and scientific models of vision and emotion to serve different purposes. As I argue, Gorgias' discussion of the emotional effects of vision relies on Democritus' theory about *eidola* and enhances with novelty an *epideictic* speech whose author professes to tell the truth about the trivial, albeit demanding, topic of Helen's responsibility for her elopement to Troy. In the few instances where Thucydides uses *eros* as an explanation of human motivation, models of vision and emotion are applied to his investigation of collective emotions and political communication and therefore underline his reflections on different modes of leadership.

A further answer to the first question that I raised above, namely the limits of visuality in the distinctively verbal realm of rhetoric would be that, ancient idealizations of the emotive effects of literary works, especially narratives, laying stress on the activation of listeners' *phantasia*, blur the limits between the 'eye of imagination' and bodily sensory perception.[23] Indeed, in some instances, our sources underscore the representational qualities of words on the basis of comparison with obects of sensory perception ('the real thing'), as is the case with Socrates' and his friends' voyeuristic glimpses of Theodote's naked body in Xenophon's *Memorabilia* (3.11.2–3, briefly discussed in chapter 2). But in idealized understandings of the written text, the borders between the pictures of the mind's gallery and the sights of sense-perception are commonly obfuscated.[24] The vagueness with which ancient sources deal with the limits between narrative visuality and what one sees with one's own eyes is also relevant to the question of whether

---

[21] On the interfaces between *peitho*, politics, and rhetoric, see Sprague-Rothwell Jr. 1990: 26–43.
[22] I borrow the locution "material process" from Cairns (2011: 40).
[23] On *phantasia* and *enargeia*, see Webb 2009; see also Meijering 1987: 29–53; Zanker 2004: 8–9.
[24] See Blundell *et al.* 2013: 12.

the understanding of vision as a material process, and its implications for emotions, leaves sufficient room for cognitive, i.e. appraisal-oriented, analysis.

As I argue in detail (chapter 3), ancient discussions of *enargeia* emphasize the representational qualities of words, and, more importantly, indicate that the main effect of 'vividness' is the arousal of audiences' emotions. This emphasis on emotions is particularly pertinent to rhetoricians' advice that the mental images that visual narratives construct must appeal to major cultural understandings shared by listeners. A requisite for *enargeia* is verisimilitude and, hence, the deployment of images reflecting audiences' shared cultural knowledge makes it possible for their members "to supply information from [their]... knowledge of the narrative background" (Webb 2009: 194). As I show on the basis of a discussion of forensic narratives in chapter 3, the requirement of verisimilitude is implicit to speakers' attempts to summon up images whose social meaning listeners are invited to unravel. The activation of audiences' imagination is therefore a process that induces them to get cognitively involved in the narrated events. Cognitive analysis, therefore, the topic of the following section, not only is compatible with, but also facilitates a better understanding of the emotive aspects of visuality in rhetorical practice, in so far as it points to the implications of the appraisals that mental images encourage listeners to endorse.

## Emotions, cognitions, and rhetorical argument

It is only natural, that, when we discuss emotions, we sense that we are dealing with a particularly familiar phenomenon. We all have emotions and our common experience suggests to us that emotions define us as human beings. Yet, being an inextricable element of our humanness, emotions are no exception to the rule that, when we discuss topics which appear to be particularly familiar to us, we tend to project on them our own presumptions.[25] In the study of emotions, the danger of presumptiveness is particularly salient, because, apart from being something that we experience,[26] emotions are also a diagnostic criterion that we

---

[25] As Cairns points out (2008: 46), "native speakers' own definitions typically tend towards the prescriptive, ignoring the full range of a term's applications in favour of those that come most readily to mind or best suit the speaker's purposes".

[26] Indeed, inability to experience certain emotions may be a symptom of pathological situations, as, of course, is the persistence of emotional conditions such as anxiety or irascibility.

use to evaluate the behaviour and motivations of others in our social interactions with them.[27]

The prominence of emotions in ethical judgments is deeply rooted in our early moral education. Moral educators not only employ sentiments, such as guilt, shame, and disgust, to control unwanted types of behaviour, but also convey –through the use of various means, especially archetypical stories– prescriptive concepts about the nature of emotions. The most salient among these concepts is that emotions are in sharp contrast with or override sensible thinking. Implicit to this concept is the assumption that passions are impulsive drives, sometimes equated with madness, which we must learn to suppress or extirpate. In fact, the identification of emotions with irrational drives is reflected in the metaphorical language that we employ to express emotional experiences.

As scholars show, emotion metaphors, reflecting overarching cultural models of understanding, frequently construe the agents of sentiments as passive recipients of uncontrollable, external forces.[28] Indeed, agents' expression of uncontrollability and passivity (one is 'seized', 'captured', or 'overwhelmed' by a certain emotion) may be used as a criterion that determines how prototypical an emotion is. The metaphorical mapping of emotions not only reflects the ways in which different cultures construe emotional experience, but, by virtue of metaphors' ability to yield mental images and invest abstract notions with immediacy and specificity,[29] it is also commonly deployed in moralizers' attempts to restrain passions.[30]

The normative conceptualization of emotions in our cultures has significant implications for the ways in which we read ancient oratory, especially the forensic speeches, a genre in which normativity is salient. On what may be labelled as

---

[27] Cp. Frank's (1998) evolutionary explanation of emotions in the frame of his commitment model.

[28] For example, madness is a common 'source domain' in ancient and modern emotion metaphors, indicating the emotion's intensity and the agent's sense of uncontrollability, see Kövecses 2000: 37, 73–75. On Greek 'anger' and madness, see Harris 2001: 62–62.

[29] Cp. Aristotle's discussion of metaphors in the *Rhetoric* (esp. 1410b 33–34), where he emphasizes metaphors' ability to 'set the scene before our eyes' thereby suggesting that metaphors convey abstract notions by making them perceptible.

[30] A good example of moralizers' use of figurative, vivid language to restrain emotions and desires, is offered in the scripts of disgust that John Chrysostom puts together in his attempt to harness lust (see Spatharas forthcoming).

the 'mechanistic view' of emotions,[31] identifying sentiments with irrational jolts, emotions seem to have no other obvious origin than the dark, inexplicable workings of our psyche. The mechanistic view, thus, fails to account for the fact that emotions are a complex cognitive phenomenon involving appraisals. When we meet a friend boiling with anger, we need to know *what* caused her emotional response. Succinctly, interpretation of her present situation involves a *why*. The answer to this *why* is vital to our evaluation of her behaviour. She may be angry because she was verbally abused by a passerby or because she found out that her partner attempted to rape her daughter. If the cause of her anger is verbal abuse, we may think that her reaction is irrational, in the sense that it displays excessive irascibility. By contrast, if the cause of her anger is sexual abuse, we might be ready to listen sympathetically to a story involving aggressiveness, even physical violence, against her partner. But in both cases, our understanding of her emotional behaviour requires a normative evaluation concerning the wrong that she has suffered, even as, of course, our assessment is shaped by our own personal emotion style or cultural biases.

As I pointed out earlier, Aristotle was the first to define emotions on the basis of a cognitive approach –i.e. by endorsing an appraisal-oriented analysis– and it is not a matter of coincidence that his systematic treatment of social emotions appears in his *Rhetoric*. The main reason for the inclusion of emotions (*pathe*) in a treatise that defines, classifies, and interprets systematically different types of proofs is that emotions not only require appraisals, but also affect listeners' judgments (κρίσεις, 1378a 19–21) –even if Aristotle does not make clear how emotions operate to 'change' listeners' judgments.[32] We may assume, however, that because Aristotle pursues an appraisal-oriented analysis his statement that emotions affect, i.e. change audiences' judgments, requires the notion that the appraisals involved in the emotion scripts put together by speakers invite listeners to endorse beliefs corresponding to the pivotal aspects of the judgements that give rise to individual emotions. For example, a script of pity would change dikasts' evaluation of a defendant's behaviour by inducing them to turn their attention to appraisals concerning undeserved misfortune. In Athenian courts, where defendants always plead not-guilty, punishment is identified as a major,

---

[31] I borrow the term from Kahan-Nussbaum (1996). According to their definition, "The mechanistic conception sees emotions as forces that do not contain or respond to thought; it is correspondingly skeptical about both the coherence of morally assessing emotions and the possibility of shaping and reshaping per-sons' emotional lives" (273).

[32] On Aristotle's definition of πάθη and the notion that emotions affect, i.e change' one's outlook, see Dow 2015: 134–135, 137–142; Konstan 2006: 36–37.

unwarranted misfortune. In other words, as a distinct type of proofs, emotions invite contextualized assessments of others' behaviour.

Aristotle's treatment of emotions in the *Rhetoric* reveals the flaws of the mechanistic view which was unreflectively endorsed by authors of handbooks (see discussion above). Indeed, if emotions were just impulsive drives, they would be of no practical use to public speakers. Unlike evaluative beliefs, raw impulses cannot be manipulated through discursive means of persuasion, including storytelling, individual characterization, or discussion of litigants' place in social hierarchy. Furthermore, if emotions were just impulses, it would be impossible for Aristotle to treat sentiments in antithetical pairs (e.g. 'indignation', what he calls τὸ νεμεσᾶν, is the opposite of 'pity', ἔλεος) –opposite cognitions generate opposite sentiments ('pity' focuses on undeserved suffering, while 'indignation' focuses on undeserved prosperity). In addition, Aristotle's definition of emotions in antithetical pairs is in pace with their uses in rhetorical practice, in so far as, especially in forensic contexts, the competing stories told by litigants reflect diametrically opposed understandings of the kind of sentiments that they or their opponents deserve.

Commentaries on and interpretations of forensic speeches usually carry the imprints of emotions' normative conceptualization as irrational drives and, hence, identify sentiments such as anger or pity with raw impulses that *affect* listeners. The cliché 'appeal to emotion X' is commonly used in scholarly works on the orators to describe instances in which emotion X is named in the text. In these uses, leaving unexplained how speakers are able to 'arouse' listeners' emotions through the use of arguments, the phrase 'appeal to emotion' seems to equate emotion labels with magic spells, in so far as it fails to explain the process which gives rise to emotional experiences and, thereby, focuses on the end. Traditional discussions of *pathopoiia* thus seem to reflect the assumption that emotions are not analyzable, an assumption which is also salient in modern views about the place of emotions in legal practice.[33] The traditional and, as I argue, unsatisfactory, approach to 'appeals to emotions' partly results from scholars' tendency to look for emotions only in instances where relevant emotion labels, such as *orge*, *eleos*, or *phobos* appear.[34] But looking for emotions only in passages

---

[33] On this point, see Bandes-Blumenthal 2012: 162, arguing that the category emotion "has long functioned as catchall category for much of what law aspires to avoid or counteract: that which is subjective, irrational, prejudicial, intangible, partial, and impervious to reason". For a convenient overview of the relationship between emotions and the law, see Bandes' article in the Emotion Researcher http://emotionresearcher.com/what-roles-do-emotions-play-in-the-law, consulted on August 1, 2017).

[34] Harris 2017 is a good example of the shortcomings of label-centered approaches.

where we find relevant lexical markers means that we turn a blind eye to rich emotional scenarios.

In the language of emotion studies, the term 'emotion scripts' refers to mini-narratives including information about fundamental aspects of an emotion's phenomenology: the causes that prompted an emotional episode, its 'output' characteristics, i.e. changes in the physiology of the body and its physical manifestations (e.g. tears in the cases of sadness, pride or joy), and the actions to which a sentiment leads, what specialists describe as 'action tendency of emotions' (fear, for example, typically elicits fight or flight).[35] 'Emotion scripts' have been advocated by researchers working in diverse fields, while their use in the field of Classics was introduced by Robert Kaster in his pioneering book on Roman passions.[36] The advantage of using scripts in the study of emotions is that they provide contextualized understandings of emotions and, thereby, remove the danger of projecting onto the cultures that we study our own biases or anachronistic readings of their literary products.

Because our pieces of evidence about emotions in the ancient cultures that we explore are provided by literary (or, indeed, non-literary) texts, 'emotion scripts' enable historians of emotions to overcome the problems of translatability which are inherent in the rendering of ancient emotion terms into their working modern languages. Modern Greek, for example, includes a substantial number of emotion labels which also appear in the ancient texts that we study. Let me adduce an example: in modern-Greek, it makes perfect sense to say 'I feel δέος at the sight of Crete's rocky mountains'. As this example shows, in my native language δέος primarily denotes an agent's feelings for something which she perceives as awe-inspiring. However, it would be wrong to use modern Greek δέος to designate an agent's fear in, say, fourth-century Athens, as is the case with the locution ἀδεές ... δέος δεδιέναι from Plato's *Symposium* ('to experience fearless fear', 198a). To put it simply, there is no one-to-one relationship between lexical markers designating emotion in different languages.

I would suggest, however, and this would not come as a surprise to classicists, that our focus on 'emotion scripts' is not mutually exclusive with an approach that takes into account labels, at least in cases where labels are available in our sources. Lexical makers are heuristically useful, in so far as we bear in mind that the emotional experience to which they refer may be fully at play in passages that omit them. Furthermore, labels always appear in contexts in the wider frame of which they acquire their full significance –fragments of literary

---

35 For a discussion of emotion scripts, see Cairns 2008: 46. See also Sanders 2014: 5–7.
36 Kaster 2005: 8–9.

works are good examples of the problems of interpretation arising from insufficient contextual information. In this respect, the study of ancient emotions presents obvious affinities with the study of ancient concepts and values in general.[37] E.g. Kenneth Dover's book on popular morality is an invaluable contribution to the study of ancient ethics, because it provides careful analysis of the labels that Greeks employed to designate pivotal moral values by discussing their uses in relevant *contexts*. Without this contextualized approach the study of concepts, and for that matter the study of emotions, would be impossible.

One of the major problems of studies that overemphasize labels is reductionism. Lexical approaches typically look for the ancient equivalents of emotion words that we use in our own spoken languages. Consequently, when researchers who rely on lexical markers fail to find an ancient word corresponding to a modern member of the category emotion, e.g. English 'jealousy' or modern Greek 'ζήλια', they wrongly assume that the emotion was unknown to the speakers of these languages. For example, David Konstan, a scholar whose pioneering work has enhanced significantly our knowledge of ancient emotions, suggests that, because he is unable to find the equivalents of 'erotic jealousy' and 'pride' in the Greek sources of specific periods, these emotions were not experienced or expressed in the societies that produced the texts under investigation.[38] A further difficulty that arises from this approach is the construction of a posteriori generalizations about the distinctive cultural characteristics of the societies that attract our attention to explain alleged emotion-gaps. In other words, reductionist lexical approaches arbitrarily grant questions of semantics with cultural implications. Lastly, advocates of lexical approaches sometimes historicize specific emotions in an arbitrary fashion by suggesting that the emergence of previously unattested emotion words in specific periods is causally related to wider cultural and social changes.

The use of emotion scripts, along with contextualized lexical approaches, is important for the study of emotions in rhetoric and oratory. An approach that relies on scripts enables students of *pathopoiia* to overcome the difficulties caused by the mechanistic view identifying emotions with irrational jolts and gives specific meaning to the vague expression 'appeal to emotions'. This is especially so, because, as I argue, the emotions that appear more prominently in the orators revolve around normative concerns, in other words they surround evaluations concerning social, ideological, or ethical issues.

---

[37] See Cairns 2008: 46.
[38] On 'jealousy', see Konstan 2006: 221; on 'pride', Konstan 2006: 90. Both examples are discussed in Cairns 2008: 53–58.

Do, however, forensic speakers themselves treat emotions as irrational drives? In some cases, litigants, especially defendants, invite dikasts to act as rational legal decision makers and, therefore, remain unaffected by emotions. Yet, do these warnings indicate that speakers treat emotions as irrational drives? This question affords two possible interpretations. On a prescriptive level, speakers sometimes emphasize that emotions are an inappropriate criterion for legal decision-making. Defendants, for example, sometimes ask dikasts to listen to them carefully and remain unaffected by their opponents' attempts to cause their anger (ἄνευ ὀργῆς) –and indeed Aristophanes composed a comic play, the *Wasps*, in which anger (and moral disgust, as *Bdelykleon's* name shows) appears as the hallmark of Athenian dikasts.[39] These pleas commonly appear in contexts where defendants seek to preempt the negative effects of prosecutors' deceitful and unsubstantiated accusations, especially their attempts at character assassination. Thus, the underlying assumption of defendants' pleas for a favourable hearing is that anger affects dikasts' judgment by deceitfully diverting their attention to allegedly disagreeable aspects of their characters rather than that anger is caused by unintelligible psychic processes.

If we turn our attention to passages discussing the consequences of emotions upon dikasts' judgments and attempt to pin down speakers' understanding of how emotions are aroused, what we find are rich emotion scripts. Speakers sometimes present emotions as appealing to the heart, as is especially the case in instances where prosecutors seek to mitigate their opponents' dramatic appeals to dikasts' pity,[40] but the discursive manipulation of emotions relies on calculated arguments, narratives, or individual characterization, which appeal to dikasts' minds. Even a cursory examination of instances where speakers invite dikasts to express negative sentiments against their opponents indicates the frequent use of causal constructions supplying individual emotions' causes.[41] Furthermore, expressions such as ἄξιον/δίκαιον ὀργίζεσθαι,[42] expressions which are common currency in the speeches, suggest that appeals to emotions in forensic contexts require ethical judgments revolving around normative and ethical concerns. Finally, in several passages, emotions such as anger are presented as the result of considerate thinking. Demosthenes, for example, urges dikasts to come to realize that Meidias deserves their anger after 'reflecting' and 'considering'

---

**39** Cp. also Ant. 5.57, 69; Lys. 25. 1–5 (discussed below).
**40** Cp. Arist. *Rh.* 1386a 29–35. See Carey 1994: 33; Hall 1995; Apostolakis 2017.
**41** Cp. the following examples (concerning dikasts' anger): Aeschines 1.166; Dem. 24.218, 47.80; Lycurg. 1.58; Lys. 10.29, 12.58, 80, 90 (explanatory γάρ), 20.1.
**42** Cp. for example Lys. 14.8; 31.11; [Dem.] 59. 5; Lycurg. 1.58.

(ἐκλογιζομένοις καὶ θεωροῦσιν) that the most vulnerable victims of his opponent's insolence are the less privileged among Athenian citizens (21.123).

Let me examine briefly an example in which the speaker anticipates his opponent's attempt to cause the audience's anger against him. In Lysias 25, a speech, perhaps delivered soon after the overthrow of the Thirty, the speaker undergoes a *dokimasia* and, quite expectedly, insists that the groundless accusation that he faces is the product of sycophancy. His opponents, he says, seek to capitalize on current political concerns, because they have nothing to accuse him of. He thus invites dikasts to turn a blind eye to his opponents' attempts to associate him with the oligarchic regime. These attempts, he suggests, are intended to cause their anger against him.[43] Is the situation that the defendant refers to here commensurate with a warning against emotions' irrationality? The answer is both yes and no. No, because, rather than being an impulsive drive, dikasts' (possible) anger against the defendant requires assessment of his political preferences which, as he says, are irrelevant to the legal questions of the case –irrelevance is not irrationality. And yes, because, in the speaker's eyes, this assessment involves ill-informed criteria that may precipitate 'unwise' decision-making. But without these ill-informed criteria, revolving around the relatively recent traumatic experiences of the polis, dikasts' anger would be impossible.

Anger serves as a test-case for the 'rationality' of forensic emotions, because Athenian litigants sometimes treat the emotion as dikasts' *appropriate* response to some types of wrongdoing. These cases show with lucidity the differences between modern and ancient uses of emotions in forensic contexts and indicate the 'rationality', i.e. the cognitive nature, of 'appeals to emotion'. Modern legal systems treat anger as an emotion that, under specific circumstances, affects criminal behaviour. Hence, the emotion is taken into account at the sentence phase of trials as a mitigating factor. But it would be unimaginable to think of a judge who would admit her sentiments of anger against the defendant in her verdict. As Bandes (1999: 2) points out, "in the conventional story [sc. about emotions and the law], emotion has a certain, narrowly defined place in law. It is assigned to the criminal courts. It is confined to those—like witnesses, the accused, the public—without legal training". Hence, ideally at least, modern courts do not punish out of anger.

The extent to which anger determined ancient courts' decision making has been a topic of scholarly debate. Allen (2000: 148–151), for example, emphasizes male antagonism in classical Athens and argues that Athenian lawsuits were a

---

43 νῦν δὲ νομίζουσι τὴν πρὸς ἐκείνους ὀργὴν ἱκανὴν εἶναι καὶ τοὺς μηδὲν κακὸν εἰργασμένους ἀπολέσαι, Lys. 25.5.

competition for dikasts' sentiments of anger (and pity) regulated by the polis' institutions. As she points out, in a locution that, as far as we can see, oversimplifies the existing evidence, "each contender had to use his speech to define the pitiable and that which was worthy of anger in order to make a claim on his dikasts' votes" (2000: 149). In her careful examination of dikasts' anger, Lene Rubinstein (2004) has shown that ancient prosecutors invite dikasts to give vent to their anger only in speeches delivered in the frame of public cases or in private cases concerning incidents of violence (and hence revolving around *hybris*).[44]

Rubinstein's conclusion that scripts of anger are exclusive to public cases shows lucidly the type of appraisals that shaped the uses of emotions in Athenian legal practice. Unlike what was the case with private legal cases, in public indictments dikasts were expected to defend the interests of the community as a whole. Note, for example, that in public lawsuits the fines were paid to the state, rather than to successful prosecutors –as was the case in private cases. The conceptualization of public indictments as legal actions against criminal action that affected the polis as a whole is also reflected in the procedures that regulated public cases. Public indictments (*graphai*) were introduced to the courts either by the victim of the alleged wrongdoing or by volunteer prosecutors (ὁ βουλόμενος) –at least in public actions where there was a victim.[45] Since volunteer prosecutors acted in defence of the polis' interests at the cost of losing personal gain, their appeals to dikasts' anger was appropriate because each and every member of the jury was perceived as a victim of the alleged perpetrator's crime. Unlike private lawsuits, thus, public disputes involved a triangular relationship between the prosecutor, the defendant, *and* the dikasts.

The prominence of anger in public indictments bears witness to the importance of the ideological assumptions that lie behind emotional manipulation in Athenian courts and the norms that constituted the public discourse in the polis. These norms, it seems, made appeals to the negative emotions of anger and hatred inapplicable in private cases. The example of anger, thus, not only indicates that appeals to emotions involve the construction of conceptual frameworks which were so designed as to guide dikasts' appraisals, but also that these appraisals were directly relevant to the legal aspects and normative expectations that characterized individual cases.

---

**44** Rubinstein's conclusion in her systematic discussion of anger is anticipated in Carey 1994: 29–30. In all the existing speeches concerning cases of violence, prosecutors equate the attack that they suffered with *hybris* and, thereby, imply that the nature of the wrongdoing harms the city as a whole.

**45** See Osborne's seminal discussion (1985).

In Athenian courtroom practice, manipulation of emotions *qua* cognitions was facilitated by the procedures. Unlike what is the case in modern trials, where evidence is produced in a rather fragmented manner, Athenian litigants delivered coherent speeches including elaborate narratives that provided dikasts with a 'wide angle' of the case at hand (on forensic narratives, see chapter 3). Hence, Athenian courts took into account questions such as the social background of those involved in legal disputes, defendants' services to the city, and their conformity with the norms and values of democratic ideology. Emotions, I argue, were particularly relevant to the construction of this 'wide angle'. According to the cognitive view that I adopt, emotions are elicited by evaluative beliefs. Emotions, therefore, enabled speakers to produce conceptual frames that served their purposes of argument by appealing to dikasts' shared cultural and social values. In fact, as I argue in chapter 3, the fact that the emotion scripts that we find in forensic speeches are shaped by potent cultural understandings explains the predictable uniformity of audiences' responses.

But, if, as I suggested, arousing audiences' emotions requires the construction of appropriate conceptual frames, how are we to explain the emotional experience supposedly imparted in audiences? To put it simply, when we say that Lysias or Demosthenes seek to cause their audience's envy, does this mean that the members of their audiences *experience* the emotion? And, more importantly, if we are unable to give a positive answer to this question, what do we expect to learn from the study of emotions in the orators?

From the perspective of a student of ancient emotions, the 'arousal' of emotions in audiences does not mean that we can tell if individual members of speakers' audiences 'experienced' specific sentiments. The notional identification of emotional manipulation with emotional experience in the study of *pathopoiia* is methodologically problematic, but also raises extremely complicated questions concerning emotions' ontology. Succinctly put: is experiencing, i.e. feeling an emotion, a necessary requirement for an emotion to exist? Ultra-cognitive responses to this question, such as Nussbaum's (2001), would be negative. Aristotle would, perhaps, agree with her. One of the emotions that Aristotle defines in the *Rhetoric*, i.e. 'hatred' (*misos*), is presented as having no feeling components: it is neither painful nor pleasant, but still, it *is* an emotion and indeed one that figures prominently in the orators.[46] Goldie (2000) has recently argued against sweeping cognitive approaches and proposes that, although emotions require evaluations,

---

[46] On Aristotle's definition of hatred, see Konstan 2006: 185–200; Spatharas 2013. On the arousal of negative emotions in the orators, see Sanders 2012.

they are also characterized by feelings which are directed towards these cognitions. On a different view, feelings are integral to, i.e. constituent elements of the cognitions that arouse emotions. The muscular tension that I experience in a state of fear or anxiety invests with salience my appraisal that danger is imminent.[47]

Despite these problems of definition which, let me mention *en passant*, are symptomatic of our inability to give a definitive definition to the category 'emotion',[48] I take the view that from the perspective of a historian of emotions the empirical question of whether litigants or dikasts experienced a specific emotion is irrelevant to the study of *pathopoiia*. This, does not, of course, mean, that speakers did not expect to elicit specific emotions in their audiences or that dikasts did not respond emotionally to what they heard. All it means is that the empirical question of whether dikasts or other audiences 'really' experienced certain emotions in response to the scripts put together by speakers is one that cannot be answered with certainty. More importantly, however, to assert that Athenian audiences were predisposed towards experiencing *specific* emotions and, consequently, that speakers commonly appealed to these emotions is a logical fallacy and requires the unprovable assumption that the 'emotion scripts' that we find in our sources correspond to preexising feelings.

To make this point clear, let me discuss briefly an emotion that I treat in some length in chapters 4 and 5 of this book. According to a fairly standard view, Athenian masses 'experienced' sentiments of envy towards the elites.[49] Ober, for example, claims that the '[T]he ostentatious lifestyles of the rich provided the forensic orator with an obvious body of material which could be used in *exploiting his audiences' envy for the wealthy*' (1989: 207, the emphasis is mine). Although it is undoubtedly true that ostentatious lifestyle was deployed in scripts of 'envy', I take issue with Ober's locution for the following reasons: (a) all we know about rich opponents' "ostentatious lifestyles" derives from speakers' elaborate and highly biased descriptions; (b) the last words of his locution (emphasized), not only imply that Ober can answer the empirical question of whether Athenian audiences experienced sentiments of envy, but also that envy was a dispositional characteristic of the citizens that manned the Athenian courts.[50] By taking for granted Athenians' sentiments of envy, Ober endorses an *ideological* use of the

---

[47] See Damasio 1994: 350–412.
[48] On the question of definition, its implications for the study of emotion's phenomenology, and the relationship between 'emotion' and *pathos*, see Cairns 2008.
[49] The opposite view is taken by Fisher (2003), who criticizes the view that elite values were not understood or shared by the masses.
[50] On this point, see Cairns 2003.

emotion, i.e. a use that we find in *specific* arguments (see ch. 4 below); and lastly, why would a speaker, such as Demosthenes in *Against Meidias*, mind to explain the reasons for which his wealthy opponent *deserves* his audience's envy, if this sentiment was an unchanging psychic characteristic of his audience?

Let me adduce another example on the basis of which I propose positive reasons that should make us pay attention to speakers' expressions of personal feelings, even if we are, as I suggested, unable to ascertain if these sentiments were experienced by them. In his speech on the Embassy, Demosthenes says that Aeschines' hypocrisy makes him choke (ἀποπνίγομαι). This is a powerful use of disgust, an emotion that morphs physical into moral aversion.[51] Modern studies indicate that when we express moral disgust we experience the feelings caused by the emotion's material elicitors (e.g. excrements, rotten bodies etc.).[52] Although it is impossible to say if Demosthenes really experienced sentiments of disgust, the use of a word that designates metonymically, indeed in a distinctively embodied manner, the speaker's physical aversion to Aeschines' public career, invests with radiant salience his moral condemnation of his opponent. This highly embodied response to Aeschines' career, conceptualizing his hypocrisy as a knee-jerk reaction, appeals to the visceral aspects of physical disgust and reveals with graphic lucidity Aeschines' contempt for the polis' interests and the values that bond together decent Athenian citizens. The use of disgust, thus, operates communicatively and grants with salience Aeschines' alleged normative transgressions.

My point about Demosthenes' use of disgust indicates that although appraisal-oriented, cognitive theories of emotion are extremely useful in the study of the orators, more holistic approaches, involving non-verbal aspects of the emotions' phenomenology, enhance nuanced understandings of the emotional scenarios that we find in the speeches. Indeed, in so far as non-verbal output features of emotions' phenomenology are culturally and socially controlled, they are important sources of evidence concerning the values and norms of the societies and cultures that we explore through the study of emotions. Balinese mourners, for example, refrain from showing openly their pain, because they believe that

---

**51** For a general discussion of the ancient emotion of disgust, see Lateiner/Spatharas 2017. For a more detailed discussion of projective disgust as a means of marginalization, see Spatharas (forthcoming). On Demosthenes' uses of disgust, see Fisher 2017a.
**52** On this point, see Chapman *et al.* 2009.

grief affects their health.⁵³ Bodily movements and gestures, the 'output' components of emotions, garments, screams and silences, in other words the non-verbal aspects that constitute the rich repertoire of social performances, invest with specificity the ethical and normative evaluations of the emotion scripts that we find in the orators.

In *Against Timarchus* (131), for example, Aeschines says that if he asked dikasts to touch Demosthenes' clothes with their own hands (the clothes in which his opponent composes speeches with which he harms his fellow-ambassadors), they would be unable to tell if they belonged to a man or a woman. The activation of dikasts' sensory imagination enhances Demosthenes' portrayal as a *kinaidos*, who, is, therefore, presented as being unsuitable for the privilege of being a *symboulos*. Demosthenes' assimilation with women invites dikasts' scornful contempt. Another example from this speech concerns Timarchus' aggressive style of delivery. During an indecorous performance at the Assembly, Aeschines says, Timarchus stripped like a *pankratiast* (ἐπαγκρατίαζεν, 26). As has been noted (Fisher 2000 note *ad loc.*), Aeschines focuses here on the ageing body of his opponent, a body that in the prime of Timarchus' youth had attracted many lovers. As Aeschines claims, Timarchus' body reflects the disgustingness of his excessive lifestyle. Internal spectators' responses to Timarchus' naked body –Athenians cover their eyes out of shame–, bears witness to the repulsiveness of the object of dikast's gazes. As I argued elsewhere, shamelessness, a fundamental characteristic of Timarchus' presentation in the speech, is enhanced by scenarios which blur the limits between physical and moral defilement.⁵⁴

This negative presentation is further substantiated in this passage by Aeschines' comparison of Timarchus' indecent style of delivery with a statue of Solon (25), which, according to Aeschines' idealized, inaccurate, and anachronistic interpretation, reflects the ideals of self-constraint and decorousness.⁵⁵ This passage, therefore, exploits body language, nakedness, and the physical condition of a major politician's body to construct an emotion script that revolves around shame and disgust. As is typically the case with relevant narratives (see chapter 3), internal spectators' gazes and responses reflect the normative concerns and shared values privileged by 'healthy' Athenian citizens. In this passage, thus, the

---

53 On Balinese grief, see Nussbaum 2001: 240–241, discussing the findings of the Norwegian anthropologist, Unni Wikan. The sanitization of grief in the American funeral industry, a business dominated by euphemism, is wonderfully depicted in the TV series *Six feet under*, whose literary predecessor is Evelyn Waugh's novel *The loved one*.
54 See Spatharas 2017. On Aeschines' emphasis on Timarchus' body, see Sissa 1999 and Carey 2017.
55 On Solon in Aeschines' speech, see Farenga 2006: 333–339.

non-verbal aspects of a prominent citizen's social and civic performances underscore the cognitions that give rise to the emotion script that Aeschines puts together in the vehement attack that he launches against his opponent.

## Outline of the book

On the basis of the topics discussed in the ensuing chapters, this book may broadly be divided into two parts. Chapters 1–3 deal, albeit in distinct ways, with emotions –especially *eros*, *pothos*, and anger–, and visuality, while chapters 4–5 focus on the role of envy in the public discourse of classical Athens.

In chapter 1, I discuss Gorgias' theorizing about vision in the *Encomium of Helen*. In the fourth major argument that Gorgias employs to defend Helen, he claims that the objects of our sights elicit emotions that lead us to specific actions. As I argue, Gorgias' speech is an *epideixis* and, as such, one of the author's main concerns is to advertise the novelty of his approach to the traditional topic of Helen's responsibility for her travel to Troy. The novelty of Gorgias' treatment of the case lies in his use of probability arguments (*eikos*). The emotive power of vision enhances one of the probability arguments that Gorgias employs to exculpate Helen. As I suggest, Gorgias defends Helen on the basis of the traditional conceptualization of erotic love as a distinctively ocular emotion, a conceptualization that literature commonly employs to suggest the destructiveness of Helen's beauty. As far I can see, Gorgias' treatment of this traditional topic is enhanced by current theories about vision, especially Democritus' *eidola* theory, which Gorgias employs to refute traditional accounts about Helen's responsibility.

In chapter 2 I turn my attention to *eros*, *pothos*, anger and, to a lesser extent, envy in Thucydides' narrative. I argue that the emphasis that recent scholars place on visuality in Thucydides' narrative has significant interfaces with his problematization of emotions in political communication and leadership. As I suggest, Thucydides employs cultural models of vision and emotion to delineate the different ways in which leaders (especially Pericles, Nicias, and Alcibiades) substantiate their rhetoric. On the one hand, Pericles enlists the emotive aspects of vision in the frame of erotic communication in support of his attempt to induce citizens to indicate their wholehearted commitment to the city. In post-Periclean Athens, and especially during the preparation of the Sicialian expedition, the emotive potentialities of vision facilitate self-interested or ineffective types of political communication. I also suggest, that Archidamus' speech in Book 2 reflects several similarities with Gorgias' arguments about vision of emotion, even as anger does not usually fit emotion models associating affective experience with sights.

In chapter 3, I discuss forensic narratives, a topic which is undeservedly under-explored. On the basis of modern legal and literary theory exploring the importance of narrativity for the dispensation of justice, I look into the interconnections between emotions and forensic storytelling. My focal point in this chapter concerns the notion of *enargeia*, i.e. vivid storytelling and its relationship with *pathopoiia*. Ancient literary theory and rhetorical treatises unequivocally associate 'vivid' stories with listeners' emotional involvement in the narrated events, but at the same time emphasize that *enargeia*, and the mental images that it elicits through activation of audiences' imagination, requires appeals to audiences potent cultural understandings. I, therefore, use a number of forensic narratives concerning incidents of violence to indicate how narrative specificity, and internal spectators' responses to the events, enhance scenarios of pity and anger.

Chapter 4 focuses on the ideological uses of what I call 'legitimate envy', roughly corresponding to Aristotle's 'indignation' (τὸ νεμεσᾶν). On the basis of Quentin Skinner's theoretical work about the language of ideology, I argue that although envy was generally thought as a socially destructive emotion, some uses of legitimate envy in the orators indicate that in the democratic environment of classical Athens the label φθόνος acquired a new field of application encompassing instances in which wealthy and self-interested citizens exhibited a deviant type of *philotimia*. This negative type of *philotimia* revolves around evaluations about the privilege of the demos to grant honours to citizens who offered their services to the city. My argument about this ideological use of legitimate envy relies on Demosthenes' speeches *Against Leptines* and, especially, *Against Meidias* and on other forensic speeches. In *Against Meidias*, I argue, the prosecutor stigmatizes his opponent's ostentatious lifestyle and anti-democratic ethos through the use of *enargeia*.

In chapter 5, I turn my attention to self-praise and envy in the Attic orators. In my analysis of *periautologia*, vision is not as prominent as in the previous chapters, even if Demosthenes' 'epiphany' in *On the crown*, the Ur-example of self-praise in classical antiquity, offers one of the most spectacular descriptions of an individual's public appearance in the corpus of the orators. As I argue in this chapter (which may be seen as complementary to my discussion of envy in chapter 4), self-praise is sometimes useful to forensic speakers, but it impinges on wider cultural and political concerns. As Plutarch points out in his short, stylistically unimpressive treatise on *Praising oneself inoffensively*, a treatise that, along with modern anthropological material and cognitive approaches to emotions serves as the basis for my analysis, self-praise compromises listeners' sense of honour and may therefore reflect badly on speakers. One of the most obvious dangers involved in the use of self-praise is listeners' envy. My discussion emphasizes that in the egalitarian environment of classical Athens, speakers deploy specific discursive strategies that enable them to highlight their achievements without isolating themselves from the majorities of civic bodies.

# 1 Vision and emotions in Gorgias

## 1.1 Preliminaries

According to Athenaeus, Gorgias dedicated a golden statue of himself at Delphi. Some years later, Eumolpus, Gorgias' grand-nephew, dedicated a statue of his grand-uncle at Olympia.[1] Gorgias' dedication to a sanctuary where he delivered one of his epideictic speeches in front of a Panhellenic audience quite literally *embodies* his tendency to elevate his epideictic performances to spectacles.[2] His fascination with the pleasures of the eye and visual illusion is plainly depicted in his frequent references to tragedy in the extant fragments,[3] but also in the predominant role of vision in the arguments that he produces in the *Encomium of Helen* (15–19).

Judging from his extant works, visual perception is also fundamental to the epistemological assumptions that underlie his theorizing about persuasion and the nature of arguments from probability: for Gorgias, firm knowledge, as opposed to slippery 'belief' (δόξα), can only be the product of autopsy.[4] Correlatively, Gorgias treats 'speech' (λόγος) as a medium of representation that makes

---

**1** In 1876, archaeologists found the base of the statue near the temple of Zeus at Olympia (see Buchheim 1989: 203). For discussion of Gorgias' and Eumolpus' dedications, see Morgan 1994.
**2** Cp. A9 DK. On the affinities of Sophists' displays with rhapsodic performances, see O' Sullivan 1992: 66–67; Worman 2002: 112; Spatharas 2008. According to Aelian *VH* 12.32, Gorgias appeared in front of his audience in the purple robe of the rhapsodes (cp. also Pl. *Hp. Mi*.363c); in Pl. *Prot.* 317a–b, poets are presented as disguised Sophists (see Ford 2002: 202–203). The word κόσμος that Gorgias associates with the truthfulness of his speech in the *priamel* that stands at the very beginning of *Helen* alludes to the 'orderly' (κατὰ κόσμον) narratives of epic poetry. But Gorgias undercuts the authority of these narratives by suggesting emphatically (note ἐγὼ δέ) that the κόσμος of his own composition relies on logical reasoning (λογισμόν). His own method, thus, transcends the limits of narrative specificity and orderliness (cp. τὸν χρόνον τὸν τότε τῷ λόγῳ νῦν ὑπερβάς, 5) and offers an interpretation centering on what Aristotle labels τὰ ὑπάρχοντα πιθανά (*Rh*. 1355b 10). Hence, Gorgias' own approach achieves the 'universality' that Aristotle recognizes in tragedy (as opposed to history, *Po*.1451b5–11) to the extent that "it demonstrates the general rule" (I borrow the phrase from Eden 1986: 70, who masterfully brings out the analogies between rhetoric and fiction).
**3** For a recent discussion, see Halliwell 2011: 266–284. On ancient and modern theories of viewing and vision, see Blundell *et al.* 2013; on ancient optical theories in early Greek philosophy, see Rudolph 2016.
**4** On Gorgias' notion –mainly expressed in the *Defence of Palamedes*– that firm knowledge can only be the product of sensory perception, especially autopsy, see Spatharas 2007 and 2008. The arguments that he puts forward in *On not being* are incompatible with the stress that he lays on

invisible things visible to the eye of the mind mainly through the use of *eikota*, i.e. arguments that offer verisimilar approximations of factual reality.[5] The power of 'speech' to fabricate likenesses of factual reality is also pivotal to the way in which Gorgias construes deception.[6]

In this chapter, I focus my attention on the relationship between vision and emotions in Gorgias' *Encomium of Helen*, a topic that has attracted some scholarly attention, but has not as yet received detailed discussion.[7] In the fourth major part of his *Encomium of Helen*, a speech that seeks to defend Helen against poets' accounts holding her responsible for her elopement to Troy, Gorgias theorizes about the ways in which the objects of vision shape our emotions. As I shall attempt to show, Gorgias' discussion of the relationship between vision and emotions seems to draw on a pattern of thought that is common in archaic and classical poetry. Yet, the existing evidence makes it possible to suggest that Gorgias modifies cultural models of vision and emotion that he finds in the literary tradition which he seeks to refute.

Gorgias' treatment of the psychological impact of images upon our emotions, I argue, is enhanced by theories of vision developed during his lifespan. This enhancement is symptomatic of the salient tendency of sophistic *epideixis* towards novelty. In addition, my discussion shows, I hope, that Gorgias' arguments about the impact of vision upon human psychology displays cognitive elements which I find to be particularly relevant to his arguments about verbal persuasion. As we

---

autopsy in *Palamedes*, a speech, however, which is more akin to forensic oratory and, thereby a speech to which the issue of discursive representation of factual evidence is pivotal.

**5** Cp. Gorgias' argument emphasizing that arguments of 'natural philosophers'' (μετεωρολόγοι) can make 'invisible' and 'unbelievable' things, visible to the 'eyes of belief' (*Hel.* 13). For a similar argument from the realm of medicine, see the Hippocratic treatise *De arte* 11.2 and cp. Spatharas 2007 and especially Mann 2012: 27–28 with notes *ad loc*. On Gorgias' use of *eikota* and other patterns of argument see Spatharas 2001; Gagarin 1994; Kalligas 2003; Balla 2004; Spatharas 2008. As Kalligas has suggested, my argument (Spatharas 2001) that Gorgias does not use probability arguments in *Helen* is wrong. Gorgias invents the causes that may have prompted Helen's elopement to Troy on the basis of probability arguments. However, in his *Defence of Palamedes eikota* are dispersed throughout the speech.

**6** Deception in Gorgias has been discussed by Rosenmeyer 1955 and Verdenius 1981 and more recently by Halliwell (2011: 266–284). In Spatharas 2008, I discuss *Helen* 11 and argue that, in Gorgias' eyes, false speeches are persuasive, because audiences lack the holistic knowledge that archaic poetry ascribes to the Muses. In Gorgias' eyes, deception is possible because speakers fabricate *logoi* that resemble empirical reality to the effect of being indistinguishable from it. On deception and sophistic *epideixis*, see also Worman 2002: ch. 5.

**7** The relationship between emotions and 'serious' poetry (especially epic and tragedy) are discussed by Segal (1962) in an article of remarkable vigour. More recent discussions are included in Taplin 1978, ch. 10; Heath 1987: 7–17, 40; Halliwell 2011; LaCourse Munteanu 2012: ch. 2.

shall see, even as Gorgias explains the generation of emotions on the basis of a physicalist approach that combines philosophical theory with relevant folk patterns of thought, at the same time his argumentation emphasizes the power of emotions to impair our beliefs and generate emotions that affect our volition.

## 1.2 Vision and the generation of emotions in the *Encomium of Helen*

Gorgias' *Encomium of Helen* is an epideictic speech that, according to its author's own words (1, 21), aims to praise Helen, a woman whose praiseworthiness can by no means be taken for granted.[8] Yet the choice of this apparently paradoxical topic fits the generic aims of rhetorical display (*epideixis*): by choosing to praise Helen, Gorgias sets himself a difficult task and, thereby, advertises his ability to elaborate on a traditional mythological theme with great originality.[9] Gorgias embarks on his encomium by attacking the poets who blamed Helen for her elopement to Troy and promises that he will attempt to remove the 'infamy' (δύσκλεια) from her through 'logical reasoning' (λογισμός) rather than on the basis of a new narrative version about the circumstances of her travel to Troy. As Gorgias says, hence suggesting that his aim is to address the issue of Helen's responsibility rather than dispute matters of 'factual' reality,[10] his own method of argument does not require telling a story that includes events that are known to everyone. Such

---

**8** In his own *Encomium of Helen* (14), Isocrates applauds Gorgias for choosing to praise Helen, but criticizes his line of argument, because, as he says, it would be more suitable for a defence than for an encomium. Isocrates' criticism would better be explained as an attempt on his part to advertise the authority of his own composition (on contradiction as a means of asserting originality, see Griffith 1990: 193).

**9** Yet, the iconographical evidence discussed by Shapiro (2005) shows that in the time of Gorgias' composition, usually placed in the last thirty years of the 5th century, vase painters treat Helen favourably. It is also worthy of our note, that, according to Shapiro, during the last quarter of the 5th century, Helen's responsibility acquires distinctive prominence in red-figure vase painting. Cp. his discussion of the narrative on a perfume vessel from the workshop of the Meidias painter reflecting Zeuxis' portrait of Helen at Croton. The painter depicts Εὔκλεια plaiting a wreath for Helen and, therefore, the stance that he adopts towards her coincides with Gorgias' intention to compose a speech that will extirpate her 'infamy' (δύσκλειαν, 21; cp. also τοῦ ὀνόματος φήμη at 2.).

**10** Gagarin (1997: 8 and 122) is therefore right to claim that in both Antiphon's and Gorgias' work we can trace the first imprints of *stasis*-theory. *Helen* belongs to what later rhetorical meta-language describes as *status qualitativus*; cp. Cole 1991: 75–76.

a storytelling, Gorgias suggests, would make his speech 'more credible but less charming'.[11]

The originality of Gorgias' composition, therefore, lies in that he attempts to exculpate Helen through an argumentation that employs probabilities (εἰκότα), i.e. arguments that offer verisimilar approximations of truth whose persuasiveness is dependent upon audiences' common experience.[12] He thus claims that Helen went to Troy for one of the following reasons: either because it was the will of the gods, or because she was violently abducted, or because she was persuaded by words, or because she fell in love with Paris.[13]

The first two causes receive only brief discussion by Gorgias. But his arguments concerning the third and the fourth causes, i.e. 'speech' (λόγος) and 'erotic desire' (ἔρως) include much theorizing that focuses on the psychological impact of words and images respectively (8–14 and 15–19). As Gorgias explains by adducing a number of examples, both speech and vision can affect our sentiments by instilling into our souls positive or negative emotions.[14] Emotions are hence

---

**11** Note that in the *Palamedes* (26), Gorgias concedes that Odysseus' argumentation in the speech of prosecution exhibited traces of novelty (καινὸς ὁ λόγος); yet, novelty is not sufficient, because Odysseus' arguments are contradictory. On the significance of novelty in public speaking and its association with the pleasure (ἡδονή) offered by words, cp. Cleon's criticism of Athenian audiences articulated in a distinctively Gorgianic fashion (Th. 3.38.24–25) and see Macleod 1983: 93–95; Hunter 1986: 423–426; Yunis 1996: 91–93; Gagarin 2002: 14; Worman 2002: 111; D' Angour 2011: 22; cp. also Ar. *Nu.* 547–8. Attempts at novelty must be associated with the agonistic environment in which sophistic *epideixis* developed (see Lloyd 1987: 94–98; Thomas 2000: chs. 7–8); this is just another characteristic that early rhetoric shares with poetry (see Griffith 1990: 187). Cp. for example Gorgias' dispute of previous versions foisting mortal parentage on Helen (4), which he substantiates on the basis of the common sophistic polarity between 'being and appearing'. On the deployment of parentage as a means of establishing authority and originality, see Griffith 1990: 194–196.
**12** 'Exculpation' does not necessarily mean that Gorgias' aim is to persuade his audience about Helen's innocence. As Gagarin convincingly shows, the purpose of the work under discussion, and indeed of the Sophists' work in general, was to display skill and offer pleasure rather than persuade (2001) –even as Gorgias' method, especially his use of *eikos* arguments, is widely used in orators' attempts to convince their audiences in real life situations.
**13** On the thread that binds together the four causes proposed by Gorgias, see Porter 1993: 274.
**14** The model of external causation that Gorgias employs to explain emotions aligns his discussion of vision with his arguments about divine intervention, physical violence and speech. In all these cases individuals are reduced to passive recipients of powers that either harm them or affect them externally (on passivity as a common intercultural phenomenon of emotional experience, see Kövecses 2000: 42). His approach to the affective power of words and images can therefore be paralleled to those instances in the poetry of Homer, where emotions (and *ate*) enter the individual externally. Yet, nowhere in his *Helen* does Gorgias claim, as Homer does (*Od.* 4. 261), that Aphrodite instilled love in Helen. By contrast, Gorgias employs hunting imagery (ψυχῆς

pivotal to Gorgias' arguments for Helen, because, on the view that he endorses, they induce us to do things that we would not have wanted or attempted to do if we were not under their control. In other words, emotions have a central role to the notion of acquiescence, the most typical aspect of ancient conceptualizations of verbal and non-verbal persuasion (πειθώ).[15]

Gorgias' arguments about *eros*, the fourth cause that may have prompted Helen's elopement, stress the psychological impact of perceived images upon our souls. From the outset of this discussion, Gorgias expresses programmatically his intention to make vision the central theme of his arguments about the compulsion of erotic love through the use of the following gnome:[16]

ἃ γὰρ ὁρῶμεν ἔχει φύσιν οὐχ ἣν ἡμεῖς θέλομεν ἀλλ' ἣν ἕκαστον ἔτυχε. διὰ δὲ τῆς ὄψεως ἡ ψυχὴ κἀν τοῖς τρόποις τυποῦται.

'Things that we see do not have the nature which we wish them to have but the nature which each one of them actually has; and by seeing them the mind [ψυχή] is moulded in its character too'. (15)

The first part of this formulation emphasizes the uncontrollability of the sights that viewers take in through sensory perception. Just as words penetrate our body and affect us emotionally (e.g. poetry 'goes into listeners, εἰσῆλθε, 9)[17] so do the

---

ἀγρεύμασι) to show that Helen fell prey to erotic love (ἔρως, 19). For Gorgias 'love' is not a divine agent *per se*. It is an agent that, as is also the case with speech, *possesses* divine power. For a survey of similar cases in Homer, showing that ate (and emotions) do not *necessarily* require divine agency (as Dodds 1951, ch. 1 suggests), see Cairns 2012: 14, with n. 25.

**15** On this topic, see Introduction.

**16** Note that towards the end of the speech (19), Gorgias underlines the compelling power of erotic love by employing the words that he uses earlier to discuss divine intervention (2). On the political terminology of these passages and its affinities with Empedocles (31B115 DK), see Buchheim 1989: 163.

**17** The materialistic approach that Gorgias endorses in his arguments about vision and emotions is also present in his discussion of 'speech' (λόγος), which he construes as a dynast with a 'minute body'. Furthermore, according to Gorgias, the power of speech to affect the soul's disposition is parallel to the drastic effects of 'drugs' (φάρμακα) on the humours of the human body (14). Depending on its 'arrangement' (τάξις), a drug (either a poison or a medicine) can cure the human body or cause its death. Hence, drugs' 'disposition' (τάξις) parallels speech's 'orderliness' (κόσμος) that Gorgias associates with truth at the opening *priamel* of *Helen*, thereby enhancing the authority of his own account. The ambivalent function of speeches-as-drugs is comparable to the objects of sight, which, depending on their nature, produce negative or positive emotions. In both cases, individuals cease to be agents of volition. On drugs in Gorgias, see Segal 1962: 104–105; Ford 2002: 173–187. On rhetoric and medicine, see Lloyd 1979: 88–98; Croally 1994: 32, nn. 55–56; Jouanna 2012: ch. 3.

images that we perceive through vision *enter into* our bodies physically and affect the disposition of our souls after coming into contact with them. When exposed to persuasive speeches or sights, human volition is extirpated (cp. [sc. persuasion] τὴν ψυχὴν ἐτυπώσατο ὅπως ἐβούλετο, 13). Furthermore, as the examples that he discusses later indicate (16–19), images are construed by Gorgias as bearing emotional charge: a frightful sight engenders fear, while the sight of a beautiful body inflicts erotic desire or longing. The word that Gorgias uses to denote what I have rendered with the word 'affect' is τυποῦται, whose literal meaning is 'to stamp' or 'to imprint'.[18]

The explanation of vision's psychological impact in physical, materialist terms is a salient feature of Gorgias' treatment of the function of vision (ὄψις) that markedly highlights viewers' passivity: at 16, vision is said to 'go' to the soul (ἐλθοῦσα, 16) and, more importantly, at paragraph 17, vision is presented as 'imprinting' images on the mind. In Gorgias' eyes, hence, emotions are not generated *in* or *by* the soul, but rather *enter into it* externally and shape it through the agency of perceived images (or, as he shows, in 9–10, through words).

Ancient popular and 'scientific' models of explanation construe vision as a haptic sense. Furthermore, these models may broadly be divided into two distinct categories: the active or emmissionist, positing that the eyes play an active role by casting rays on the objects of sensory perception and the passive, emanationist, according to which the eye receives effluences emitted by the objects of sights.[19] Although the difficulties of interpretation involved in the theories of vision proposed by the major representatives of these categories are immense, it is important to note that "[T]hese folk and scientific models are important because in their different ways they are compatible with beliefs that *the eyes may cause or lay one open to a variety of profound and often unwelcome physical changes*. Such, for example, is the belief that diseases such as eye-infections and epilepsy, and physical-cum-spiritual afflictions such as *miasma* (pollution) may be transmitted by sight" (Cairns 2011: 42).

Gorgias' physicalist approach to emotions throughout *Helen* indicates that he endorses a passive understanding of vision, emphasizing the psychological

---

**18** On τύπος, see Segal 1962: 142 n. 44, showing that τυπόω is used of 'moulding', 'stamping' *and* 'impressing'. Segal points out that τύπος "occurs in Democritus B228 with a metaphorical, ethical sense approaching 'character': τοῦ πατρικοῦ τύπου; the metaphor here would probably be adequately conveyed by the English 'stamp'. The association of the verb with τρόποις in *Hel.* 15 places the word in an ethical context similar to this fragment of Democritus". τύπος is also discussed by Roux 1961.
**19** For lucid outlines of ancient optical theories, see Cairns 2011: 140–141 and, for a more extensive account, Rudolph 2016: 36–53.

effects of sights upon beholders. This approach serves efficiently his argument, in so far as it reduces Helen, albeit, as we shall see, in a subversive way, into a victim of the external and uncontrollable power of vision. In doing so, he presents vision –qua elicitor of strong emotions– as an agent of coercion whose effectiveness is comparable with divine will, physical violence, and persuasion. Note, for example, that at the conclusion of his discussion of visual persuasion (19), Gorgias says that it was Helen's eye, rather than Helen, which was pleased at the sight of Paris' body.

In this chapter, I argue that Gorgias deploys current scientific theories of vision in order to promote his epideictic argument and show that Helen was not responsible for her travel to Troy. His appropriation of scientific theories of vision is compatible with folk assumptions concerning vision's importance for the onset of erotic love in earlier literature. In Gorgias' speech, Helen, the archetypical object of amazed male erotic gazes in earlier literature (and in Gorgias' encomiastic prelude in this speech, emphasizing the godlike beauty of her body, 4),[20] becomes the victim of Paris' beauty. Current theories of vision are thus put to the service of Gorgias' attempt to fly in the face of poets, presented collectively as ignoramuses, by using their own weapons.

As I suggested, throughout his treatment of the psychological impact of sights, Gorgias seems to deploy emanationist approaches. His gravitation towards emanationist, intromissive models of vision is anticipated in the opening of the fourth major argument (15), indicating the passivity of the beholder. For example, when he says that the objects of our sight have the nature that *they happen* to have, rather than the nature that we would want them to have, he emphasizes the uncontrollability of the psychic effects caused by the multiformity of sights to which humans are exposed. Thus, *physis* is construed as commensurate with natural (or divine, cp. πέφυκε at 6) necessity.

As is commonly the case in ancient philosophy and literature, chance is construed here as the equivalent of 'necessity' (*ananke*). Note, for example, that chance and necessity are conjoined in Gorgias' formulation about the indefensible compulsion exercised by divine will (ἢ γὰρ Τύχης βουλήμασι καὶ θεῶν βουλεύμασι καὶ Ἀνάγκης ψηφίσμασιν ἔπραξεν ἃ ἔπραξεν, 5).[21] 'Necessity' and 'chance' are also employed by Gorgias to qualify the compulsion of persuasive speeches (ἀνάγκης εἶδος ἔχει μὲν οὔ, τὴν δὲ δύναμιν τὴν αὐτὴν ἔχει, 12) and the

---

**20** πλείστας δὲ πλείστοις ἐπιθυμίας ἔρωτος ἐνειργάσατο, ἑνὶ δὲ σώματι πολλὰ σώματα συνήγαγεν ἀνδρῶν.
**21** Cp. Empedocles B 115.

overwhelming effects of visually inflicted *eros* in the conclusive points of his argument about the emotive potentialities of sights. At that point, Gorgias uses a gnomic aorist and a common conceptual metaphor for erotic love to indicate that Helen travelled to Troy (a) because she was ensnared by chance (τύχης ἀγρεύμασι), rather than because she decided to do so, and (b) because she was forced by the compulsion of love (ἔρωτος ἀνάγκαις), rather than because she carefully contrived her elopement. As Guthrie (1965) points out in his discussion of 'chance' and 'necessity' in Empedocles (on whom Gorgias perhaps draws at the passage from paragraph 5 cited above),[22] "[I]t must be remembered that for a Greek chance and necessity could be much the same thing" (163); for the Presocratics, "*Physis*...is a natural necessity inherent in each separate thing or substance, not a law of interaction between them".

If, as I suggested, Gorgias deploys an intromissive view to establish the uncontrollability of sights' psychological impact, our next task is to explore whether he appropriates specific theories of vision to serve his epideictic purposes. The existing evidence makes it impossible to identify *with certainty* a specific 'scientific' theory of vision favoured by Gorgias in *Helen* and, on account of the epideictic nature of the speech, one may reasonably argue that he was guided by creative selectivity rather than commitment to a specific scientific model of explanation. Notably, however, one of the most distinctive characteristics of Gorgias' discussion of vision in *Helen* is the emphasis that he places on images' 'imprinting' of the soul through the mediation of vision. In addition to images' stamping of the soul (τυποῦται) at the outset of his discussion of vision, in his example of the destructive psychological impact of frightful sights Gorgias says: οὕτως εἰκόνας τῶν ὁρωμένων πραγμάτων ἡ ὄψις ἐνέγραψεν ἐν τῶι φρονήματι, 17.

During Gorgias' lifespan, Democritus developed a theory of vision according to which *eidola* flow towards the eye and are imprinted *on the air*.[23] Furthermore, as far as one can see, Gorgias is the first to speak of 'impressions' of images *on the soul* (or, indeed, *phronema* –on this term see discussion below) in the frame of a discussion concerning the emotive impact of sights. Although it is impossible to tell with certainty if Gorgias owes the notion of 'imprinting' to Democritus, there are some reasons that make this hypothesis possible. As I argue, this speculation gains some support from the fact that in Gorgias' formulation at 17 vision is said to imprint on *phronema* '*images* of sights', rather than effluences of sights or sights themselves

---

[22] See Buchheim 1989, note *ad loc.*
[23] For a recent discussion of Democritus' theory, recognizing the observer's active role, see Rudolph 2011.

(εἰκόνας τῶν ὁρωμένων),[24] but also from the possibility that, like Gorgias, Democritus used his physicalist approach to vision to explain ethical or psychological issues.

Before I discuss Gorgias' possible appropriation of Democritus' theory of *eidola*, it would be useful to investigate briefly an external piece of evidence associating Gorgias with Empedocles' theory about colour perception. This passage does not dispute my hypothesis that Gorgias draws on Democritus' *eidola* theory.[25] By contrast, it furnishes further evidence that Gorgias took a selective interest in previous or current 'scientific' theories of vision which enabled him to enhance his epideictic arguments.

According to some pieces of evidence,[26] Gorgias was a disciple of Empedocles. Even if this evidence is the product of later doxographers' attempts to impose anachronistically on Presocratic philosophers the notion of 'schools of philosophy', we know for certain that Gorgias came from Leontini, a small Sicilian town, while Empedocles' native town was Acragas. Furthermore, scholarship has identified several instances in which Gorgias' work echoes Empedocles' philosophy.[27]

In *Meno* 76c–e, Socrates claims that both Meno, who is introduced in the dialogue as one of Gorgias' disciples, and Gorgias himself adhere to Empedocles' explanation of colour-perception:

ΣΩ. Βούλει οὖν σοι κατὰ Γοργίαν ἀποκρίνωμαι, ᾗ ἂν σὺ μάλιστα ἀκολουθήσαις;
MEN. Βούλομαι· πῶς γὰρ οὔ;
ΣΩ. Οὐκοῦν λέγετε ἀπορροάς τινας τῶν ὄντων κατὰ Ἐμπεδοκλέα;
MEN. Σφόδρα γε.
ΣΩ. Καὶ πόρους εἰς οὓς καὶ δι' ὧν αἱ ἀπορροαὶ πορεύονται;
MEN. Πάνυ γε.
ΣΩ. Καὶ τῶν ἀπορροῶν τὰς μὲν ἁρμόττειν ἐνίοις τῶν πόρων, τὰς δὲ ἐλάττους ἢ μείζους εἶναι;
MEN. Ἔστι ταῦτα.
ΣΩ. Οὐκοῦν καὶ ὄψιν καλεῖς τι;
MEN. Ἔγωγε.

---

**24** Cp. Pl. *Tht.* 191c–d; *Phil.* 39a–b; Arist. *de An.* 2.424a19; 3.425b23, 3.434a29; Stoics: *SVF* 2.53, 55, 56.
**25** To look for systematicity in Gorgias' speech for *Helen*, a speech which he qualifies as a *paignion*, means to miss the point of his *epideictic* attempt which invests in novelty. On this point see Gagarin (2001a: 278), emphasizing that Gorgias was not the first to defend Helen, but the first to deal in an elaborate manner with the question of her responsibility.
**26** DK 82 A 3, A10.
**27** On Gorgias as Empedocles' pupil, see DK A 2, 3, 14; Segal 1962: 99 with further references in n. 4; Buchheim 1985.

ΣΩ.  Ἐκ τούτων δὴ "σύνες ὅ τοι λέγω," ἔφη Πίνδαρος. ἔστιν γὰρ χρόα ἀπορροὴ σχημάτων ὄψει σύμμετρος καὶ αἰσθητός.
ΜΕΝ.  Ἄριστά μοι δοκεῖς, ὦ Σώκρατες, ταύτην τὴν ἀπόκρισιν εἰρηκέναι.

(Plato, *Meno* 76c–e)

Socr: Shall I answer in the manner of Gorgias, to make it easy for you to follow? Men. Yes, please. Of course I'd appreciate that. Socr: All right, then. Do you and Gorgias agree with Empedocles that there are certain emanations from things? Men.: Definitely. Socr: And that there are channels into which and through which the emanations travel? Men.: Yes. Socr: And that some of the emanations fit some of the channels, while others are too small or too big? Men.: That's right. Socr.: Now, you acknowledge the existence of something called 'sight', don't you? Men.: Yes, I do. Socr: So now you're in a position to 'mark well what I say', as Pindar puts it: colour is an emanation emitted by shapes which is commensurate with sight and so is perceptible. Men.: I think this is a truly excellent answer, Socrates (transl. Waterfield).

According to this (abbreviated) version of his theory, Empedocles postulated that colours emit material effluences that 'go to' our eyes (πορεύονται) and enter into them through some kind of openings or 'pores' (πόροι; cp. φέρεσθαι δὲ τὰ χρώματα πρὸς τὴν ὄψιν διὰ τὴν ἀπορροήν in Theophrastus' version of Empedocles' theory, and ἐλθοῦσα [sc. ἡ ὄψις] in *Helen* 16).[28] Furthermore, according to this version of Empedocles' theory, the perception of colours requires that the size of the 'effluences' (ἀπορροαί) emitted by individual objects is commensurate (σύμμετρος) with the pores of our eyes. As the use of the word ἁρμόττειν shows, colour-perception can be achieved only when the effluences *fit exactly*, i.e come into contact with, the pores of our sense organs. Hence, as is typically the case with ancient optical theories, Empedocles construed vision as haptic and one may also note that in Theophrastus' account, effluences are said to 'touch' the sense-organs (ἁπτόμενα, *De sensibus* 7). Hence, Socrates' emphasis on the movement of effluences towards the eye, endorsed, as Meno ascertains, by Gorgias, is compatible with modern intromissive interpretations of Empedocles' theory, which cast doubt on Aristotle's interactionist description of it.[29]

---

[28] Note that the use of the schema etymologicum (πόροι/πορεύονται) –further highlighted through the use of acoustic repetition (**πόρ**οι, **ἀπορρ**οαί, **πορ**εύονται)– adds to Socrates' exposition of Empedocles' theory the tonality of Gorgias' prose style.

[29] See Long 1966 and O'Brien 1970. On Theophrastus' account of Empedocles' explanation of colour perception in *De sensibus* 7, presenting colours as being transmitted to the eye 'by effluence' (φέρεσθαι), see Ierodiakonou 2005. For a recent overview of Empedocles' colour perception theory, see Rudolph 2106: 44–46.

What, however, is absent from Empedocles' theory about colour perception[30] is the notion of 'imprinting' that figures predominantly in Gorgias' discussion of vision. In fact, Rudolph (2016: 51) has recently argued that "the imprint theory supplements rather than contradicts the notion of vision by effluences". In what follows, I argue for the possibility that in his discussion of the emotional power of sights Gorgias relies on Democritus' optical theory, which, as we shall see, is relevant to his ethics.

Atomists' optics display several difficulties of interpretation, but according to some ancient sources discussing the psychological impact of vision indicate that, according to Democritus, the *eidola* of the objects of perception bear emotional charge. The most instructive among these pieces of evidence is a passage from Plutarch (682F–683A), where one of the interlocutors, Gaius, explains envy and *baskania* ('the evil eye'):

> Ἐμοῦ δὲ παυσαμένου, Γάιος ὁ Φλώρου γαμβρός τῶν δὲ Δημοκρίτου , ἔφη, εἰδώλων, ὥσπερ Αἰγιέων ἢ Μεγαρέων, ἀριθμὸς οὐδεὶς οὐδὲ λόγος; ἅ φησιν ἐκεῖνος ἐξιέναι τοὺς φθονοῦντας, οὔτ' αἰσθήσεως ἄμοιρα παντάπασιν οὔθ' ὁρμῆς, ἀνάπλεά τε τῆς ἀπὸ τῶν προϊεμένων μοχθηρίας καὶ βασκανίας, μεθ' ἧς ἐμπλασσόμενα καὶ παραμένοντα καὶ συνοικοῦντα τοῖς βασκαινομένοις ἐπιταράττειν καὶ κακοῦν αὐτῶν τό τε σῶμα καὶ τὴν διάνοιαν.

> When I had stopped, Gaius, Florus' nephew, said, 'Is there no mention nor discussion of Democritus' *eidola*? Is he to be left out "like the Aigeans or Megareans"? Democritus says that envious people emit these *eidola*, which are not entirely without a share in perception nor impulse and are full of their senders' bitterness and malevolence. Filled with this and preserving it they come into contact with those who are 'bewitched' and disturb and harm both their bodies and thoughts. That at least is what I think Democritus thinks, and it is what he says in marvelous and impressive language. (transl. Warren)

As Gaius' account makes clear, the *eidola* emitted from enviers are 'full' of (ἀνάπλεα) senders' negative psychological disposition (μοχθηρίας καὶ βασκανίας). Furthermore, Gaius notably uses the word συνοικοῦντα, which implies that *eidola* enter into the body of the viewer, or rather the target of *baskania*, and 'lodge in' it or even become parts of it, as ἐμπλασσόμενα (perhaps corresponding to Gorgias' notion of *typos*) seems to suggest. The image of the emotion's cohabitation with the target's body corresponds to a common conceptual metaphor, according to which the body is construed as the container of a substance, frequently a fluid. But it is noteworthy that in Gaius' explanation the intrusion of *eidola* into targets' bodies is used to explain, in a materialist fashion, the disturbance (ἐπιταράττειν)

---

[30] Traces of Empedocles' philosophy can be found in Gorgias' discussion of painting at 18 (see Buchheim 1989, note *ad loc.*).

and harm (κακοῦν) that they inflict on targets' souls and bodies. Admittedly, Plutarch's account of Democritus' theory poses several problems of interpretation, which, however, are not directly relevant to my discussion.[31] For example, what are the implications of the conceptualization of *eidola* as *agents* of sense perception? And how are we to account for the fact that in another passage from the same work (734F–735B), discussing the role of *eidola* in divination, *eidola* are presented as being alive ('as if they are alive', ὥσπερ ἔμψυχα)?

In a recent discussion of the passage under review, Warren (2007: 99) argues that "according to Democritus, *eidola* given off by people, especially people in extreme emotional states, carry and preserve the imprint of that psychic state. When they lodge in the soul of someone else, therefore, this psychic imprint can affect the perceiver's soul too… In this way, therefore, Democritus is able to offer a physical, atomist account of the mechanism of interpersonal psychic harm". On Warren's understanding, thus, Democritus' physicalist explanation of the psychological impact of *eidola* has important implications for atomist ethics and serves to explain instances, such as 'mass hysteria' or panic, where groups of people are overpowered simultaneously by the same emotion.[32]

Gorgias' (possible) appropriation of Democritus' physicalist approach may offer an example of how "la théorie des simulacres constitue une explication générale susceptible d'applications multiples" (Morel 1996: 319). My hypothesis that Gorgias uses for his own purposes Democritus' theory gains some support from the fact that, in his formulation at 17, indicating the psychological harm done by frightful images, Gorgias says that vision imprints on *phronema* 'images of sights', i.e. copies of sights, rather than 'sights' themselves (εἰκόνας τῶν ὁρωμένων).[33] In other words, Gorgias not only seems to employ Democritus' notion of images' 'imprinting' the soul, a notion that as far as I can see is unattested elsewhere in the Presocratics, but also seems to be in line with Democritus' view that the objects of sight emit 'images' (rather than effluences, as is the case with Empedocles). Furthermore, as we saw, both at the beginning and at the end of his argumentation about vision, Gorgias emphasizes the randomness of images' sights, which he associates with the emotions that they produce (cp. οὕτω τὰ μὲν λυπεῖν τὰ δὲ ποθεῖν πέφυκε τὴν ὄψιν, 18). Hence, Gorgias not only postulates

---

31 As a Platonist, Plutarch's representation of Democritus' theory must have been influenced by the *Phaedrus*, on which see Cairns 2013.
32 For an approach to 'mass psychology' in Gorgias and Thucydides, see Hunter 1986.
33 Cp. Pl. *Tht.* 191c–d; *Phil.* 39a-b; Arist. *de An.* 2.424a19; 3.425b23, 3.434a29; Stoics: *SVF* 2.53, 55, 56.

viewers' passivity, but, rather correlatively, seems to attribute to the images emitted by sights emotional charge which is transmitted to and imprinted on the soul. Note for example, that, in his discussion of humans' response to acute danger Gorgias says that people frequently lose their mind at the very moment that they are exposed to frightful sights. Furthermore, as is the case with Gaius' Democritean explanation of the destructive power of enviers' gazes (ἐπιταράττειν), Gorgias says that the frightful sight of the enemy's armour alarms vision (ἐταράχθη) and, in its own turn, vision alarms the soul (ἐτάραξε, 16). Finally, the notion that the malicious *eidola* of *baskania* lodge in beholders' souls (συνοικοῦντα) parallels Gorgias' use of the verb εἰσῳκίσθη to convey images' inhabitation in beholders' souls.

The traces of Democritus' theory about *eidola* in Gorgias' theorization may also be discerned in his division of sights into two distinct categories according to their hedonic valence: sights are either pleasurable or distressful. This bipolar division is encapsulated in Gorgias' concluding remark that, by their own nature (πέφυκε, 18), some images make vision experience sorrow (λυπεῖν), while others make it experience longing (ποθεῖν, and note the antithetical construction τὰ μέν...τὰ δέ). The polarity distressful/pleasurable (sights) is also reflected in the examples adduced by Gorgias: panic caused by frightful sights (16–17), yearning and erotic desire as a response to the products of visual arts (17–18).

According to later doxographical evidence, Democritus recognized two distinct types of *eidola*: those which are harmful and those which are beneficial.[34] Although this is not the place to discuss the question of whether *eidola* are intentionally malicious (as Taylor suggests), or dispute Sextus' theist understanding of *eidola*, it seems possible to argue that Democritus' bipolar division of *eidola*, emphasizing their impact on the viewer, perhaps served as the basis for Gorgias' antithetical classification of images –a classification dictated by natural necessity (πέφυκε)– according to the psychological effects that each member of this antithesis prompts. This hypothesis is supported by the fact that, as we saw, Gorgias' treatment underscores the role of 'chance' (τύχη) in the visual transmission of emotions. The randomness with which perceived 'images' operate to transmit emotions, thereby reducing beholders to a state of passivity, is also a distinctive characteristic of Democritus' theory positing the existence of two distinct types of *eidola*.

According to Plutarch (*De def. or.* 419A) and Sextus (*Math.* 9.19), Democritus distinguished between malevolent and benevolent *eidola* which he qualified as

---

[34] On whether eidola are intentionally harmful, see Warren 2007: 98, n. 21 with further bibliography.

εὔλογχα ('benevolent', 'beneficial'). The qualification of 'positive' *eidola* with a word indicating that the beholder's perception of either type of *eidola* is random seems to correspond to Gorgias' emphasis on 'chance' (ἔτυχεν) that I discussed earlier. Furthermore, in Plutarch's and Sextus' accounts of *eidola* theory, Democritus is presented as praying to meet propitious *eidola* (εὔχεσθαι). Both sources, thus, underscore beholders' inability to control the *eidola* that they happen to meet. Indeed, in Sextus' account the role of 'chance' is made explicit in his presentation of the contents of Democritus' prayers (εὔχετο εὐλόγχων τυχεῖν εἰδόλων).

Gorgias' endorsement of Democritus' two contrasting types of *eidola* with corresponding psychological qualities may also lie behind the inclusion of harmful sights in the examples that he uses in *Helen* (16–17). At first sight, fear or panic are not directly relevant to Helen's case. However, the inclusion of these emotions serves the important purpose of giving the impression that Gorgias' model of explanation is 'holistic'. As we noted, his defence of Helen relies on *eikota*, i.e. all encompassing arguments of general applicability rather than on narrative specificity. In other words, the negative example of fearful sights, relying on his listeners' knowledge of collective panic in the battlefield, not only indicates vision's power to vitiate cognition to the extent of causing madness (17), but also makes Helen's amazement at the sight of Paris' body look like just another example supporting the general rule of the indefensible compulsion exercised by the images that sights 'imprint' on our souls.

In what follows, I engage in a closer reading of Gorgias' treatment of visually inflicted fear (16–17). As we shall see, despite Gorgias' unsystematic treatment of the topic, this section of the speech allows us to discern the ways in which he construes emotions' impact upon cognition –and in this sense, emotions *are* a cognitive phenomenon. On the basis of a comparison with Aristotle's treatment of emotions' interference with cognitive processes, I conclude that Gorgias takes a more negative stance towards emotions. Unlike Aristotle, Gorgias seems to view visually inflicted emotions as a vehicle of cognitive impairment, especially in so far as emotions prompt human action. I then turn my attention to his discussion of the emotional potentialities of visual arts, which I discuss in comparison with his arguments about the power of speech.

## 1.3 Emotions, vision, and cognitive impairment

The impact of emotions upon assessment of any given situation explains in part why Aristotle endorses in the *Rhetoric* an appraisal-oriented approach to *pathe*. As he says:

> ἔστι δὲ τὰ πάθη δι' ὅσα μεταβάλλοντες διαφέρουσι πρὸς τὰς κρίσεις οἷς ἔπεται λύπη καὶ ἡδονή, οἷον ὀργὴ ἔλεος φόβος καὶ ὅσα ἄλλα τοιαῦτα, καὶ τὰ τούτοις ἐναντία.

> The emotions [*pathe*] are those things through which, by undergoing change, people come to differ in their judgments and which are accompanied by pain and pleasure, for example, anger, pity, fear, and other such things and their opposites. (transl. Kennedy)

Aristotle's locution emphasizes two things: first, that *pathe* affect the way in which one evaluates a situation and, indeed κρίσις is, as he avers, the objective of rhetoric (1377b 20–24)[35] and, second, emotions' phenomenological aspects, the pleasure and pain that accompanies them. Unlike Gorgias who seems to endorse a physicalist approach to his theorizing concerning the generation of emotions, in the *Rhetoric* Aristotle stresses that for an emotion to come into being its agent *must* endorse a certain belief.[36] However, as the passage that I cited at the beginning of this section indicates, Aristotle also observed that emotions affect our assessments. In other words, for Aristotle emotions not only require beliefs, but also shape them decisively.[37] As I argue, in Gorgias' eyes visually inflicted emotions act with an extreme immediacy and, thereby, impair rather than affect cognition.

The first example that Gorgias adduces concerns the fear experienced by soldiers when they face the enemy's weapons. On such occasions, Gorgias claims, the soldiers' vision, filled with panic, transmits fear to soldiers' souls:

> αὐτίκα γὰρ ὅταν πολέμια σώματα [καὶ] πολέμιον ἐπὶ πολεμίοις ὁπλίσῃ κόσμον χαλκοῦ καὶ σιδήρου, τοῦ μὲν ἀλεξητήριον τοῦ δὲ † προβλήματα, εἰ θεάσεται ἡ ὄψις, ἐταράχθη καὶ ἐτάραξε τὴν ψυχήν, **ὥστε πολλάκις κινδύνου τοῦ μέλλοντος <ὡς> ὄντος φεύγουσιν ἐκπλαγέντες**. (16)

---

[35] ἐπεὶ δὲ ἕνεκα κρίσεώς ἐστιν ἡ ῥητορική…ἀνάγκη μὴ μόνον πρὸς τὸν λόγον ὁρᾶν, ὅπως ἀποδεικτικὸς ἔσται καὶ πιστός, ἀλλὰ καὶ αὐτὸν ποιόν τινα καὶ τὸν κριτὴν κατασκευάζειν.

[36] Note, however, that in *De anima* 403a 3–13, Aristotle suggests that philosophers define emotions by emphasizing the appraisals that cause them while 'natural philosophers' stress bodily changes.

[37] For a modern discussion of this issue from a cognitive perspective, see Frijda/Manstead/Bem 2000: ch. 1.

For instance, when the sight surveys hostile persons and a hostile array of bronze and iron for hostile armament, offensive array of the one and shields of the other, it is alarmed, and it alarms the mind, so that often people flee in panic when some danger is imminent as if it were present. (transl. D.M. MacDowell)

The object of soldiers' vision in the present example, i.e. the enemy's weaponry, stirs *ekplexis* in their souls. *Ekplexis* commonly signifies the paralysing wonder, surprise or stupefaction experienced by a person who is unprepared to deal with a sudden, embarrassing or threatening situation.[38] The situation that Gorgias describes here must have been particularly familiar to his audience. In the *Iliad*, the appearance of Achilles' body is enough to cause intense sentiments of fear (e.g. *Il.* 18. 247–8). Furthermore, in descriptions of battle-field scenes, shields, and especially shields decorated with apotropaic images that return fierce gazes, are presented as having paralysing effects upon viewers.[39]

Gorgias' example of the effects of frightful sights, however, is not identical with the numerous instances that we find in Homer. At a crucial moment in the *Iliad*, for example, the sight of Achilles' blazing weapons give Hector the shivers (*Il.* 22.131–37):

Ὣς ὅρμαινε μένων, ὁ δέ οἱ σχεδὸν ἦλθεν Ἀχιλλεὺς
ἶσος Ἐνυαλίῳ, κορυθάϊκι πτολεμιστῇ,
σείων Πηλιάδα μελίην κατὰ δεξιὸν ὦμον
δεινήν· ἀμφὶ δὲ χαλκὸς ἐλάμπετο εἴκελος αὐγῇ
ἢ πυρὸς αἰθομένου ἢ ἠελίου ἀνιόντος.
Ἕκτορα δ', ὡς ἐνόησεν, ἕλε τρόμος· οὐδ' ἄρ' ἔτ' ἔτλη
αὖθι μένειν, ὀπίσω δὲ πύλας λίπε, βῆ δὲ φοβηθείς.

Thus he pondered, waiting, while Achilles approached him— the equal of Enyalios, that bright-helmed warrior!— above his right shoulder wielding his spear of Pelian ash, so fearsome, while all about him the bronze now glinted like blazing fire or the rays of the rising sun. As Hektor looked, trembling seized him, he no longer dared to stand fi rm: the gates left behind him, he fled in terror (transl. Green).

The present passage not only indicates the literary tradition on which Gorgias' treatment of emotions draws, but also indicates the novelties of his epideictic approach. Just like the epic narrative, Gorgias emphasizes the immediacy with which sights cause strong sentiments, but also highlights the power of emotions to prompt action. Furthermore, just like the epic, Gorgias gives as a glimpse of the threatening materiality of the hostile armament, even as his imagery is not as

---

**38** Cp. Huart 1968: 119; Worman 2002: 132, 165, 174.
**39** For discussion, see Lovatt 2013: 197–204.

enhanced as the imagery that grants Achilles with salient visuality. But unlike the description of Hector's reflexive response to the sight of Achilles in Homer, emphasizing Hector's immediate action, Gorgias seems to suggest that fearful sights cause cognitive impairment. The overwhelming emotion of panic (*ekplexis*) is transmitted through vision to soldiers' souls and, thereby, forces them to *perceive the danger as present*.

Emotions' power to affect our assessment of sensory experience is discussed by Aristotle in a passage from *De somniis*.[40] I cite the relevant passage in full, because it seems to me to be particularly relevant to Gorgias' line of argument:

> πρὸς δὲ τούτοις ὅτι ῥᾳδίως ἀπατώμεθα περὶ τὰς αἰσθήσεις ἐν τοῖς πάθεσιν ὄντες, ἄλλοι δὲ ἐν ἄλλοις, οἷον ὁ δειλὸς ἐν φόβῳ, ὁ δ' ἐρωτικὸς ἐν ἔρωτι, ὥστε δοκεῖν ἀπὸ μικρᾶς ὁμοιότητος τὸν μὲν τοὺς πολεμίους ὁρᾶν, τὸν δὲ τὸν ἐρώμενον· καὶ ταῦτα ὅσῳ ἂν ἐμπαθέστερος ᾖ, τοσούτῳ ἀπ' ἐλάσσονος ὁμοιότητος φαίνεται. τὸν αὐτὸν δὲ τρόπον καὶ ἐν ὀργαῖς καὶ ἐν πάσαις ἐπιθυμίαις εὐαπάτητοι γίνονται πάντες, καὶ μᾶλλον ὅσῳ ἂν μᾶλλον ἐν τοῖς πάθεσιν ὦσιν. διὸ καὶ τοῖς πυρέττουσιν ἐνίοτε φαίνεται ζῷα ἐν τοῖς τοίχοις ἀπὸ μικρᾶς ὁμοιότητος τῶν γραμμῶν συντιθεμένων. καὶ ταῦτ' ἐνίοτε συνεπιτείνει τοῖς πάθεσιν οὕτως, ὥστε, ἂν μὲν μὴ σφόδρα κάμνωσι, μὴ λανθάνειν ὅτι ψεῦδος, ἐὰν δὲ μεῖζον ᾖ τὸ πάθος, καὶ κινεῖσθαι πρὸς αὐτά. (460b 4–16)

> And moreover that we are easily deceived about our perceptions when we are in emotional states, some in one state and others in another; e.g. the coward in his fear, the lover in his love; so that even from a very faint resemblance the coward expects to see his enemy, and the lover his loved one; and the more is one under the influence of emotion, the less similarity is required to give these impressions. Similarly, in fits [sc. states] of anger and in all forms of desire all are easily deceived, and the more easily the more they are under the influence of emotions. So for those in a fever, animals sometimes appear on the wall from a slight resemblance of lines put together. Sometimes the illusion corresponds to the degree of emotions so that those who are not very ill are aware that the impression is false, but if the malady is more severe, they actually move in accordance with appearances. (transl. Leighton, based on Hett)

Aristotle shows lucidly here how emotions affect, indeed deceive sensory perception (ἀπατώμεθα περὶ τὰς αἰσθήσεις), thereby giving rise to false beliefs. Because Aristotle recognizes in emotions intentionality, i.e. emotions are *about* something, his discussion emphasizes how our sentiments affect our sensory perception of individual emotions' elicitors. On his view, emotions push agents to attribute meaning to what they take in by putting together (συντιθεμένων) arbitrarily the random indications that they perceive through sight. Aristotle,

---

[40] On this passage, and relevant points made by Aristotle in the *Nicomachean Ethics* (1149a 24–31), see Leighton 1982: 149–154.

however, makes another important point in this passage, namely that the degree of the agent's misperception depends on the intensity of the emotion that she experiences. The reason for this is that when we are overpowered by a certain emotion, we are more prone to misinterpret the objects of our sensory perception. In other words, we are led to believe that what we see *is* what we take it to be. Hence, the more we are affected by a certain emotion, the more the differences between our false-beliefs and what we take in through our senses are obfuscated. As Aristotle observes, intense emotions require a small degree of similarity to prompt illusory effects. Finally, as Aristotle avers, the degree of our self-deception determines our readiness to act (cp. κινεῖσθαι πρὸς αὐτά).

Although Gorgias shares with Aristotle the emphasis on emotions' power to affect judgment and prompt action, on account of its being fundamentally physicalist, his approach differs from Aristotle's discussion of emotions' impact on judgment in one significant respect: unlike Aristotle who proposes that emotions affect our cognitive processing of sensory experience, thereby providing us with deceitful cognitions that intensify the emotion, Gorgias construes vision (or the eyes) as an entrance through which emotionally charged images find their way to the soul. In the concluding lines of his example, Gorgias maintains:

> ἰσχυρὰ γὰρ ἡ ἀμέλεια τοῦ νόμου διὰ τὸν φόβον εἰσῳκίσθη τὸν ἀπὸ τῆς ὄψεως, ἥτις ἐλθοῦσα ἐποίησεν ἀμελῆσαι καὶ τοῦ καλοῦ τοῦ διὰ τὸν νόμον κρινομένου καὶ τοῦ ἀγαθοῦ τοῦ διὰ τὴν δίκην γιγνομένου. (16)
>
> So strong is the disregard of law which is implanted in them because of the fear caused by the sight; when it befalls, it makes them disregard both the honour which is awarded by obeying the law and the benefit which accrues for doing right.[41]

This passage seems to take Gorgias' previous argument a step further. As the text stands, disregard for normative considerations and possible profit are presented as a situation that enters into and 'lodges in' the soul, because of the fear caused by the frightful sight of the enemy. This argument has significant ethical implications which are directly relevant to Helen's exculpation.

As I suggested, Gorgias appropriates Democritus' physicalist theory of vision postulating that *eidola* have emotional and ethical charge. As Warren convincingly argues (2007), Democritus put his emanationist theory, proposing the ex-

---

**41** Note that 'sight' is here presented to 'go' (ἐλθοῦσα), just as eros is said to 'go' (ἦλθεν γὰρ ὡς ἦλθεν) at 19: in both cases Gorgias employs gnomic aorists and in both cases individuals are presented to be overridden by external forces able to extirpate their volition.

istence of beneficial and harmful *eidola*, to the service of psychological and ethical questions, such as mass 'hysteria', public panic, or *stasis*. If we accept that Gorgias endorses Democritus' model of explanation, Gorgias' example about of the wave of panic that overpowers soldiers in battlefields, with all the stress that it lays on the consequences of visually transmitted fear upon agents' sense of normative obligations and expediency, gains further significance for the argument of this epideictic piece. Helen, Gorgias seems to imply, is no more responsible for her actions than the soldiers who flee the battlefield. The 'ignorance' of her soul (ψυχῆς ἀγνόημα) is the result of a sight's, i.e. Paris' body, emotional impact upon her soul's 'character' (τρόποι, 15).[42] Just as soldiers neglect their social and moral obligations on account of the overwhelming emotion of fear, so did Helen displayed disregard for her family.

That Gorgias (perhaps selectively) understands vision as a medium capable of cognitive impairment is further highlighted in the next lines, where he turns his attention to the effects of frightful sights perceived in the past:

> ἤδη δέ τινες ἰδόντες φοβερὰ καὶ τοῦ παρόντος ἐν τῶι παρόντι χρόνωι φρονήματος ἐξέστησαν· οὕτως ἀπέσβεσε καὶ ἐξήλασεν ὁ φόβος τὸ νόημα. πολλοὶ δὲ ματαίοις πόνοις καὶ δειναῖς νόσοις καὶ δυσιάτοις μανίαις περιέπεσον· οὕτως εἰκόνας τῶν ὁρωμένων πραγμάτων ἡ ὄψις ἐνέγραψεν ἐν τῶι φρονήματι. καὶ τὰ μὲν δειματοῦντα πολλὰ μὲν παραλείπεται, ὅμοια δ' ἐστὶ τὰ παραλειπόμενα οἷάπερ <τὰ> λεγόμενα (17).

> And some people before now, on seeing frightful things, have also lost their presence of mind at the present moment; fear so extinguishes and expels thought. And many have fallen into groundless distress and terrible illness and incurable madness; so deeply does sight engrave on the mind images of actions that are seen. And as far as frightening things are concerned, many are omitted, but those omitted are similar to those mentioned.

What Gorgias seems to suggest here is that extremely frightful sights lead individuals to lose their 'mind' (φρονήματος). Although Gorgias appears to be unsystematic in his use of words denoting the human mind in particular and cognitive processes in general, it seems to me that the word φρόνημα that he employs here

---

[42] Cp. Segal (1962: 107): "Here the physical stimulus affects even the internal 'character,' the *tropoi*, of the psyche, a term which may itself have physical connotations like the taxis of the psyche in 14.46 The *tropoi* probably refer more immediately to the ordinary ethical values upon which the stability of the psyche in society rests, but these values are forgotten under the impact of a powerful *opsis*, just as *phobos* at the end of 16 'drives out' *nomos*". If, as Segal suggests, *tropoi* has physical connotations, one may wonder if Gorgias envisages an 'atomist' soul which, when imprinted by sights, sustains physical change. The notion of change is attested in Gorgias' discussion of magic, where he claims that the power of incantations 'alter' (μετέστησεν) the soul by witchcraft (10).

designates one's ability to make sensible judgments. I therefore take it to be a close synonym of the word νόημα that he also employs in the passage under discussion. That both these words signify 'sensible thinking' can be gleaned from the next lines, where the 'stamping' of frightful images on φρόνημα are identified as a cause of madness.[43] Since madness is a condition in which we have worries 'for which there is no real justification',[44] φρόνημα should be construed as signifying 'sensible thinking'. In this connection, it is also important to note that, even as Gorgias refers here to the impact of traumatic events experienced in the past upon individuals' cognitive ability, he does not speak of 'memory' (μνήμη). Instead, he suggests that frightful sights affect one's mind *at the time* of their perception, thereby causing a permanent injury to one's mental sanity.[45] The immediacy with which fearful sights lead individuals to mental insanity is another indication that Gorgias endorses a physicalist approach, according to which individuals are powerless to control the impact of what they see upon their souls.

## 1.4 The fabrication of likenesses: visual arts, speech, and emotions

Gorgias' points on vision and emotions are relevant to his views about persuasive speech and deception. In the following pages, I turn my attention to his arguments about *logos* (9–14) in comparison with his points about the impact of visual arts. In Gorgias' discussion, *logoi* share with visual arts at least two characteristics: they are products of human craftsmanship and they persuade, i.e. they make listeners acquiesce in speakers' beliefs (*doxai*), by causing emotions. As we shall see, the analogies between the emotional power of speech and sights are salient and, taken jointly, may give us a clearer image about Gorgias' conceptualization of persuasion and deception.

Just like sights, *logos* is perceived by Gorgias as entering into the human body externally and affecting the 'disposition' of one's soul. Hence, in Gorgias' eyes,

---

[43] For this meaning of the phrase ἐξήλασεν τὸ νόημα, cp. E. *Ba.* 853: ὡς φρονῶν μὲν εὖ/οὐ μὴ θελήσῃ θῆλυν ἐνδῦναι στολήν,/ἔξω δ' ἐλαύνων τοῦ φρονεῖν ἐνδύσεται.

[44] This definition of madness would fit modern descriptions of anxiety, especially cases of general anxiety disorder involving panic attacks during and after which sentiments of impending doom are predominant.

[45] In the *Defence of Palamedes* (25), Gorgias construes madness as a condition in which one engages in pointless tasks (ματαίοις πόνοις); for a similar description of madness, cp. Dem. 21.69 and see Padel 1995: 206–207. For a recent treatment of the vocabulary of insanity, see Thumiger 2013.

persuasion is not achieved, as scholars commonly argue, solely through the use of incantatory verbal style or probability arguments. As Ford argues (2002: 175), Gorgias' style grants *logos*, conceived as mouldable raw material, with corporeality and, thus, visuality.[46] This is a plausible suggestion, but, as I suggest, Gorgias' materialistic understanding of *logos* is a distinctive characteristic of his views about the interfaces between emotion, persuasion, and deception that invites comparison with his discussion of the psychological impact of sights.

By virtue of emotions' ability to affect our cognitive abilities, psychological control enables speakers to beguile their audiences into false beliefs. The prominence of emotional manipulation in Gorgias' theorizing about persuasion is clearly depicted in his points about the language of poetry (9). In Gorgias' eyes, the realm of poetry's 'speech acts', to use John Austin's terminology, is listeners' souls, in which *logos* instills sentiments (πάθημα) of pity, fear, and grief for the sufferings of others. For Gorgias corporeal *logos* (8) is a powerful dynast capable of divine achievements *because* of its (or rather His) psychotropic qualities. As I argue, these qualities are directly relevant to *logos*' visuality.

The first example that Gorgias introduces to discuss vision as an elicitor of positive emotions is painting:

ἀλλὰ μὴν οἱ γραφεῖς ὅταν ἐκ πολλῶν χρωμάτων καὶ σωμάτων ἓν σῶμα καὶ σχῆμα τελείως ἀπεργάσωνται, τέρπουσι τὴν ὄψιν (18).

But when painters complete out of many colours and objects [/bodies] a single object [/body] and form, they please the sight.

Gorgias' emphasis on painters' appropriate selection and arrangement of colours and shapes as prerequisites for achieving the illusory effects of a perfect painting is vividly exemplified in an anecdote about Zeuxis' portrait of Helen. According to Cicero (*De inv*. 2.1.1),[47] when Zeuxis was commissioned to produce a portrait of Helen for the temple of Hera at Croton, he asked the locals to show him the five most beautiful virgins of the city. He then proceeded to create his work by imitating the most attractive bodily parts of each one of them. This anecdote eloquently

---

[46] Ford 2002: 182. I discuss the visual aspects of *logos* below, but one may note that Gorgias is conceived as having a body (9). On probability arguments, see n. 5 above with Spatharas 2001 and 2008.

[47] The anecdote is also preserved by Dionysius of Halicarnassus (*On Imitation* fr. VI, pp. 203–204, U.-R.); for discussion of this version, see Hunter 2009: 110ff. Shapiro (2005: 55) suggests that Zeuxis' painting is perhaps depicted on a vessel from the workshop of Meidias Painter. His suggestion relies on Sutton's view (1997/1998) that Zeuxis' painting was showing Helen bathing. On Gorgias and Zeuxis' portrait of Helen, see Ford 2002: 181–182; Tanner 2005: 177–178.

brings out the vital importance of mimetic accuracy in the process of producing a fine work of painting, but also highlights that visual arts aim at idealization.[48]

As the wording of the passage under discussion indicates (τελείως ἀπεργάσωνται), Gorgias insists on completed, i.e. perfected works of painting, which he presents as products of a process requiring appropriate selection and orderly arrangement of many different colours and shapes.[49] Harmonious synthesis of individual elements produces a unity that hides its constituents from viewers. The beguiling effects of paintings are thus commensurate with the impact of Helen's body upon those who gaze at it. The beauty of Helen's godlike body embodies in its singularity the effects of paintings produced by harmonious composition of individual elements.[50] The notion that emotionally affective paintings are illusory *likenesses* of beauty is underlined by Gorgias' vocabulary.[51] The bodies depicted on paintings and their psychological effects that they have on viewers parallel the emphasis on the collective sentiments of erotic desire caused by Helen's body (ἑνὶ δὲ σώματι, 4) in the encomiastic section of the speech. In this connection, it is also important to note the salient visibility of Helen's beauty. As Gorgias says, Helen did not hide her godlike beauty from men's eyes (ὃ λαβοῦσα καὶ οὐ λαθοῦσα ἔσχε, 4).

The limits between model and representation are blurred. In their depiction of beauty, perfected paintings are indistinguishable from reality and reality is indistinguishable from the works of art. This bidirectional relationship is underlined by the common psychological effects caused by visual arts and living bodies. The objective of realistic representations of beauty, a process of composition relying on idealized mimesis of real life models, is, as Gorgias says, viewers' pleasure (ἐτέρψατο).

---

[48] Gorgias' points in this context are relevant to Socrates' discussion with Parrhasius at Xen. *Mem.* 3.10. See Rouveret 1989: 14–15; Goldhill 1998. Halliwell (2000: 100–103) suggests that the passage under review reflects 5th century debates; see also Brancacci 1995: 118–119; Halliwell 2002: 122–123; Bandini-Dorion 2011: 362–373.
[49] On τελείως, cp. Pollitt 1974: 168–169. Gorgias' discussion of painting is reminiscent of –and perhaps draws on– Empedocles' B23 DK discussing the combination of the four elements (see Buchheim 1989, note *ad loc.*). As Ierodiakonou points out (2005: 5), the notion of 'mixing' different colours in Empedocles must not be construed as "completely blending pigments of various colours in order to produce new hues". By contrast, 'mixing' signifies the appropriate arrangement of "pigments of various colours side by side in order to portray the world realistically."
[50] Cp. Gorgias' emphasis on the 'oneness' of Helen's body at 4.
[51] On paintings and deception, see Elsner 2007: 197.

Gorgias' text underlines through repetition the similarities between painters' work and written composition of persuasive speeches.[52] When completed (note τελείως ἀπεργάσωνται), a finely crafted work of painting offers pleasure to its viewers. The same holds true for speeches. As Gorgias says in a programmatic statement, the aim of his composition is to offer pleasure to his audience (τέρψιν, 5) through an argumentation which is intended to strike the audience with the originality of his approach. As I suggested earlier, the novelty of his composition consists in his attempt to exculpate Helen on the basis of arguments from probability, what he calls 'reasoning' (λογισμός), rather than on a new narrative version contradicting previous unfavourable accounts.

What adds κόσμος to his composition then, κόσμος signifying both the harmoniousness and decorativeness of his speech (and indeed a term which resonates with Helen's attractiveness) is the extremely orderly, well sign-posted, and cohesive exposition of arguments that he ties together in an impenetrable web. In the *priamel* that introduces the speech (1), Gorgias says that κόσμος for a body is beauty, while κόσμος for a speech is truth. Like the poetic predecessors that he seeks to refute, Gorgias appeals to the truthfulness of his account thereby underscoring the authority of his own treatment of Helen's elopement, a treatment that relies on 'reasoning' (λογισμός). Hence, composition of speeches is similar to the work of painters in that it requires careful selection and orderly arrangement of individual elements. Finely crafted *logos* possesses a body (cp. 8) whose harmoniousness (κόσμος) is comparable to that of the bodies depicted on paintings. Lastly, like paintings, a speech based on probabilities produces likenesses of reality, in so far as it produces images of truth.

The next example that Gorgias adduces derives from sculpture. Viewers of statues, like viewers of paintings, experience sentiments of longing (πόθος), an emotion that appears to be particularly relevant to the purposes of the present argument. The pragmatics of prototypical understandings of πόθος in Greek literature involve situations in which the agent's desire is prompted by something or someone distant or absent.[53] Gorgias, for example, uses the word πόθος in the concluding lines of his *Funeral Speech* (fr. 6) to describe –in a locution character-

---

[52] On the significance of realistic representation as a means of attaining deception both in tragedy and painting, cp. *Dissoi Logoi* 3.10.
[53] Cp. Pl. *Crat.* 419b and Ar. *EN* 1187a6; see Vernant 1990: 41–50; Bettini 1999: 7–9; 40–42; Whitmarsh 2011: 139–177; on statues and *pothos*, Steiner 2001: ch. 4.

istic of his style– the 'undying' (ἀθάνατος) sentiments experienced by the relatives for the loss of the deceased,[54] a use which is akin to the 'longing for grief' (πόθος φιλοπενθής) caused by serious poetry (9).

Given the centrality of absence to the feeling of πόθος, at least in the most prototypical uses of the emotion, statues generate a bittersweet emotional situation, which, if we accept Dobree's emendation at *Helen* 18,[55] is experienced by spectators as a pleasant disease: on the one hand, verisimilitude produces illusory effects that inflict upon viewers sentiments of strong erotic desire; on the other hand, however, statues are lifeless products of human craftsmanship. Consequently, they are tantalizingly similar to, but never identical with what can be one's real object of erotic desire. As Steiner (2001: 191) points out, in the extant literature "no lover ever erects an image or directs his passion toward the figurine when the living object of desire is close at hand".[56] This 'utilitarian' conceptualization of the image qua a substitute for the real object of desire in erotic contexts is particularly relevant to the idealization of mimetic verisimilitude which we trace in Gorgias –and elsewhere. When we gaze at statues, what is present is (and is also designed to be) a constant and sorrowful reminiscence of what is absent.[57]

Statues, however, also lend themselves as an analogy for the representational nature of *logos*. As we have seen, for Gorgias speech possesses corporeal qualities (σώματι, 8) and, more importantly, it is conceived as mouldable material. As he says, speakers achieve persuasion by 'fabricating' (πλάσαντες, 11) false speeches. The products of this 'moulding' are likenesses –the etymology of *eikota* is particularly relevant here– that resemble reality to the effect of being indistinguishable from it. Speech is thus construed once more as a medium that can add visibility to the invisible: in Gorgias' own words, speech can make the invisible visible to the 'eye of belief' (13). However, speech is not just 'mouldable' material.

---

54 The full text runs as follows: τοιγαροῦν αὐτῶν ἀποθανόντων ὁ πόθος οὐ συναπέθανεν, ἀλλ' ἀθάνατος οὐκ ἐν ἀθανάτοις σώμασι ζῇ οὐ ζώντων. Cp. also Pi. *Ol* .6.16. See Loraux 2006: 81–83 and Vernant (1990: 102) on the associations of erotic πόθος with death.

55 Dobree changes ὅσον into νόσον. Looking at statues can be described as a 'sweet disease', because of the paradoxical coexistence of presence and absence which is intrinsic to the sentiments of πόθος triggered by statues. It is particularly relevant to compare here Menelaus' emotional response to Helen's absence in Aeschylus' *Agamemnon*. As Bettini (1999: 15) writes, "this πόθος for the absent lover is [nevertheless] understood in terms of images...Helen's absence is figured in images".

56 For the notion of falling in love with statues in antiquity and later literature and art, see Hersey 2009. The prototypical example of such instances is, of course, Pygmalion; see Elsner 2007: 122–131.

57 On the psychology and aesthetics of 'replacement' in ancient Greek sculpture, see Steiner 2001: esp. 3–25.

As Gorgias says, thereby underscoring the similar effects of sights and *logos*, πειθώ moulds listeners' souls as it wishes (ἐτυπώσατο ὅπως ἐβούλετο, 14). Speech, thus, shares with images their emotive potentialities and the ability to physically approach the soul and imprint on it speakers' beliefs (14). Speakers give shape to *logos* and *logos* in its own turn shapes the soul. Hence, *logos* shares with statues and Helen –whom Gorgias construes as a body rather than as a person– the power to charm and, thereby, generate in listeners' souls erotic desire.[58]

Gorgias' emphasis on the visuality of *logos* raises a question which is directly relevant to its emotional potentialities. If *logos* is characterized by or is productive of visuality, does this mean that it operates to affect the souls in the way that objects of sight operate to transmit emotion to the soul? For example, is the expression 'eyes of belief' (13) just a conceptual metaphor denoting the perception of mental images (of things which we are unable to see with our eyes) or should we postulate that the soul possesses an independent receptive faculty?[59] And if, as I argued, the emotions caused by sights impair human cognition, should we, on the basis of the analogies between the psychological impact of sights and words in the speech, also say the same about *logos*?

I find it impossible to give a definitive answer to these questions. In regard with the first question, Blundell *et al.* (2013: 13) have recently pointed out that, "there is no absolute distinction here, in Greek literary and rhetorical theory, between the forms of viewing encouraged by direct visual spectacle and the visualization that verbal narratives excite in their audiences". On account of this indeterminacy and the frequency with which the metaphor is employed in later sources, it would be unnecessary to adopt Ford's strongly materialist (atomist) interpretation, according to which the 'eyes of belief' are "an organ of the soul that translates verbal impressions into images" (2002: 179). To the extent that persuasive, i.e. verisimilar, speech is presented as being able to grant with visibility what is otherwise invisible and, thereby, affect one's beliefs, it has the same power as the images that are transmitted to the soul through the eyes. Just like paintings and sculptures, verisimilar *logoi* produce mental images which 'imprint' the soul as they wish. Visual speeches thus share with the objects of sights and the products of arts the same overmastering emotive power, but, as far as I

---

**58** Worman (2002: 158) views Gorgias' style as a means through which he attempts to add visuality to his speech, thereby emulating the aesthetic effects of visual arts, especially painting. On Pindaric poetry and statues, cp. *N*. 5.1–6 and see Steiner 2001: 259–265; cp. also Isocrates' speech on the *Antidosis* (7), where he claims that his speech, 'an image of his thoughts', is much finer than bronze statues. Cp. also *Euagoras* 73–74, with Alexiou 2010 note *ad loc.*
**59** This hypothesis is endorsed by Ford (2002: 178, n. 67).

can see, it is impossible to ascertain, on the basis of what Gorgias says, that their perception requires an independent receptive faculty.

The answer to the second question is also speculative. Gorgias does present, as we saw, speech in materialist terms and also claims that, just like sights, words –as the examples of poetry and incantations show– enter into the soul and cause (or remove) specific sentiments. Gorgias' point about the psychological impact of magic is not unattested elsewhere, but, the fact that he adduces the examples of *both* magic and medicine in the same context points to the selectivity of his epideictic approach.

Gorgias' relationship with medicine is well attested in the sources. In Plato's *Gorgias* (456b 1–5), for example, he is presented as visiting his brothers' patients and persuading them to endure painful treatments, thereby underscoring the superiority of rhetoric to all other arts, including medicine. On the basis of this comparison, he boasts that rhetoric possesses the δυνάμεις of all other arts, thereby overpowering them. The use of δύναμις, a medical term employed by Gorgias in *Helen* (see below), in a context indicating the superiority of rhetoric on the basis of its ability to remove patients' fear, perhaps suggests that Plato puts to Socrates' interlocutor's mouth aspects of the quasi-scientific arguments that Gorgias employs in his own composition.

From a doctor's perspective, however, the blurring of the limits between magic and medicine that Gorgias attempts in *Helen* would be unacceptable.[60] Note, for example, that the author of the treatise *On the sacred disease* castigates magicians' charlatanism by employing a language that presents obvious affinities with Gorgias' discussion of incantations' psychotropic effects.[61] For Gorgias, incantations and medicaments have a drastic power (δύναμις) that disarranges the order of the soul: incantations 'change' the soul (μετέστησεν, 10), while *logoi* qua *pharmaka* have a power (δύναμις) which affects the soul's order –in the way that drugs affect the 'nature' (φύσις) of bodies. In both cases, δύναμις retains its materiality, in so far as it is presented as entering the human body and affecting it externally by affecting its disposition. This meaning of δύναμις, a medical term that denotes the 'capacity' or 'effectiveness' of medicines or other substances,

---

**60** The anonymous reader usefully suggests to me that from a lay perspective the blurring of the limits between magic and medicine was quite common, since people seem to have been eclectic in recourse to medical assistance (cf. Pind. *P*.3.47ff.).

**61** ὅστις γὰρ οἷός τε περικαθαίρων ἐστὶ καὶ μαγεύων ἀπάγειν τοιοῦτον πάθος, οὗτος κἂν ἐπάγοι ἕτερα τεχνησάμενος, καὶ ἐν τούτῳ τῷ λόγῳ τὸ θεῖον ἀπόλλυται, 3.

e.g. food to affect the nature of the body is attested in medical texts,[62] but its parallel uses in magic are philosophically investigated in Plato's *Charmides* (156b) where δύναμις has the same meaning as the one that we find in Gorgias, i.e. it denotes the 'effectiveness' of a magic spell.

On the basis of this evidence, the comparison of drugs with *logoi* and, by extension, the parallelisms between visually, i.e. physically caused emotions, and the power of *logos* to affect the soul are not just analogies on a conceptual level. As I argued, on account of its materiality, *logos* seems to affect the soul in the way that visions do, but this does not necessarily mean that 'the eyes of belief' are an independent bodily faculty. In my view, Gorgias' materialist approach to *logos* also appropriates Democritean doctrines centering on the alterations sustained by the soul on account of verbal and visual stimuli.

According to Democritus, teaching (ἡ διδαχή) 'changes' or 'rearranges' a person (μεταρυσμοῖ τὸν ἄνθρωπον, 68 B 33). As has been suggested, the verb μεταρυσμοῖ reflects the atomist notion of ῥυσμός, namely the shape of atoms within a compound (cp. Ar. *Met.* 985b 13–19).[63] As Warren says (2007: 100), citing further bibliography, "it is not an implausible thought that Democritus considered teaching to involve the impact of the teacher's words and image on the pupil's soul, whether or not the vocabulary in this fragment conclusively demonstrates that this was indeed his view". Hence, on this physicalist interpretation, teaching would involve the impact of *eidola* on pupils' soul.[64] On the basis of this evidence, it may be possible that Gorgias' notion that magic 'changes' or 'reforms' the soul (μετέστησεν, 10)[65] and his analogy between drugs and *logos* –which, as we saw, affects the 'order' (τάξις) of the soul– relies on an appropriation of Democritus' atomist soul.

This hypothesis is perhaps supported by another Democritean fragment B7, postulating that humans know absolutely nothing about anything and that, therefore, each man's opinion is something that 'flows in' (ἐπιρυσμίη ἑκάστοισιν ἡ δόξις) or, according to an alternative translation, taking ἐπιρυσμίη as a noun (rather as an adjective) reflecting the atomist meaning of ῥυσμός, 'opinion is a reshaping'.[66] On this view, humans' cognitive abilities or their evaluations are affected by the ever changing phenomena to which our senses are exposed. This

---

62 On *dynamis* in *On ancient medicine*, see Miller 1952.
63 See Taylor 1999: 233, Warren 2007: 101–112.
64 Taylor 1999: 233.
65 Note that the verb is causal, i.e. incantations make the soul 'change'.
66 See Taylor 1999: 11, with n. 4.

epistemological observation is comparable with Gorgias' abundantly attested depiction of *doxa* (both in *Helen* and in *Palamedes*) as an unreliable cognitive condition. At paragraph 11, which, as I argued elsewhere relies on the epistemology of Hesiod's *Theogony*,[67] Gorgias claims that because audiences have restricted cognitive abilities, they give credence to uncertain and slippery beliefs (ἡ δὲ δόξα σφαλερὰ καὶ ἀβέβαιος οὖσα) fabricated by deceptive speeches (ψευδῆ λόγον πλάσαντες). Furthermore, in his examples indicating the impact of persuasion's imprinting of the soul (13), he argues, as we saw earlier, that 'natural philosophers' replace a *doxa* with another, thereby making invisible and incredible things visible to 'the eye of belief'. In the same context, the exchange of philosophical arguments is presented as altering swiftly listeners' beliefs. Lastly, magic spells alter the soul, because their drastic power (δύναμις) 'meets' or even 'penetrates' (συγγιγνομένη) the soul's *doxa* (10).

If my hypothesis that Gorgias' approach to *logos*' impact on the soul relies on selective use of Democritean doctrines, and is, thereby, essentially materialistic, the ties between his treatment of visually inflicted emotions and the psychological impact of speeches become stronger. Like vision, speech is productive of emotions by virtue of its physical ability to affect the soul. Although the evidence does not make it possible to determine if the notion of images' (*eidola*) imprinting is applicable to verbal means of changing the soul in Democritus' theory, it seems clear that in Gorgias' *Helen* the imprinting of the soul is achieved both verbally and visually –to the extent, of course, that it is possible to draw a clear-cut distinction between these two categories. Like visions, speeches imprint the soul, but in some cases they also affect its 'order', i.e. they alter it physically. Speech thus shares with visions the quality of 'materiality' by virtue of which it affects the soul in a compulsive manner.

But is it possible to explain why the notion of the 'alteration' of the soul which we find in Gorgias' discussion of *logos* is omitted from his treatment of sight's psychological impact? Again, no sweeping answers are possible. I would venture, however, to argue, that, in spite of the fact that Gorgias grants *logos* with materiality and visuality, the privileged place of vision in cultural models of emotion, as well as its irrefutable epistemic prominence in Greek culture in general, may explain sight's more commonsensical and less elaborate treatment in *Helen*. I would also speculatively suggest that the core of Gorgias' elaborate discussion of *logos*, relying on several examples, is modeled, at least on a conceptual level, on his discussion of vision.

---

67 Spatharas 2008.

A possible objection to this argument would be that the emotive effects of words are central to Greek poetics as early as Homer and Hesiod. But the extent to which Gorgias employs visuality, and especially the notion of 'imprinting', to explain the psychological impact of 'material' speech is perhaps based, as far as I can see, on an extension of vision and emotions cultural models to encompass the emotive abilities of *logos*. For example, *eikota*, i.e verbal likenesses of empirical reality, conceptually require deceptive likenesses on a purely visual level. The cultural models of vision, emphasizing the immediacy with which sights evoke emotion, provided Gorgias fertile ground to indicate the overpowering emotional potentialities of speech. *Logos*, Gorgias says, is a great ruler who, despite his finest and almost *invisible* body, achieves divine deeds (λόγος δυνάστης μέγας ἐστίν, ὃς σμικροτάτῳ σώματι καὶ **ἀφανεστάτῳ** θειότατα ἔργα ἀποτελεῖ, 8).

## 1.5 Helen's eyes, Gorgias' *epideixis*, and the poets

In this concluding section, I turn my attention to the uses to which Gorgias puts his appropriation of cultural models of vision and emotion in the frame of his *epideictic* composition.

Helen's name is almost absent from the speech. It appears in paragraphs 2, 5, and 6, i.e. in the opening of the speech and in the encomiastic passages that precede Gorgias' discussion of the causes that may have caused Helen's travel to Troy. Apart from one occurrence at paragraph 12, Helen's name reappears only after Gorgias has completed his argumentation. Notably, in this late reemergence of Helen (19), Gorgias emphasizes her eye, rather than Helen, whose name appears in the form of a possessive genitive. Helen's eye, Gorgias says in a chiastic formulation, was pleased by Paris' body (τῷ τοῦ Ἀλεξάνδρου σώματι τὸ τῆς Ἑλένης ὄμμα ἡσθέν, 19). This formulation corresponds to the climax of a *Priamel*. This *Priamel* started with a gnome about vision's nature and psychological effects (15); proceeded with several examples showing how vision inflicts negative and positive emotions (16–17); and, now, concludes with its focal element, i.e. Helen's desire for Paris.[68]

---

[68] The notion that Gorgias' examples about the psychological impact of vision are constructed in the form of an extensive *priamel* is put forward by Race 1989.

The examples that Gorgias adduced in the preceding paragraphs to show the emotional potentialities of vision contextualize Helen's case.[69] Helen is just another example of the psychological compulsion exercised by vision –and note that, because Gorgias uses *eikota*, he presents the pleasures of Helen's gaze as a possibility (εἰ οὖν, 19). However, it is particularly noteworthy that Gorgias places the climax of his *priamel* immediately after the example of statues. As Steiner (2001: 195) points out, in some pieces of existing evidence from archaic and classical literature, "the beloved instigates passion precisely because he or she displays the properties that belong to finely crafted objects ... [T]he object suggests itself because it offers a paradigmatic instance of the *charis* which the supremely attractive body also displays".

Helen, construed by Gorgias mainly as a body in the rest of the speech (cp. 5), is transformed here into a victim of male radiant beauty. But this reversal of her traditional role involves a paradox: in Gorgias' version, Helen becomes the agent rather than the object of vision: a spectator rather than the notorious woman whose distinctively visible beauty attracted prominent suitors. As Lovatt points out in her discussion of the *teichoskopia* (2013: 221), when the old men look at Helen on the walls, "they think of her as a cause, an abstract reason for what has happened and not as a person". In Gorgias' speech, Helen becomes a passive viewer of Paris' attractive body and falls for him. Gorgias, thus, flies in the face of tradition by using its own weapons. Reduced to a body, and, thereby, an object of Helen's gaze, Paris is nothing more than the cause of Helen's elopement. In Gorgias' version, Paris becomes a new Helen. Notably, this substitution is saliently emphasized through the use of verbal mirroring: at the purely encomiastic part of his composition (4), Gorgias praises Helen for the unifying power of her charms with the following words:[70]

> πλείστας δὲ πλείστοις ἐπιθυμίας ἔρωτος ἐνειργάσατο, ἑνὶ δὲ σώματι πολλὰ σώματα συνήγαγεν ἀνδρῶν ἐπὶ μεγάλοις μέγα φρονούντων. (4)
>
> In very many she created very strong amorous desires; with a single body she brought together many bodies of men who had great pride for great reasons.

Towards the end of the speech, Paris is a body that Gorgias groups among finely crafted, albeit lifeless objects, which stimulate desire and longing:

---

[69] By reducing Helen to another example in an argument that relies on analogies, Gorgias brings to our mind another Helen, that of Sappho's fr. 16 (see Race 1989: 19 and Pelliccia 1992).
[70] On the locution λαβοῦσα καὶ οὐ λαθοῦσα, cp. n. 40 above.

πολλὰ δὲ πολλοῖς πολλῶν ἔρωτα καὶ πόθον ἐνεργάζεται πραγμάτων καὶ σωμάτων. εἰ οὖν τῷ τοῦ Ἀλεξάνδρου σώματι τὸ τῆς Ἑλένης ὄμμα ἡσθὲν προθυμίαν καὶ ἅμιλλαν ἔρωτος τῇ ψυχῇ παρέδωκε, τί θαυμαστόν; (18)

Many things [sc. that we see] create in many people love and desire of many actions and bodies. So if Helen's eye, pleased by Alexander's body, transmitted an eagerness and striving of love to her mind, what is surprising?[71]

Gorgias' argument about the power of vision to cause erotic desire has a long tradition. In many relevant passages from early Greek poetry, reflecting the vision and emotion cultural model, erotic desire is identified as a distinctively visual experience.[72] Emmisionist or emanationist understandings of vision are commonly reflected in poet's accounts and convey distinct aspects of *eros'* phenomenology. One of the earliest examples and indeed a *locus classicus* appears in the *teichoskopia* (*Il.* 3.141–160) that we saw earlier. In this context, the poet highlights Helen's beauty indirectly by emphasizing the stupefying effects that it has upon the old men of Troy who come into visual contact with her. Another example can be traced in Sappho's fragment 31V, a poem including a marvelous description of the bodily symptoms experienced by the female narrator at the sight of a girl who speaks to a man sitting next to her. In Alcman 3.6–12, the paralysing effects of the beloved girl's gaze are said to be stronger than sleep and death. In other instances, poets present *eros* as a kind of destructive emanation emitted from the eyes of the lover's object of desire. In Ibycus 287.1–4 *PMG*, for example, personified *Eros* dwells under the eyelids of the beloved's eyes and his glance overwhelms the lover with erotic desire.[73] In Aeschylus' *Agamemnon*, the Chorus describes Helen's glances as soft darters (742–743; cp. also Eur. *Hipp.* 525–526 on desire). Lastly, in some (less typical cases) poets emphasize lovers' attempts to attract their beloved's attention by looking at them amorously (cp. for example Aesch. *Supp.* 1003–1005).

---

[71] Gorgias perhaps uses θαυμαστόν to allude to the 'marvel' that Paris' body would elicit. On θαῦμα as a term denoting admiration at the sight of perfectly crafted works, see Steiner 2001: 282–283.
[72] On the typology of erotic gazes and the ideological or normative implications of the visual relationship established between the lover and the beloved, see Cairns 2011 with comprehensive evidence.
[73] On this passage, see Davies 1986 (cp. also Pl. *Charm* 155c–d). On erotic gazes in vase-paintings, see esp. Frontisi-Ducroux 1996 and Sutton 1997/1998.

All in all, if, as I suggested, Gorgias' explanation of the psychological power of sights is based on an appropriation of 'scientific' theories about vision,[74] our next task is to see how this appropriation serves the purposes of his rhetoric. One of the most salient characteristics of Sophistic *epideixis* and, indeed, one that Gorgias self-consciously emphasizes in the programmatic statements of his *Helen*, is the need for novelty.[75] However, epideictic novelty is parasitic upon tradition.[76] In Plato's disparaging words reflecting common rhetorical *topoi*, Gorgias was able to make 'new topics appear old and, conversely, old topics appear new' (*Phaedrus* 267b 1–2).[77] The assumption that vision, conceived as a tactile sense, generates erotic love or desire is common in Greek thought and appears extremely frequently in archaic poetry and tragedy,[78] namely the tradition that Gorgias seeks to refute through his prose encomium. In the light of this evidence, Gorgias' theorizing about the psychological function of vision, relying on current philosophical approaches to vision, seems to be symptomatic of the generic tendency of sophistic *epideixis* to make the audiences be struck with the originality of arguments, the parade of visual images that speakers' flamboyant, 'poetic' style evokes, and the easiness with which the speaker deals with his topic.[79] Gorgias' use of intromissive models of vision invest his composition with the aura of a scientific explanation and enables him to present Helen as a powerless, passive victim of Paris' beauty, thereby identifying her with the limitless number of men who are presented in poetic tradition as falling prey to her charms.

---

**74** As Democritus' theory about the psychological effects of *eidola* indicates, it is impossible to draw a clear line of distinction between 'scientific' exegetical models and folk assumptions. As Guthrie points out (1965: 482), "Here at least the limits of materialist explanation seem stretched to breaking point in order to accommodate the popular beliefs of his time. The superstition of the evil eye is justified in similar terms: envious people emit images which convey their own ill-will and power for harm and by implanting themselves in the victim injure him both bodily and mentally".
**75** On novelty, see n. 11 above.
**76** Cp. D' Angour 2011: 88, who claims that "the status of the perceiver is often key to the attribution of newness. Even if an object's identity is stable, in a changed context or in altered surroundings it may seem to be something new".
**77** Cp. also Isocr. 4.8, with Marincola 1997: 276–277; Nicolai 2004: 75–76, 129–131; see also D' Angour 2011: 88–89.
**78** The bibliography is vast; for a convenient collection of examples, see Calame 1999: 20–23.
**79** On *ekplexis* in epideictic speeches, see Worman 2002 *passim*. Gorgias' expressions indicating the self-confidence with which he argues for Helen are located in 8 (οὐδὲ πρὸς τοῦτο χαλεπὸν ἀπολογήσασθαι), 13 (χρὴ μαθεῖν), 15 (καὶ ὅτι μέν, εἰ λόγῳ ἐπείσθη, οὐκ ἠδίκησεν ἀλλ' ἠτύχησεν, εἴρηται), and the concluding, self-referential remarks at the end of the speech at 21 (ἀφεῖλον τῷ λόγῳ δύσκλειαν γυναικός, ἐνέμεινα τῷ νόμῳ ὃν ἐθέμην ἐν ἀρχῇ τοῦ λόγου), to which one may add the qualification of the whole composition as a 'plaything' (παίγνιον).

As Pelliccia (1992) has accurately observed, the core of Gorgias' defence already exists in the poetic tradition that gave rise to her infamy. If one is ready to endorse poets' accounts presenting Helen's beauty as a captivating weapon able to dominate those who come into visual contact with it, one must also be ready to accept that Paris' eye-arresting beauty could elicit equally strong erotic sentiments.[80] From a literary historian's perspective, however, it is plausible to suggest that Gorgias may well have been the first to invest the traditional vision/eros pattern with the quasi-scientific dimensions that it has in a long chain of later authors, starting with Plato –whose *Phaedrus* seems to set the pattern– and extending to the Greek novel.[81]

---

**80** As we saw, in the purely encomiastic part of his composition (3–4), Gorgias can boastfully claim that Helen's divine parentage bestowed on her 'godlike beauty' which she displayed openly (λαβοῦσα καὶ οὐ λαθοῦσα, 4). Shapiro (2005: 52–53) discusses a vase-painting in which Paris is introduced to Helen (perhaps in Menelaus' palace). Helen sees Paris and turns away in distress caused by 'her first glimpse of Paris's devastating good looks' (53). Conversely, in the *agon* of Euripides' *Troades*, (discussed in comparison with Gorgias' *Helen* in Spatharas 2002), Hecuba's disparagement of Helen emphasizes Paris' attractiveness on account of which Helen's mind was overtaken by Aphrodite (ὁ σὸς δ' ἰδών νιν νοῦς ἐποιήθη Κύπρις, 987–988 cp. also 991–996).

**81** For the role of Presocratic theories of vision in the imagery of eros in *Phaedrus*, see Cairns 2013. Cp. also the 'etymology' of ἔρως from ἐσρέω ('to flow in') in Plato's *Cratylus* 420a9–b4, a passage that also seems to draw on Empedocles (the tragic poet Agathon, perhaps a disciple of Gorgias, writes: ἐκ τοῦ γὰρ ἐσορᾶν γίγνετ' ἀνθρώποις τὸ ἐρᾶν). Cp. also Plutarch, *Quaestiones convivales* 681 A-F; Heliodorus, *Aethiopica* 3.7.5, with Dickie 1991 (suggesting that Heliodorus relies on Plutarch) and see Cairns 2011: 45–48. In Achilles Tatius (1.9.4), gazing at beauty is described as 'copulation at a distance', because the effluences emitted by the beloved's body penetrate the soul: ὀφθαλμοὶ γὰρ ἀλλήλοις ἀντανακλώμενοι ἀπομάττουσιν ὡς ἐν κατόπτρῳ τῶν σωμάτων τὰ εἴδωλα· ἡ δὲ τοῦ κάλλους ἀπορροή, δι' αὐτῶν εἰς τὴν ψυχὴν καταρρέουσα, ἔχει τινὰ μίξιν ἐν ἀποστάσει. For discussion of this passage, see Goldhill 2001: 169–170; on vision in Achilles Tatius' narrative and its intertextual relationship with the *Phaedrus*, see Morales 2004. Krier (1990) discusses emanations and vision in later European literature.

# 2 Vision and collective emotions in Thucydides: *eros*, *pothos*, and anger

## 2.1 Introductory notes

In recent years, the implications of vision, visuality, and spectatorship for Thucydides' work have attracted much scholarly attention. Most of the relevant studies concentrate on the Sicilian expedition, a narrative that displays distinctive vividness (ἐνάργεια) and that frequently, especially at its most crucial moments, problematizes the relationship between sensory perception and deception, displays of power and financial realities.[1] The emphasis of Thucydides' narrative on ways that emotions shape human behaviour can be gleaned from his frequent references to individual sentiments both in the *erga* and the *logoi*.[2] In the relevant passages, emotions are integral to his interpretation of the underlying reasons or motives that determine human action. In this chapter, I propose to explore Thucydides' appropriation and fashioning of cultural models emphasizing the role of vision in significant aspects of the phenomenology of emotions, especially their onset. My focal points are the few instances in which *eros* and *pothos* make their presence in Thucydides' narrative, but also the deployment of anger in Archidamus' speech in Book 2. This chapter may therefore be seen as complementary to my discussion of vision and emotions in chapter 1, in which my focal point was Gorgias' appropriation of scientific and folk cultural models of vision and emotion.

Thucydides physicalist explanation about the emotive potentialities of vision and its implicarions for his investigation of the persuasive, even if deceptive, power of sights or spectacles appeals to emotion models –both 'scientific' and non-scientific– in which vision seems to play a significant role.[3] The immediacy with which sights prompt emotional responses is employed by Thucydides' authorial voice as a means of highlighting the versatility of the masses and hence

---

[1] See especially Kallet 2001: ch. 1; on the illusiveness of appearances and the Sicilian expedition, see Jordan 2000; Steiner 2001: 209; on *enargeia* in the Thucydidean narrative, Walker 1993.
[2] For an exhaustive lexical inventory of emotion words in Thucydides and extensive discussion of their semantics, see Huart 1968.
[3] Cairns' discussion of the imagery of eros in the *Phaedrus* (2011) offers useful heuristic material on the interfaces between the emotion's phenomenology and the visual and excellent discussion of Plato's revisionary appropriation of cultural models of vision and emotion to the needs of his philosophical argument. On *opsis*, love, and Socratic pedagogy, see Wohl 2012.

attests to his wider anti-emotionalist stance conceptualizing emotions as an obstacle to rational deliberation.

Before I proceed to the main topic of my discussion, however, I would like to turn my attention briefly to Thucydides' programmatic statement concerning the method that he followed in writing the speeches.[4] As he famously says, he tried '[to] make each speaker say broadly what [he] supposed would have been *needed* (τὰ δέοντα) on any given occasion' (1.22.1). Assessment of the situational context of a speech as a prerequisite for choosing the appropriate arguments, what the Greeks labelled *kairos*, was one of the pivotal concerns of ancient rhetoric. Gorgias is said to have written a treatise on *kairos*, but we know nothing about its contents.[5] However, Gorgias also seems to allude to this notion in *Helen*, when he claims that his task is 'to say what is necessary (τὸ δέον) in the right way (ὀρθῶς)' (2). This statement reveals the speaker's concern to produce an argumentation that meets the demands of the case at hand.

On the basis of Gorgias' programmatic statement in *Helen*, Macleod supported the view that Thucydides' use of τὰ δέοντα in his own methodological exposition draws on current rhetorical concerns. Macleod writes: "*τὰ δέοντα* is a two-fold notion, as indeed rhetoric is two-fold. On the one hand, it presupposes a system of practical reasoning: the orator must be aware of the relevant factors in political deliberation and be able, in the light of that awareness, to construct arguments for particular circumstances...and *τὰ δέοντα* is the application of this in any particular situation." (1983: 68). An orator's evaluation of the situational context frequently, if not always, involves assessment of the psychological disposition of his audience.[6] This is particularly obvious in Thucydides' narrative that frequently emphasizes the volatility of mass audiences.[7] What is more, prominent politicians' emotional manipulation of audiences is offered by Thucydides

---

[4] For discussion of the affinities between sophistic rhetoric and Thucydides' methods, see Plant 1999.

[5] Cp. 82 B13DK, with Donadi 2000 and Alexiou (2010) on Isocrates' *Euagoras* 34.

[6] Audiences' psychological manipulation was a particularly important issue of discussion among the Sophists. Cp. Gorgias' *Defence of Palamedes* 33, where appeals to pity are treated pejoratively as a means of securing the 'mob's' goodwill. Thrasymachus is said by Aristotle (*Rhet.* 1404a 13) to have composed a work under the title *Eleoi*, and Plato informs us that he was particularly capable of 'enchanting' his audiences through incantatory style (ἐπᾴδων κηλεῖν, *Phaedr.* 267c). According to some sources (A6 DK), Antiphon the Sophist contrived an art of removing sorrow (τέχνη ἀλυπίας) through the use of words (for an evaluation of the relevant evidence, see Pendrick 2002: 240–242). And, as we have seen, in his discussion of the power of *logos* in the *Encomium of Helen* (9–10), Gorgias highlights the performative qualities of speech by focusing his attention on its impact upon the human soul.

[7] See Hunter 1986.

as a criterion of effective political communication.⁸ In Book 2, for example Thucydides twice presents Pericles dealing successfully with the citizens' anger (2.22.1 and 2.59.1).

In the first instance, Athenians are driven by rage against Pericles, because he does not lead them to battle. Pericles realizes that it would be unadvisable to allow them to give vent to sentiments of irascibility and, hence, employs one of the most effective weapons of rhetoric –and, indeed, one that Longinus (9.2) associates with the sublime: silence.⁹ His choice presumably reflects his estimation that addressing the *demos* would allow his opponents to take advantage of Athenians' anger and dispute his policy thereby undermining his authority. In the second instance, Athenians are already exhausted by the plague. Pericles now decides to address them with a speech that focuses on public success and private worries. He wins the day, even if he is temporarily removed from office. In both cases, however, his rhetorical strategy is conditioned by accurate diagnosis of the citizens' emotions and dispositional traits. In the short passage that introduces Pericles' second speech, the authorial voice emphasizes that the urgent task that Pericles faced on the present occasion was to control citizens' irascibility –or better their 'emotional logic'.¹⁰ The wording that Thucydides employs to describe Pericles' rhetoric in this context is informed by the language of magic and is reminiscent of Gorgias' approach to the performative qualities of the incantatory *logos* of magic:¹¹

> ξύλλογον ποιήσας...ἐβούλετο θαρσῦναι τε καὶ **ἀπαγαγὼν** τὸ ὀργιζόμενον τῆς γνώμης πρὸς τὸ ἠπιώτερον καὶ ἀδεέστερον καταστῆσαι. (2.59.1)
>
> So he called a meeting... with the intention of stiffening their resolve and drawing them away from anger to a more benign and confident frame of mind.

---

**8** See Tsakmakis 2006: 168.
**9** See Halliwell 2011: 356–360.
**10** Perhaps this is one of the instances that ὀργή designates excessive passion rather than 'anger'. On this point, see Huart 1968: 157–158. On Pericles' understanding of mass psychology and the use of emotive meta-language in his attempts to control the masses' emotions, see Tsakmakis 2006: 168
**11** Cp. αἱ γὰρ ἔνθεοι διὰ λόγων ἐπῳδαὶ **ἐπαγωγοὶ ἡδονῆς, ἀπαγωγοὶ λύπης γίνονται** (*Helen* 10; cp. also Gorgias' analogy between speeches and drugs at 14). For more examples and discussion, see Segal 1962: 130; Hunter 1986: 425–426; de Romilly 1975. Cp. also Xen. *Mem.* 2.6.13, where Socrates claims, that Pericles used magic to make citizens love him (ἤκουσα μὲν ὅτι Περικλῆς πολλὰς ἐπίσταιτο [sc. ἐπῳδάς], ἃς ἐπᾴδων τῇ πόλει ἐποίει αὐτὴν φιλεῖν αὐτόν).

The psychological manipulation of the mass, however, is not restricted only to words. By contrast, sights play an integral role in the shaping of audiences' emotions, especially so in the case of Athenian audiences which, according to Cleon's paradoxical and distinctively Gorgianic locution, were liable to misidentification of speeches with spectacles (θεαταὶ λόγων, 3.38.4).[12] As we shall see on the basis of Pericles' rhetoric in the *Epitaphios*, in some cases *logoi* do, indeed, gain persuasive force by highlighting the overriding power of the objects of sight to compel emotional responses.

As recent scholarship on Thucydides has emphasized, speakers' attempts at verbal persuasion frequently involve exploitation of the dynamics of vision's impact upon cognition and, correlatively, upon audiences' psychological disposition. The most exhaustive treatment of the topic is offered by Kallett, whose excellent analysis reveals lucidly how Thucydides' narrative in books 6 and 7 throws into relief the relationship between public displays of (private) wealth and deception.[13]

In what follows, I discuss Thucydides' treatment of the emotive impact of visions or spectacles upon civic audiences. I focus my attention to three distinct emotions: *eros* and *pothos* in Book 6, and anger (ὀργή) in Archidamus' speech in Book 2. *Eros* and *pothos* are emotions whose onset 'scientific' and folk-psychology cultural models typically associate with vision. Anger is a different animal. Although, as Cairns shows (2011: 49), looks of anger are very common in literature, the eyes seem to play no significant role in the transmission of the emotion. As I argue, however, anger (along with fear) is presented by Thucydides as an emotion caused, but not transmitted through sights which generate relevant cognitions and, thus, prompts collective responses.

In Archidamus' speech Thucydides seems to employ the widely attested association of vision and emotions (see chapter 1) to indicate the masses' tendency to act unreflectively because of their misguided thought/action fusion caused by strong sentiments. Correlatively, Thucydides' deployment of the emotive potentialities of vision in his narrative underpins his presentation of distinct modes of leadership: Periclean and post-Periclean trends of political communication differ significantly in the ways that they treat the emotional potentialities of sights. The possible similarities between Gorgias and Thucydides, especially in Archidamus'

---

**12** Unlike Pericles who tries to check Athenians' overriding emotions, Cleon seeks to convince them that a right decision on the issue of Mytilene *must* rely on anger. On this point, see Yunis 1996: 90–92.
**13** See Kallet 2001: ch. 1.

speech, attest to Thucydides' "complex relationship to various intellectual currents [which] is left usually implicit rather than overtly displayed" (Thomas 2006: 88).[14]

## 2.2 Pericles' lovers of the city

I start with discussion of a famous passage from the *Funeral Speech*, where Pericles addresses the men who survived the war and invites them to keep defending the city with relentless resolution, not only by assessing the benefits of fighting against the enemy, but also by gazing at it persistently:

> τοὺς δὲ λοιποὺς χρὴ ἀσφαλεστέραν μὲν εὔχεσθαι, ἀτολμοτέραν δὲ μηδὲν ἀξιοῦν τὴν ἐς τοὺς πολεμίους διάνοιαν ἔχειν, σκοποῦντας μὴ λόγῳ μόνῳ τὴν ὠφελίαν, ἣν ἄν τις πρὸς οὐδὲν χεῖρον αὐτοὺς ὑμᾶς εἰδότας μηκύνοι, λέγων ὅσα ἐν τῷ τοὺς πολεμίους ἀμύνεσθαι ἀγαθὰ ἔνεστιν, ἀλλὰ μᾶλλον τὴν τῆς πόλεως δύναμιν καθ' ἡμέραν ἔργῳ θεωμένους καὶ ἐραστὰς γιγνομένους αὐτῆς, καὶ ὅταν ὑμῖν μεγάλη δόξῃ εἶναι, ἐνθυμουμένους ὅτι τολμῶντες καὶ γιγνώσκοντες τὰ δέοντα καὶ ἐν τοῖς ἔργοις αἰσχυνόμενοι ἄνδρες αὐτὰ ἐκτήσαντο. (2.43.1)

> The rest of us may pray for a safer outcome, but should demand of ourselves a determination against the enemy no less courageous than theirs. The benefit of this is not simply an intellectual question. Do not simply listen to people telling you at length of all the virtues inherent in resisting the enemy, when you know them just as well yourselves: but rather look day after day on the manifest power of our city, and become her lovers. And when you realize her greatness, reflect that it was men who made her great, by their daring, by their recognition of what they had to do, and by their pride in doing it.[15]

Through the use of the word ἐραστής, Pericles invites Athenian citizens to establish with the polis the kind of relationship that they would expect to have with an object of desire, an ἐρώμενος. But it is particularly significant for the purposes of my argument to note, that, in this much discussed passage, Pericles exploits the drastic and immediate effects of visual persuasion through the use of θεωμένους that serves as the contrasting pole of σκοποῦντας.[16] The object of vision suggested by θεωμένους is a spectacle of power, i.e. the polis and its robustness, earlier qualified by Pericles as a marvel (*thauma*, 2.39.4), mirrored in the discourse of the *Epitaphios*.[17] Hence, gazing *at* the city has an overwhelming and more persisting

---

**14** On Thucydides and his intellectual milieu, see Thomas 2006.
**15** I have used Hammond's translation of Thucydides.
**16** On the citizens as lovers of the city the bibliography is vast, but see Monoson 2000: ch. 3; Ludwig 2002: ch. 3, esp. 141–169; Wohl 2002: ch. 1.
**17** I take αὐτῆς to refer mainly to the city, rather than just its power. On this point, see Hornblower 1991, note *ad loc*.

psychological effect than the detached assessment (σκοποῦντας) of words *about* the benefits accrued through excellence in the battlefield. Speech, in this case a *logos protreptikos*, derives its persuasiveness from uses of *topoi* appealing to audiences' shared knowledge about the expedient, in other words it emphasizes the self-evident and may thus be irksome.[18] By contrast, the city's robust beauty, which Pericles favours (unlike other, unspecified, speakers who just repeat commonplaces, ἥν ἄν τις ... μηκύνοι), being something to be looked at, inflicts a piercing and immediate admiration.[19]

The rhetoric of the present passage invests in the immediacy with which, as we saw in chapter 1, tradition grants vision in folk models concerning the onset of *eros*. The power of vision to throw Athenians into strong amorous desire is comparable to the pleasure that Helen's eye experienced at the sight of Paris' body. Like Gorgias, self-professed rational Thucydides exploits the culturally established implications of vision for the onset of seductive *eros* to portray a leader who exhorts his fellow-citizens to display a whole-hearted commitment to the city by encouraging them to admire its distinctively visual robustness.

By complementing detached listening to involved viewing, Pericles' words deliberately problematize the limits of speech's representational ability, and, thereby, point to the restrictions of verbal persuasion. His strategy is thus one of well-calculated *tapeinosis*: by tactfully undermining his or others' arguments, emphasizing realistic calculation of 'profit', Pericles invests in the overwhelming psychological effects of vision. This is indeed rhetoric at its best by a leader who knows how to put his listeners' emotions in the service of the city's interest. The contrast between speeches and gazes, thus, enables Pericles to stress that erotic desire is the inescapable effect of citizens' visual contact with the city's grandeur.

Pericles' rhetoric in this context, relying on the superiority of sight as a means of emotional persuasion, is comparable to the invitation that Socrates teasingly addresses to his companions in Xenophon's *Memorabilia* (3.11.2–3) to absorb

---

**18** Cp. Gorgias, *Helen* 5, indicating the novelty of his approach by claiming that the inclusion of what is already known to his audience would add credibility to his speech (presumably because shared knowledge about the myth attests to its veracity), but would also detract from the pleasure (τέρψιν) that it aspires to offer.

**19** At 2.64.5 Pericles emphasizes the city's 'splendour' (λαμπρότης) by exploiting the painful emotions –especially envy– that it (allegedly) causes to those who come into visual contact with it. Note that the effects of brilliance upon watchers display remarkable immediacy (ἡ παραυτίκα λαμπρότης). On envy and vision, see Dickie 1991; Cairns 2011; chapters 4 and five in this book. Contrast the 'brilliance' of Alcibiades' *private* wealth at 6.12.2–3 (criticised by Nicias 6.12.1). On λαμπρότης (and μεγαλοπρέπεια), see Kurke 1991: 181–182; Wilson 2000: 138–143; on Alcibiades' 'brilliance', see Gribble 1999: 62–64.

with their own eyes Theodote, a beautiful courtesan posing nude for a painter.[20] As Socrates says, her beauty transcends the limits of verbal description (λόγου κρεῖττον, 11.1.1). Speech's limited representational ability pushes Socrates' companions to visit the painter's atelier. When, after a while, they leave the atelier, they experience strong sexual longing (ποθήσομεν) for Theodote. Her absence turns their desire into a bitter sentiment of emptiness that can only be soothed if they take a fresh glimpse of her. Indeed, Socrates' friends not only want to see Theodote again, but also touch her.

The implications of Socrates' lesson about the dangers involved in vision's power to compel unbridled longing help us grasp a more nuanced understanding of Pericles' rhetoric. Like Socrates in Xenophon, Pericles' erotic persuasion is fostered by the notion that once a prospective lover is overwhelmed with the charms of his beloved, he is driven by an urge to establish a permanent (visual) contact with him. Pericles' strategy, therefore, tacitly appeals to the pain of absence which is typical in prototypical scenarios of *pothos*. The purpose of his emotional persuasion is to induce his audience to establish a permanent erotic relationship with the *polis*, a relationship characterized by commitment.

A possible objection to my reading of Pericles' visual erotics would be that it encourages irrational decision-making – love relationships sometimes go wrong. However, Pericles' exhortation points to an idealized love relationship reflecting the *ethos* of citizens partaking of the democracy of *aristoi* that the *Funeral speech* envisages.[21] To argue that the *ethos* that the *Funeral speech* advertises is 'aristocratic' implies a misguided understanding of the plasticity with which the language of democratic ideology accommodates pre-democratic uses of concepts (on this point, see chapter 4). Furthermore, as Fisher (2013, with nn.1 and 3) has shown, clear-cut distinctions between 'aristocratic' or 'elite' and lower classes' understandings of pivotal values, including *charis*, are mistaken.[22] Although both *eros* and 'benefit' or rather 'profit' (ὠφελία) are tactfully presented by Pericles as

---

**20** On this passage, see Goldhill 1998; Bandini-Dorion 2011: 378–380, with further literature; Wohl 2012. We must bear in mind that, as Bandini-Dorion (2011: 381) rightly observe, Socrates exposes his friends to Theodote's charms with the intention of establishing the superiority of speech to vision (see also Azoulay 2004: 405; on 4th century warnings about the inappropriateness of desire in political life, see Steiner 2001: 209–210).
**21** On the 'aristocratic' overtones of the speech, see Loraux 1986: 180-92; Kallett 2003: 137 with n. 87.
**22** On the appreciation of noble, reciprocal homosexual *eros* "by all types of citizens", see Fisher (2013: 62, with n. 64 including references to scholars who take a different view).

citizens' free choices, i.e. the product of decisions based on their own motivation,[23] *eros* for the polis' power is privileged as an aesthetically, politically, and morally responsive choice. Calculation of benefit enhances the endurance and courageousness of the citizens of *any* polis. But showing determination and courage out of erotic love is a choice that reflects the ideal of a reciprocal erotic relationship characterized by generosity and *charis*.

Unlike the gratitude that Theodote owes to Socrates' friends on account of the monetary gain (and the reputation) that she will secure by exposing her naked body to their eyes, the relationship that Pericles imagines is one of ideal male reciprocal love. The type of *charis* envisaged by Pericles "is the longer-term *charis* evidenced in one or more chains of good will, such as good deeds, thanks, gratitude, return, and payback" (Fisher 2013: 39). Furthermore, the social dynamics of male citizens' gazes are symptomatic of the normative aspects of their *eros* for the polis. As is commonly the case with erotic persuasion, persistent gazes indicate the attractiveness of the object of desire, but at the same time they attest to lovers' endeavour to secure reciprocation of their sentiments and desire. What is more, lovers' persistent gazes, an indication of emotional enslavement to the *eromenos*, reveal their commitment to and respect for their object of desire,[24] in so far as they promise a long-lasting relationship of mutual respect.

Pericles' manipulation of citizens' gazes is in pace with a reading of the *Funeral* as a speech that constructs an idealized image of Athens with which citizens must identify themselves. The visual perception of the polis' grandiosity is reflected in the (partly) aesthetic qualification *lamprotes* ('brilliance') which, as Pericles says (2.64.5), causes the envy and loathing of citizens of other cities (ὅστις δὲ ἐπὶ μεγίστοις τὸ ἐπίφθονον λαμβάνει).[25] It is notable that in this passage, the brilliance of the city is said to cause negative emotional responses *immediately* (παραυτίκα),[26] even as in the long term rivalrous sentiments subside giving their place to eternal glory. This passage is important for the purposes of my argument for two main reasons. First, the identification of the city's brilliance as the cause of other cities' jealousy attests to Pericles' deployment of projective

---

[23] On this point, see Ludwig 2002: 321.
[24] Frontisi-Ducroux (1996: 82) discusses vase paintings where lovers' aggressive gazes are meant to compel the beloved to return the gaze, thereby indicating his interest. See also Carins 2001: 45.
[25] Cp. γενομένου δὲ Ἁρμοδίου ὥρᾳ ἡλικίας λαμπροῦ (6.54.2), a passage in which the temporal qualification ('at the prime of his youth') suggests that Thucydides' authorial voice underlines Harmodius' beauty. For discussion, see Wohl 2002: 7–9.
[26] μῖσος μὲν γὰρ οὐκ ἐπὶ πολὺ ἀντέχει, ἡ δὲ παραυτίκα τε λαμπρότης καὶ ἐς τὸ ἔπειτα δόξα αἰείμνηστος καταλείπεται.

envy as a means of indicating the target's superiority (on this use of envy, see chapter 4). Furthermore, the distinctive visuality of the city's brilliance reflects the common conceptualization of envy as an immediate response to what one physically perceives through one's eyes.[27] The city's brilliance, thus, generates the two sentiments that Greek cultural models of emotion most commonly associate with vision: its own citizens' erotic love and its enemies' envy. Under Pericles, these two distinctively visual emotions are caused by the city itself and attest to its power.

## 2.3 Lovers of sights: *eros*, *pothos*, and vision

The ocular emotions of love (and envy) reappear in Thucydides' narrative during the preparation of the Sicilian expedition. In Alcibiades' speech, we find one of the most aggressive deployments of envy in the extant literature. In that context, Alcibiades advertises his wealth and achievements, the private *lamprotes* for which he boasts, by overtly projecting sentiments of envy to his fellow-citizens. Alcibiades' *lamprotes* is of a kind that, as he openly states, ignites other citizens' inherent sentiments of envy (τοῖς μὲν ἀστοῖς φθονεῖται φύσει, 6.16.3).[28] As Kallet has pointed out (2001: 46), in post-Periclean Athens passions are presented as a destructive power.[29] "Pericles," she suggests, "is instructing the Athenians to experience an emotion...whereas earlier in the work the Athenians are empowered by the passions, which are applied to constructive use, now love and lust for victory attack them and ultimately place their very possession of money, and power, at risk" (46–47). In the following pages, I turn my attention to the role of *eros* and *pothos* in the sections of Thucydides' narrative concerning the preparation of the Sicilian expedition.

The first passage that I propose to investigate concerns Athenian responses to Nicias' second speech (6.20–23). According to Thucydides, not only did Athenians misunderstand Nicias' warnings, emphasizing the size of the 'preparations' (παρασκευή) and resources required for the expedition, but also 'a strong desire

---

[27] On envy and the eyes, see Cairns 2011 with further bibliography. For a physicalist approach to the emotion's transmission through the eyes, see chapter 1; on 'benign' envy and the visual aspects of wealthy citizens' lifestyle, see chapter 4.
[28] On this pont, see chapters 4 and 5.
[29] Manipulation of citizens' emotions is evidently implicit to Thucydides' elitist comment concerning Pericles' successors (2.65.10): οἱ δὲ ὕστερον ἴσοι μᾶλλον αὐτοὶ πρὸς ἀλλήλους ὄντες καὶ ὀρεγόμενοι τοῦ πρῶτος ἕκαστος γίγνεσθαι ἐτράποντο καθ' ἡδονὰς τῷ δήμῳ καὶ τὰ πράγματα ἐνδιδόναι.

afflicted them all alike to sail' (καὶ ἔρως ἐνέπεσε τοῖς πᾶσιν ὁμοίως ἐκπλεῦσαι, 6.24.3).³⁰ Urged by different motives, Athenians feel safe enough to embark on the expedition. The use of *eros* in this passage indicates alarmingly the shift in Athenian desire from its proper focus (under Periclean Athens), i.e. the city itself, to distant lands.³¹ In his explanation of the motives that fostered Athenians' erotic seizure, Thucydides subdivides the Athenian demos into three distinct categories: those who belonged to the first and third subgroups of citizens, corresponding to the older men and ordinary soldiers respectively, focused on realistic calculations and profit. However, those who belonged to the second subgroup, namely those in the prime of their youth, were driven by a 'longing for distant sights and the viewing of spectacles' (τῆς τε ἀπούσης πόθῳ ὄψεως καὶ θεωρίας, 6.24.3).³² Distance is what separates the young from the unknown and therefore πόθος designates their strong desire for what is absent (τῆς ἀπούσης). Notably, their present agitation contradicts the warning that Nicias addressed to them to avoid behaving like 'obsessive lovers of what is absent' (δυσέρωτας τῶν ἀπόντων, 6.13.1).³³ As has been noted, the qualification *duseros* reflects the widely attested conceptualization of erotic love as a disease.³⁴

In the context under discussion, the desire for distant sights is the intentional object rather than the cause of Athenians' yearning. Hope, a predominant motivational force in the narrative (see below), supplies the attainability of the distant object of Athenians' *pothos*. The present passage, therefore, summarizing the results of Nicias' speech, seems to reverse the invitation that Pericles addressed to

---

30 On παρασκευή in Nicias' speech, see Allison 1989: 82–84. On desire and the Sicilian expedition, see Kallet 2001: 44, n. 83; see also Wohl 2002: 188–202.
31 Ludwig 2002: 157 observes that Thucydides owes the phrase ἔρως ἐνέπεσε to tragedy and compares passages where it is used to describe desire for the plundering of Troy. Ludwig (2002: 155) takes the (conceptual) metaphor to describe the leaping of an animal or a person on the victim. Although this may be a mixed metaphor, the uses of the verb to describe a disease and its symptoms (cp. Thuc. 2.49 and in tragedy, S. *Tr.* 1253) grants the passage with more sinister overtones; on the medical meaning of the verb, see also Scott 2005: 384. Note also that Nicias asks the *prytanis* to act as a doctor (ἰατρὸς ἂν γενέσθαι, 6.14) and put the decision about the expedition to a second vote. On this metaphorical use, see Brock 2013: 117, with 81 n. 43 indicating possible associatios with the Hippocratic principle *primum non nocere*.
32 On the contrasting arguments concerning the Sicilian expedition as a conflict reflecting the protagonists' different generational concerns, see Strauss 1993: 130–211.
33 *Duseros* is employed by the speaker of Lysias 4 to describe the unbridled passion of his opponent for a slave girl whose sexual services the two men had shared for a certain period of time. The speech thus constructs a scenario of vindictive, aggressive jealousy (see Sanders 2014: 161–162).
34 See Wohl 2002: 288–189.

the Athenians to become lovers of their own city *by gazing* at it, an invitation that implies the presence of the desired object. In Pericles' speech, vision is the medium of desire, while the object of desire is the city itself. After Nicias' speech, distant sights become the very object of the frantic, indeed morbid, desire that falls upon the young. In the *Funeral Speech*, Pericles invites his listeners to become active, and, thus, manly, self-composed, and committed *erastai* of the city. But, as the conceptual metaphor ἔρως ἐνέπεσε –perhaps identifying love with a disease– indicates, after Nicias' account of the difficulties involved in the expedition, Athenians become passive agents of an emotion that they are unable to control and that, more unnervingly, guides their action. Furthermore, Pericles undermines his own *logos* in order to highlight the immediacy of the polis' *present* visible impact. By contrast, Nicias' words counter-intuitively foster Athenian fantasy with images of a remote place that they have not seen with their own eyes.

After his speech, the distant sights that the young are longing for –distance being a disquieting sign of the dangers involved in the undertaking– are less remote than Nicias would have wanted them to appear. For, as Nicias unveils the dangers hidden behind the unknown and distant land of Sicily through his description of the island, he makes the object of his listeners' desire visible. As Thucydides says by way of commenting on the impact of Nicias' second speech, 'they hastened on all the more and the reverse [of what he expected] happened to *him*' (6.24.2) –and the emphatic use of αὐτῷ implies that Nicias views his unsuccessful attempt to deter the Athenians as a nightmare that primarily affects him *personally* rather than the polis as a whole.

Ironically, Nicias' speech backfires partly because it achieves the effects that Gorgias associates with the arguments of 'natural philosophers' (μετεωρολόγοι), whose speeches are persuasive because they make 'incredible and *invisible* things visible to the eye of belief':

> ὅτι δ' ἡ πειθὼ προσιοῦσα τῷ λόγῳ καὶ τὴν ψυχὴν ἐτυπώσατο ὅπως ἐβούλετο, χρὴ μαθεῖν πρῶτον μὲν τοὺς τῶν μετεωρολόγων λόγους, οἵτινες δόξαν ἀντὶ δόξης, τὴν μὲν ἀφελόμενοι τὴν δ' ἐνεργασάμενοι τὰ ἄπιστα καὶ ἄδηλα φαίνεσθαι τοῖς τῆς ψυχῆς ὄμμασι ἐποίησαν (*Hel.* 13).
>
> To show that persuasion, when added to speech, also moulds the mind in the way it wishes, one should note first the speeches of astronomers, who substituting belief for belief, demolishing one and establishing another, make the incredible and obscure become clear to the eyes of the mind.

In this context, Gorgias shows that persuasion forces the mind (note the use of ἐτυπώσατο) to endorse beliefs that cannot be tested against experience acquired through sensory perception.³⁵ On account of its verisimilitude, speech grants with visibility what is otherwise obscure or invisible, and, thereby, injects in listeners' souls beliefs about objects which they are unable to perceive through their own senses. Speech is thus construed as possessing representational abilities by virtue of which it affects human cognition, in so far as it blurs the limits between objects of sensory perception and their illusory likenesses.³⁶

Nicias fails to deter the Athenians from engaging in the expedition, partly because he is insensitive to the drastic power of (his own) speech to invest remote places with visibility.³⁷ The manic *eros* that inflicts the younger members of his audience may, retrospectively, be taken as an ironic comment on the hopelessness of Nicias' anxious attempt –perhaps reflected in the messy style of his speech– to warn citizens about the dangers involved in the expedition. Nicias is afraid of the demos' volatility and his fear prevents him from uttering an authoritative speech that would restrain citizens' passions. He fails to realize that Athenians' attention is selective, partly because hope blinds them to his dramatic warnings, including his point that people respond with admiration to things that are farthest away (τὰ γὰρ διὰ πλείστου πάντες ἴσμεν θαυμαζόμενα, 6.11.4). All that Nicias achieves is to excite Athenians' desire to admire with their own eyes what he just described to them.

His call to the *prytanis* to act as a doctor and put the mission to a second vote intensifies the impression of a leader who is hopelessly unable to control the morbid emotions of the masses (6.14.1). The disease has already reached a point where drastic solutions are required, solutions, which, in Nicias' eyes, cannot be provided by the collective entity of the demos through deliberation.³⁸ Nicias' dramatic appeal to the *prytanis* encapsulates in a tragic manner the limitations of his own words. Nicias' problematic relationship with the demos, and, therefore with democracy, resulting in inefficient political communication, is bitterly reflected in the words with which he addresses the defeated troops in Sicily. Weakened by his illness, Nicias says that he is 'at the same cusp of danger as the meanest among you' (νῦν ἐν τῷ αὐτῷ κινδύνῳ τοῖς φαυλοτάτοις αἰωροῦμαι, 7.77.2). Even as Nicias does not, of course, display the extravagant *philotimia* of Alcibiades, his

---

**35** On this passage, and the use of ἐτυπώσατο, see chapter 1.
**36** Gorgias' remarks are comparable to a passage from *De arte*, an epideictic defence of the art of medicine from the Hippocratic corpus. The author of this treatise claims that when doctors deal with 'hidden diseases', they use thinking (cp. Gorgias' λογισμός at 2) to make what is invisible visible to the mind of belief. On this passage see Spatharas 2007 and especially Mann 2012: 27–30.
**37** For a discussion of the speech and an overview of scholarly criticism, see Kallet 2001: 42–47.
**38** On this point, see Brock 2013: 117.

fear of the expedition prevents him from looking effectively into the demos' desires and psychological disposition.

The effects of Nicias' counterintuitive use of visual persuasion are comparable with Alcibiades' deliberate and self-interested display of his own private wealth and achievements through a rhetoric that emphasizes the splendour of his 'brilliance' and μεγαλοπρέπεια (6.16.1–4),[39] which, as we saw, contrasts Pericles' emphasis on the polis' 'brilliance' as a collective entity. For different reasons, Nicias' and Alcibiades' use of visual persuasion prepare the disaster of their city. Unlike Pericles' words that exhort Athenians to become lovers of the city through gazing at its greatness, Nicias' miscalculated *enargeia* projects on listeners' 'eye of belief' unseen spectacles and, consequently, inflames in the young their existing desire to absorb these marvels with their own eyes. Alcibiades' appeal to his *private* wealth and splendour (λαμπρός) are equally deceptive, in so far as they give the false impression that the city is adequately prepared for the expedition, an expedition which serves Alcibiades' own unbridled and selfish *philotimia*.[40]

At chapter 30, the Athenian fleet is ready to depart. A great mass of people is now gathered at the Piraeus; some of them are bystanders who admire the greatness of the preparation. The whole passage is full of images and the wording is flamboyant. We rub shoulders with those who have come to see their relatives off. We can hear their bewailing which, as Thucydides says, is mixed with feelings of hope for the outcome of the expedition. Yet, we soon learn that those who are about to depart have second thoughts. Their initial 'longing' and desire for profit have now changed into feelings of fear (ἐσῄει τὰ δεινά, 6.31.1). The conceptual metaphor employed by Thucydides here typically reflects (as was also the case with the phrase ἔρως ἐνέπεσε) the intensity of Athenians' fear and their inability to control it. Their present emotional condition is contrasted by Thucydides to their confidence at the assembly. At this point, Thucydides reintroduces in

---

[39] Alcibiades argues that thanks to his own achievements and splendour of his Olympic *theoria* (τῷ διαπρεπεῖ) 'the rest of the Greeks thought that the city to be greater than it really was' (οἱ γὰρ Ἕλληνες καὶ ὑπὲρ δύναμιν μείζω ἡμῶν τὴν πόλιν ἐνόμισαν, 6.16.2). When ready to sail off, Athenians mistake the comeliness of their fleet (εὐπρέπεια, 6.31.3) for an indication of its efficacy (cp. Thucydides' comments at the beginning of 6.31.3: ἀλλὰ ἐπί τε βραχεῖ πλῷ ὡρμήθησαν καὶ παρασκευῇ φαύλῃ, οὗτος δὲ ὁ στόλος ὡς χρόνιός τε ἐσόμενος καὶ κατ' ἀμφότερα, οὗ ἂν δέῃ, καὶ ναυσὶ καὶ πεζῷ ἅμα ἐξαρτυθείς, with Kallett 2001: 57; on φαῦλος as a qualification of poor preparation for war, see Foster 2010: 54 with n. 30).

[40] On the uses of private wealth as a disquieting indication in Thucydides' narrative, see Kallet 2001: 33–34; 77–78. On Alcibiades' destructive private *philotimia*, see Gribble 1999: ch. 3 and on the political dimensions of his participation of the Olympics of 416, Gribble 2012.

his narrative the impact of vision upon the agents of action. Athenians experience emotions according to what they see. They are thus extremely volatile. They construe the brilliance of the preparation as proof of the city's power.[41] The spectacle boosts their spirit (ἀνεθάρσουν). Notably, however, the narrative omits words indicating rational thinking. The swift emotional changes prompted by different sights indicate Athanians' vulnerability.

The rapid shift in Athenians' emotional state, the product of a reflexive attachment to appearances, emphasizes their overpowering sentiments of fear and their inability to rationally control their anxiety. Thucydides contrasts the anxious 'gaze' (ὄψις) of those actively involved in the expedition to the passive 'sight-seeing' (θέα) of the stupefied foreigners and the mob of bystanders who have come to absorb an incredible spectacle (ἐπ' ἀξιόχρεων καὶ ἄπιστον διάνοιαν, 6.31.1). To the reader who knows the end of the Sicilian expedition, these viewers are alarmingly reminiscent of the young Athenian men whose deliberation at the Assembly relied on their desire for the spectacle of Sicily.[42] Spectators' gazes and their responses invite us to perceive the preparation as a spectacle that mirrors their conceptualization of Sicily as a desirable object of sight. According to Thucydides' authorial voice, beholders witness a 'glazing' spectacle that amazes them (οὐχ ἧσσον τόλμης τε θάμβει καὶ ὄψεως λαμπρότητι περιβόητος ἐγένετο, 6.31.6). The qualification περιβόητος ('famous'), resulting from the fleet's splendour, echoes Alcibiades' use of ἐπιβόητος to describe the perception of the visual aspects of his *philotimia*, especially his brilliant participation in the Olympic games (περιβόητος).[43] Hence, the narrative projects Alcibiades' self-serving exploitation of displays of private wealth upon the collective mission of the polis.

As we saw, Thucydides contrasts passive viewers' sight-seeing (θέα), eliciting emotions of marvel and admiration, to soldiers' psychologically involved gaze (ὄψις) that produces a storm of conflicting sentiments. This contrast eloquently brings out an important quality of emotions:[44] that their objects are intentional or, to put it differently, that emotions are felt for things that have significant importance for our wellbeing. Athenians' fear requires their becoming

---

[41] On the pivotal notion of πολυτέλεια in this context, see Kallet 2001: 52–58.
[42] On the verbal similarities between the scene in the Piraeus and the narration of Athenians' destruction at Syracuse (also emphasizing vision's impact upon emotions), see Walker 1993: 355–357; Jordan 2000: 76–79.
[43] Jordan (2000: 65) discusses the verbal similarities between the presentation of the Athenian fleet at the Piraeus with Alcibiades' self-qualification as ἐπιβόητος and the ocular aspects of his private *philotimia*.
[44] On emotions and vulnerability, see Nussbaum 2001: 42. Note that Thucydides uses emotion words only for the soldiers and their relatives.

conscious of their vulnerability. This consciousness materializes only at the point where the *erga* are threateningly imminent and the distance between the anticipatory representations of hope and disquieting realities diminishes. As we saw, Athenians' sense of vulnerability is reflected in their volatility: the sight of the preparation offers them some comfort because it (misleadingly) leads them to turn their attention to appearances that offer temporary relief.[45] But as the rest of the Greeks realize, Athenians' competition looked more like a "display (ἐπίδειξιν) of power and capability than a preparation for war" (6.31.4).[46]

The deceptiveness of the spectacle is emphasized by the comment that Thucydides makes immediately after his description of dazzled beholders' reactions to it (ὄψεως λαμπρότητι): the unprecedented expedition was motivated by the greatest hopes for the future, hopes which, however, were not commensurate with the size of available resources (ἐπὶ μεγίστῃ ἐλπίδι τῶν μελλόντων πρὸς τὰ ὑπάρχοντα ἐπεχειρήθη, 6.31.6).[47] This passionate, highly desiderative and motivational, but unrealistic hope looks back to the *eros* and positive expectations (εὐέλπιδες) inflamed by Nicias' arguments and operates as a sinister indication that the fear of those ready to sail at the Piraeus would have served as a more useful and safer guide than the deceptive spectacle that encourages comforting, albeit unrealistic assessments of the situation.[48]

Crucial aspects of the phenomenology of *eros*, *pothos* (and to a lesser extent envy) play an important role in Thucydides' narrative concerning the preparation of the Sicilian expedition. As I suggested, Thucydides seems to make use of the strong cultural affinities of these emotions with vision –a relationship that as I showed in the previous chapter is widely attested in literature –, and the different ways in which cultural models of emotion conceptualize the implications of vision for the onset of *eros* and *pothos*. One of the most typical characteristics of

---

**45** On vision and deception, see Kallett 2001, and especially 71–79 where she discusses the Egestan story at 6.46. Athenians' responses in this context are reminiscent of Aristote's treatment of the relationship between emotions and sensory experience in *De somniis* 460b 4–16 that I discuss in chapter 1.
**46** On the use of εἰκάζειν in Thucydides' present comment (in comparison with 1.10), see Kallett 2001: 55–56.
**47** On hope in this passage, see Lateiner (2018), with further bibliography and Kallett 2001: 65; on *elpis* and Athenian expansionism, Arrowsmith 1973.
**48** On the deceptiveness of *eros* and *elpis* as motivational drives (on account of their 'invisibility'), cp. Diodotus' words (3.45.5): ἥ τε ἐλπὶς καὶ ὁ ἔρως ἐπὶ παντί, ὁ μὲν ἡγούμενος, ἡ δ' ἐφεπομένη, καὶ ὁ μὲν τὴν ἐπιβουλὴν ἐκφροντίζων, ἡ δὲ τὴν εὐπορίαν τῆς τύχης ὑποτιθεῖσα, πλεῖστα βλάπτουσι, καὶ ὄντα ἀφανῆ κρείσσω ἐστὶ τῶν ὁρωμένων δεινῶν.

these models is the immediacy with which sights engender erotic desire, an aspect of their conceptualization that gives Thucydides the opportunity to emphasize the masses' liability to emotion shifts. The importance of vision for the onset of emotions also enhances post-Periclean leaders' deceptive exploitation of spectacles as a means of guiding masses' sentiments which contrast strongly Pericles' confident deployment of the seductions of the eye as a means of urging citizens to indicate a passionate commitment to the city that incorporates an idealized version of homoerotic relationships.

## 2.4 Archidamus, vision, and anger

In this section I turn my attention to the role of anger in Archidamus' anticipatory arguments concerning Athenian responses to the sight of Spartans' invasion of Attica during the first years of the war. As Cairns points out (2011: 49–50), "we have no warrant to generalize from the physical efficacy or vulnerability of the eye in some scenarios to an all-encompassing universal belief in the physical effects of seeing and being seen; these models of vision are enlisted in support of cultural models of emotion where they fit, modified where they fit less well, and ignored when they do not fit at all." Indeed, as Cairns further points out (49), if agents of anger were able to harm their targets with their aggressive gazes, they would not cut off eye-contact, as is usually the case with persons indicating their feelings of offence in emotion scripts that we find in literature.

As we shall see, however, in his speech in Book 2, Archidamus supports his anticipation of the psychological effects of Spartans' and their allies' invasion in Attica on the basis of a rhetoric that rests on the emotive power of vision. Although it is impossible and perhaps unnecessary to provide a definitive answer to the question of whether the discussion of sights' psychological effects in this speech draws on Gorgias' theorizing, the verbal similarities between Archidamus' arguments and Gorgias' points in *Helen* make this suggestion possible, especially in view of the fact that anger is not an obvious candidate in ancient conceptualizations of vision's impact on human sentiments.[49] As I argue, Archidamus' analysis of Athenian (and especially Acharnians') responses to the devastation of their land includes appraisals revolving around the recent history of the city and its collective identity, but at the same time reflects vision's pivotal role in ancient

---

[49] On the suggestion of K.R. Jackson, Connor (1984: 55–56 n. 10) points out that throughout Book 2 there are striking parallels between Gorgias' *Helen* and the ways in which Thucydides' narrative thematizes vision and emotions.

sceientific and folk cultural models of emotion. Thus, Thucydides extends the *epideictic* use of these models in Gorgias to construct a speech conveying the predictions that shaped Archidamus' response to Pericles' strategy. These predictions revolve around the irrationality of initiatives that rely on unchecked emotions. The emotions caused by what Athenians see are intensified by their dispositional characteristics.

Archidamus' speech is rather unimpressive and it may well be the case that Thucydides had restricted evidence about its contents. In a detailed comparison of Archidamus' words with the ensuing account of the *erga*, Hunter (1973) points out that Thucydides models his analysis concerning Archidamus' motives and prognostication retrospectively, on the basis of his knowledge about the events and the outcome of the Spartans' and their allies' first invasion.[50] Archidamus delivers this brief speech at the Isthmus in front of the generals and the officers of the Spartans' allies. The main bulk of his arguments focuses on an assessment of the enemy's traits of character and present psychological disposition and, accordingly, includes prediction about the action that the Athenians will take at the sight of the devastation of their land.[51] At this early stage of the war, the population of Attica had withdrawn within the city walls and abandoned Attica to the invaders. According to Thucydides, Archidamus' present prediction was that Athenians (and especially Acharnians) would not tolerate the devastation of Attica and, consequently, they would leave the city walls and join them in battle.[52] What Archidamus achieves through his policy is to direct Athenians' anger against Pericles. Like Archidamus who earlier in the narrative triggers soldiers'

---

[50] However, Pelling (1991: 128) rightly emphasizes that in Archidamus' speech Thucydides gives an account of what Archidamus *said* rather than what he thought. On 'inferred motivation' in Thucydides, see Rogkotis 2006: 59 and n. 7 with further literature.

[51] Hence, Archidamus departs from what he says at 1.80ff. On this 'contradiction', see Pelling 1991: 126–127, who rightly stresses that in this context Archidamus delivers a *logos protreptikos* and, therefore, his present rhetorical strategies are different from those that he employs in his *logos apotreptikos* at book 1. Pelling further points out that Archidamus follows a policy that he "regarded as only second- or even third-best, presumably because it relied on the other side making mistakes and being irrational: he had always preferred to posit an enemy more like himself (cf. 1.84.3–4). Yet, now that he finally turns to his irrationalist policy, it very nearly wins success" (128).

[52] Note that in his digression on Athenian habitation, Thucydides stresses citizens' emotional attachment to their demes which they identified as their own city (πόλιν τὴν αὑτοῦ ἀπολιπὼν ἕκαστος, 2.16.2; cp. Parker 1987: 137).

rage on account of his 'slowness', Pericles must now exercise his ability at emotional control and check citizens' unbridled emotions.[53] He does so by postponing the meeting of the assembly (2.22.1).[54]

As this brief summary of the main contours of Archidamus' speech suggests, the policies that determined the first invasion and the turmoil that it elicited revolve around psychological interpretation and emotional control. As Connor (1984: 54–55) has pointed out, anger is the determinant factor of the majority of events described in Book 2. At the beginning of his speech, Archidamus focuses on the great power of Athens. The massive force with which invaders have come to Attica, Archidamus claims, will not deter Athenians from engaging them in battle.[55] War is unpredictable, especially so because sometimes people are motivated by anger rather than sensible thinking. Athens is very well prepared for war and, therefore, Spartans and their allies must be alert to the possibility that the Athenians will decide to fight. After these remarks, Archidamus proceeds to an evaluation of the present situation and comments on specific characteristics of the attitudes and personality traits of the enemy.

Archidamus estimates that even if the Athenians have not yet deployed, they will certainly do so as soon as they see his army devastating their land. For, as he explains:

> πᾶσι γὰρ ἐν τοῖς ὄμμασι καὶ ἐν τῷ παραυτίκα ὁρᾶν πάσχοντάς τι ἄηθες ὀργὴ προσπίπτει· καὶ οἱ λογισμῷ ἐλάχιστα χρώμενοι θυμῷ πλεῖστα ἐς ἔργον καθίστανται. (2.11.7–8)
>
> Anger enters all men when they have in front of their own eyes the immediate sight of damage they have never seen before: and when reason retreats, passion advances as the determinant of action.

Archidamus' present analysis of the enemy's motives has the flavour of a *gnome* concerning human behaviour, but this *gnome* is notably overshadowed by present concerns.

According to Archidamus, anger is inflicted through viewers' perception of a damage to which they are unaccustomed. Emotion therefore enters humans, in this case the Athenians, through sensory perception. Furthermore, anger is here conceptualized as an external force, perhaps a disease, as the metaphorical use

---

[53] For a comparison between Archidamus' and Pericles' responses to the 'mob's' anger, see Pelling 1991: 129.
[54] On this issue, see Hornblower 1987, note *ad loc.*
[55] On παρασκευή in Archidamus' speech, see Allison 1989: 45–60. For a discussion of Archidamus' call for cautiousness in the first part of the speech, see Pelling 1991: 125–126.

of προσπίπτει may indicate. Along with παραυτίκα, the metaphorical conceptualization of the emotion as attacking its agents externally indicates that the transmission of anger displays physical immediacy. The psychological turmoil caused by visually inflicted anger urges the emotion's agents to act instinctively, without proper judgement of the situation at hand.

Archidamus' arguments present obvious similarities with Gorgias' *Helen* (see chapter 1): (a) vision is productive of emotion. Like Gorgias' soldiers who experience ἔκπληξις and fear at the sight of the frightful weapons of the enemy (16), in Archidamus' eyes Athenians will react spontaneously as soon as they see the devastation of their land; (b) emotion impairs judgement: in Gorgias' example, the emotional turmoil that accompanies visually inflicted fear blinds soldiers to the prospect of a positive outcome; in Thucydides, emotion removes sensible thinking and calculation, thereby jeopardizing Pericles' strategy requiring rational restraint of overwhelming emotions. (c) Finally, both in Gorgias and Thucydides emotions have specific action tendencies causally related to agents' evaluations. In Gorgias' example, fear causes soldiers to retreat in disarray, whereas in Archidamus' speech anger will, as the speaker asserts, lead the enemy to fight. Archidamus' predictions concerning the enemy's response, however, include an important element that Gorgias seems to neglect: evaluation of the agent's character.

As Archidamus explains on the basis of an argument from probability (*eikos*), Athenians' anger will lead them to action, because 'they presume the right to empire and expect to invade and ravage others' territory rather than see it done to their own' (οἳ ἄρχειν τε τῶν ἄλλων ἀξιοῦσι καὶ ἐπιόντες τὴν τῶν πέλας δῃοῦν μᾶλλον ἢ τὴν αὑτῶν ὁρᾶν, 2.11.8). This formulation reveals that Athenians' anger involves specific cognitive content which affects the way in which they see things: what intensifies their agitation is their sense of superiority, which, as Archidamus says, makes Athenians more irascible than any other enemy suffering comparable harm. The intentional object of Athenians' emotion is, therefore, causally related to both the way in which they determine their self-identity and, correlatively, the course of action that they are ready to take.

Thucydides' inclusion of Athenian personality traits in Archidamus' prognostication adds to his analysis of human behaviour an element that figures predominantly in Aristotle's cognitive analysis of the emotions in the *Rhetoric*. In that context, discussion of emotions typically focuses on features of the agent's and the target's personalities. Furthermore, Aristotle stresses the ways in which the relationship between agent and target, as well as their relative position in social hierarchy, affects the intensity of emotions.[56] According to Aristotle, anger is

---

56 On this point, see Konstan 2003: 212–213.

caused by 'conspicuous slight' and prompts a desire for retaliation (*Rh.* 1378a 30–33). Furthermore, since anger requires a one-to-one relationship (*Rh.* 1378a 33–35), the way that agents perceive their status in social hierarchy is extremely relevant (*Rh.* 1378b 35–1379a 4). Because *orge* is caused by the belief that one has been slighted, individuals feel anger 'at those who have been accustomed to honor or respect them (τοῖς εἰθισμένοις τιμᾶν) if, instead, they do not associate with them in this way' (*Rh.* 1379b 4–5) and 'at those opposing them (τοῖς τἀναντία ποιοῦσιν αὐτοῖς) if these are inferiors; for all such evidently show contempt, the latter as though looking down [on someone] as inferior to themselves' (*Rh.* 1379b 7–10).

Aristotle's points are particularly relevant to Archidamus' predictions: anger inflicted by vision will make Athenians lose contact with sober reasoning, because their inherent sense of superiority and their dispositional inclination to believe that they are entitled to rule others rather than be ruled by them will make them perceive the devastation of their land as a serious slight. Hence, their emotional agitation will shape their evaluation of the present situation and will push them to reconsider their initial decision to refrain from fighting back against the invaders.

In Thucydides' narration of the *erga*, Archidamus' predictions partly come true. A few chapters later in the narrative, we find the Spartan force under Archidamus occupying Acharnae. Thucydides gives a number of reasons that allegedly made the Spartan general choose this location to establish himself, one of them being that the younger members of the Athenian demos would not 'tolerate the sight of their land being devastated' (περιιδεῖν 2.20.2).[57] Indeed, as soon as the Athenians *saw* the invaders seizing Acharnae –note that Thucydides highlights the proximity of this deme to the city of Athens thereby stressing its visibility– they reacted in the way that Archidamus had predicted.

ἐπειδὴ δὲ περὶ Ἀχαρνὰς **εἶδον** τὸν στρατὸν ἑξήκοντα σταδίους τῆς πόλεως ἀπέχοντα, οὐκέτι ἀνασχετὸν ἐποιοῦντο, ἀλλ' αὐτοῖς, ὡς εἰκός, γῆς τεμνομένης **ἐν τῷ ἐμφανεῖ, ὃ οὔπω**

---

[57] Huart (1968: 85 n. 2) points out that quite expectedly the verb appears mainly in the narration of the first invasion. The verb περιορῶ ('overlook') sometimes designates passive viewing of a suffering (cp. for example Th. 1.24.6 with *LSJ* II ). Commenting on the use of the verb, Rusten (1989: 112) adduces several uses from Thucydides and points out that speakers usually emphasize that rage is more intense "at the instant a wrong is suffered…Archidamus suggests the same here, but adds that being an inactive *watcher* of sufferings *makes rational deliberation even more difficult*". In the light of Aristotle's analysis, passivity would intensify the agent's sentiments because anger is accompanied by desire for retaliation (ὄρεξις μετὰ λύπης τιμωρίας, 1378a 30).

ἑοράκεσαν οἵ γε νεώτεροι, οὐδ' οἱ πρεσβύτεροι πλὴν τὰ Μηδικά, δεινὸν ἐφαίνετο καὶ ἐδόκει τοῖς τε ἄλλοις καὶ μάλιστα τῇ νεότητι ἐπεξιέναι καὶ **μὴ περιορᾶν**. (Thuc. 2.21.2–3)

But when they saw the army in Acharnae, less than seven miles from the city, this was beyond their tolerance. Their land was being devastated in open view, something which the younger men had never seen before, and the older men only in the Persian Wars. Naturally enough, they regarded this with horror, and they thought, especially the young among them, that they could not simply stand by but should go out on the attack.

Attica is now being devastated 'in open view'. This sight is one that the younger men had never experienced in the past and the older men only during the Persian Wars. What was an argument from probability (*eikos*) supporting Archidamus' points in the speech that he delivered at the Isthmus, in the present account of the *erga* becomes an explanation of Athenians' reaction to the implementation of the Spartan's strategy. What is new in Thucydides' account of Archidamus' calculations, as depicted in the *erga*, is the division of the Athenian demos into two categories: the young and the old.

As Thucydides writes when he explains the reasons that made Archidamus choose Acharnae as the basis for his expedition, he was hoping that the populous Athenian youth would feel a strong desire to retaliate.[58] His calculations therefore included evaluation of one more personality trait of the enemy: the irascibility of the youth. Archidamus' opinion may reflect nothing more than current stereotypes concerning the recklessness of the young, but it is particularly important that it appears in a context that exemplifies with extreme lucidity the significance of psychological evaluation for military action. Furthermore, his emphasis on the young's unfamiliarity with similar situations looks back to his own observation that when an agent of anger is unaccustomed to suffering a slight, the sentiments that he experiences are more intense.[59]

All in all, Archidamus invests in a policy that relies on evaluation of the opponent's psychological disposition. He therefore adheres to a strategy that earlier in the narrative he saw fit to castigate. This strategy carries the imprints of current intellectual discussion about the impact of vision upon emotions. As scholars have emphasized, this is not the only instance in which Archidamus appears to speak the language of the Sophists. According to Tompkins (1993: 100), in contrast to the distinctively Spartan speech that he delivers in Book 1, the speech

---

**58** Whitehead (1986: 399) points out that this is the only time in the narrative that a "*deme* qua *deme*" acquires prominence.
**59** Aristotle's remarks concerning the *ethos* of the young in the *Rhetoric* are particularly relevant; cp. esp. 1389a 9–13.

under discussion (and the subsequent one at 2.72–74) betrays an Archidamus who appears to be sensitive to 5th century stylistic innovations.[60] Because of Pericles' ability to restrain the demos' anger, Archidamus does not achieve his primary goal, yet his evaluation of the enemy's possible emotional response is correct. Passions do lead to actions, but Athens is presently ruled by a leader who can control emotional logic. However, Archidamus' policy is not totally ill-founded: he manages to place significant psychological pressure upon Athenians and, thereby, forces Pericles to confront a threatening tide of opposition. The salient role of anger in the narrative surrounding the *logoi* and the *erga* of the first invasion attests to the importance of group emotions in political deliberation and also to the rhetorical potentialities of emotional persuasion.

## 2.5 Conclusions

The examples that I discussed in this chapter touch on different uses of vision as a means of eliciting passions. In the *Funeral speech*, Pericles puts the erotic potentialities of gazing in the service of persuasion in order to inspire citizens with a vision of civic unity, self-sacrifice, and loyalty to the common good. In post-Periclean rhetoric, the emotional impact of vision facilitates the deceptiveness of appearances and is thereby used by self-interested politicians as a lever to promote their questionable and sometimes destructive policies. Alcibiades exploits displays of his private wealth as a means of convincing Athenians about the efficiency of his leadership, while Nicias, in fear of the Sicilian expedition and the demos, delivers a speech that intensifies Athenians' desire to see Sicily. Furthermore, the distinctively vivid narrative with which Thucydides introduces the preparation for the Sicilian expedition reveals Athenians' psychological volatility by stressing their responses to the spectacular, even as inefficient, preparations of the fleet.

Thucydides' presentation of the masses' responses to sights and spectacles, or their discursive manipulation by public speakers, relies on recognizable cultural models of emotion in which vision plays a predominant role. His narrative, and especially the speeches, brings to the fore significant aspects of sceientific and cultural emotion models of *eros*, *pothos* and, to a lesser extent, envy. The most salient among these aspects are: the central role of vision and visuality in

---

[60] On Archidamus' use of sophistic methods in the speech that he delivers in book 1, see Allison 1989: 49.

emotions' phenomenology, especially at the phase of their onset; their conceptualization as forces that affect humans externally; and, in the case of Pericles' *Funeral speech*, the notion that the persistent gazes of the *erastes* indicate his commitment to the object of his desire. Furthermore, Archidamus' speech in Book 2 may be taken as an instance in which Thucydides extends the use of emotion and vision models to encompass anger. Pericles' political communication is successful because he is able to control Athenian citizens' unreflective emotional responses to a sight which is so orchestrated as to cause their anger.

As I suggested at the beginning of this chapter, recent scholarship has elucidated the relationship between visual displays of power or wealth with deceptiveness in Thucydides' narrative and the implications of this relationship for different modes of leadership. My discussion of Thucydides' possible appropriation of scientific or cultural models extends this discussion by focusing on significant aspects of the role of vision in the phenomenology of emotions. The most prominent of these aspects is the immediacy with which vision generates emotions, an immediacy which, as we saw in the previous chapter, is relevant to the physicalist conceptualization of *opsis* as an haptic sense. Along with immediacy, the intensity of emotional responses to sights, especially in cases of erotic desire, enhances Thucydides' elitist thematization of the masses' impulsiveness and volatility and is therefore directly relevant to the ways in which his narrative explores distinct types of leadership (Pericles/Archidamus, Alcibiades, and Nicias) and political communication. Furthermore, I argued that, in view of its similarities with Gorgias' treatment of vision and emotions in *Helen*, Archidamus' arguments in the speech that he delivers in Book 2 (and the ensuing description of *erga*) may indicate that Thucydides extends the use of vision and emotion models, typically centering on erotic desire and envy, to include anger. If this is so, the presentation of Archidamus' strategy, relying on Athenians' instinctive reaction to the devastation of their land, is another instance in which the inflammatory immediacy of vision's emotional impact is employed by Thucydides as a means of problematizing the masses' emotionalism and the implications of emotions for leadership.

# 3 *Enargeia*, emotions, and violence in forensic storytelling

## 3.1 Forensic narratives: some preliminary observations

In the previous chapters, I focused on the implications of ancient models of vision and emotion for persuasion. In this chapter, I shift my attention to the 'ocular' qualities of narratives in forensic oratory. Vision thus remains the main thread of my argument, even if my discussion emphasizes the persuasive force of audiences' emotional responses to mental images rather than sights. The importance of narratives in *modern* courtroom deliberation has attracted much attention in the last decades.[1] In the field of Classics, narratology has been used widely in the interpretation of literary genres, such as epic, tragedy or the novel –sometimes mechanistically as a substitute for more imaginative interpretational approaches. This chapter does not rely on structuralist orthodoxy or narratological formalism. My aim here is to discuss the use of emotions in forensic storytelling, by emphasizing the implications of narratives for forensic persuasion.[2] As Amsterdam and Bruner claim (2000: 110), "law lives on narrative for reasons both banal and deep". Legal theorists suggest that dispensation of justice would have been impossible, if judges were not, as we all are, equipped with narrative skills (Brooks 2002 and 2005). These skills not only enable judges to put together the highly fragmented material that they are presented with and smooth over the complications of individual cases, but also make it possible for them to construct cohesive verdicts. Hence, narratives are fundamental to legal decision making at least in

---

[1] For a critical overview of the topic, see Olson 2014. Good introductions to the topic are Brooks 2002 and 2005. See also Brooks/Gewirtz 1998 and Scheppele's seminal paper (1989). A pioneering work is White 1985. On ancient forensic storytelling, see Gagarin 2003; Johnstone 1999 (esp. ch. 2); Edwards 2004. On Apollodorus' storytelling, see Spatharas 2009 and recently Kapparis 2017. Wohl 2010 emphasizes the literary qualities of forensic stories. Forensic storytelling was the topic of a panel at the 9th Celtic Conference in Classics (Dublin, 2016). Revised versions of the papers read at Dublin will appear in Edwards and Spatharas (forthcoming).
[2] A recent book edited by Douglas Cairns and Ruth Scodel (2014) under the title *Defining Greek Narrative* has no chapter on storytelling in the Attic orators. One suspects that this omission, reflecting the broader scarcity of scholarly work on narratives in the orators, is due to the fact that the speeches are commonly treated as sources of evidence about the law and social history of classical Athens rather than as literary pieces (notable exceptions are Wohl 2010 and more recently O'Connell 2017 who fruitfully takes into account the conclusions of the Law and literature movement –see discussion below). Needless to say, that this was not the case with ancient literary criticism.

two distinct, albeit correlative, ways: on the one hand, they are inextricable components of the cognitive abilities that make it possible for judges to flesh out the legal significance of the evidence that they take in during the trial; on the other hand, they enable them to put together verdicts, ideally reconstructing and representing the 'story' that gave rise to the legal dispute more accurately than any other narrative heard in the court.[3]

Despite our assumptions about the 'objectivity' of courtroom deliberation, stereotypically viewed as the product of impartial measuring of evidence against existing statutes, one need not be a legal theorist, nor even a survivor of criminal action, to realize that legal cases attest to the fact that a story can be retold in many different ways, even when the main contours of the events that constitute the nucleus of the case are not disputed by the involved parts. The beginning, the middle, and the end of forensic stories (as Aristotle would put it), i.e. stories revolving around legally significant events, are crucial to speakers' argumentation. Let us examine briefly Judge Cole's dissent in the much discussed *State v. Rusk* case of rape to indicate the extent to which "law lives on narrative":[4]

> While courts no longer require a female to resist to the utmost or to resist where resistance would be foolhardy, **they do require her acquiescence in the act of intercourse to stem from fear generated by something of substance**. She may not simply say, "I was really scared," and thereby transform consent or **mere unwillingness** into submission by force. These words do not transform a seducer into a rapist. She must follow the natural instinct of every proud female to resist, by more than mere words, the violation of her person by a stranger or an unwelcomed friend. She must make it plain that she regards such sexual acts as abhorrent and repugnant to her natural sense of pride.

Judge Cole's dissent is in tune with much of what he said during the trial, sometimes with over sarcasm: "[T]his was not a child. This was a married woman with children, a woman familiar with the social setting in which these two met." When the victim walked up to his room, "[s]he certainly had to realize that they were not going upstairs to play Scrabble."

Judge Cole's formulations bring out extremely lucidly, and, indeed, cynically, the power of forensic narratives to invest with unequivocal meaning events with legal significance. In the case under discussion, there was no dispute as to the facts of the 'story'. However, Judge Cole's interpretation of the events is determined by his own highly prejudiced assumptions about –among other things– 'violence', 'fear', 'honour', 'willingness', 'resistance' and 'women's pride'. Judge

---

3 On this topic, see Brooks 2005.
4 The case is discussed by Brooks 2002.

Cole, for example, is unwilling to understand the meaning of the victim's, in his own words, the 'married woman's' statement, that she was scared because of 'the look in his [sc. the defendant's] eyes'. What Judge Cole refuses to take into account, i.e. the woman's response to Rusk's facial expression and gestures, is exploited rhetorically by Demosthenes in order to establish the difficulties involved in conveying verbally the hybristic aspects of a violent attack that he suffered from Meidias: 'there are many things', Demosthenes says, 'that [a *hybristic*] hitter might do' some of which the victim 'might not even be able to report to someone else –*in his bearing, in his look, in his voice*' (Dem. 21.71–73, see discussion below and Spatharas 2017a).[5] Judge Cole's dissent not only treats with contempt the victim's version of the story, but also invites us to conceive her as a treacherous and shameless person: treacherous, because her emotions of fear are feigned rather than real (cp. the following locution from his verdict: "[he] 'started lightly to choke' her, *whatever that means*", the emphasis is mine) and shameless, because Judge Cole projects on the woman an 'ideal self', the 'ideal self' of a married woman, whose demands the victim's behaviour failed to meet.

As Peter Brooks has observed (2002: 3), Judge Cole's dissent and the three verdicts that preceded it used different 'narrative glue', i.e. "the way incidents and events are made to combine in a meaningful story, one that can be called 'consensual sex' on the one hand or 'rape' on the other". Brooks' formulation raises issues that are particularly pertinent to the purposes of my discussion. Firstly, it shows that narratives are integral to forensic practice because they are an indispensable tool of signification. The narratives heard at a trial are so designed as to ascribe specific legal meaning to actions. The second point may appear as self-evident, but its implications for the nature of legal narratives are significant. Unlike other forms of narratives, forensic narratives are so constructed as to produce unequivocal meaning (see discussion below). This is due to the fact that forensic stories revolve around a guilty/non-guilty verdict and must therefore fit relevant legal prescriptions. In the case of rape that serves as my example here, the two competing stories heard at the trial predictably revolved around the notion of 'consent'. Forensic stories, therefore, seem to operate differently from other forms of stories in that they anticipate their significance from their outset.

---

**5** Despite the prevalence of *hubris* in ancient Greek texts, it is impossible to provide a definitive definition of the term. For a seminal article on *hubris*, see MacDowell 1976, emphasizing the personality traits and psychological disposition of the agent of *hubris* (and, crucially, the non-theological applications of the term). In his meticulously researched book, Nick Fisher (1992) highlights the consequences of *hubris* upon the victim (loss of face). MacDowell's and Fisher's non-incompatible theses are critically reviewed by Cairns 1996.

Unlike the literary narratives that Winkler has in mind when he concludes that "[I]n the structure of a narrative, the story's ending gives all the story's facts their final significance" (1991: 98), forensic stories fix their 'final significance' from their very first words, because litigants *compete* for judges' unequivocal understanding of the legal and social dimensions of their cases,[6] especially so in ancient trials where defendants always claimed that they were victims of their opponents' wrongful accusations. For example, as I show in my examination of the speech's strory (see below), the meaning of the much admired narrative of Demosthenes' *Against Conon* is encapsulated in the very first word uttered by the young prosecutor: *hubristheis*.

An important issue that Brooks' discussion invites us to address is the relationship between narratives and the questions of definition which surround legal issues. The question of 'consent' in the frame of a trial concerning a case of rape is not just a matter of linguistic signification. It is hardly possible to imagine a situation where the meaning of 'consent' in the following example from Oxford Online Dictionaries would be disputed: "he had consented to serve as external assessor on the panel". If 'he' had not consented, the panel organizers would have to look for somebody else to serve as an assessor. Compare, now, the use of 'consent' in this sentence, which evidently does not require a high degree of conceptual contextualization to become intelligible, with Judge Cole's calculated use of narrative material viewing the incident from the post factum perspective of the trial. This perspective attributes meaning to 'consent' through the narrative specificity of his verdict.

As Skinner observes in his discussion of the uses of concepts in the language of ideology (see chapter 4), in many cases disagreements centering on the meaning of concepts arise from social rather than linguistic complexities. As he says (2002: 165), "we may...find ourselves arguing over whether a given set of circumstances can be claimed to yield the criteria in virtue of which the term is normally employed". In our example, the criteria that determine the applicability of the word 'consent' are saliently social and, as Judge Cole's dissent shows, they are inextricably interwoven with potent normative presumptions by virtue of which their meaning is fixed. Judge Cole's story, for example, construes resistance as an act of aggressive, physical self-defence commensurate with the perpetrator's act of sexual assault. This, one may suggest, is due to his understanding of sexual abuse as a zero-sum competition in which one primarily defends one's honour

---

6 On this point, see Burns 1999: 163, who views lawyers' competition for the jurors' imagination as an indispensable element of opening statements.

rather than one's life and physical integrity. Predictably, then, Judge Cole's cultural biases blind him to the fact that most survivors of rape usually resist by saying 'no' and that their 'no' means 'no' rather than a weak 'yes'.[7]

Judge Cole's dissent displays graphically the extent to which legal professionals' or juries' responses to human action, behaviour, and sentiments are shaped by potent cultural assumptions. This is another important reason that makes narratives standard fare in forensic practice. The distinction between what is acceptable and unacceptable, the normative rules that condition our behaviour and the cognitions that foster our social emotions, and, indeed, the prejudices that so often guide our judgments are embedded in the narratives that constitute the cosmos of our moral and social education. As Cover (1983: 11) claims in a seminal essay on narratives and the law, "[T]he intelligibility of normative behavior inheres in the communal character of the narratives that provide the context of that behavior. Any person who lived an entirely idiosyncratic normative life would be quite mad. The part that you or I choose to play may be singular, *but the fact that we can locate it in a common 'script' renders it 'sane'* –a warrant that we share a nomos." Narratives are, therefore, an indispensable tool of persuasion because they offer dikasts a conceptual frame of recognizable and commonly accepted cultural understandings that enable them to contextualize the case at hand and invest it with specificity.

As we shall see in the next section, the typical characteristics of Athenian courtroom practice allowed litigants to make extensive use of storytelling, thereby providing a 'wide angle' of their cases. The stories that Athenian litigants tell in their speeches commonly place individual behaviour in the wider context of social and normative concerns, they locate it in 'common scripts' to use Cover's locution. This narrative contextualization of the legal aspects of ancient cases, I suggest, is very important for Athenian litigants' emotion scripts.

## 3.2 Forensic narratives and Athenian courts

All legal disputes live on stories. When a client met a logographer, say Lysias or Demosthenes, the first question he would have to answer was: 'What happened'? –and it is notoriously stupid to lie to your lawyer (or your logographer). Clients' stories were the first step in the development of a dispute into a legal case. Clients' stories helped logographers understand the main contours of the

---

[7] On the *State v. Rusk*, rape reform, and changes in the conceptualization of date rape, see Gersen 2013.

cases assigned to them. Furthermore, since forensic stories revolve around legal questions –even if Athenian laws were sometimes distinctively vague–[8] logographers were able to predict their opponents' competing stories and preempt their effectiveness. Besides the preparation of cases by professional logographers, narratives were also pivotal to the early procedural stages of a case's hearing. For example, they predictably played an important role during the *anakrisis*,[9] in the frame of which a magistrate had to be convinced that the case should be heard at a trial. Furthermore, it would be on the basis of narrative specificity that magistrates fathomed out the legal nature of individual disputes and, where necessary, called prosecutors to harmonize their accusations with the prescriptions of a statute. Narratives would also play a significant role in instances, such as private suits, where cases were allocated to an arbitrator (*diaitetes*). Finally, it is evident that witnesses' testimonies are essentially mini-narratives concerning specific aspects of the history of any given legal dispute.[10]

My focal point in this chapter, however, is the interface between rhetorical uses of forensic storytelling and emotions rather than generally the role of narrativity in the procedures of Athenian law or the importance of storytelling for the representation of factual evidence.[11] Hence, in what follows I outline significant aspects of forensic storytelling and discuss the interconnections between some distinctive characteristics of the legal system of Athens and forensic storytelling on the basis of the conclusions of the Law and literature movement.

As I suggested in an earlier publication where I outlined the main conclusions of legal theorists' work on narrativity and the law in the frame of the 'Law and literature movement' (Spatharas 2009a: 99–100), "Stories contextualize events; by means of this contextualization apparently indefinable or meaningless actions acquire specificity. As a legal scholar claimed, legal stories widen

---

**8** On the 'open texture' of Athenian law, see Harris 2000 and 2013: chs. 5 and 6; on its implications for decision making, see Lanni 2016, ch. 2.
**9** On *anakrisis*, see Harris 2013: 182.
**10** On (obligatory public) arbitration in private disputes, cp. *Ath. Pol.* 53 with Rhodes note *ad loc*. On arbitration in general, see Scafuro 1997: 117–153; Hunter 1994: 55–67, esp. in the frame of family disputes.
**11** *Enargeia* is, of course, a quality that enhances speakers' narrative fashioning of their cases' legally significant 'events' as these events were described in the indictment. A famous example from the orators is Lysias' description of Euphiletus' house in which the dead body of Eratosthenes was found. On Dionysius' discussion of Lysias' *enargeia* (*Lysias* 7), see Zanker 1981.

the angle (Scheppele 1989: 2096).¹²" Similarly, the author of the *Rhetorica ad Alexandrum* advises speakers to reveal their opponents' villainy through *detailed* accounts of their lives (πραγματολογοῦντες), because narratives (λόγοι) are like images of men's characters and attitudes (1441b16–23). Furthermore, "Competing stories predictably invest with radically different meanings any single action of legal significance (see my discussion of 'consent' above)". "Storytelling" also "enables lawyers to smoothen the legal or other technical complications of their cases and present dikasts with simple yet often misleading questions. Lawyers often achieve simplification through the use of generic stories including recognizable patterns". Lastly, "legal stories are conditioned by considerations of timeliness, or what the Greeks labeled *kairos*. In the words of a student of legal storytelling, 'like all professional storytellers... lawyers shrewdly orchestrate myriad elements to make a convincing story...the evidence [has to be] molded to fit potent cultural understandings' (Schrager 1999: 8)" (see Spatharas 2009a: 99–100).

Unlike what is the case in modern courtroom practice, Athenian litigants delivered cohesive and relatively uninterrupted speeches on the basis of which dikasts had to decide the case at hand.¹³ These speeches were frequently the product of well-crafted and considerably costly *written* composition by professional logographers who acted as 'ghost' writers. Thus, unlike what is the case in modern trials where evidence is presented in a rather fragmented way, in 4th century Athenian courtroom practice legally significant pieces of evidence, such as witnesses' testimonies or relevant documents were submitted in written form before the trial and were read during the procedure by a clerk.¹⁴ One may, mutatis mutandis, compare ancient narratives' scope with Burns' points about modern (American) trials' practices: "the storytelling of direct examination stands in stark contrast to that of opening statement" (2001: 53); ideally the opening statement "presents to the juror what the evidence will *show*, not what the evidence will *be*...[T]he opening has an 'argument. But it is like the argument of a novel,

---

12 This aspect of forensic narratives is especially pertinent to ancient forensic speeches, where speakers commonly focus on the social background of their legal disputes, see Humphreys 1985: 248. Lanni 2009 classifies and discusses the social norms that litigants commonly appeal to.

13 On the length of public trials, see Worthington 2003, with a critical overview of previous scholarly work on the topic. On the topic of forensic *thorubos* which interrupted the delivery of forensic speeches, cp. e.g. Dem. 19.75; 23.18–19; 41.17; 49.63. The topic is discussed by Bers 1985 and Hall 1995. Lanni 1997: 188–189 discusses courtroom hubbub in her wider discussion of bystanders.

14 On evidence in Athenian courts, see Todd 1990.

deriving from all the sources of plausibility that pure narratives can have". Similarly, being the products of careful composition involving the selection and effective arrangement of details, ancient forensic narratives –or digressions– are, despite handbooks' artificial division of speeches into distinct sections, such as prologue, *diegesis*, and proofs, indistinguishable from 'argument'.

The fact that Athenian litigants defended themselves or supported their prosecutions through delivery of relatively uninterrupted speeches gave logographers the opportunity to construct cohesive stories, the products of written composition, even as speakers commonly advertise their inexperience and sincerity by emphasizing that their stories reflect unembellished accounts of the raw facts of the case.[15] Ancient logographers, thus, put together narratives which incorporated important features of fictional stories. They manipulated the temporal arrangement of their stories, they stressed the causal relationships between individual events, or they condensed the time of their stories when they dealt with incidents that they wanted to pass over. Furthermore, they employed direct speech in order to give voice to members of social categories, such as women, which were excluded from the courts (cp. for example, Lysias 1 and 32)[16] and invest their speeches with dramatic force.

Logographers' narrative skills are more obvious in cases where their storytelling shares significant features with other narrative genres. The Attic orators, for example, offer the first extant examples of extensive 'autobiographical' accounts in antiquity, even as these accounts construct an objective, rather than a subjective self on which speakers project social and civic norms, or, as is the case with Demosthenes' *On the crown*, the ideals of the Athenian past (see chapter 5). Furthermore, at least in the frame of major political trials, forensic speakers produced lengthy, albeit markedly biased, digressions referring to the polis' history. In Apolldorus' *Against Neaira* we find a long digression on the history of the Plataeans and in *Against Meidias*, Demosthenes provides a relatively lengthy narrative of Alcibiades' life to which he compares the life of his self-serving and insolent opponent.[17]

In other instances, forensic speakers not only recite literary narratives, but also interpret them. These instances indicate the importance of literary *paideia*

---

**15** On this topic, which reflects Athenians' suspicion about the written text and legal expertise, see Johnstone 1999: 87–92. On appeals to inexperience, see Dover 1974: 24–28; Schloemann 2002: 139–142; Todd 1996; Christ 1998: 203–208; Montiglio, 2000: 118–122.
**16** On the use of direct speech and a woman's voice in Lysias 32, see Gagarin 2001.a.
**17** On Apollodorus' digression about the Plateans, see Trevett 1990; Patterson 1994: 209–211; Kapparis 1999: 375–388; Pelling 2000: 61–67. On Alcibiades in *Against Meidias*, see MacDowell 1990, notes *ad loc.* and Gribble 1999: 31–34, 68–69, and 142–143.

for the cultivation of speech-writers' narrative skills and their understanding of literature as a repository of shared values.[18] Lastly, narratives are pivotal to the historicization of the city's legal system: stories establish and canonize the normative status of law. In the extant speeches, the law's historicization is typically achieved through narratives centering on archetypical lawgivers, above all Solon. The stories about the establishment of laws contextualize law's prescriptions by placing them in the frame of wider 'master plots', such as the city's democratization.[19] These master plots are frequently employed to indicate how an opponent's behaviour is in breach with overarching normative concerns exemplified by lawgivers such as Solon.

One of the most evident aspects in which Athenian courtroom practice differs from modern procedures, however, concerns litigants' use of arguments that appear to be irrelevant to the legal issues of individual cases. In modern trials, the evidence produced in the courts is regulated by rules of relevance. By contrast, ancient courts –exceptions are discussed by Lanni (2006)– took extensively into account what Lanni has recently described as 'extra-statutory norms'.[20] Hence, speakers embark recurrently on extensive references to the social background of their cases, their public services, especially their liturgic and military records, their loyalty to their families, or their relationships with friends, neighbours, and lovers (see Lanni 2009). Athenians, thus, normatively favoured "contextualized and individualized justice" (Lanni 2009: 60).[21] The fact that Athenian courtroom

---

**18** On the use of poetry in forensic contexts, see Perlman 1964; Wilson 1996 (on tragedy); Ford 1999 (on Aeschin. 1, with Fisher's notes on paragraphs 141–154 of the speech); and Scodel 2007.
**19** I borrow the term from Olson 2014: 379. On appeals to the authority of past lawgivers, see Thomas 1994; on the use of lawgivers' authority for the purposes of orators' argumentation, see Johnstone 1999: 25–33. On the use of the civic past in forensic oratory, see Westwood 2014 (and Yunis 2000 on the uses of 'heroic fiction' and the Athenian past in Dem. 18).
**20** The extent to which rules of relevance restricted ancient forensic speakers is a debatable topic. See Lanni 2005 and 2006, but contrast Rhodes 2004 and Harris 2009/10. For a critical overview of the debate, see Cohen 2005: 10–12.
**21** Scholars who defend the importance of relevance are particularly concerned with defending the primacy of the 'rule of law' in classical Athens (see n. 74 below). Enforcing the law is not necessarily incompatible with the deployment of extra-statutory norms. In fact, Athenian speakers commonly construe the laws as reflecting the polis' shared values –and in some cases, as in Aeschin.1– the laws are subjected to interpretation along with literary texts. One may also compare the importance of social norms for the determination of actions that constitute 'adequate provocation' in *modern* murder cases involving marital infidelity –i.e in the frame of trials regulated by strict rules of relevance. In these cases, norms surrounding male and female 'honour' (Greek *time*) seem to determine the severity of the punishment (cp. Kahan-Nussbaum 1996: 308–309, whose discussion of material from relevant legal cases abounds with features which are

speakers supported their cases on the basis of speeches rather than on fragmented presentation of evidence or examination of witnesses gave them the opportunity to deploy narratives in such a way as to locate their cases within a frame of probability.

As we shall see in the next section, Athenian speakers' tendency to conceptualize their cases through the use of stories that revolve around wider normative concerns is pertinent to the emotive potentialities that ancient rhetorical theory associates with visual narratives. Through their appeal to shared values and common social knowledge, effective visual narratives elicit predictable emotional responses.

## 3.3 *Enargeia*, verisimilitude, and emotions

As we have seen, the 'wide angle' perspective achieved by forensic stories appeals to potent rather than peripheral social and cultural understandings on account of which narratives acquire verisimilitude. In this section, I turn my attention to the visual qualities of forensic stories, what ancient literary theory labels as *enargeia*. As we shall see, *enargeia* raises questions concerning speeches' representational potentialities, but is also pertinent to the emotive qualities of storytelling, in which this chapter finds its focus.

Our most important sources about *enargeia* derive from treatises composed much later than the speeches of the Attic orators. Yet, the authors of the *progymnasmata* or literary critics, such as ps.-Longinus or Quintilian, whose treatment of the concept is exhaustive, do not develop a systematic theoretical meta-language that would enable us to fully understand how they construe this important concept.

In her study on *ekphrasis*, Ruth Webb (2009) has done much to elucidate ancient rhetorical treatments of 'vividness'. Furthermore, Kathy Eden (1986: 71–72) has plausibly pointed out that theories of *enargeia* developed in classical Greece for cases where "the narrator set out to reproduce the vividness of ocular proof through language. Only later was this theory applied to discussions of poetry and other forms of literature". In view of the emphasis that early rhetoricians place on the problems arising from the fact that forensic deliberation relies on ex post facto verbal representations of past events, Eden's remark gains significant plausibility.

---

reminiscent of the arguments produced by Euphiletus in Lysias 1). On the interfaces between ancient and modern conceptualizations of honour and shame, see Cairns 2011a.

As we saw in chapter 1, Gorgias' epistemological assumptions concerning 'arguments from probability' (*eikos*) are deeply rooted in the tradition of epic poetry and problematize the representational potentialities of speech.[22] Gorgias seems to endorse the view –although systematicity is not a distinctive feature of his writings– that true knowledge can only be the product of first-hand, sensory experience and, hence, dispensation of justice unavoidably rests on the slippery ground of verbal representations. In the *Defence of Palamedes*, knowledge of *erga* is sharply contrasted with the *doxai* produced by *logoi*. Similarly, in The *Encomium of Helen* (11), the limitations of audiences' knowledge are presented as the cause of deceptive speeches' persuasiveness, while *written* courtroom speeches are also qualified as deceptive (13). Arguments from probability are verisimilar because they produce likenesses of empirical reality. Speech, for example, projects on the mind's eye verisimilar 'images of truth', to use William Blake's phrase out of its context, and, thereby, deceives listeners into taking these mental images as undistinguishable from sensory perceptions. Belief (*doxa*), as opposed to knowledge, is slippery because it is the product of speeches that add visibility to the invisible. Physical philosophers (μετεωρολόγοι), for example, can make visible to the 'eye of belief' what otherwise remains remote and thus invisible (ἄδηλα and ἄπιστα, *Helen* 13).

According to Webb, one of the most salient features of ancient discussions of *enargeia* is their emphasis on narratives' ability to affect listeners' emotions.[23] Vivid storytelling not only makes listeners feel that they are present to the narrated events, but also induces them to get emotionally involved in the story as it is told by the speaker. Dionysius of Halicarnassus, for example, says that Lysias' vivid narratives induce listeners to believe that they are able to converse (ὁμιλεῖν) with the characters (*Lysias* 7). Hence, *enargeia* operates as a mechanism of emotional involvement through which speakers lead listeners to experience the emotions that *they* experienced when they composed their narratives. But, as Webb, emphasizes, a crucial point concerning ancient theories of *enargeia* is that they take audiences' emotional responses to be unequivocal (2009: 109). In other words, when composing a vivid description of an event, the orator takes it for granted that there will be no room for individual or subjective emotional responses to his storytelling. As Webb says, the predictable conformity of listeners' responses, a requirement for effective uses of *enargeia*, is due to the fact that: "[T]he production of *enargeia* involved a competence which was more than

---

[22] On the interfaces between probability arguments and epic poetry in Gorgias' theorizing about deception, Spatharas 2008.
[23] On *enargeia* and emotions in ancient literary theory, see Webb 1997.

simply lexical; rather it was a cultural competence, a familiarity with the key values of a culture and the images attached to them" (2009: 124–125).

The notion that the deployment of overarching cultural, normative, and ideological understandings is a requisite for the verisimilitude of vivid stories and the objectification of listeners' emotional responses is particularly relevant to my argument.[24] Given that forensic speakers attempted to achieve persuasion, it is hardly surprising that their narratives appeal to 'mainstream' rather than peripheral or marginal ideological assumptions, social norms or values. In so far as forensic speakers seek to elicit *specific* emotional responses directed against their targets, it is only natural that the cognitive framing of their narrative accounts is shaped not only by easily recognizable, but also by widely accepted normative schemata.[25] It is for this reason that forensic narratives can serve as a heuristic tool that helps us investigate with better hopes of accuracy the web of values favoured by the ideology and social priorities of classical Athens.

The study of forensic narratives, however, intersects with the study of emotions for an additional reason. Modern approaches in psychology view emotions as a cognitive phenomenon.[26] To put it simply, emotions require evaluations, which, in the case of forensic oratory centre on social and ideological concerns. More importantly, however, because stories are a significant medium of signification they are also pivotal to the cognitions that give rise to emotions. The importance of stories for the communication of emotional experience is easily understood if we take into account the extent to which we use narratives in order to convey our sentiments in our social interactions.[27] Furthermore, modern students of emotions use scripts, i.e. mini-narratives, in order to pin down the complexities of an emotional episode, involving the evaluations that gave rise to it, the embodied cognitions that inform it and the actions to which it urges its agents.[28] Emotion

---

**24** On the requirement of verisimilitude and probability, cp. Quint. *Inst. Or.* 6.2.30 and 6.2.31. Ps.-Longinus (15.8) stresses that the mental pictures fabricated by the orators, unlike those fabricated by the poets, are more attractive when they are closer to reality (τῆς δὲ ῥητορικῆς φαντασίας κάλλιστον ἀεὶ τὸ ἔμπρακτον καὶ ἐνάληθες).
**25** Webb (2009: 124–125) aptly compares Susan Smith's story about the abduction of her children by a black man. The police believed her story and started a manhunt. Smith's account relied heavily on stereotypes and, as some evidence suggests, it was based on a known individual. Subsequently Smith confessed to the murder of her children.
**26** For further discussion, see Introduction.
**27** On the narrative structure of emotions, see Nussbaum 2001: 236. On narrative thinking and emotions, see Goldie 2012. For an overview of the role of emotions in literary narratives, see Johnson/Oatley 2016.
**28** On emotion scripts, see Introduction 12–13.

scripts are, thus, particularly relevant to the study of forensic narratives, because they indicate the importance of context specific and particularized appeals to emotions. Lastly, the emotions which are pertinent to forensic practice may be labelled 'social' emotions, in so far as they typically require appraisals pertinent to social transactions.[29]

So far, I have emphasized the importance attributed by early rhetoricians to the representational qualities of speech. I also pointed out that a requirement for the construction of persuasive narratives is their appeal to cultural, normative, or ideological understandings. Yet, the emotive potentialities of *enargeia* are also intextricably interwoven with the visual qualities of verbal narratives. More frequently than not, scholars explore the theatricality of ancient oratory by looking into speeches' 'dramatic' aspects or their literary affinities with tragedy.[30] However, as early as Gorgias, ancient rhetoricians foreground the affective qualities of visual *logos*. In Aristotle's eyes, *opsis* can arouse the emotions which are characteristic of tragedy, but these emotions, pity and fear, should properly be aroused by the plot itself (*Po.* 1453b 1–12). Indeed, as Blundell et al. point out (2013: 12) "ancient Greek authors regularly comment on the greater power and persuasiveness of what one sees with one's own eyes by comparison with what one merely hears about...but it seems to have been an implicit ideal of Greek narrative to efface the distinction as far as possible". In other words, there is no clear-cut distinction between physically perceived images (and their effects) and the mental images elicited through the activation of listeners' *phantasia*.

The idealized conceptualization of verbally produced mental pictures as equivalent to sights has important implications for the affective power of visually enhanced storytelling. As Webb (2009) shows, ancient authorities construe *phantasia* as 'mimetic', i.e. 'imagination' appeals to listeners' real experience (and, one may add, to their autobiographical memory). What listeners' respond to, therefore, are familiar and culturally specific images. The 'realism' of mental representations thus partly explains the strong language with which ancient rhetoricians convey listeners' emotions to narratives. Ps.-Longinus, for example, says that good visual narratives 'enslave' listeners (*douloutai*, 15.9), while Quintilian claims that they 'penetrate' audiences' emotions (8.3.62). Modern cognitive research on human responses to fiction shows that the emotional responses caused by verbal narratives may be different in degree but not in kind from the sentiments that we experience in our real life interactions. Cognitive approaches also

---

[29] On social emotions, see Konstan 2006: 23–24.
[30] See for example, Bers 1994; Hall 1995; Fantham 2002; Harris 2017.

emphasize that the mental abilities that we activate when we are exposed to verbal narratives are not different from the abilities that we employ in our social transactions, such as mind reading and imagination.[31]

As the examples that I use as test cases indicate, forensic narratives are characterized by careful selection and description of socially significant details. These details grant stories with cultural meaning. Gestures, common social practices, physical manifestations of emotions, material objects, and the ideological connotations of private or public space are orchestrated to evoke meaningful mental images familiar to forensic audiences. By virtue of their familiarity, the mental images that narratives produce induce audiences to supply the stories' meaning by activating their social competence and, thereby, engage them actively in the narrative world. As Webb points out (2009: 122), "the more a scene corresponds to the empirical, or culturally acquired, knowledge stored in the audience's minds, the easier it will be for them to supply the images suggested by the orator's words, and the easier it will be for the orator to predict the audience's response".

A good example of how forensic speakers invite dikasts to employ their social knowledge in order to supply the meaning of what they are told belongs to *Against Meidias* (73). In this passage, Demosthenes puts the limitations of the representational power of *logos* to the service of his rhetoric in the frame of an attempt to convince dikasts that the violence that he suffered was commensurate with *hybris*.[32] This example is useful for two main reasons. First, because it deals with *hybris*, a crime whose exact nature notoriously resists interpretation. Second, it anticipates the meta-language of later treatments of *enargeia*.

Demosthenes claims that it is practically impossible to describe verbally the *hybristic* aspects of Meidias' behaviour (παραστῆσαι), because these aspects are incorporated in the perpetrator's gestures. *Hybris*, he says, is reflected in the attacker's 'bearing, in his look, in his voice'. The bodily signs of *hybris* (cp. 'the look in his eyes' in the case of rape that I discussed in my preliminary remarks) constitute the repertoire of a socially meaningful performance with visible and audible features. However, as I argued elsewhere (2017a), Demosthenes' emphasis on the limitations of verbal description and the use of elliptical language encourage his audience to activate their social knowledge (and, perhaps, their autobiographical

---

**31** On this topic see Blundell *et al.* 2013: 13–14, with references to modern experimental approaches to the emotion responses elicited by visual and verbal narratives.
**32** I discuss this passage, including terms pertinent to *enargeia*, in Spatharas 2017a. Demosthenes' emphasis on the visual clues of *hybris* is partly due to the fact that, unlike other victims of violence, such as Teisis and Ariston that I discuss in the following section, he suffered no serious injury.

memory) and supply the meaning of Demosthenes' account by formulating relevant mental pictures. The fact that dikasts are able to mentally picture the violent attack that Demosthenes suffered and thus meaningfully rewrite the 'script' of this attack in the scripts of their own civic lives grants Demosthenes' account with credibility. Demosthenes' elliptical description of what constitutes *hybris* relies on the 'everyone knows' *topos*, here revolving around dikasts' common social knowledge, on the basis of which he identifies his opponent's attack with *hybris*.

## 3.4 *Enargeia*, emotions, and stories about violence

In what follows, I discuss a number of forensic stories concerning incidents of violence. Lysias' *Against Teisis* and Demosthenes' *Against Conon* are prosecution speeches composed for delivery in the frame of *aikeia* ('battery') cases.[33] The other two stories that attract my attention appear in the course of speeches delivered in the frame of major political trials: Demosthenes' *On the false embassy* and Aeschines' *Against Timarchus*. As will be argued, these narratives are so designed as to elicit sentiments of pity for the victims and anger against the perpetrators, while emotions such as erotic jealousy, shame, and disgust are also present. For reasons of conceptual clarity, however, I anticipate my main argument that the emotion scripts that ancient stories put together rely on wider social concerns rather than personal trauma, by discussing briefly the role of emotions in modern Victims Impact Statements (VIS) which I use as comparative ground.[34]

In some American courts, VISs are read by or on behalf of victims at the sentencing phase of criminal cases. The nature of the narrative material that we find in these statements is relevant to my discussion, especially because of the distinctively strong emotional language that they employ, the mental pictures that they produce, and the attempts that they make to divert jurors' compassion to the victims of criminal action. Furthermore, VISs offer good, albeit fervently disputed examples of non-professional legal storytelling. The scripts that we find in VISs help us outline more lucidly the characteristics of the emotional scenarios of ancient forensic stories.

In cases of murder, VISs, read by or on behalf of victim's relatives after the defendant's guilt has been established, give voice to the speechless victim of the crime. The mini-narratives that we find in VISs typically include accounts of the victim's character and the emotional impact of the defendant's criminal action

---

[33] Violence in Athenian forensic speeches is discussed by Riess 2012: ch. 2.
[34] For a general presentation of VIS and their history, see Stevens 2000.

upon his or her relatives. Unsurprisingly, the appropriateness of VISs is a highly disputed topic among legal theorists, even among those who defend the use of narratives as a means of non-professionals' integration into the unintelligible legal procedures, especially because of the central role that inflammatory emotions have in the stories told by victims of criminal action.[35]

A desirable approach to the place of emotions in courtroom practice would first and foremost dispute the common assumption that emotions override reason. Quite the contrary, a sober approach would look into emotions' 'logic' and thus emphasize their cognitive aspects.[36] On the basis of this cognitive analysis, reflexive emotions such as disgust and attributes that elicit the emotion, e.g. 'heinousness', are inappropriate tools for measuring the severity of criminal action, because they dehumanize their targets and invite evaluations which are irrelevant to the crime itself.[37] Another obvious candidate that invites discussion about the emotions' role in courtroom deliberation is compassion for the victim.[38] VISs frequently highlight victims' moral and emotional merits.

I give here an example of a VIS. This statement was read to the penalty-phase jury in *Booth v. Maryland* (I cite the text from Gewirtz 1996: 140):

> The victims' son reports that his children first learned about their grandparents' death from the television reports. "Since the Jewish religion dictates that birth and marriage are more important than death, the granddaughter's wedding had to proceed on May 22nd... She had been looking forward to it eagerly, but it was a sad occasion with people crying. The reception, which normally would have lasted for hours, was very brief. The next day, instead of going on her honeymoon, she attended her grandparents' funerals....The victims' granddaughter, on the other hand, vividly remembers every detail of the days following her grandparents' death. Perhaps she described the impact of the tragedy most eloquently when she stated that it was a completely devastating and life altering experience. "The victims' son states that he can only think of his parents in the context of how he found them that day, and he can feel their fear and horror. It was 4:00 P.M. when he discovered their bodies and this stands out in his mind. He is always aware of when 4:00 P.M. comes each day, even when he is not near a clock.

The mini-narratives included in this statement revolve around the ways in which relatives' lives were affected by the death of the victim. Their language is distinctively emotional: "she had been looking forward to it [her wedding] eagerly, but

---

35 For a criticism from a legal theorists' point of view, see Gewirtz 1996.
36 For a cognitive approach to emotions and the law, see Kahan/Nusbaumm 1996; see also Deigh 2008. For a general discussion of the interfaces between emotions and the law, see Bornstein/Wiener 2010.
37 On the inappropriateness of disgust in criminal law, see Kahan 1998.
38 On pity and the law, see Konstan 2001: ch. 2.

it was a sad occasion with people crying"; "it was a completely devastating and life altering experience"; "he can only think of his parents in the context of how he found them that day, and he can feel their fear and horror". These are the overwhelming *personal* feelings of individuals who suffered a great loss because of the condemned perpetrator's criminal action. Furthermore, their stories center on aspects –more or less important– of 'common' peoples' private lives: a wedding that had to take place before the funeral because of religious concerns, a cancelled honeymoon, going to school, preparing for work etc. As we shall see, Athenian prosecutors' narratives in cases of violence differ from these accounts in a significant respect: the emotion scripts that they construct encourage appraisals concerning the *public* dimensions of criminal action, even in cases, just like the suits of battery, where prosecutors equate punishment with revenge (*timoria*).[39]

In *Against Conon* that I discuss below, Ariston fears that a possible acquittal of his opponent will make him suffer additional *hybris* (προσυβρισθείς, 43). In other words, if he fails to get Conon punished, he will be pitiable because dikasts will double the *shame* –loss of face and loss of *time*– that Conon's crime caused him to experience. This piece of evidence does not, of course, show that ancient narratives about violence do not thematize personal harm at all. Ariston, for example, uses narrative specificity to describe his state of health immediately after Conon's brutal attack (11) and the emotional responses of the female members of his family at the sight of his wounded body (9). However, as will be argued below, unlike the VISs' emphasis on personal trauma, the emotions that Ariston and other prosecutors seek to elicit gravitate towards cognitions centering on wider social, political, or, more generally, public concerns. The emphasis on the crime's impact upon the community (rather than upon the victim) explains why in Athenian courtroom practice prosecutors invite openly dikasts to express their sentiments of anger towards the defendant, an invitation, that, as we saw, would be unthinkable in a modern trial.

---

[39] On *timoria* in Athenian homicide speeches, see Cairns 2015. Cairns concludes that "Athenian legal discourse is built up out of ordinary social, ethical, and emotional language; that language is not transformed by its use in legal contexts, but still its use in such contexts gives it a distinctively legal shape... The honor that is enjoyed by all Athenian citizens alike...is not something entirely different from the varieties and degrees of honor that are at stake in purely personal interactions; but it is not merely that either. It is also something in which the state as such has a legitimate interest, both as guarantor of the honor of its members and as a bearer of honor in its own right." (665). For a recent discussion of enmity in classical Athens, see Alwine 2015.

## 3.4.1 *Against Teisis* (Carey fr. 279)

One of the most fascinating narratives concerning a case of assault can be found in *Against Teisis*, a speech that belongs to the corpus of the extant fragments of Lysias (fr. 279 Carey). Despite its rhetorical qualities and its significance as a piece of evidence about the social history of classical Athens, the speech has not received due attention and I therefore discuss it in some detail.[40] In this speech of prosecution, the victim of a violent attack, including whipping, is a certain Archippus, not the speaker. The person who delivered the speech acted as Archippus' *synegoros* or as a volunteer prosecutor.[41] On the balance of evidence, it is plausible to suggest that this is a private case of battery (*dike aikeias*) rather than a case of *graphe hybreos*. Hence, the unknown speaker who delivered the speech as a *synegoros* was a relative or a friend of Archippus –(note that in fr. 278 he describes himself as an *epitedeios*, a qualification that designates a relative *or* a friend).

The portion of the speech that we possess is a fascinating narrative that includes all the *topoi* that we find in other similarly themed speeches: the presentation of the violent attack as an act of *hybris* that affects the community as a whole; the dramatic display of the victim's wounded body to passersby; a preliminary narrative suggesting the prehistory of the litigants' enmity; and emphasis on the elites' sympotic activities, including the pursuit of erotic companions. Yet, its conciseness makes one wonder if the text that we have is a revised version of the speech delivered by the *synegoros* at the trial. Teisis scheme is concocted by a certain Pytheas ('the informed'), whom the speaker presents as Teisis' lover. After Archippus' whipping, a certain Antimachus (an *anterastes*?) goes to Teisis' house to deal with the consequences of the householder's drunken and outrageous violence. Although the meaning of these speaking names is not sufficient evidence about the nature of the speech, the fact that they feature in such a short narrative, incorporating the rhetorical *topoi* of other, longer *diegeseis* concerning cases of assault, may lead us to the very tentative conclusion that the narrative that Dionysius preserves is a revised version of a longer speech perhaps composed for circulation as a model-speech. In any case, my discussion of the story's persuasiveness is not affected by the nature of the text in its present form, in so

---

**40** A notable exception is O'Connell (2017: 152–157); Riess (2012, ch. 2 *passim*) also discusses the speech in his treatment of violence in Athenian courtroom practice. For a general discussion of the speech's rhetoric and legal questions, see Spatharas 2006a. See also Cohen 1995: 137–138.
**41** See Rubinstein 2000: 67–68. Fisher 1990: 126 claims tentatively that the speech may concern a *graphe hyreos*; on the legal nature of the speech, see also Spatharas 2006.

far as it incorporates recognizable rhetorical strategies deployed in other similarly themed speeches of prosecution.

Dikasts' cultural knowledge that Lysias seeks to activate through the details of his story emphasizes Teisis' underhanded tactics, the *hybristic* maltreatment of a free citizen, and stereotypes surrounding wealthy young men. Typically, Lysias' main narrative is preceded by a preliminary story providing limited and obfuscated information about a fight between the litigants that took place in a *palaestra*. The speaker recounts in a sufficiently neutral manner the event in the wrestling ground without assigning responsibility for the outbreak of the quarrel to the side of the accused: the two opponents disrobed together as they were preparing to train and at some point they began to argue, exchanging heavy insults. However, as is typical in speeches composed for cases of assault, Archippus suppresses the narrative time between the fight in the *palaestra* and the incident of the assault that gave rise to the legal dispute.[42] The events of this unspecified period of time are focalized by the speaker who emphasizes that Archippus avoided Teisis. As the speaker says, immediately after the incident in the *palaestra*, Teisis hastened to inform Pytheas, his guardian and lover, about all that happened, and the latter advised him to reconcile with Archippus, albeit watching for the chance to find him somewhere alone. This post factum version of the events, the product of hearsay (ὡς ἡμεῖς ἔκ τε τῶν πεπραγμένων ᾐσθήμεθα καὶ τῶν εὖ εἰδότων ἐπυθόμεθα), enhances Archippus' characterization as a non-vindictive, quiet young man.

The neutral presentation of the incident by the speaker –according to Lysias' story, neither Teisis nor Archippus used bodily violence in the *palaestra*–[43] does not reveal anything in connection with Teisis' guilt or innocence. It is of course possible that Archippus insulted Teisis first for his relation with Pytheas. In Fisher's words (2001: 197), "one may suspect that the slavery motif was introduced by Archippos' insults directed perhaps at Teisis' voluntary sexual 'enslavement' to his lover/guardian".[44] Nevertheless, Teisis is found in a difficult position: if he claimed that Archippus attacked him first in the wrestling ground, he would not in any way be able to explain why he did not prosecute him at that point, but preferred to avenge him in the crude way that the speaker presents.

---

42 Suppression of narrative time is also evident in Lysias 3 and Demosthenes 54.
43 On the social implications of the *palaestra* and the *gymnasium*, see Fisher 1998. On relevant legal prescriptions, see MacDowell 2000.
44 In the case of Pittalacus' whipping discussed below, "there are clear signs that Hegesandros and Timarchos claimed Pittalakos actually was a slave, asserting illegally some citizen rights" (Fisher 2001: 197).

In anticipating Teisis' arguments, the speaker claims that his line of defence will be founded upon the allegation that Archippus entered uninvited to the house and rudely attacked the members of the household (5). The side of the defendant thus would present Archippus as a vindictive youth, who, despite having first insulted Teisis, never forgot the hostility between them, and being drunk, violently entered his house with the intention of committing *hybris* against him and his family. Following this line of argument, Teisis would perhaps present to the court the testimonies of the members of his family and his friend that the events did indeed occur in such a manner. This position can be compared –despite the individual differences of the cases– with the position of the sons of Conon, who, likewise hybristic, violent, and in a state of drunkenness, wished to continue their conflict with Ariston when they returned to the city from the garrison in Panacton (see discussion below). Perhaps Lysias understood that Teisis –denying that he acted according to Pytheas' advice– would present himself as a quiet young man and assert that his desire to reconcile with Archippus was sincere and thus that it was his own decision not to continue the conflict that occurred in the wrestling ground. This self-presentation is similar to the position taken by the speaker in Lysias' *Against Simon* (Lys. 3) or the prudent position of Ariston, who prefers to avoid people like the sons of Conon.

Unaware of Pytheas' plan, in Lysias' script, Archippus adopts a relatively easygoing behaviour toward Teisis, in order to make it clear that he was a victim of Pytheas' machinations: he does not hesitate to pass in front of the house of Teisis –even if the speaker feels the need to explain that this happened because they were neighbours– and he accepts to make an appearance at night at the *komos* to which Teisis invited him, even if Lysias saw fit to make the speaker convey Archippus' reservation when he claims that at first the defendant refused to dine with him. However, the fact that Archippus ultimately accepts the invitation of Teisis, as well as the absence of any reference whatsoever –at least in the extant portion of the text– to particular events which would prove the shift in Teisis' behaviour are two elements which invite suspicions concerning the credibility of the speaker. They also lead us to assume that in the intervening period between the meeting of the two men in the wrestling ground and the invitation to dinner there may be things that the speaker prefers to conceal. In the narrative however, the speaker has every reason to highlight the hypocritical, underhanded, and nonsensical (εἰς τοῦτο μανίας) behaviour of Teisis, who happily receives Archippus in his home only to flog him a little later.

Lysias therefore inserts in his narrative the information that Teisis mentioned to Pytheas all that happened in the *palaestra* and that he advised him to reconcile with Archippus and to avenge him later, in order to deal with the basic weakness of his client's case. The flogging of Archippus happened in the house of Teisis and the only possible witness of the former, namely the speaker of the speech, was violently (and suspiciously) ousted –as is also the case with Ariston's friend, Phanostratus, in *Against Conon*.

The narration of the event in the *palaestra* and the description of the scheme allegedly conceived by Pytheas are intended to prejudice the dikasts, while at the same time –and this is perhaps more important– to fill a logical gap in the presentation of the case, because they supply the motive of the defendant's act: Archippus, who mocked Teisis for his deliberate erotic enslavement to Pytheas, was himself treated like a slave.[45] This version of the events would make Teisis appear as a particularly vindictive young man. This characterization is also underpinned by Teisis' presentation as a rich heir who came of age recently.

The initial quarrel in the *palaestra* and Archippus' state of health after the flogging are *prima facie* the only pieces of evidence that the side of the prosecutor would be able to support on the basis of testimonies of people not involved in the case. However, if Teisis denied that he himself or his slaves flogged Archippus, it is quite possible that at some point of his speech the speaker would mention that Archippus challenged Teisis to hand over his slaves in order to produce testimonies with the process of *basanos* and that the latter rejected the *proklesis*.[46] In this case, we would be faced with a situation in which Archippus would threaten with torture his own torturer, i.e. the slaves who were asked by Teisis to bind him to the pillar and flog him. Although we must exclude the possibility that this *basanos* took place, a possible mention to this challenge in the trial would emphasize the complete reversal of roles and consequently highlight the excessively *hybristic* behaviour of Teisis.

If Lysias intentionally leads dikasts to believe that Archippus playfully insulted Teisis by indicating his sexual subordination to Pytheas, in order to present the defendant's outrageous *hybris* as an act of incommensurate revenge – note that according to the narrative Teisis had Archippus whipped twice–, the visual story that he constructs and the cultural assumptions that this story appeals to gain further significance. The prosecutor spoke first and Lysias predicted that Teisis would tell a story in which *he* rather than Archippus would be the victim of aggressive behaviour. The details of the story are therefore tailored to pre-

---

[45] This line of argument is followed by Cohen 1995: 137.
[46] On *basanos*, a widely discussed topic, see Thür 1977, the most extensive treatment of the topic; see also Hunter 1994: 89–95; Gagarin 1996.

empt Teisis' line of argumentation and direct dikasts', anger against the defendant. In the emotion script that Lysias devises, Archippus is treated like a disobedient slave by a young man who 'enslaved' himself to an older *erastes*.⁴⁷

The normative transgressions that inform this fascinating narrative's emotion script focus, as happens so often in speeches delivered for assault, on the body as a legal object and as a marker of social status. Although, as O'Connell suggests (2017: 156), Lysias' use of deictics induces dikasts to construct mental pictures of Teisis' wounded body at the time of the attack and thereby emphasize personal harm, it is particularly notable that the agents of Archippus' second whipping are slaves and that Teisis has him imprisoned privately in what the speech describes as an *oikema*.⁴⁸ A short story told by Apollodorus in *Against Nicostratus* brings eloquently to the fore the social significance of Teisis' act.⁴⁹ In that speech (53.15–16),⁵⁰ the speaker claims that his opponents, wishing to ensnare him, urged a free child to enter his estate and cut roses, in order to cause the prosecutor to bind the boy and hold him illegally in his house like a slave and thus bring legal action against him with *graphe hybreos*. This story not only reflects the legal significance of private imprisonment, but also reveals how a citizen's control over his body marks off his status. Furthermore, although the narrative does not emphasize Archippus' state of health after the attack, the exposition of his body to the sight of passersby, a typical element in speeches composed for assault, introduces to the text internal spectators whose emotional responses guide the listeners' sentiments.

Notably, at the sight of Archippus' wounded body spectators complained that the polis does not enforce summary execution of the perpetrator rather than indicate compassion for his personal suffering and his maimed body. The

---

**47** Slavery is one of the conceptual metaphors that inform the imagery of *eros* in early poetry (see Cairns 2013: 240 n. 13, with discussion of Plato's appropriation of the metaphor in the *Phaedrus*). Metaphors of slavery reflect the importance of status for acceptable types of male homoerotic behaviour. The topic is discussed by Harper 2013, in an approach that fruitfully explores how the Christian notion of sin departs from earlier sexual ethics emphasizing one's relevant position in social hierarchy.
**48** On the pillar and the torturing of slaves, see Hunter 1994: 166–168.
**49** Private imprisonment was possible when an adulterer was caught in the act by the *kurios* of the *oikos*. On the legal regulation of adultery in Athens, a widely discussed topic, see, among others, Cohen 1991: 131–215; Todd 1993: 276–279, 1998: 107–180; Carey 1995; Omitowoju 2002: 72–115.
**50** On this story see Fisher 1992: 40, 56–57 and Scafuro 1997: 334–336 and 339, discussing the theatricality of the description.

wounded body, displayed on the *deigma* (the samples market), elicits social evaluations surrounding the interconnected matters of status, *hybris*, and punishment as deterrence.[51] Spectators' responses thus emphasize their anxiety, indeed anger, about the legal system of the polis.[52] Their 'verdict' is directly relevant to Lysias' rhetoric in general –and *pathopoiia* in particular. By stressing the public consequences of privately inflicted violence on the body of a citizen, internal spectators' 'spontaneous' response indicates that violence is a crime that affects the citizens as a whole.[53] Their emotional response, therefore, which is notably granted with propositional content (τῆς πόλεως κατηγορεῖν, ὅτι οὐ δημοσίᾳ οὐδὲ παραχρῆμα ... τιμωρεῖται), determines the appraisals that must shape dikasts' sentiments towards Teisis: his criminal action deserves their anger because his act is a threat to each and every member of the jury.

At the same time, as is typically the case with cases of violence, the emotion script that Lysias constructs is also a script of pity. Because Teisis' outrageous violence has public implications, pity is informed by social evaluations revolving around the body as a legal object. His humiliation, indeed the fact that he is treated like a slave, is undeserved, because his body is a citizen's body and therefore a boundary of status. The onlookers' emotional responses, therefore, induce dikasts to self-consciously reflect on their role as protectors of the social order, especially so because, as the narrative suggests, the perpetrator's *hybris* is prompted by his wealth. The bystanders' informal verdict in the narrative, thus, sets the example for the dikasts who will soon cast their vote.[54] Their anger against the prosecutor asserts the public dimensions with which Lysias grants the case by presenting Teisis as an archetypical *hybristes*. It is the viewing of the outrageous incident (δεινά) from a public perspective that allows Lysias to invite

---

[51] On violence and the body of the free citizen, see Fisher 2005. The display of the body at the *Deigma* in the Peiraeus, where many citizens and foreigners gathered to look at goods for sale, underscores the social implications of the body. Archippus' brothers wanted to show him to both sets of people to encourage a response of anger. This encourages the dikasts to feel the same anger and act on it. Cf. Pittalacus' self-display in the agora as an assembly was about to start (discussion below).

[52] On internal spectators' focalization of the narrated events and their importance for guiding listeners (or in the case of visual arts –ancient and modern) viewers' sentiments, see Blundell *et al.* 2013: 13.

[53] Rubinstein (2013) rightly argues that forensic speakers appeal to dikasts anger only in public cases or private cases concerning incidents of violent attacks. The prevalence of anger in cases of assault is due to the fact that violence is conceptualized as hybristic and is therefore seen as an action that threatens the city as a whole.

[54] On bystander intervention in the speech under discussion, see Sternberg 2006: ch. 3 and Christ 2012: 32–35.

dikasts to give vent to their anger against a defendant from whom they have not suffered personally.

### 3.4.2 *Against Conon* (Dem. 54)

My next example concerns the narrative of Demosthenes' *Against Conon*, a speech composed for a case of *aikeia* ('battery'). Dionysius of Halicarnassus compares the *diegesis* of this speech with *Against Teisis*, in order to reveal its Lysianic merits, especially the convincingness of individual characterization and its neat style. If we did not know to whom each of these two speeches belonged, Dionysius says, it would have been impossible to tell their respective authors (*Demosthenes* 13). The similarities of the rhetoric employed in the two narratives are also reflected in the adjective ὑβριστική with which Dionysius qualifies them (11). As we shall see, Demosthenes' speech makes extensive use of the word *hybris* and its derivatives. Note that the very first word of the speech is ὑβρισθείς, a word that signifies the insolent nature of the violence that the defendant suffered at the hands of Conon. The use of the most important buzz word of the speech at its outset offers a good example of how forensic narratives anticipate their final meaning from the very beginning, thereby framing dikasts' perception of their stories.

Conon and his sons, young Ariston says, were drinking at a party in the deme of Melite, when Conon and his friend Phanostratus, who were taking a walk in the agora, encountered Ctesias, one of Conon's sons. The latter insulted the defendant and Phanostratus and immediately went up to Melite and made Conon and his friends get up. A few minutes later, they all proceeded to the agora. One of them pinned Phanostratus, who like Archippus' friend in *Against Teisis* also disappears from the narrative, while Conon, his son and the son of a certain Andromenes threw themselves upon Ariston. The description of the incident underlines the sympotic context of the assault and thus makes intelligible Demosthenes' choice to mention in his preliminary *diegesis* that Conon's sons were habitual and bad-tempered drinkers.[55]

---

[55] On the sympotic aspects of the case and their political implications, see Murray 1990; for an overview of sympotic violence in Greece, see Murray 2016. On sympotic drunkenness and hybris, see Fisher 1990. As Carey (1989: 63) points out, the *sympotic* hyperactivity of Conon's sons, in effect a family tradition indicating the unacceptable moral education that the boys received from their father, is reminiscent of the excesses of Alcibiades' son.

In the rest of this section, I turn my attention to the visual qualities of the narrative and emphasize the social significance of the details that Demosthenes inserts in the description of the assault. Narrative specificity is one of the most salient characteristics of Ariston's account. The story about the defendant's humiliation, very probably a post eventum reconstruction of events for which Ariston produces no palpable evidence in the speech,[56] is portrayed as a choreography of *hybris* with salient performative features. Conon's gestures in this comic,[57] albeit humiliating enactment of superiority, are culturally specific and invite dikasts to recognize their meaning by activating their cultural knowledge.

Ancient art and literature attests to the fact that in antiquity cocks were conceptualized (ambivalently, as Csapo's discussion indicates –triumphalism requires a victim) as a social marker of agonistic masculinity,[58] sometimes symbolizing the opposite of the Ur-effeminate category of *kinaidos*. Note, for example, that in ancient cockfights the losing cock was called a 'slave' (*doulos*). In this agonistic framework, the demeaning posture of Ariston's body implies that what he suffers is a symbolic rape. An unidentified comic poet writes: 'You'll never see a cock that is a *kinaidos*' (Com. adesp. 1213 Kock).[59] The triumphant cock's *hybris* was proverbial: 'the cock treads upon [its victim]'. As Csapo points out (2006: 18), "the meaning of the proverb arises from the ambiguity of ἐπιπηδᾶν which denotes both physical assault and the mounting of a hen" (cp. Arist. *Hist. An.* 539a 32). The proverb's meaning is "something like rubbing it in" (Csapo 2006: 28). In other instances, ἐπιπηδᾶν describes homosexual intercourse, while in the *Wasps* it is employed to convey metaphorically dikasts' (perhaps visible ithyphallic) aggression against Cleon's enemies (705).

The culturally significant connotations of Conon's display of superiority are further enhanced by the strong associations between birds and *phalloi*. Although the existing literary evidence is meagre, ancient art commonly presents winged *phalloi*, nests of phalloi, and phallic headed birds. The pedestal of the enormous ithyphallic column at the entrance of Dionysus' shrine at Delos, to mention a memorable example, depicts a phallus headed cock. Furthermore, as Csapo

---

56 For a brief discussion of the weaknesses of Ariston's case, see the Introduction to the speech in Carey/Reid 1985. For a discussion of social violence and legal violence in the speech, see Wohl 2010: 71–82, with further literature on readings of the speech (esp. Cohen 1995) as evidence that the courts asserted litigants' honour rather than regulated legal disputes.
57 On the comic aspects of Ariston's humiliation and the ambivalent conceptualization of laughter as a 'consequential' or 'playful' gesture, See Halliwell 2008: 33–37.
58 For a reading of the speech focusing on masculinity and youth, see Roisman 2005: 17–21.
59 See Winkler 1990: 181 with n. 28.

points out, "[T]he victorious cock was perceived as 'phallicity' itself. Ancient writers lovingly describe the way it swells up, flutters its wings, lifts its entire body, rises on tiptoes, stretches head and neck skywards and crows while gathering its wings into a ball. Greek art leaves no doubt that the cock, at its climactic moment, became a winged phallus."[60]

This literary and material evidence indicates that Demosthenes' description of the skirmish in the agora is tailored to embed an imagery that reflects recognizable cultural patterns surrounding sexual activity and virility. The recognizability of these patterns is attested by the fact that Conon and his friends associate with violent gangs called the 'Erects' (*Ithyphalloi*) or *Autolekythoi*, a word whose meaning is obscure,[61] but most probably refers to aggressive sexual activity.[62] Conon thus enacts a role of sexual domination in the context of a social script focusing on the construction of male hierarchies, esteem, and shame.

The visual qualities of the narrative are significantly enhanced by the presence of spectators. The gazes of Conon's fellow-symposiasts turn Ariston's humiliation into a spectacle of violence, which brings shame to the victim. The abusive language with which onlookers respond to what they see and hear verbalizes Conon's gestures and asserts Ariston's loss of face.[63] As Halliwell suggests (2008: 34–45), the audience of Conon's performance may be seen as a chorus that supports "the prancing of a comic actor". A few paragraphs later, however, another chorus, consisting of Ariston's female family members, engages in a performance of tragic mourning. This chorus responds with cries of grief to the sight of Ariston's wounded body. As was the case with bystanders' responses to Archippus' maltreated body, internal spectators' emotional responses are deployed here to guide audiences' sentiments from a third person perspective. The weeping of this

---

**60** Csapo 2006: 25, with 40 n. 52 including further examples from Greek literature. Mitchell (2009: 131) discusses a red-figure Pelike in Tarquinia depicting a prostitute's client inspecting her genitals in the presence of a cock.
**61** See Carey/Reid 1985: 87; Borthwick 1993. As I hope to show elsewhere on the basis of visual evidence, *autolekythos*, a person who carries his own oil-flask, has connotations of sexual aggressiveness.
**62** Conon's and his friends are characterized by *aselgeia*, a word signifying extreme aggressiveness and violence and uncontrolled sexual indulgence. Note also that the rich imagery is characterized by mobility, with many striking-words (προσπίπτει, ὑποσκελίσαντες καὶ ῥάξαντες, ἐναλλόμενοι, τὸ μὲν χεῖλος διακόψαι, τοὺς δ' ὀφθαλμοὺς συγκλεῖσαι, 8).
**63** One may imagine that Conon's performance also included crowing, on whose associations with contempt, see Halliwell 2008: 34–35 with n. 89. Conon's mimicry is also reminiscent of ritual humiliation of the enemy in the epic and other battlefields (see Halliwell 2008: 34 n. 88).

audience contrasts sharply the loud and hybristic laughter of superiority that we heard at the agora.

Another set of spectators are the doctors who examined Ariston's body (cp. ἔδειξαν, 9). The semi-scientific vocabulary that Demosthenes' employs here indicates professionalism and is thus intended to make a strong impression upon dikasts (12). But notably, the detailed account of doctors' diagnosis encourages dikasts to imagine Ariston's body, i.e. the body of the young man who delivers the speech, as an object of medical observation.[64] Note for example that the description emphasizes the 'swellings' and 'bruises' on his face (11) –which mirror Ariston's 'unscientific' description of the physical harm that he suffered in the agora.[65] Ariston's immobile body –during and after the attack– is the object of agile spectators' viewing. The sonorous responses of Conon's friends to his comic and violent performance and the screams of anxiety and grief of the female tragic chorus in the victim's house are sharply contrasted with Ariston's silence and inability to act.[66] Ariston's forced silence enhances a scenario that emphasizes the terrible consequences of insolence upon defenceless victims and, hence, underscores dikasts' normative role as helpers of the defendant (cp. 2, 42).

The grief of Ariston's female relatives indicates the gravity of the attack and is therefore intended to arouse the dikasts' pity for the defendant. Indeed, their grief was so intense that it reflected their fear that Ariston was dead (ὡσπερανεὶ τεθνεῶτός τινος, 20). Women's screams were so loud, the speaker says, that their neighbours were alarmed, another indication of the agitation caused by the attack.[67] But since the speech stresses the hybristic nature of Conon's aggressiveness and its implications for the community as a whole, Demosthenes contextualizes the incident by appropriating in the emotion script that he puts together evaluations concerning the maltreatment of a free citizen rather than just the personal suffering of Ariston.

In the following paragraphs of this fascinating narrative, Ariston frames his own suffering by emphasizing both his wealthy opponent's social activities, including sympotic violence, deviant sexuality, erotic pursuits of courtesans and

---

64 Ariston's 'neutral' nakedness when he is the object of medical observation and his forced half-nakedness at the time of the attack reveal the rich social contextualizations of the body in the ancient (and modern) cultures that attract our attention, but in both cases the exposure of his body is intended to elicit dikasts' pity. On forced half-nakedness and humiliation, see Bassi 1995.
65 On the medical aspects of the diagnosis, see Holmes 2010: 150–151; on doctors as witnesses, see Humphreys 1985: esp. 327.
66 Cp. οὕτω δὲ κακῶς ἔχοντα κατέλιπον, ὥστε μήτ' ἀναστῆναι μήτε φθέγξασθαι δύνασθαι. κείμενος δ' αὐτῶν ἤκουον πολλὰ καὶ δεινὰ λεγόντων, 8.
67 On cries and other noises –or silence– in Greek tragedy, see Stanford 1983.

young boys, and disgusting, indeed sacrilegious practices, such as the consumption of purificatory pigs' testicles (39). Furthermore, Ariston's story throws into relief Conon's and his friends' antidemocratic political predilections.[68] At 34 for example, he says that Conon and his friends endorse aspects of Spartans' lifestyle and physical appearance. Hence, even as Ariston predictably highlights the almost fatal consequences of Conon's attack, the fact that he devotes a large portion of his forensic story to reveal his opponents' social background and oligarchic inclinations shows that he contextualizes the violence that he suffered and the personal harm that he sustained by indicating its wider social implications. Lastly, because cocks in general and cockfights in particular are typically associated with boys and youths, Conon's performance foregrounds his intrinsic *hybris* and indicates his problematic socialization.[69] As Ariston says, Conon endorses and exemplifies a youthful behaviour which is in breach with his status as a middle-aged adult.[70] The self-indulgence that he displays identifies him with his arrogant, insolent, and aggressive sons.

The 'wide-angle' framing of the case that Demosthenes attempts with his story, relying on cultural assumptions about sympotic *hybris*, suspicions about the political engagements of elite commensalities, and norms surrounding the inviolability of the citizen's body, is in pace with Ariston's use of the law as an argument. Because Conon's attack is commensurate with *hybris*, dikasts' pity requires appraisals concerning the public nature of the wrongdoing. Indeed, in the course of the trial Ariston has the clerk read the laws of *hybris* and clothestealing rather than the law of *aikeia*.[71] His story, thus, invites dikasts' empathetic sentiments towards Ariston, by stressing that the violence that the prosecutor sustained is a crime that the polis punishes in the frame of public lawsuits (*graphe hybreos*). The public concerns shaping the evaluations that give rise to dikasts'

---

**68** On the political aspects of the symposium and the *hetereia* (including discussion of Dem. 54), see Murray 1990; recently Hobden 2013: ch. 3. On the symposium and suspicions about oligarchic conspiracy, see Roisman 2006: 70. On Demosthenes' attitudes to Sparta and Spartanising, see Fisher 1994. The main point here is the contrast between pompous, old-fashioned moralising austerity and nocturnal debauchery and violence.
**69** On violence and socialization in Greece, see Fisher 2017a.
**70** See Roisman 2005: 20. On the pejorative qualification *neanikos* and *neanieuesthai*, see Dover 1974: 103–104.
**71** On this point, see Lanni 2006: 65. The crucial question in the law of *aikeia* was who started the attack. In our case, this question is addressed by Ariston in the socially and culturally contextualized description of the incident at the agora, where he says that Conon and his sympotic company attacked him first. On *aikeia* as a legal term, see Todd 1993: 269–270, 360.

compassion may also explain the prominence of anger in this private speech. Because Conon's insolent behaviour is directed against the polis as a whole, his act of violence must be seen as an offence inflicted on each and every member of the audience. Consequently, Ariston invites dikasts not only to consider the consequences of a possible acquittal upon his honour, but also conscientiously reflect on their role as guarantors of social order.

In his attempt to contextualize the violence that he suffered, Ariston's story also lays stress on the social implications of laughter. Laughter is an ambiguous gesture: it sometimes gravitates towards playfulness, but it is also used as a public display of superiority that brings shame to its targets.[72] In Ariston's eyes, Conon's and his companions' laughter is part of a zero-sum game which requires the victim's shame. When, for example, Ariston describes the skirmish, he employs *deinosis* and hence uses military vocabulary (cp. ἀνεμείχθημεν 8). Unlike Conon's and his sons' playful understanding of violence, Ariston's seriousness and self-restraint are in accordance with his socially responsive perception of aggression as an antidemocratic trait of the elites' social activities. Ariston's interpretation of his opponents' laughter reflects Demosthenes' attempt to provide a wide angle of the case at hand. Conon deserves dikasts' anger because his and his companions' laughter is consequential rather than just playful. Their aggressive and humiliating laughter, or rather their taunting, indicates contempt for the law and reflects an archetypically antidemocratic behaviour. What Conon takes as a joke is a serious threat for democracy and social order.

The narrative of *Against Conon*, thus, indicates how visual narratives activate dikasts' social competence through the use of culturally significant gestures. It, therefore, offers another example of how a script of pity for the maltreatment of a citizen encourages dikasts to direct their anger against an opponent who poses a serious threat to the community as a whole.[73] Indeed, Ariston suggests overtly that he will be more pitiable than his opponent, if dikasts' double the *hybris* that he suffered by succumbing to his opponent's unwarranted attempts to appeal to their compassion (43). Each and every member of the jury is a possible victim of hybristic elites. Furthermore, through its specificity, the narrative contextualizes the shame experienced by Ariston. Because through compromising less powerful

---

**72** On this distinction, see Halliwell 2008: 19–38.
**73** Cp. ὥσπερ ἂν αὐτὸς ἕκαστος παθὼν τὸν πεποιηκότ' ἐμίσει, οὕτως ὑπὲρ ἐμοῦ πρὸς Κόνωνα τουτονὶ τὴν ὀργὴν ἔχειν, καὶ μὴ νομίζειν ἴδιον τῶν τοιούτων μηδὲν ὃ κἂν ἄλλῳ τυχὸν συμβαίη, ἀλλ' ἐφ' ὅτου ποτ' ἂν συμβῇ, βοηθεῖν καὶ τὰ δίκαι' ἀποδιδόναι, καὶ μισεῖν τοὺς πρὸ μὲν τῶν ἁμαρτημάτων θρασεῖς καὶ προπετεῖς, 42.

citizens' sense of self-esteem members of the elite insolently showcase their superiority, the outcome of the trial has important social implications. Indeed, as we saw, Ariston claims that Conon's acquittal would double the shame that he suffered (40). But before reaching this point, the narrative emphasizes the repercussions of *hybris* upon the *polis*' interests and especially upon the honour and integrity of the less powerful among its citizens.

### 3.4.3 Aeschines, an Olynthian woman, and sympotic *hybris* (Dem. 19. 196–199)

In this and the next section I turn my attention to incidents of violence described in speeches concerning major political disputes. The protagonists of these violent incidents are the prosecutors' political enemies: Aeschines in Demosthenes' *On the false embassy* and Timarchus in Aeschines' *Against Timarchus*. These narratives primarily serve purposes of character-assassination, but they also have wider implications for the speeches' political concerns.

Sympotic violence is central to a story told by Demosthenes (196–199) in the frame of his embassy speech (Dem. 19). This story, reflecting Aeschines' unbridled insolence and unpatriotic feelings, displays saliently the qualities that ancient theory associates with vividness: careful selection of details, detailed descriptions of socially significant gestures encouraging audiences to supply their meaning, appeals to major cultural understandings and activation of listeners' emotions.

Athenian ambassadors, Demosthenes says (196), were invited to a symposium hosted by a certain Xenophron –indeed, an intriguing name for an ancient host. From the outset of his narration Demosthenes prudently informs dikasts that he refused to participate in the symposium, obviously with the purpose of disassociating himself from its aggressive and indecorous outcome. As he claims, he was subsequently informed about the incidents that took place in the symposium by Iatrocles who was present.

The story concerns the humiliation and sadistic violence that an Olynthian woman, qualified by Demosthenes as freeborn and modest, suffered at the hands of Aeschines. At first, Demosthenes says, the symposiasts let the woman eat and drink quietly, but when they got drunk they ordered her to recline and sing for them. In a state of embarrassment and anxiety, the woman refused to do as she was told. Irritated by her refusal, which they took as an indication of inappropriate arrogance, Aeschines and Phrynon, utterly drunk, ordered a slave to whip her. The slave undressed her and gave her a number of lashes on the back. Aeschines' and Phrynon's drunkenness was such that they remained unmoved by her begging and tears. After the torture, the woman was so angry that she overturned a table and fell at the knees of Iatrocles in supplication.

Modern commentators of the speech point out that the story told by Demosthenes includes a number of inaccuracies and suggest that it is irrelevant to the prosecution.[74] Yet, in my view, not only is the story relevant to the wider scope of the speech but also the inaccuracies that it includes are important for its meaning. As I pointed out earlier, Demosthenes was not present at the symposium and, as he suggests, the characterization of the woman as a freeborn and modest Olynthian results from her responses to the violence that she sustained within the limits of the script that he puts together.[75] Demosthenes, therefore, fabricated the story post factum by carefully selecting the material that he saw fit to include in it. The meaning that his distinctively visual narrative produces, I would like to suggest, centres on the woman's status and thereby offers a wider conceptual frame revolving around sympotic decorousness, the tension between *xenia* obligations and Athenian interests, and normative assumptions about the body as a social marker and a legal object.

---

[74] See for example MacDowell's note on 196. In a recent publication, Harris (2017) takes the view that ancient litigants and supporting speakers refrained from "sensational descriptions of acts of violence and that they aroused dikasts' anger or pity they avoided 'giving the impression that they were attempting to distract the judges from the legal issues" (226). The extent to which individual narratives are 'sensational' is a question liable to subjective assessment, but I find the description of Pittalacus' maltreatment by Timarchus and Hegesandrus (see discussion below) 'sensational' enough, even if it does not focus on the victim's wounded body as much as Ariston does in *Against Conon*. Harris (230) also points out that in *Against Conon* Ariston "never describes his own sense of humiliation". Quite the contrary: this is he what he does when he starts his speech with the word *hybristheis* (the occurrences of *hybris* and cognates in the speech are extremely frequent, 22X, while in *Against Meidias*, a much longer speech, which, as Harris believes was composed for a *graphe hybreos*, the word recurs 44 times) and when he says that immediately after the attack 'they left me in such a state that I could neither get up nor utter a sound.' Furthermore, Harris' argument that Ariston's reference to his wounds is due to the fact that the speech concerns a case of battery is weak. In the law of *aikeia* the bodily harm sustained by the victim was legally irrelevant. On the basis of lexical comparison with other speeches, Harris concludes that the passage from the embassy speech that I discuss here is unusual in that it employs extremely graphic language. Interestingly, Harris (236) puts Aeschines' refutation (2, 153–158) to the service of his own argument. For example he uses as *evidence* Aeschines' statement that Athenians responded with *thorubos* to Demosthenes' story presumably because it was false. Lastly, Harris calculates speakers' 'sensationalism' or lack thereof on the basis of labels rather than scripts. For a discussion of this method's limitations, see the Introduction.

[75] On Aeschines' 'correction' of the story, see previous note.

As has been noted, Xenophron, the host of the symposium in Macedonia was not the son of Phaedimus. Perhaps he was the son of Phaedrias, whose name appears in Xenophon's list of the Thirty.[76] Furthermore, in his own account of the story, Aeschines says that the 'host' (*xenodocus*) was a *hetairos* of Philip, not a person associated with the Thirty. More importantly perhaps, Demosthenes' account "glosses over", as Hobden suggests, "an important detail":[77] that at the time of the symposium, the Olynthian woman was a slave, presumably one of the captives who ended up in Philip's court after the sack of Olynthus. It would, therefore, be well known that the woman, like any Olynthian present at the Macedonian court, was now a prisoner and hence might be treated by the conquerors as a slave, and sold on, but also might, if they chose, be ransomed. But Demosthenes implies that, on account of his anti-Athenian sentiments, his opponent turns a blind eye to the woman's previous status and the events which prompted her enslavement. Demosthenes' handling of the woman's status is thus reminiscent of, albeit not identical with, Aeschines' dubious rhetoric when he tells the story of how Pittalacus, presented ambivalently as a freedman and a public slave, was humiliated by Timarchus (see discussion below).

The woman's status and the host's political inclinations are particularly important for the meaning that Demosthenes' story produces by way of inducing dikasts to understand Aeschines' conduct from a wide angle perspective. At the same time, his story incorporates culturally and socially specific material thereby providing dikasts with an emotion script to which the speaker urges them to respond. As we saw, the Olynthian woman's status is transvaluated by Demosthenes' authorial voice. If for Demosthenes and any Athenian patriot it would only be natural to treat the Olynthian woman as a freeborn lady, whose personal misfortune resulted from Philips' threatening expansionism, Aeschines not only treats her as a slave, but is also insensitive to the fact that her presence in the symposium is in breach with her previous status as a free woman.[78] Indeed, Demosthenes implies that her refusal to recline and sing was due to the fact that she was freeborn and, therefore, had no experience in men's sympotic entertainment. And it is also important for the presentation of the woman's status that Demosthenes does not provide her name.[79]

---

[76] See MacDowell 2000: 287.
[77] Hobden 2009: 76.
[78] In his own speech, Aeschines preserves the same uncertainty on her status: at 2.4 he reports without comment Demosthenes' labelling her as *eleutheran* and at 158 he calls her a prisoner (*aichmalotos*).
[79] On not-naming respectable women, see Schaps 1977.

Aeschines therefore not only misrecognizes the woman's prideful behaviour and misidentifies it with *hybris*, but also displays *hybris* by treating the woman as a *hetaera* and more seriously by whipping her on account of her disobedience.[80] Aeschines' maltreatment of the woman is reminiscent of Neaira's barbarous maltreatment by Phrynion in [Dem.] 59.35 (ἀσελγῶς προὐπηλακίζετο, also called *hybris* by 'Neaira' 37), which ultimately urged her to abandon him. As Apollodorus says, Phrynion abused Neaira during his nightly revels and in some cases forced her to have sex with him in public (33) by way of insolently displaying his power of dominion over such a beautiful woman. Neaira's reaction to Phrynion offers evidence as to the limits of the aggressive laddishness that a courtesan would tolerate and the dikasts' understanding of these limits. A fortiori then, Aeschines' maltreatment of an Athenian captive woman that any decent citizen would respect, if not pity, is an outrageous act that betrays his disregard for human dignity.

The insolence that Aeschines' commits in the symposium is emphasized by the alleged political associations of the host, especially so because this is a symposium that takes place in Macedonia. Demosthenes' story is compatible with Athenian suspicions about the political aspects, especially the anti-democratic orientation, of elite symposia in Athens.[81] Hence, the insinuation that the host's father was one of the Thirty is reminiscent of the way in which Demosthenes 'politicizes' Conon's conduct and sympotic activities in the private speech that he wrote for Ariston. Indeed, the fact that the symposium that Demosthenes describes took place in Macedonia where Aeschines was dispatched by the polis in order to negotiate a peace treaty with Philip adds to his story further significance.

Although it is not easy to understand the Macedonian symposium on account of the fact that the sources that we possess,[82] like the passage under discussion, display Athenocentric biases, recent scholarship shows that the symposia organized in the Macedonian court differed from Southern or Athenian symposia in some respects, but, as Murray (2016) suggests, sympotic excess is one of the ways that hostile sources emphasize Macedonian kings' un-Greekness. For the purposes of my discussion be it sufficient to suggest that Macedonian symposia were

---

[80] I discuss Phrynion's relationship with Neaira and Kapparis' reading of it (1999) in Spatharas 2009a: 107–108. The presumption that a prostitute does not say no, because he takes money from his clients is implicit to Aeschines' rhetoric in *Against Timarchus*.
[81] See n. 68 above.
[82] For a general overview of Macedonian symposia, see Sawada 2010. On the problems surrounding our understanding of Macedonian symposia and instances of drunken violence, see Murray 2016: 201–205; see also Hobden 2013: 182–189. On the excesses of Macedonian symposia and political propaganda, see Carney 2007.

characterized or thought to be characterized by excessiveness and heavy drinking (Carney 2007). Although, as I suggested earlier, Aeschines' behaviour transgresses the rules of Athenian symposia, it is plausible to assume that Demosthenes' description invests in stereotypes surrounding formal Macedonian commensalities. That Demosthenes places Aeschines' excessive drinking and *paroinia* in the *andron* of an Athenian with oligarchic predilections who now lives in Macedonia and tolerates the humiliation of an Olynthian woman in his own house may be taken to reflect Aeschines' identification with Macedonian cultural practices and excess.[83] If this is so, Demosthenes exploits the tension between complying with the rules of *xenia* in the Macedonian court and acting in the best interests of the polis. Demosthenes' abstinence from the indecorous symposium, therefore, substantiates the presentation of his patriotic stance to which he contrasts Aeschines' assimilation into Macedonian *truphe*.

The rich emotion script that Demosthenes puts together in this brief narrative must be understood in its wider context. The story about the Olynthian woman is preceded by another short narrative recounting the behaviour of Satyrus during a banquet in the frame of a *thysia* that took place after the sack of Olynthus (193–195). On that occasion, Demosthenes says, Satyrus asked Philip to give him as a gift the daughters of his dead friend Apollophanes who had been taken captive. Demosthenes also adds the detail that the young women were of marriageable age. This story of altruism, which also takes place in the frame of Macedonian commensalities, is used by Demosthenes as the appropriate comparative ground on the basis of which he asks dikasts to evaluate Aeschines' behaviour in Xenophron's symposium. Unlike Satyrus, who decorously takes advantage of the festive commensality and Philip's self-serving, autocratic generosity to support his request and, thus appeals to the previous status of the girls and emphasizes that the time is ripe for their marriage, Aeschines is so mesmerized by Macedonian luxury and Philip's gifts that he unreflectively treats the Olynthian woman as a courtesan and mistakes the defence of her status for arrogance. Contradistinctive characterization is also underscored by the fact that Satyrus, whose words are given in direct speech, points out that he has nothing to gain from his request, but also that he is willing to contribute to the girls' dowry.[84]

---

**83** Aeschines' cultural assimilation is discussed by Hobden (2009: 87). On the manipulation of *xenia* and friendship in the frame of Demosthenes' and Aeschines' dispute, see Herman 1987: 3–4; Harris 1995: 86–87; Mitchell 1997: 183–187. On the eventual endorsement of Macedonian practices by southern Greeks, see Dalby 1993: 152.

**84** βούλομαι δέ σ' ἀκοῦσαι καὶ μαθεῖν οἵαν μοι δώσεις δωρειάν, ἂν ἄρα δῷς, ἀφ' ἧς ἐγὼ κερδανῶ μὲν οὐδέν, ἂν λάβω, προῖκα δὲ προσθεὶς ἐκδώσω, 195.

It is particularly noteworthy, that the story about the Olynthian woman is followed by one of Demosthenes' most vehement attacks on Aeschines focusing on his private life before becoming a *symboulos*.[85] Aeschines' sympotic *hybris* and disrespect for the Olynthian woman elicits one of the strongest responses of disgust to be found in the orators: Aeschines' attempt to defend his career with theatrical grandiosity makes Demosthenes choke (ἀποπνίγομαι).[86] Demosthenes' moral disgust is also corroborated by the qualification *katharma* which he attributes to his opponent. Far from being irrelevant to the main contours of Demosthenes' accusation, therefore, his story about the Olynthian woman substantiates his opponent's hypocrisy and unpatriotic feelings. In fact, as Demosthenes bitterly avers, there was a time when Aeschines was capable of empathetic feelings towards Olynhtians. When in the past Aeschines crossed paths with thirty Olynthian captives, women and children, led by the Arcadian friend of Philip, Atrestidas (305–306), he burst into tears (δακρῦσαι καὶ ὀδύρασθαι τὴν Ἑλλάδα, 306) and complained about the plight in which Greece was getting entangled. Indeed, later in the speech, Demosthenes poses the following rhetorical question: is it possible for the man who expressed his abhorrence for Atrestidas to cooperate with Philocrates, who brought free-born Olynthian ladies to this city for sexual exploitation (ἐφ' ὕβρει, 309)?

The story about the Olynthian woman is so designed as to arouse dikasts' anger against Aeschines. Their anger is fostered by the cognitions that elicit their pity for the woman's undeserved suffering. Demosthenes' story guides dikasts' sentiments through its distinctive visuality and the mental pictures that it produces. These pictures result from the details that he inserts in his account. The overturning of the table not only reflects the woman's unrestrained anger for the humiliation that she suffered, but also indicates a serious violation of the rules of *xenia* prompted by Aeschines' drunken *hybris*.[87] Her gesture perhaps transgresses the limits of her gender, but it is commensurate with her forced presence in the symposium and reflects the extremity of her despair at her humiliation. Furthermore, her bodily gestures, including her forced reclining and her silence when she refuses to sing are powerful markers of her social status and the habits that it

---

[85] On the use of slander in this part of the speech, see Worman 2008: 249–250.
[86] On forensic uses of disgust, see Fisher 2017 and Spatharas 2017.
[87] See Hobden 2009: 80, providing examples from the epic.

entailed (cp. οὔτ' ἐπισταμένης, 197). Furthermore, the embarrassment experienced by the woman was perhaps intensified by the nature of the songs that she was asked to sing.[88]

The rich imagery of the description reaches a climax when a slave undresses her and whips her. The vividness of the narration is underpinned by Demosthenes' identification of the instruments of torture: as Harris points out (2017: 235), the use of a *rhyter*, 'a bridle', is humiliating because it indicates that a human being is restrained like an animal; her *chitoniskos* is a garment associated with slaves; and the verb *xaino* conveys "the image of the sharp whip lacerating the woman's flesh". Lastly, the woman's emotional condition is carefully focalized through words reflecting her thoughts or emotional state (ἀδημονούσης, 197, ἔξω δ' αὐτῆς οὖσα, 198), while her anxiety and anger are reflected in her gestures: she sheds tears (δακρύσασα); she is restless, as the overturning of the table shows; and lastly she embraces Iatrocles' knees in a typical scene of supplication.

The sentiments of pity that Demosthenes imparts in his audience are therefore elicited by appraisals concerning the woman's present status rather than just her personal suffering. Just like Ariston's humiliated body, the Olynthian woman's body is primarily construed as a social marker of status –even if the emotive implications of Demosthenes' description is undoubtedly enhanced by its appeal to physical pain and forced nakedness. But given the wider political issues that this speech addresses, the treatment of her body is also elevated to a criterion of patriotism, or lack thereof. Unlike Ariston's or Teisis' bodies, the woman's social body in the Macedonian symposium is ambiguous and therefore open to interpretation: Aeschines *chooses* to treat her body as the body of a slave, an object of sexual satisfaction and sadistic corporeal punishment, because his excess and insolence make it impossible for him to turn his attention to the cultural and social history of the woman and, thereby, display sympathy for her. More importantly, his selective understanding of the woman's status reflects the mentality with which he approaches his duties as an ambassador. He humiliates the woman because his unpatriotic feelings lead him to turn a blind eye to her past and the past of her polis' relationship with Athens. Furthermore, the supposed language which he and Phrynon allegedly used of the Olynthians in general (θεοῖς ἐχθρῶν, ἀλειτηρίων, 197) indicates their total adoption of Philip's attitude of hatred and contempt towards the unfortunate Olynthians for whom most Athenians felt pity and perhaps guilt that they had not done more for them.

---

**88** Nick Fisher usefully suggests to me that at Dem. 2.19 'poets of obscene songs' are listed among other types of amusers who parade at the symposia of the Macedonian court. On the erotic nature of courtesans' songs, see Davidson 2000.

In fact, Demosthenes emphasizes the repercussions of Aeschines' sympotic *hybris* upon Athens' reputation by letting his audience know that the story became common talk all over Greece (198). These Panhellenic audiences not only vouch for the veracity of the story and underscore the public nature of Aeschines' misconduct, but also add to the emotion script that Demosthenes constructs shame. Aeschines' behaviour belittles Athens and compromises its power.

### 3.4.4 Timarchus, Hegesandrus, and Pittalacus (Aeschin. 1. 53–62)

My last example derives from *Against Timarchus*, a speech that Aeschines composed by way of pre-empting Demosthenes' allegations about his misconduct on the embassy of 346. The passage that I discuss in this section concerns an incident of violence directed against a victim whose status is presented ambiguously. Throughout the speech, the prosecutor seeks to establish that Timarchus, one of Demosthenes' political friends, prostituted himself when he was young thereby inflicting *atimia* upon himself.[89] The narrative of the speech focuses mainly on Timarchus' sexual relationships with a number of men by way of establishing that he was receiving money for his sexual services. In order to satiate his unbridled desires, Aeschines says, Timarchus accepted to be penetrated by a limitless number of men, including merchants and foreigners. One of the most ocular stories included in his narrative concerning Timarchus' career as a prostitute centres on his opponent's relationship with a certain Pittalacus whose status Aeschines deliberately blurs. This short story concerns an incident of violent intrusion into Pittalacus' gambling house and the legally significant events that took place immediately after it.[90] Like the story about the Olynthian woman, the story about Pittalacus, presented both as a freedman and a public slave,[91] offers a good opportunity to consider how appeals to potent cultural understandings determine the verisimilitude of vivid stories and the emotions scripts that they construct.

After having been ousted by one of his previous lovers, a certain Misgolas, Aeschines says (52–53), Timarchus moved to the gaming house of Pittalacus, a

---

**89** On the legal questions of the speech (*dokimasia rhetoron*), see Fisher 2001: 36–52, Efstathiou 2014.
**90** Fisher 2001: 189 takes the inclusion of the attack on Pittalacus in the hypothesis of Demosthenes 19 and in Tzetzes (*Chil.* 6.56) as an indication of its "impact on later scholars and perhaps on contemporaries".
**91** Fisher 2001: 191 accepts the view of Todd (1993: 192–194) and Hunter (1994: 231) that at the time of the narrated events Pittalacus was a freedman.

man qualified twice as a public slave and a servant of the city. The monetary nature of Pittalacus' relationship with Timarchus, a relationship that Timarchus saw as an opportunity for monetary gain, is figuratively described by Aeschines as a *choregia* (54). The qualification *choregos* with which Aeschines sarcastically grants Pittalacus enhances significantly Aeschines' rhetoric, in so far as the speech emphasizes, albeit on the basis of unsubstantiated rumors,[92] the tension between private life and public interests. Instead of aspiring to be a wealthy *choregos* for the city, Timarchus not only dissipated the wealth that he inherited from his family, but also allowed a public slave to operate as his private sponsor in exchange for accepting to be buggered by him.[93] However, after his arrival at Athens, a certain Hegesandrus crossed paths with Timarchus. Hegesandrus, Aeschines claims, was away from Athens because he served as treasurer. This service, Aeschines insinuates, offered Hegesandrus the opportunity to acquire a large amount of money, no doubt the product of expropriation.[94] When Hegesandrus saw the defendant, he fell for him. He therefore immediately asked Pittalacus to hand Timarchus over to him. Pittalacus refused to do as he was told, but Hegesandrus persuaded Timarchus to go off with him. Pittalacus, however, subsequently made a pest of himself and, thus, kept visiting Hegesandrus' house on account of his jealousy and because he thought that he had wasted much money.

The following lines in Aeschines' narrative (57–62) exhibit several qualities that ancient theory associates with visual stories. Because Hegesandrus and Timarchus were frustrated by Pittalacus' behaviour, they violently entered into his house. Aeschines' description of Pittalacus' domestic space is characterized by specificity: for example Aeschines names the items of Pittalacus' gambling equipment. Furthermore, as is typically the case with other forensic stories detailing instances of violence, in this brief narrative the perpetrators' act is associated with sympotic excess. Timarchus and Hegesandrus burst into Pittalacus' house in a state of drunkenness (58) and in the company of an unspecified number of unnamed men, and, therefore, it is possible to assume that before the attack they were drinking in a symposium where they organized the nightly attack. Their aggressiveness is reflected in their manic agility: they destroyed the equipment of the gaming house and threw it into the street –shaking knucklebones and

---

[92] Indeed, Aeschines appeals to deified Rumor (*Pheme*) to substantiate his ungrounded accusation (125–131). On gossip and *pheme* in Athenian courtrooms, see Hunter 1994: ch. 4; Eidinow 2016: 191–206.
[93] The speech allows us to understand that Pittalacus was well-off (Fisher 2001: 191).
[94] For a detailed prosopography, see Fisher 2001: 188–189. On the political dimensions of Timarchus' erotic relationships, see Davidson 2007: 354–355. On Hegesandrus' and his brother's political careers, see Davies 2011: 11–24.

dice-boxes. They also killed the quails and the cocks, of which, as Aeschines hastens to add, Pittalacus was particularly fond.[95] The story reaches a climax when Pittalacus and Hegesandrus, just like Teisis in Lysias' speech that I analysed above, bound Pittalacus to a pillar and 'gave him the worst beating imaginable in the world, for such long time that even the neighbours heard the outcry' (59).

On the next day Pittalacus appeared half-naked in the agora and took refuge to the altar of the Mother of the Gods.[96] When a crowd appeared, Hegesandrus and Timarchus panicked, because they realized that their hybris would become common talk in the polis. The scenes of supplication that Aeschines describes to convey Hegesandrus' and Timarchus' attempts to cajole Pittalacus into getting up from the altar indicate his opponent's overt hypocrisy and manipulative behaviour: Timarchus not only begs a public slave, but also promises that he will offer him afresh the sexual favours that he denied him when he got off with Hegesandrus. Timarchus trades his sexual passivity for Pittalacus' silence. Yet, in what follows, Aeschines informs his audience that Pittalacus prosecuted both Hegesandrus and Timarchus for their *hybris*.[97] But when the case was about to be heard in a trial, Hegesandrus claimed that Pittalacus was his slave, thereby attempting to lead a freedman to slavery.

As we saw earlier, Pittalacus' wealth and his involvement in legal actions indicates that he was a freedman rather than a slave. But for his purposes of argument Aeschines treats him contradictorily: when he wants to foreground Timarchus' self-inflicted humiliation, he presents him as a slave. Aeschines' elliptical language when he refers to Timarchus' willing submission to Pittalacus mobilizes dikasts' imagination and notably the veracity of his 'account' is underscored by a powerful oath.[98] Furthermore, as Fisher suggests (2001: 192), Aeschines' appeal

---

**95** As Fisher rightly points out (2001: 196), the killing of Pittalacus' domestic animals is meant to cause dikasts' sympathy, even if ancient sensitivities to animals were not as strong as their modern counterparts. However, this detail underlines Hegesandrus' and Timarchus' hostility towards Pittalacus and may therefore be seen as part of a wider script of erotic jealousy, in which anger, vindictiveness, and machismo play an important role.
**96** His half-nakedness is deliberate, as it invites passers by to look at his wounds, but also prompts dikasts to activate their imagination. On the exposure of victims' wounded bodies, see my discussion of *Against Teisis* above.
**97** The text does not specify the type of the legal action that Pittalacus took, but Fisher (2001: 199–200) rightly points out that his status would have prevented him from bringing a *graphe hybreos*, i.e. a public case. *dike aikeias*, *dike biaion* or *dike blabes* are possible on account of Timarchus' and Hegesandrus' actions described by Aeschines.
**98** At the same time, Aeschines avoids *aischrologia* (discussed by Halliwell 2008: 219–237). For a good example of how Aeschines avoids *aischrologia* and at the same time 'reveals' Timarchus' allegedly shameful sexual practices through the use of *double entendres*, cp. 80–84.

to Zeus reflects the gravity of Timarchus' transgression of social standards. But the (visual) details of Timarchus' sexual practices must be supplied by the dikasts: Timarchus, a free man, allows willingly a slave to penetrate him anally and thereby shamelessly compromises his honour. Furthermore, Aeschines uses three disgust words in this context to describe Timarchus and his acts. Timarchus is *miaros*, his debauchery is equated with *bdelyria*, but more importantly his shamelessness does not allow him to recoil at his willing sexual subordination to a slave.

As I suggested elsewhere (see Lateiner/Spatharas 2017 and Spatharas forthcoming), social status is directly relevant to projective uses of disgust, because status determines the extent to which one's 'vile' bodily substances or sexual organs are perceived as contaminating. In other words, Aeschines' attempt to make dikasts imagine Timarchus being anally penetrated by and giving oral sex to Pittalacus invests in the identification of low status with moral and physical dirt. This identification commonly underlies the appraisals, or rather ideations that give rise to disgust. No doubt, the same strategy is followed by Aeschines when he says that Timarchus sold his body to merchants and foreigners like a common prostitute (40). The 'law of contagion', one of the two laws of sympathetic magic that informs the cognitions of disgust, involving the notion "once in contact, always in contact" is fully at play throughout the speech. Timarchus' sexual submission to a limitless number of men defiles his body and reflects his insensitivity to dirt, an insensitivity prompted by his insatiable appetites. Timarchus quite literally embodies a problematic cultural history –whose visible signs are fully exploited by Aeschines in his description of decent Athenian men's responses to his nudity at 25–26 (see Fisher 2001, notes *ad loc.*). Here and elsewhere in the speech, thus, the visceral emotion of disgust enhances a rhetoric of social exclusion and marginalization. Timarchus is morally and physically defiled and must therefore be removed from public life.

As we saw, Aeschines' contradictory account of Pittalacus' status is relevant to the manipulation of dikasts' emotions. But it should be noted that it is mainly the nonchalance with which Timarchus compromises his own status that Aeschines stresses with the narrative about Pittalacus. On account of his position in social hierarchy, Pittalacus is deployed as the touchstone of Timarchus' deviance. Dikasts' empathy for Pittalacus' suffering, therefore, facilitates Timarchus' portrayal as a self-interested, greedy, and unrelenting sex worker whose only concern is monetary gain. This portrayal is enhanced by the focalization of Pittalacus' sentiments. Furthermore, when Hegesandrus comes to Athens and meets Timarchus, Aeschines' opponent is reduced to a body that attracts other men's gazes rather than a citizen possessing manly *sophrosyne*. He is also a person whose deviant nature, i.e. his shameless, but promising sexual activity is easily detected by men like Hegesandrus (57). Timarchus' lack of self-restraint urges him to follow Hegesandrus, because he becomes aware of the latter's recently acquired wealth. Note that Hegesandrus' first move is to approach *Pittalacus* rather than Timarchus (as his gambling mate), a former slave rather than a man who would normatively be expected to act out of free choice. Timarchus is thus treated by his lovers like a female courtesan, an object of others' monetary transactions who possesses no control upon the uses of his body.[99]

Pittalacus on his own part, qua public slave and therefore a powerless *erastes*, is more responsive to the ideal of erotic reciprocity.[100] For not only does he refuse to hand Timarchus over to Hegesandrus, but also fervently seeks to re-attract his attention. Pittalacus' jealousy, thus, also enhances Timarchus' presentation as the equivalent of a courtesan, a presentation that no doubt exactly suits the case as the terms for the offence are *hetairein/hetairesis* as well as *porneia*. Jealousy and a strong sense of individual property are also pivotal to Lysias 4, where, in the aftermath of an *antidosis*, the involved parties, most probably rival lovers, struggle for the attentions of a slave-girl.[101] Timarchus' manipulative behaviour and nonchalance encourage dikasts' pity for betrayed Pittalacus, the victim of an attack which Aeschines conveys in a description full of mobility, acoustic, and mental images. Pittalacus' loud groans during the whipping reach the neighbouring houses, while, as we saw, dikasts are urged to construct images of the destruction of Pittalacus' equipment and the killing of his cocks and quails.

The scenario of pity for Pittalacus' maltreatment in his house, however, prepares the ground for the scene of public supplication where Timarchus will become the suppliant's, i.e. Pittalacus', suppliant. This scene emphasizes Timarchus' anxiety that his shameless private life will become known to the polis. And this is exactly what Aeschines' speech achieves. The scene is once more full of agitation and abounds with images. The crowd that runs to the altar in the agora where Pittalacus takes refuge half-naked enhances the visuality of the story. Notably, this is an unusually populous crowd whose members represent the body of citizens, because, as Aeschines says, an assembly was about to take place. As was the case in other stories of violence that we examined, onlookers constitute an

---

[99] In this respect, the narrative of the present speech, recounting Timarchus' relationships with several lovers resembles Apollodorus' presentation of Neaira's (and Phano's) career (on Apollodorus' narrative, see Spatharas 2009).
[100] On *charis* in the frame of erotic relationships (including discussion of the speech under review), see Fisher 2013.
[101] For a discussion of this speech, see Spatharas 2006.

internal audience which guides dikasts' gazes to the object of their autopsy. But the fact that the members of this crowd are about to attend a meeting of the Assembly also points to the civic privileges of which Timarchus is in danger of depriving himself in the future on account of a shameless private life that pushes him to lower his status in front of a slave. Timarchus' public exposure as a man who prostituted himself at the civic epicenter of the polis in front of ecclesiasts enhances the scenario of self-inflicted shame that Aeschines' opponent so anxiously seeks to forestall by appeasing Pittalacus. Note that while the other members of the aggressive and intoxicated gang that attacked Pittalacus attempt to assuage him through verbal persuasion, it is only Timarchus who *enacts* the role of a supplicant (ὑπογενειάζων τὸν ἄνθρωπον, 61).

Timarchus' dramatic gestures in front of onlookers are socially meaningful. Still a young man of good looks (οὔπω μὰ Δία ὥσπερ νῦν ἀργαλέος ὢν τὴν ὄψιν, ἀλλ' ἔτι χρήσιμος, 61),[102] Timarchus manipulates his beauty in order to beguile Pittalacus into standing up from the altar. But at the same time, this is an affectionate gesture that, as numerous courtship scenes depicted on vase-paintings reveal, indicates self-abasement and promises erotic commitment.[103] Timarchus goes to the forefront of the scene to make himself visible to Pittalacus, or perhaps establish eye-contact with him, because he calculatedly anticipates that the suppliant will succumb to his charms. This is an instance of erotic deception at its best: it involves calculation of one's irresistibility, feigned self-abasement and remorse (equating a prominent politician with a duplicitous young boyfriend), and ultimately exploitation of another's vulnerability and hopeful expectations through cheap promises (τευξόμενος τῶν δικαίων, 61).[104] But given the relevant position of the two men in social hierarchy, Timarchus' stagy appeal to Pittalacus' pity, indeed an erotic supplication, is a shameful act, undoubtedly the result of Timarchus' fear about the consequences of a private life that he attempts to hide and the speech 'reveals'.

---

102 As Nick Fisher suggests (personal communication), χρήσιμος may perhaps cleverly indicate both that Timarchus is still 'useful in appearance', i.e. good material to be 'used' by his lovers and also that he is, ironically, ensuring by his consensual acts that he cannot ever be a 'useful citizen' for the city.
103 On visual evidence, see for example, Shapiro 1981. On the importance of gazes for persuasion in male homoerotic behaviour, see Cairns 2011. See also Frontisi-Ducroux 1995 *passim*.
104 In erotic contexts, ἀδικεῖν indicates unreciprocated erotic desire; cp. Sappho, 1V; [Theognis] 1283 West, Antiphon 1.15. See Dover 1978: 176–177.

## 3.5 Conclusion

In this chapter I argued that, unlike other types of narratives, forensic stories revolve around a single act of legal significance and thus *compete* for jurors' imagination. Ancient theories of *enargeia* emphasize that stories' verisimilitude is a requisite for persuasion, but also highlight that effective visual narratives stir listeners' emotions. In the stories about violence that I used as test cases, verisimilitude is achieved through the deployment of shared cultural and social knowledge. Speakers also manipulate details in such a way as to reflect socially and culturally significant gestures. The stories told by forensic speakers invite jurors to employ their cultural competence and supply the meaning of the details –e.g. gestures, physical manifestations of emotions, social symbols, material culture– that orators insert in their narratives. Furthermore, I argued that, because forensic stories require verisimilitude, the cognitions that inform the emotional responses elicited by the scripts that I examined –mainly responses of anger against the perpetrator anger and pity for the victim– appeal to dikasts' horizon of expectations and thereby reflect mainstream rather than peripheral ideological priorities or stereotypes. I also suggested that in comparison with modern uses of emotions in courtroom practice, commonly emphasizing personal harm, ancient *pathopoiia* centers on wider social concerns. Hence ancient forensic stories are so designed as to appeal to overarching social norms. Lastly, I argued that as it typically the case with literary narratives, forensic stories guide dikasts' emotional responses through the responses of internal spectators who are perceived as representing the body of citizens' as a whole.

# 4 The ideological uses of 'legitimate envy' in classical Athens

What's irritated me about the whole direction of politics in the last 30 years is that it's always been towards the collectivist society. People have forgotten about the personal society. And they say: do I count, do I matter? To which the short answer is, yes. And therefore, it isn't that I set out on economic policies; it's that I set out really to change the approach, and changing the economics is the means of changing that approach. If you change the approach you really are after the heart and soul of the nation. Economics are the method; the object is to change the heart and soul.

Margaret Thatcher

## 4.1 Introduction

καὶ γὰρ αὖ τοῦτο. τῶν ἄλλων ἁπάντων τῶν ἐπιδόντων τριηράρχων παραπεμπόντων ὑμᾶς ὅτε δεῦρ' ἀπεπλεῖτ' ἐκ Στύρων, μόνος οὗτος οὐ παρέπεμπεν, ἀλλ' ἀμελήσας ὑμῶν χάρακας καὶ βοσκήματα καὶ θυρώμαθ' ὡς αὐτὸν καὶ ξύλ' εἰς τὰ ἔργα τὰ ἀργύρει' ἐκόμιζεν, καὶ χρηματισμός, οὐ λητουργία γέγονεν ἡ τριηραρχία τῷ καταπτύστῳ τούτῳ.

(Dem. 21.167)

Consider this point next. When all the other trierarchs who contributed provided escort when you sailed back from Styra, this man alone did not provide escort, but without a shred of concern for you he shipped stakes, livestock, and doorposts for himself and timber for his silver mills. This disgusting man made his trierarchy into a way of doing business instead of service to the state.

(transl. E.M. Harris)

The present passage from Demosthenes' *Against Meidias* reveals the way in which forensic speakers manipulate the tensions between private interests and public concerns. Meidias' greed is highlighted through a description of his conduct as a wealthy *liturgist*.[1] This description enhances the contradistinctive characterization of the speech, in so far as Demosthenes compares, here and elsewhere, his own adherence to fundamental democratic values, especially his *metriotes*, with Meidias' excessive lifestyle. The presentation of Meidias' self-in-

---

[1] In this passage, Demosthenes refers to Meidias' behaviour during a military campaign that took place in 357. The Athenians helped the Euboeans to fight back the Thebans who were forced to withdraw (cp. Aeschin. 3.85, Diodorus 16.7.2). For an outline of these events and their relationship to Demosthenes' argument, see MacDowell 1990: 380–381.

terested behaviour in the present passage is thus enlisted in support of Demosthenes' attempt throughout the speech to denigrate his opponent's ethos, by describing him as a wealthy member of the elite who shows contempt for the cooperative values of the polis,[2] and even worse, exploits the service assigned to him by the city in his own interest. Furthermore, the description of Meidias' private transactions in the frame of a military campaign indirectly encourages the audience to evaluate his opponent's hybristic behaviour on the basis of criteria reflecting the symbolic significance of financial transactions.[3] Meidias' absorption with monetary gain serves as a touchstone of his irresponsiveness to the democratic values that bond citizens together. His greed betrays his disregard for the ideological implications of liturgies and their significance in the wider context of the democratic values that regulate the relationship between wealthy and less well-off, ordinary citizens.

Demosthenes' description of Meidias' behaviour is comparable to the ways in which public communication in our societies thematizes the luxuriousness of politicians' lifestyle. The portrayal of corrupt politicians' excessive lifestyle is frequently employed by political opponents as a means through which they stir their voters' negative emotions such as indignation and anger. At the same time, the details of politicians' private lives attract the attention of bloggers, social media followers, and the few remaining newspaper readers. Despite the obvious differences between ancient and modern democracies and the ways in which political communication operates in them, the lifestyle of prominent politicians is an issue that gains individuals' attention.

The civic space of the Athenian courtroom provided prominent Athenians who were actively involved in the city's public life the opportunity to attack their political opponents by highlighting condemnable aspects of their private lives. As recent scholarship has shown, in the trials heard by Athenian courts speakers offered particularlized accounts of the legal disputes in which they were involved

---

[2] On the terms 'mass' and 'elite', see Griffith 1995: 65 n. 9 and especially Ober 1989: 11–17. The problems involved in the use of the term *aristocracy* to describe ancient 'aristocracies', see the excellent discussion by Fisher/van Wees 2015.

[3] On the "symbolic world of transactions", see Parry/Bloch 1989: 28, who point out that we tend to disapprove of the exploitation of long-term financial transactions for short-term gain or even worse instances in which "grasping individuals will divert the resources of the long-term cycle for their own short-term transactions" (27). A typical example can be found in Apollodorus' treatment of Phano's marriage in *Against Neaira*, where Stephanus is presented as taking advantage of the girl's marital status in order to extort money from her use as a prostitute (see Gilhuly 2009: 23–24).

and, as we saw in the previous chapter, provided dikasts with a 'wide angle' perspective of their cases, by emphasizing normative rather than just statutory prescriptions.⁴ This highly contextualized presentation of legally significant events commonly involved evidence about litigants' commitment to civic obligations and their adherence to the shared values of the polis' ideology.⁵ For this reason, significant portions of the extant forensic speeches emphasize the social background of litigants' disputes, commonly through presentation of highly biased evidence concerning their private lives. In a good deal of the speeches from the corpus of the Attic orators, especially those delivered in the frame of major political disputes, speakers provide detailed, albeit fabricated accounts of their opponents' private lives, centering, among other things, on their commitment to family obligations, professional engagements, and sexual activity.⁶ Furthermore, when speakers attack wealthy citizens, Demosthenes' *Against Meidias* offers a good example, they lay stress on the antisocial and hybristic behaviour of their opponents and emphasize their reluctance to offer their services to the city.⁷ Hence, the ideological web of values that speakers appeal to, especially values revolving around wealth which are more akin to the emotion of legitimate envy that concerns me here, may be viewed as the product of the social tensions caused by social inequalities. Appeals to cooperative values, such as positive *philotimia* and *charis*, may be viewed as ways of negotiating the frictions caused by social inequalities in an egalitarian political environment.

In my analysis, social tensions are construed as productive of the public discourse of classical Athens. I take the view that, as Fisher has shown in a series of studies on *charis*,⁸ the values that constituted democratic ideology in fourth century Athens were understood both by the elites and the masses. Equally important for my purposes of argument is the notion that the language of ideology is performative rather than just descriptive and that for this reason it imposes restrictions upon the actions taken by its advocates. As Skinner argues (2002: 156) in his Weberian analysis, innovating idelogists "cannot hope to stretch the application of existing terms indefinitely; so they can only hope to legitimise, and

---

4 For a detailed discussion of these topics, see chapter 3.
5 On the term 'ideology' and its implications for democratic Athens, see Ober 1989: 38–43.
6 On the deployment of the elites' private lives as a means of controlling prominent citizens, see Fisher's Introduction to *Against Timarchus* (2001).
7 As is well-known, Athenian litigants delivered their speeches in person or alternatively they were supported by *synegoroi* (on 'supporting speakers', see Rubinstein 2000). When I use the term 'speakers' I refer either to logographers' clients or people like Demosthenes who were able to compose and deliver their own speeches.
8 Fisher 2006; 2008; 2010. See also Fisher 2003.

hence to perform, a correspondingly restricted range of actions. To study the principles they invoke will thus be to study one of the key determinants of their behaviour". This, one may argue, was especially so in classical Athens, where, ideally at least, through their participation in the civic bodies of the polis, all citizens were able to engage actively in decision making by forming majorities and thereby controlling the protagonists of the civic life. Especially in Athenian courtrooms, where speakers appealed to "extra-statutory" norms (Lanni 2009), the uses of key ideological concepts operate to evaluate specific behaviours in the frame of a wide angle, paricularlized presentation of litigants' private lives and civic conduct. Hence, on the basis of Skinner's analysis, I take the view that ideology is not a fiction, and especially not a fiction which remained unintelligible to the masses that manned the Assembly or the courts of law, even if, of course, ideology supported rhetorical fictions that served individual speakers' arguments. Implicit to my understanding of the language of ideology as performative is the notion that the public presentation of wealthy citizens' private lives in the Athenian courts served as a means through which the masses controlled more privileged citizens by setting the rules of their competition for honours.

In its depictions in the public discourse of classical Athens, the language of democratic ideology constrains individualization through the emphasis that it places on values that assert and perpetuate the exclusive privilege of the majorities to grant affluent citizens honours. In our sources of evidence, especially in legal disputes concerning major political issues, the private lives of wealthy individuals are so narrativized as to reveal behaviours which are in breach with the norms and values of democratic ideology, especially the fundamental values of equality –reflected in the many *iso-* compound constructions (*isonomia, isegoria* etc.)– *metriotes,* and cooperative *philotimia.*[9]

The discursive representations of wealthy citizens' private lives in the forensic speeches, these highly elaborate constructions characterized by narrative specificity, are so designed as to correspond to dikasts' horizon of expectations and for this reason speakers derive material from a stock of recognizable values and normative prescriptions. Hence, the depictions of prominent citizens' private lives in the forensic speeches reflect public concerns and emphasize the submission of individuality to the public interest. The predictability of speakers' conformity with dikasts' horizon of expectations explains the recurrent appeals to

---

[9] Perhaps the most telling example of a speech relying on the private life of a major protagonist of the polis' public life is Aeschines' *Against Timarchus*. On the extensive use of gossip and rumors in this speech, see Fisher 2001: 53–61. On gossip in the Athenian courtroom, see Hunter 1990.

the same cluster of values in the speeches, even as, of course, the legal nature of individual cases necessitated contextualized treatments of commonplaces. The recurrence of these *topoi* in the speeches provides further evidence that the so called 'elite values' were shared and understood by the masses, because it is only natural for forensic speakers to put forward intelligible arguments which are suitable for their cases.

I offer these preliminary points in an attempt to outline some of the methodological, and hence, practical issues that underlie my discussion of the ideological uses of envy in classical Athens, especially in contexts where the emotion appears in scripts revolving around private wealth and, thereby, thematize social inequalities. My discussion therefore relies on appraisal-oriented analysis of emotions and for this reason takes into account the wider contexts in which relevant emotion scripts appear.[10] As we shall see, perhaps the most prominent among the values that give specific meaning to the envy scripts that I discuss is *philotimia*, a notion that primarily revolves around competitive ambitiousness and is therefore sometimes identified with public spending.

The pivotal importance of envy in forensic or other contexts has recently attracted the attention of a number scholars, whose work elucidates the emotion's uses in the public discourse of the polis and its implications for our understanding of the ideology of classical Athens.[11] My discussion focuses on forensic uses of the emotion and, hence, pins down the ways in which envy enhances forensic speakers' *pathopoiia*, especially in Demosthenes' speeches *Against Leptines* and *Against Meidias*. These speeches are directly relevant to the questions that I raise in this chapter for two main reasons: (a) because envy is central to the wider rhetorical strategies deployed by Demosthenes and (b) because, on account of the diametrically opposed uses to which Demosthenes puts the emotion in these speeches, the envy scripts that we find in them provide wider scope of investigation. In the next section I outline, and where appropriate, I comment on recent scholarship about the ideological uses of envy in classical Athens. More particularly, on the basis of recent work on the emotion and Skinner's analysis of the language of ideology, I argue that earlier projective uses of the emotion, serving the stigmatization of egalitarian claims through the attribution of the morally irresponsive, dispositional envy to the masses, was an ideological concoction of

---

10 I discuss these methodological issues in the Introduction.
11 See Walcot 1978; Cairns 2003; Fisher 2003. The most extensive treatment of the topic is Sanders 2014. See also recently Eidinow 2015, focusing on women's depiction in forensic contexts. See also Spatharas 2017b.

the elites through which they attempted to restrain egalitarian demands. As Alcibiades' speech in Thucydides indicates (6.16), the ideological deployment of dispositional envy was founded on essentialist claims –a further indication of its reactionary nature.

Quentin Skinner's work on the language of ideology enhances the appraisal-oriented approach that I endorse and provides a tool that enables us to look into the semantic changes of 'envy' by focusing on the mutual relationship between social realities and language rather than on a history of the label *phthonos*. On the basis of Skinner's approach, I, therefore, suggest that the uses of (what John Rawls describes as) 'benign envy' in the public discourse of classical Athens may reflect the democratization of aggressive uses of envy by the elites. As I argue, the evaluations that inform the cognitions of 'benign' or, what I will be calling 'legitimate' envy, correspond to Aristotle's description of 'indignation', an emotion that he labels with the obsolete phrase τὸ νεμεσᾶν, in so far as it is a *pathos* caused by appraisals centering on undeserved prosperity.[12] As the uses of the emotion that I discuss indicate, under specific conditions legitimate envy becomes a democratic, commendatory term.

The fact that in the public discourse of classical Athens the democratic uses of this socially specific emotion concept is still designated by the word *phthonos* is, as Skinner's approach to the ideological uses of concepts suggests, the most common strategy employed by advocates of new ideologies. The uses of *phthonos* to indicate 'legitimate envy' in democratic contexts relies on a reversal of the criteria of application of the elites' projective uses of the masses' allegedly dispositional envy for the elites, i.e. their *phthonos*. A note of caution is here necessary: my argument *is not*, of course, that bad envy is not at play in our sources. But I hope that my approach is helpful for two reasons: first, it indicates that the denigrating accounts of the masses' attitude to the elites' wealth reflects the ideological uses of bad envy to which the democratic ideology responded. A history of concepts is a history of their uses in arguments and counterarguments. The second reason is that by emphasizing the ideological uses of *phthonos* in the public discourse, we avoid interpretations that overemphasize 'moral' concerns thereby ignoring the social tensions that determine the ideological uses of pivotal values. Hence, as I argue, Aristotle's use of τὸ νεμεσᾶν to describe 'legitimate envy' is due to the prominence of *phthonos* in antidemocratic ideological discourse. In the last section I turn my attention to a significant passage from Demosthenes' *Against*

---

[12] I prefer the term 'legitimate envy' because it reflects the notion of 'desert' which is integral to the appraisals that shape the emotion scripts that we find in the speeches –and to Aristotle's definition of τὸ νεμεσᾶν.

*Meidias* where the speaker highlights the excessive and ostentatious lifestyle of his opponent. This passage helps us understand with better hopes of accuracy, I suggest, the emotion of 'legitimate envy', a sentiment, which, in its democratic uses, is morally responsive, because it requires evaluations concerning wealthy citizens' adherence to and respect for political equality and commitment to the interests of the polis.

## 4.2 Equalities, inequalities, and the envy of the *hoi polloi*

In her address to the delegates of the Conservative party on October 13, 1978, Margaret Thatcher accused her political opponents that they deployed social envy for personal political gain.[13] According to Thatcher, her opponents' claims for just distribution of wealth –and indeed wealth gap has increased dramatically since the late 70's–, revealed their envy for the more industrious and successful members of society –even as Thatcher disclaimed the use of the term 'society' altogether:

> This [sic] spirit of envy is aimed not only at those privileged by birth and inherited wealth, like Mr. Wedgwood Benn. It is also directed against those who have got on by ability and effort. It is seen in Labour's bias against men and women who seek to better themselves and their families. Ordinary people—small businessmen, the self-employed—are not to be allowed to rise on their own. They must rise collectively or not at all. Object to merit and distinction and you're setting your face against quality, independence, originality, genius, against all the richness and variety of life. You are pinning down the swift and the sure and the strong, as Gulliver was pinned down by the little people of Lilliput...Envy is dangerous, destructive, divisive—and revealing. It exposes the falsity of Labour's great claim that they're the party of care and compassion. It is the worst possible emotion to inspire a political party supposedly dedicated to improving the lot of ordinary working people.

---

[13] I cite Thatcher's speech from http://www.margaretthatcher.org/document/103764, consulted for the purposes of this revised version of my 2014 study on August 25, 2017. For an admirable discussion of ancient uses of projective envy in comparison with the 'politics of envy' in Britain, see Cairns 2003, who outlines the main ideological countours of British politics under Thatcher and the theoretical work on which neo-liberalists relied, especially Schoeck's book (1987, first English translation 1969). A sample of Schoeck's argumentation (criticized by Cairns 2003) is offered in the following statement: "The utopian desire for an egalitarian society cannot, however, have sprung from any other motive than that of an inability to come to terms with one's own envy, and/or with the supposed envy of one's less well-off fellow men. It must be obvious how such a man [sic], *even if only prompted by his unconscious*, would carefully evade the phenomenon of envy or at least try to belittle it" (127, the emphasis is mine).

Thatcher's rhetoric in this context offers useful comparative ground that allows us to understand in a more nuanced way the ideological uses of envy in the frame of political or social disputes. The most obvious characteristic of this use of envy is that the emotion is arbitrarily projected onto a group of people, in this case Thatcher's political opponents. Envy is thus offered as an all encompassing interpretation of one's opponents' sentiments which eliminates other, more reprehensible, evaluations of their possible motives. On account of the emotion's moral baseness, projective uses of envy make it impossible for its alleged agents to claim that they foster morally responsive sentiments caused by appraisals revolving around the prosperity of others. Indeed, as Thatcher pointed out in her speech, albeit relying on the arbitrary assumption that her opponents' arguments were the product of envy, Labour politics betray insensitivity to the emotion that allegedly characterizes their political agenda, namely compassion. Their aggressive envy destroys industrious people. According to Thatcher, the socially destructive sentiment of envy targets indiscriminately the prosperous and the successful, that is the hardworking and committed members of society, individuals who merit the qualification 'ordinary' people –the businessmen and the self-employed. Lastly, the metaphorical use of Gulliver, the powerful giant who is immobilized by the small enviers who outnumber him, is extremely important, because it indicates lucidly the impact of collectivity upon personal distinction.[14] As Thatcher put it, "[T]hey must rise collectively or not at all".[15] As we shall see, the issue of individual distinction is pivotal to the ideological uses of envy in the public discourse of classical Athens.

Thatcher's use of envy to stigmatize her opponents' motives displays similarities with ancient elite authors' treatment of the emotion in their criticism of democracy. The most obvious examples are perhaps offered in Isocrates' *Antidosis*,

---

**14** On the notion of (methodological) individualism in neoliberalism, see Harvey 2005: 23.
**15** It is noteworthy that in her speech, Thatcher classifies the targets of envy into two distinct categories: those who have inherited their wealth and the self-employed who distinguished themselves through their industriousness. The emphasis that she places on the second social group –even as Thatcher notoriously claimed that "there's no such thing as society. There are individual men and women and there are families"– enhances her rhetoric, in so far as it lays stress on the small-minded pettiness of envy's agents. Note that in recognizing the social aspects of envy Aristotle points out that the nouveau-riche (νεόπλουτοι) are more vulnerable to projective uses of envy because they give the impression that their wealth does not belong to them. As he says, what is long established seems closer to nature (*Rh.* 1387a 16). Furthermore, since being an ἀρχαιόπλουτος is a matter of chance, the envy that targets people of noble birth is more palatable (on envy and chance, see Ben Ze'ev 2003: 110).

which I discuss in chapter 5.¹⁶ In ancient political theory and antidemocratic discourse, the less privileged masses of citizens are presented as putting pressure on members of the elite commonly by abusing the legal system of the polis or through the assignment of liturgies. In addition, Thatcher's line of argument offers useful comparative ground which helps us understand David Konstan's hypothesis (2006: 125–126) that from 6th century onwards envy becomes a vehicle through which the elites express their contempt for the masses of lower class people. In the light of this analysis, an analysis that, however, lays much emphasis on the semantic changes of the lexical markers that the Greeks used to indicate 'envy', the projection of dispositional envy upon the masses may be understood as an ideological invention of the elites that emerged at a point in which they started to feel threatened.

Konstan's approach is supported by Aristotle's discussion of *stasis* in the *Politics* –although Aristotle was not a natural friend of democracy. In his discussion of the causes that prompt *stasis* in the cities, Aristotle emphasizes the notion of equality and endorses the view that poorer citizens covet the privileges of the rich. At the same time, however, because of their greed, the rich not seek only to protect their interests, but also increase the existing inequalities.¹⁷ Hence, in his discussion of *stasis* Aristotle seems to depart from other elite authors' presentation of envy as a dispositional and unchanging feature of the masses by interpreting their envy as a dynamic phenomenon caused by social tensions.¹⁸ Note, for example, that in Aristotle's analysis, the *hybris* of the powerful and the rich plays a significant role in their attempts to establish and perpetuate their superiority (*Pol.* 1301b 2–14). Furthermore, Aristotle suggests that envy is not just a bottom-up emotion, in so far as it is also experienced by those who are significantly superior to others on account of their fear that they may lose their privileges (*Rh.* 1387b 28–32). Hence, the *philotimoi* are more inclined to experience envy than those who are less ambitious. This, Aristotle avers, is due to the fact that people

---

**16** On the deployment of envy in Isocrates' *Antidosis*, see Saïd 2003.
**17** καὶ ὅλως δὴ δεῖ τοῦτο μὴ λανθάνειν, ὡς οἱ δυνάμεως αἴτιοι γενόμενοι, καὶ ἰδιῶται καὶ ἀρχαὶ καὶ φυλαὶ καὶ ὅλως μέρος καὶ πλῆθος ὁποιονοῦν, στάσιν κινοῦσιν· ἢ γὰρ οἱ τούτοις φθονοῦντες τιμωμένοις ἄρχουσι τῆς στάσεως, ἢ οὗτοι διὰ τὴν ὑπεροχὴν οὐ θέλουσι μένειν ἐπὶ τῶν ἴσων ("And generally, it should be remembered that those who have secured power to the state, whether private citizens, or magistrates, or tribes, or any other part or section of the state, are apt to cause revolutions. For either they envy of their greatness draws other into rebellion, or they themselves, in their pride of superiority, are unwilling to remain on level with others" Arist. *Politics* 1304a 33–38, transl. Everson). On *hybris* and greed as causes of *staseis*, cp, Arist. *Pol.* 1302b 1–14.
**18** See Cairns 2003: 240–242 and Fisher 2003: 182–185.

who are superior to others believe that they deserve everything: they interpret others' privileges as stolen property.

From these points, it becomes clear that, unlike other elite authors, Aristotle interprets the political dimensions of envy as a result of social inequalities and emphasizes the tensions that these inequalities cause. Furthermore, Aristotle lays stress on the repercussions of the contradiction resulting from social inequalities in environments of political equality. If, in these environments, the poorer citizens covet the privileges of the rich, on account of their (characteristically undemocratic) hybristic disposition the rich aspire to eliminate the masses' egalitarian pressures.

In order to get a better grasp of the uses of envy as a means of denigrating and neutralizing the masses' egalitarian claims, we may turn our attention to a much discussed passage from Thucydides (6.16), in which Alcibiades defends his right to lead the Sicilian expedition:

> ὧν γὰρ πέρι ἐπιβόητός εἰμι, τοῖς μὲν προγόνοις μου καὶ ἐμοὶ δόξαν φέρει ταῦτα, τῇ δὲ πατρίδι καὶ ὠφελίαν. οἱ γὰρ Ἕλληνες καὶ ὑπὲρ δύναμιν μείζω ἡμῶν τὴν πόλιν ἐνόμισαν τῷ ἐμῷ διαπρεπεῖ τῆς Ὀλυμπίαζε θεωρίας, πρότερον ἐλπίζοντες αὐτὴν καταπεπολεμῆσθαι, διότι ἅρματα μὲν ἑπτὰ καθῆκα, ὅσα οὐδείς πω ἰδιώτης πρότερον, ἐνίκησα δὲ καὶ δεύτερος καὶ τέταρτος ἐγενόμην καὶ τἆλλα ἀξίως τῆς νίκης παρεσκευασάμην. νόμῳ μὲν γὰρ τιμὴ τὰ τοιαῦτα, ἐκ δὲ τοῦ δρωμένου καὶ δύναμις ἅμα ὑπονοεῖται. καὶ ὅσα αὖ ἐν τῇ πόλει χορηγίαις ἢ ἄλλῳ τῳ λαμπρύνομαι, τοῖς μὲν ἀστοῖς φθονεῖται φύσει, πρὸς δὲ τοὺς ξένους καὶ αὕτη ἰσχὺς φαίνεται. καὶ οὐκ ἄχρηστος ἥδ' ἡ ἄνοια, ὃς ἂν τοῖς ἰδίοις τέλεσι μὴ ἑαυτὸν μόνον ἀλλὰ καὶ τὴν πόλιν ὠφελῇ. οὐδέ γε ἄδικον ἐφ' ἑαυτῷ μέγα φρονοῦντα μὴ ἴσον εἶναι, ἐπεὶ καὶ ὁ κακῶς πράσσων πρὸς οὐδένα τῆς ξυμφορᾶς ἰσομοιρεῖ· ἀλλ' ὥσπερ δυστυχοῦντες οὐ προσαγορευόμεθα, ἐν τῷ ὁμοίῳ τις ἀνεχέσθω καὶ ὑπὸ τῶν εὐπραγούντων ὑπερφρονούμενος, ἢ τὰ ἴσα νέμων τὰ ὅμοια ἀνταξιούτω.

> Those pursuits for which I am criticized bring me personal fame, as they did my family before me, but they also bring benefit to my country. My outstanding performance at the Olympic festival made the Greeks revise and even exaggerate their estimate of the power of Athens, when they had expected the city to be exhausted by war. I entered seven chariots – more than any private citizen had ever done before. I won the victory, and second and fourth place too: and my whole display at the games was of a piece with my victory. Quite apart from the regular honour which such successes bestow, the plain fact of their achievement also hints at reserves of power. And then again my sponsorship of productions and any other public duty on which I may "preen" myself, though naturally exciting envy at home, does make its own contribution to the impression outsiders form of our strength. So there is use in this sort of "folly", when a man expends his own resources for national as well as personal benefit. And there is nothing wrong if someone with good cause for pride does not treat others as equals, just as those in poor state do not expect others to share their misfortune. If we are in trouble, people shun us: by the same token no one should complain if the successful look down on him –or else he should give others equal treatment before claiming parity of esteem for himself. (transl. M. Hammond)

If Alcibiades, or Thucydides' Alcibiades, endorsed in a 4th century courtroom the aggressive rhetoric that he endorses in this passage, by appealing openly to his listeners' envy, it is highly probable, if not certain, that he would have caused dikasts' anger.[19] Indeed, this kind of aggressive deployment of envy would be suicidal. For example, despite the aggressive uses of envy that we find in the *Antidosis*, a speech composed for private reading, Isocrates is careful enough to suggest that on account of the possible psychological pressures that his (self-adulatory) statements might place on his readers he gave it the form of a forensic defence.[20] Yet, Alcibiades not only attributes openly sentiments of envy to his fellow-citizens, but also qualifies their envy with the word φύσει, thereby endorsing an essentialist interpretation of their sentiment.

Alcibiades' essentialist approach is of decisive importance for our understanding of the ideological matrix that fosters the uses of envy in anti-democratic arguments. As Douglas Cairns (2003: 240) points out in his discussion of Alcibiades' rhetoric, "[I]f a claim to equality can be stigmatised as envy, then there is no genuine claim to be satisfied, and the inequality between patient and target which envy identifies may be legitimately maintained". But I would like to take Cairns' helpful suggestion a step further and emphasize the importance of the word φύσει with which Alcibiades' qualifies citizens' envy.[21]

In his book under the title *Distinction*, Pierre Bourdieu (1984: 24) points out that "[A]ristocracies are essentialist. Regarding existence as an emanation of essence, they set no intrinsic value on the deeds and misdeeds enrolled in the records of and registries of bureaucratic memory. They prize them only insofar as they clearly manifest, in the nuances of their own manner, that their one inspiration is the perpetuating and celebrating of the essence by which they are accomplished". He also claims, that the discourse of all aristocracies is characterized by "essentialist faith in the eternity of natures, celebration of tradition of the past, the cult of history and rituals, because the best they can expect from the future is the return of the old order, from which they expect the restoration of their social

---

**19** I discuss this passage in chapter 2, where I emphasize the visual qualities of Alcibiades' private *philotimia*. On Alcibiades' exceptionally overt and aggressive reference to the conflict between liturgists and the masses, see Wilson 2000: 154 and Fisher 2003: 189. See also Gribble 1999: 70–72 and 2012.
**20** On this point, see chapter 5.
**21** The presentation of envy as an innate characteristic of the masses reflects the fundamental role of the bipolar pair nomos/physis in ancient political theory (see Ostwald 1986: 260–266). In his discussion of Alcibiades' use of the term in the passage under discussion, Ostwald (264) points out that "*Physis* becomes the true character of a man, to which he must not be false". See also Donlan 1980: 178–179.

being". The projective use of envy in Thucydides' passage reflects an extremely aggressive attempt at self-praise, which is in pace with Thucydides' depiction of Alcibiades' excesses in his private life and possibly the negative responses caused by his ostentatious liturgic style. Alcibiades competes with his ancestors for everlasting, immortal honour, which 'naturally', as he claims, causes his inferiors' begrudging.[22] Alcibiades' essentialist approach conceives inferiors' envy as an inherent characteristic, an inextricable element of what they *are*. On this view, the social order, and, thereby inequalities, is a static, unchanging phenomenon the order of things in society is irrelevant to the tensions caused by social inequalities. In Alcibiades' eyes, society is a divided entity comprising those who are superior by nature and inferiors who *on account of their inferiority* are prone to sentiments of envy.

Alcibiades' rhetoric reflects a method commonly endorsed by the enemies of arithmetic equality.[23] By highlighting his nobility, the glorious past of his family, and his contribution to the glory of Athens though his personal success at the Olympic games, Alcibiades seeks to extend his monopoly over birth and wealth to every aspect of the city's activities, including its public offices.[24] He therefore invites his inferiors, practically each and every member of the demos, to tolerate ungrudgingly the contempt of their superiors. By interpreting the masses' envy as a dispositional characteristic, Alcibiades establishes the perpetuation of his natural superiority.

---

**22** See Gribble 2012: 48–49.

**23** On this topic, see Morris 1996: 23.

**24** Cp. Aristotle, *Politics* 1282b 23–30: ἴσως γὰρ ἂν φαίη τις κατὰ παντὸς ὑπεροχὴν ἀγαθοῦ δεῖν ἀνίσως νενεμῆσθαι τὰς ἀρχάς, εἰ πάντα τὰ λοιπὰ μηδὲν διαφέροιεν ἀλλ' ὅμοιοι τυγχάνοιεν ὄντες· τοῖς γὰρ διαφέρουσιν ἕτερον εἶναι τὸ δίκαιον καὶ τὸ κατ' ἀξίαν. ἀλλὰ μὴν εἰ τοῦτ' ἀληθές, ἔσται καὶ κατὰ χρῶμα καὶ κατὰ μέγεθος καὶ καθ' ὁτιοῦν τῶν ἀγαθῶν πλεονεξία τις τῶν πολιτικῶν δικαίων τοῖς ὑπερέχουσιν ("For very likely some persons will say that offices of state ought to be unequally distributed according to superior excellence, in whatever respect, of the citizen, although there is no other difference between him and the rest of the community; for those who differ in any one respect have different rights and claims. But, surely, if this is true, the complexion or height of a man, or any other advantage, will be a reason for his obtaining a greater share of political rights", transl. Everson). For discussion, see Ostwald 1986: 117; Lintott 1992: 117–118; Morris 1996: 23.

## 4.3 The democratization of envy: 'indignation' and democratic ideology

If, as I suggested in the previous section, the masses' envy is an ideological invention of the elites and a vehicle of aggressive display of one's superiority, our next task is to explore the ways in which envy was appropriated in the ideological discourse of democratic Athens. In his *Rhetoric* (1385b 11–15), Aristotle defines *eleos* ('pity') as an unpleasant emotion which is caused by our assessment that a person who is 'like us' in some relevant respect suffers a misfortune of considerable importance without deserving it (τοῦ ἀναξίου). *Phthonos* by contrast is an emotion that targets indiscriminately people who prosper and are in some respect similar to or equal with us. In other words, according to Aristotle envy may also target people who *deserve* their prosperity (1386b 16–20). For this reason, Aristotle criticizes those who employ the word *phthonos* to refer to cases in which the emotion's targets are people who prosper undeservedly. In Aristotle's systematization of emotions, the sentiment that we foster for people who prosper undeservedly is 'indignation' (τὸ νεμεσᾶν). Hence, in Aristotle's eyes, those who present envy as the opposite of pity are wrong.

Aristotle's use of the obsolete term τὸ νεμεσᾶν for a sentiment which, as his definition shows, corresponds to the emotion that, at least in some passages, the orators designate with the word *phthonos* (I discuss some examples below) is not just an exercise in conceptual clarity. This can be gleaned from the fact that, although Aristotle's definitions of negative emotions are generally morally neutral, in the case of *phthonos* he states that the emotion is φαῦλον and characterizes those who are φαῦλοι (1388a 36). Unlike other negative emotions, thus, *phthonos* is offered by Aristotle as a diagnostic criterion for the ethical standards of its agents. Why does Aristotle treat 'envy' as unequivocally 'bad' and, correlatively, why does he introduce the obsolete articular infinitive τὸ νεμεσᾶν, an artificial construction that no Greek would normally use, to designate the morally acceptable emotion of 'indignation'?

A recent attempt to answer this question is offered by Sanders (2014) in his book length study of envy and jealousy. On the basis of comparison with the *Nicomachean Ethics*, Sanders (2014: 64) rightly argues that the meaning of φαῦλον is flexible: its fields of application are both social and moral. In its social uses, the word designates 'commoners' or just the 'poor'. The fact that a 'moral' term has social implications or that it derives its appraisive force from its social implications is standard fare in Greek ethics. For example, in Aristotle's eyes, to become ἐπιεικής or χρηστός, the opposite of φαῦλος, requires moral education, a privilege, which, in classical Greece was exclusive to the leisure class rather than to poorer citizens described by the term *phauloi* – in the 'social' meaning of the word. In his discussion of *phthonos* in rhetorical practice, however, Sanders points out that "('bad') *phthonos* was so socially unacceptable that orators felt uncomfortable using the word even to mean morally acceptable resentment" (2014: 94). This hypothesis, emphasizing the moral reprehensibility of bad *phthonos* (essentially Aristotle's version of the emotion) fails to explain the instances in which forensic speakers use the word *phthonos* to indicate what Aristotle labels τὸ νεμεσᾶν, i.e. morally responsive evaluations concerning others' prosperity. Furthermore, it underplays the social meaning of *phaulos*, which, as Sanders acknowledges, is undistinguishable from its moral meaning. One may thus wonder why Aristotle chooses the ideologically marked word *phaulos* to describe the type of people who are prone to this emotional response.[25]

As Konstan suggests (2006: 127), Aristotle's treatment of envy as a 'bad' emotion reflects his and other elite authors' understanding of the emotion as "a vice endemic to democracy, one that is excited by the prosperity of those we deem our equals". Aristotle's understanding of envy as a sentiment which characterizes the lower classes is therefore directly relevant to his negative view of arithmetic equality, i.e. the equal share of political powers among all citizens. The destructive effects of envy in 'extreme' democracy, advocating equality among citizens, is brought out in a passage from the *Politics* (1318b27–1319a3) where Aristotle refers favourably to an 'ancient' democracy in which the masses of citizens (πλῆθος) live by farming and, to their satisfaction, they have little access to government.[26] In this type of democracy, holders of office are elected, but the importance of their office varies according to the size of their property. Furthermore, the masses of citizens conduct audits of the elected officials (εὐθύνειν), i.e. the propertied minorities of citizens which are competent in governance. According to Aristotle, this polis is governed prudently by 'good' citizens (ἐπιεικεῖς), but the masses of farmers are not totally powerless. More importantly for the purposes of my study, however, in this type of government, lower classes do not envy their social superiors, namely the *epieikeis* citizens who are responsible for its governance.

---

25 Adduce here some examples of elitist uses of φαῦλος to describe socially inferiors: Nicias' (extremely irritated use at a time of desperation) at Thuc. 7.77.2; Isocr. 1.1 (opposed to σπουδαίων); Xen. *Mem.* 4.2.31 ('worse' than the slaves); Xen. *Cyr.* 2.2.24 (opposed to σπουδαῖοι). Note also that *phaulos* is sometimes used positively to describe the lower classes: Thuc. 3.37.4; Eur. *Bacch.* 430; *Ion* 834–5.
26 On this 'moderate' democracy, essentially an oligarchic regime, see Ober 1998: 334–339.

The 'ancient democracy' described by Aristotle in this passage differs saliently from the democracy of classical Athens. Indeed, it is not a democracy at all. A better description of this constitution would be moderate oligarchy. Aristotle does not explain why the exclusion of the masses from governance extirpates the masses' envy for the propertied office holders.[27] His silence indicates that in this context he takes poorer citizens' envy for their social superiors for granted. Furthermore, on the basis of Aristotle's definition of envy in the *Rhetoric* it is possible to suggest reasons that may explain the absence of the emotion from this moderate democracy. As we saw, on Aristotle's view envy is directed against one's equal or similar. For this reason, it is less likely to envy those who stand far above us (*Rh.* 1388a 1–14).[28] Consequently, a constitutionally prescribed exclusion of the masses of farmers from offices would, ideally at least, make it impossible for poorer citizens to experience the socially destructive sentiment of envy for the *epieikeis*. In other words, because the system of governance described by Aristotle is characterized by political inequality, envy is (conceptually) impossible. As Cairns suggests (2003: 240), actual equality heightens perceived inequality. From Aristotle's description it becomes clear that in 'extreme' democracies, favouring arithmetic equality, poorer citizens' envy is an unavoidable symptom.

Unlike Aristotle's 'democracy' which constitutionalizes social inequalities, in 4th century Athenian democracy political equality gave citizens the opportunity to control the elites of wealth and thereby regulate social inequalities. This is particularly obvious in pieces of evidence laying stress on the repercussions of social inequalities upon ordinary citizens' status.[29] But it is also important to note, that, as Cartledge suggests, ancient *isotes* did not mean "sameness or identity, but rather similitude or likeness" (1996: 178). This observation is crucial for our understanding of the ideological uses of legitimate envy, because, as I suggest below, the evaluative appraisals that constitute the deployment of this emotion in the public discourse of the polis center on wealthy individuals' adherence to

---

**27** Note, however, that in the *Rhetorica ad Alexandrum*, 2.14–15, the author proposes a mixed system of governance in which the important offices are held by elected officers, while the less important offices are filled by lot and are therefore accessible to all citizens. In this constitution, the participation of the *plethos* in the election of officers eliminates the masses' envy for the distinguished office-holders (ἐπιφανεστέρους), while the fact that officers are characterized by *kalokagathia* secures citizens' benevolence.
**28** On this point, see Elster 1999: 170; Sanders 2014: 69–71.
**29** Speeches' concerning cases of violence commonly emphasize wealthier citizens' hybris and its impact upon ordinary citizens' honour: cp. for example Dem. 54 and Lysias fr. 279 (discussed in chapter 3); Isocr. 20 with Spatharas 2009c.

cooperative values rather than their wealth as such.[30] In other words, Athenian ideology did not encourage dikasts to cast their votes guided by sentiments of (bad) envy against wealthier citizens' property, because it accommodated the notion that a minority of citizens is comparatively 'unequal' and that this minority must ideally collaborate with the demos for the polis' interests. As Fisher (2003: 212) puts it, "the *demos* could proclaim to the more cooperative members of the elite its adherence to the motto 'let envy be absent' (φθόνος δ' ἀπέστω)". By contrast, the opponents of democracy advocated the masses' innate envy as a means of extending existing inequalities by emphasizing that comparative inequality indicated the incongruity of absolute (political) equality.

In my view, thus, the most plausible explanation of Aristotle's partially negative presentation of envy in the *Rhetoric* must be attributed to his unfavourable view of immoderate democracy. Despite what Aristotle says in his *Rhetoric*, however, in some instances forensic speakers do invite dikasts to express their envy against their opponents. To restate my question: if the masses' dispositional envy is an ideological invention of the elites by means of which they attempted to protect their privileges, namely a top-down response to bottom-up egalitarian claims, how should we explain the admittedly small number of cases in which forensic speakers ask dikasts to give vent to their legitimate *phthonos*? To put it differently, how can we explain the uses of *phthonos* in the context of democratic Athens, in such a way as to correspond to Aristotle's morally responsive τὸ νεμεσᾶν?

In order to answer this question I briefly outline some pivotal aspects of Quentin Skinner's theoretical approach to the language of ideology and the history of concepts. In several studies, Skinner investigates the relationship between the linguistic signification of concepts in the frame of emerging ideological schemata and social realities. Central to Skinner's approach is the notion that "The only histories of ideas to be written are histories of their uses in argument" (2002: 86). Hence, the meaning of concepts changes according to the uses to which they are put by emerging ideological schemata and according to the changes that their advocates intend to bring about. Furthermore, according to Skinner, whose approach relies on John Austin's theory of language, the ideological uses of concepts is primarily performative. As he says in his discussion of the use of concepts by "innovative ideologists" (2002: 148): "The special characteristic of this range of terms is thus that ... they have a standard application to perform one of two contrasting ranges of speech acts. They can be used, that is, to perform such acts

---

[30] On this point, see Cairns 2003 and Fisher 2003.

as commending and approving –or else of condemning and criticising– whatever actions they are employed to describe".

According to Skinner, ideological disagreements about the meaning of appraisive concepts in their uses in arguments are not just a matter of semantics on a linguistic level. As he puts it, to understand the meaning of a concept "we need...to know what range of attitudes the term can standardly be used to express". But even when this is the case, disputes may arise from the following reasons: either "because a given set of circumstances can be claimed to yield the criteria in virtue of which the term is normally employed" (165) or because, "a group of language users may be open to the charge of having a mistaken or an undesirable social attitude" –even when agreement on the circumstances that allow the use of a certain term has been attained (169).

Skinner's theoretical approach suggests possible ways of understanding the democratization of *phthonos*.[31] First, it is clear that in the political and social uses of 'envy' that concern me here, the term is not just the name of an emotion. As we saw, the attribution of dispositional envy to the masses is the product of social tensions, a top-down response to egalitarian claims advocated by the elites who primarily targeted the 'absurdity' of equality among un-equals. In the words of e.e.cummings' aphorism, "equality is what does not exist among equals". Furthermore, Skinner's emphasis on the causal relationship between the 'appraisive' function of concepts and their social criteria of application indicates that the question that we are dealing with is not empirical. We do not know if the dikasts who manned the jury in, say, Meidias' trial experienced envy. Instead, our task is to investigate public speakers' discursive strategies in an attempt to pin down competing views of social realities and the means through which new social perceptions were established. Lastly and more importantly, Skinner's approach gives us a sense of the ways in which democratic discourse responded to the stigmatization of egalitarian quests through projective uses of envy, a good example of which is Alcibiades' speech in Thucydides that we saw earlier. In what follows

---

[31] As Skinner (2002: 183–185) suggests, the main aspects of his analysis of the language of ideology can be traced back to the works of ancient rhetorical theory, which qualify the change or reversal of the appraisive function of concepts such as παραδιαστολή (cp. Quint. *I.O.* 9.3.65). Note also that the dramatic change of the criteria of concepts' application is a central topic of Thucydides' treatment of the *stasis* in Corcyra: καὶ τὴν εἰωθυῖαν ἀξίωσιν τῶν ὀνομάτων ἐς τὰ ἔργα ἀντήλλαξαν τῇ δικαιώσει, 3.82.4 ("They reversed the usual evaluative force of words to suit their own assessment of actions", transl. Hammond). On democrats' appropriation of 'aristocratic' values, see Brock 1991, who rightly disputes Loraux's argument (2006: 415–416) that democratic ideology was aphasic.

I suggest that the uses of legitimate envy in democratic contexts rests on the modification of the criteria of its application.

The new criteria of application that facilitated the use of *phthonos* to indicate a morally responsive sentiment are directly relevant to the cognitive structure of Aristotle's τὸ νεμεσᾶν and especially the 'socialization' of the evaluations that determine the desert of one's prosperity. Hence, legitimate envy requires a contextualized approach that takes into account the performative function of other concepts, such as *philotimia* and *charis*, which constitute the web of values favoured in the democratic ideology of 4th century Athens. The modification of (bad, dispositional) *phthonos*' criteria of application corresponds to social realities and reflects the poorer citizens' power to form majorities and control through their decisions prominent citizens' personal distinction. The ideological uses of 'legitimate envy' are a locus in which the public discourse of classical Athens negotiates the contradictions prompted by the coexistence of political equality with social inequalities and the repercussions of social inequalities upon 'equal' citizens' status. Legitimate envy is therefore an emotion that contributes to the masses' control over politically ambitious citizens, a commendable evaluative term targeting antisocial and antidemocratic behaviour.

In his recent book on envy and jealousy, Sanders shows that "justified envy", non-divine "phthonos-as-censure", appears for the first time in the 5th century and that all the relevant passages are written by Athenian authors and "relate to the abuse of political position or wealth." (2014: 44). Sanders further points out that this may be due to the fact that we possess very little literature composed outside Athens. This is, of course true, but, as Cartledge (1996: 178) puts it, "of all ancient cities, Athens was surely the one that most fervently preached the gospel of equality". The very fact that legitimate envy appears in Athenian sources, reflecting typically Athenian ideals, invites our attention.

By way of introducing my approach to the uses of legitimate envy, I propose to discuss briefly a fragment of Hippias of Elis that we find in Stobaeus (quoted from Plutarch), which Sanders takes to indicate that by the end of the 5th century legitimate envy has become a moral sentiment "across Greece" (44). The fragment (B 16 DK) runs as follows:

> Λέγει [sc. Hippias} δύο εἶναι φθόνους· τὸν μὲν δίκαιον, ὅταν τις τοῖς κακοῖς φθονῆι τιμωμένοις, τὸν δὲ ἄδικον, ὅταν τοῖς ἀγαθοῖς. καὶ διπλᾶ τῶν ἄλλων οἱ φθονεροὶ κακοῦνται· οὐ γὰρ μόνον τοῖς ἰδίοις κακοῖς ἄχθονται ὥσπερ ἐκεῖνοι, ἀλλὰ καὶ τοῖς ἀλλοτρίοις ἀγαθοῖς.

> Hippias says there are two types of *phthonos*: the just type, when someone envies bad men who are honored, and the unjust type, when he envies the good. And the envious suffer double the distress of others; for not only are they aggrieved, as others are, at their own troubles, but also at other peoples' good fortunes (transl. Sanders, slightly modified).

It is impossible to say with certainty if the fragment belongs to Hippias of Elis. But if it does, it is likely that, like the rest of the passages in which Sanders traces early uses of justified envy, it reflects Athenian attitudes. Like most of the so-called Sophists, Hippias traveled extensively and spent considerable time in Athens. And, what is more, would the uses of 'legitimate' envy be practicable in the public life of a city like Sparta or Pherae in Thessaly? And if yes, how? Be that as it may, Hippias, or whoever the author of this fragment is, might well be one of those that Aristotle criticizes for the use of the label *phthonos* to describe the moral sentiment of 'indignation' (τὸ νεμεσᾶν). It is noteworthy, however, that the novelty of the thesis expressed in this passage requires the established view that envy is reprehensible, because the fragment would otherwise state the self-evident. In other words, Hippias' saying offers a good example of how by reversing the criteria of application of a key concept it acquires a new performative function. When it involves morally and socially appropriate evaluations, legitimate envy is commendable. Furthermore, it is also notable (and perhaps an indication of its Athenocentric perspective) that the fragment identifies justified envy with instances in which bad people receive unwarranted honours. As we shall see, the notion of τιμή and the rules according to which honour is conferred on prominent Athenian citizens are fundamental to scripts of legitimate envy in the Attic orators.

The fragment under discussion offers useful comparative ground that helps us glean the semantic changes of the word *phthonos* in its uses in the ideological discourse of classical Athens, insofar as it telescopes its more elaborate deployment in the orators to which I now turn my attention. In what follows, I propose to discuss two passages from Demosthenes' speeches *Against Leptines* and *Against Meidias*.

*Against Leptines* was delivered by Demosthenes, who acted as a *synegoros* supporting Apsephion's charge against a law passed by Leptines in 356.[32] Leptines' law abolished exemptions from *liturgies* awarded to wealthy Athenians or foreigners for their services to the city. The passage that I focus on runs as follows:

ἔστι δὲ πάντα μὲν ὡς ἔπος εἰπεῖν ὀνείδη φευκτέον, τοῦτο δὲ πάντων μάλιστ', ὦ ἄνδρες Ἀθηναῖοι. διὰ τί; ὅτι παντάπασι φύσεως κακίας σημεῖόν ἐστιν ὁ φθόνος, καὶ οὐκ ἔχει πρόφασιν δι' ἣν ἂν τύχοι συγγνώμης ὁ τοῦτο πεπονθώς. εἶτα καὶ οὐδ' ἔστιν ὄνειδος ὅτου πορρώτερόν ἐσθ' ἡμῶν ἡ πόλις ἢ τοῦ φθονερὰ δοκεῖν εἶναι, ἁπάντων ἀπέχουσα τῶν

---

[32] For a convenient presentation of the legal and historical aspects of the case, see Harris 2008. For a more detailed discussion of the speech, see the recent commentaries by Kremmydas (2012) and Canevaro (2016). Demosthenes' treatment of equality in this speech has been discussed by Mossé 1987: 167–173.

> αἰσχρῶν. τεκμήρια δ' ἡλίκα τούτου θεωρήσατε. πρῶτον μὲν μόνοι τῶν πάντων ἀνθρώπων ἐπὶ τοῖς τελευτήσασι δημοσίᾳ [καὶ ταῖς ταφαῖς ταῖς δημοσίαις] ποιεῖτε λόγους ἐπιταφίους, ἐν οἷς κοσμεῖτε τὰ τῶν ἀγαθῶν ἀνδρῶν ἔργα. καίτοι τοῦτ' ἔστι τοὐπιτήδευμα ζηλούντων ἀρετήν, οὐ τοῖς ἐπὶ ταύτῃ τιμωμένοις φθονούντων. εἶτα μεγίστας δίδοτ' ἐκ παντὸς τοῦ χρόνου δωρεὰς τοῖς τοὺς γυμνικοὺς νικῶσιν ἀγῶνας τοὺς στεφανίτας, καὶ οὐχ, ὅτι τῇ φύσει τούτων ὀλίγοις μέτεστιν, ἐφθονήσατε τοῖς ἔχουσιν, οὐδ' ἐλάττους ἐνείματε τὰς τιμὰς διὰ ταῦτα. πρὸς δὲ τούτοις τοιούτοις οὖσιν οὐδεὶς πώποτε τὴν πόλιν ἡμῶν εὖ ποιῶν δοκεῖ νικῆσαι· τοσαύτας ὑπερβολὰς τῶν δωρειῶν αἷς ἀντ' εὖ ποωιεῖ, παρέσχηται. ἔστι τοίνυν πάντα ταῦτ', ὦ ἄνδρες Ἀθηναῖοι, δικαιοσύνης, ἀρετῆς, μεγαλοψυχίας ἐπιδείγματα.
>
> (Dem. 20. 140–142)

> Generally speaking, one should avoid all shameful actions, men of Athens, and most of all, this one. Why? Because spite is undoubtedly an indication of an evil nature, and there is no excuse that would entitle someone who feels it to any sympathy. Beyond that, there is no criticism that our city, which shuns all forms of shameful conduct, deserves less than the charge of being spiteful. Consider how much evidence proves this point. First, you are the only people in the world who hold public funeral orations for the dead, in which you celebrate the deeds of brave men. Indeed, this is the way men act if they admire outstanding achievement, but not if they are jealous of men who are honored for this. Next, you have throughout history given the most generous awards to those who win crowns in athletic contests. Just because these crowns are naturally granted to few men, you are not jealous of those who win them, nor do you reduce their honors for that reason. Besides virtues like these, no other place has ever gained a reputation for outdoing our city in granting awards. This is how far our city outdoes others in granting prizes as rewards for the benefits we receive. All these things, men of Athens, provide examples of our justice, outstanding character, and magnanimity (transl. E. M. Harris).

My second example is a passage from Demosthenes' *Against Meidias*. The speech concerns the attack that Demosthenes suffered in the theatre of Dionysus in Athens, when his opponent, Meidias, struck him on the face while he was acting as a choregos for his tribe. The passage that I propose to discuss in comparison with *Agianst Leptines* is the following:

> μεγάλην μεντἂν ἀρχήν, μᾶλλον δὲ τέχνην, εἴης εὑρηκώς, εἰ δύο τἀναντιώταθ' ἑαυτοῖς ἐν οὕτω βραχεῖ χρόνῳ περὶ σαυτὸν δύναιο ποιεῖσθαι, φθόνον ἐξ ὧν ζῇς, καὶ ἐφ' οἷς ἐξαπατᾷς ἔλεον. οὐκ ἔστιν οὐδαμόθεν σοι προσήκων ἔλεος οὐδὲ καθ' ἕν, ἀλλὰ τοὐναντίον μῖσος καὶ φθόνος καὶ ὀργή.
>
> (Dem. 21. 196)

> You would certainly have discovered a great source of power—or rather of deceit—if you are able to gain for yourself two things that are most completely at odds with one another: loathing for the way you live and pity for your hypocrisy. There is no way that pity is the appropriate response for you, not in any respect, but the opposite: hatred and loathing and anger
>
> (tranls. E.M. Harris).

In the passage from *Against Leptines* that I cited, *philotimia* plays a predominant role. *Philotimia* indicates the ambitiousness of prominent citizens (see also discussion below) and, just like good and bad envy, it is a concept that as far as we can see over time acquired new criteria of application. Although in 5th century sources *philotimia* signifies primarily the over-ambitiousness of wealthy citizens and their destructive struggle for public displays and power, in 4th century Athens it becomes a commendable virtue for which citizens were honoured publicly. As a socially cohesive virtue, 4th century *philotimia* appears in contexts referring to wealthy citizens' public expenditure on account of which the demos expresses its sentiments of gratitude (*charis*) by granting them in return different types of material and immaterial honours. The idealized reciprocal relationship between wealthy and poorer citizens helps Demosthenes ask his audience to display their magnanimity and thereby avoid the danger of appearing envious towards useful members of the elite.[33] In order to support his argument, Demosthenes compares *ateleia*, the exemption from liturgic assignments, with the honours that Athenians grant to the dead of war, which the polis praises wholeheartedly through the funeral speeches delivered in their honour. In instances of institutional competition reflecting the values that constitute the polis' identity, Demosthenes claims, personal distinction does not cause citizens' envy. Quite the contrary, due to their magnanimity, Athenians respond to distinction by expressing the noble sentiment of *zelos,* an emotion that Aristotle associates with people who have received moral training and are therefore *epieikeis* (Rh. 1388a 35).

Demosthenes' treatment of envy in this passage is extremely circumspect. His reference to his listeners' possible sentiments of envy is significantly mitigated by the encomiastic tone that he endorses, a tone that must be explained by the fact that his speech touches on the sensitive issue of wealthy citizens' prominence in an environment of political equality. For example, the expression 'you are the only people' (μόνοι τῶν πάντων ἀνθρώπων) is a recognizable encomiastic formulation which imports in Demosthenes' speech the epideictic tone of the funeral speeches, i.e. speeches which, as he says, not only are the trademark of Athenian ethos, but also indicate citizens' magnanimous responses to eminence.[34] Furthermore, as Kremmydas points out (2012: 413), the words ὀνείδη and αἰσχρά "have epideictic overtones". Demosthenes thus places his projective use of envy in an encomiastic context which, through the use of second person plural,

---

**33** On Demosthtnes' presentation of Leptines as *acharistos*, a key issue of the speech, see Fisher 2003: 193–200; Cairns 2003: 246–247; Sanders 2014: 89–91.
**34** On the encomiastic *topos* of emphasizing the 'Athenianess' of the Funeral speeches, see Loraux 2006: 25–26.

construes dikasts collectively as representatives of the polis' ideals, especially their positive response to distinction.

Demosthenes' rhetoric in this passage presents envy as a sentiment unworthy of his audience. This becomes especially clear in the opening construction of the passage that I cited above, where he claims, in a markedly solemn tone (cp. παντάπασι), that the emotion is a sign of a bad *physis*. Athenian competitive institutions are ἐπιδείγματα, 'proofs', but also 'public displays', that reveal Athenians' magnanimity. The depiction of the polis' collective identity is significantly enhanced by Demosthenes' appeal to dikasts' shame (ὀνείδη) which supports his argument for *ateleia*. Demosthenes avoids an overt attribution of sentiments of envy to his audience by putting together a script of shame that typically involves anticipatory appraisals about one's (here the whole citizenry's) failure to meet the standards of an ideal self. Shame helps Demosthenes warn his audience that their decision to abolish *ateleia* will be interpreted as a consequence of their envy and that this will be a fatal blow on the city's good reputation.

Demosthenes' treatment of bad envy in this context is particularly relevant to the ideological uses of the emotion that concern me in this chapter. *Ateleia* may be seen as one of the ways in which the demos reciprocated wealthy citizens' services to the city. Although Demosthenes' rhetoric revolves exclusively around bad *phthonos*, which, as we saw, he treats as a sign of villainy, the contextualization of the emotion through references to typical Athenian responses to institutional competitions offers comparable ground indicating the circumstances under which *phthonos* is a justifiable, morally responsive, and democratic sentiment. His reference to the few citizens who, on account of their outstanding physical skills, engage in athletic achievements is an allegory for the public-spirited members of the elites of wealth who contribute to the city's power. Demosthenes' circumspect treatment of citizens' *possible* sentiments of envy, reflecting the emotion's more aggressive uses by elite authors, must be explained by the unpopular nature of Demosthenes' argument. Unlike Aristotle who emphasizes the badness of *phthonos* by omitting from the cognitions that give rise to the emotion the notion of 'desert' (ἀξίως), the ideological discourse of classical Athens emphasizes criteria on the basis of which the polis normatively decides when a citizen deserves others' envy.

Demosthenes' *Against Meidias* is perhaps the most lucid source of evidence concerning legitimate envy's appropriate criteria of application.[35] Centering on

---

[35] On the question of whether the speech was delivered in an Athenian court, see MacDowell 1990: 23–28. The answer to this question does not affect my discussion of the uses of legitimate envy in the speech.

the insolent and antidemocratic nature of his wealthy opponent, Demosthenes underscores Meidias' self-interested character and deviant competitiveness. Meidias is presented throughout the speech as an overambitious citizen who embodies egotistic *philotimia*. Despite his unwillingness to spend his considerable wealth for the city, Meidias is thirsty for honours. Furthermore, the speech relies heavily on contradistinctive characterization, in so far as Demosthenes takes pains to present himself as a 'middling' (*metrios*) citizen who acts in the interest of less privileged citizens. Meidias, by contrast, not only is hybristic, but through his antidemocratic, aggressive behaviour he has destroyed poorer citizens, as Straton's, the poor arbitrator's example clearly indicates (83–96). Indeed, as has been observed (see below), Meidias is characterized by tyrannical traits.

The passage from *Agianst Meidias* that I cited above offers one of the most aggressive uses of legitimate envy. In conformity with Demosthenes' rhetoric throughout the speech, this passage stresses in an overtly sarcastic tone, that on account of his *hybris* and contempt for the common good, Meidias deserves citizens' justified envy –rather than their pity (cp. esp. 154–157). In anticipating his opponent's attempts to appeal to the dikasts' compassion, Demosthenes constructs two competing emotion scripts. Despite Meidias' theatrical attempts to make his audience take pity on him, presumably by emphasizing Demosthenes' deceptiveness, the sentiment that he deserves (προσήκων) is legitimate envy (along with anger and hatred). Aristotle, we may be reminded, insists in the *Rhetoric* that the opposite of envy is not pity, as some unidentified authors suggest (presumably authors of handbooks), but τὸ νεμεσᾶν. The passage thus shows not only that uses of legitimate *phthonos* do not reflect badly on speakers who appeal to the emotion, but also that it was sufficient for speakers to encourage feelings of indignation through the label *phthonos* on the condition that they specified the criteria of application of the term. Hence, this passage is a good example of Skinner's suggestion that new ideological uses of old terms rely on modifications of the criteria of their application so as to correspond to new social perceptions. Although these criteria are not expressly mentioned in this passage, the wider context of the speech indicates sufficiently enough that dikasts' legitimate *phthonos* revolves around appraisals concerning Meidias' selfishness and manic desire to display his superiority in a typically undemocratic way that misrecognizes the demos' privilege to grant honours. *Phthonos* in this context reverses the performative function of the word, that is the evaluative force that it has in the frame of its anti-egalitarian uses, and describes a morally responsive sentiment.

In the last section of this chapter, I analyze in detail a rich emotion script of legitimate envy from Demosthenes' *Against Meidias* which shows lucidly the appraisals that inform this democratic emotion. Before I reach this point, however, it would be useful to discuss briefly other instances of legitimate envy from the orators. In the pseudo-Demsothenic speech *Against Phaenippus* concerning a *diadikasia*, a trial in which, after an unsuccessful *antidosis*, the dikasts would decide which of the two litigants would undertake a liturgy, and hence revolves around public expenditure, the unnamed speaker claims that wealthy citizens who willingly engage in public spending must not meet with their fellow-citizens' envy (22). Indeed, in his comparison of his opponent's poor liturgic record with that of his ancestors, the speaker says: "I do not envy them". As he suggests, the well-off must be useful citizens and offer willingly their services to the city. Notably, the expression χρησίμους αὐτοὺς παρέχειν τοῖς πολίταις ('making themselves useful to the citizens') that the speaker employs here is a formulaic locution that we find in honorific inscriptions after the second half of the 4th century.[36] The use of envy in this speech is the opposite of the one that Demosthenes makes in *Against Meidias*, in so far as the speaker's opponent's ancestors spent profusely on the city. They thereby do not deserve citizens' envy.

Even if, however, the speaker of *Against Phaenippus*, does not invite dikasts to express openly their envy against his opponent, the contradistinctive characterization that he endorses, contrasting Phaenippus' public record with that of his parents, provides appraisals which are relevant to legitimate envy scripts. In his attempt to convince dikasts that Phaenippus must undertake the liturgy, he claims that the only *philotimia* that his opponent can display is his horse-breeding, a trademark of the elites' luxurious lifestyle, and his purchase of a chariot (24). The reference to Phaenippus' *hippotrophia*, emphasized by the statement that his opponent sold his war-horse, is clearly intended to make dikasts realize that the money that he saves by avoiding the undertaking of liturgies is used to support his ostentatious lifestyle. However, it is also noteworthy that the speaker enhances his personal attack against Phaenippus by associating his *hippotrophia* with his young age and power. Young age, power, and luxuriousness are typical characteristics of antidemocratic *hybris*, and, hence, are deployed here as a means of causing dikasts' anger against Phaenippus.

Although the detailed account of Phaenippus' property in the speech is explained by the nature of the legal case –but note that the speaker is obliged to admit that Phaenippus did indeed include the chariot in the inventory list during the *antidosis*–, it provides a competing version of his ancestors' public *philotimia*. Phaenippus is thus characterized by the main traits that inform scripts of justified

---

**36** On *philotimia* and other 'cardinal' values, see Whitehead 1983; 1993. Whithehead (1983: 67–68) shows that *philotimia* appeared on honourary decrees from the 340's onwards. For a recent discussion of *philotimia* in the orators, see Ferrucci 2013.

*phthonos*: unwillingness to engage in public spending, ostentatious lifestyle, and a hybristic inclination to showcase superiority and power.

Another example that provides useful evidence concerning the ideological uses of legitimate envy is Isaeus' *On the estate of Philoctemon* (Is. 6). Towards the end of his speech for this inheritance case, the speaker, a friend of Chaerestratus' family, claims that if Philoctemon's property is adjudicated to Chaerestratus' opponents, they will squander thereby causing dikasts' envy. By contrast, despite his young age, Chaerestratus has an impressive liturgic record which guarantees that, if he gets Philoctemon's property, he will take care of the polis' interests. Indeed, Chaerestrarus spends more money on the polis than on himself (60). Furthermore, in his attempt at character assassination, the speaker claims that his opponents try to deceive dikasts into believing that they are poor, while Chaerestratus is rich. Again, in his a anticipation of dikasts' possible sentiments of envy towards a substantially rich man (and his sister) who claims the inheritance of his (allegedly) adoptive father, the *phthonos* script that Isaeus constructs revolves around considerations of justice. It is Chaerestrarus' opponents rather than public-minded Chaerestratus who, through their selfishness, will eventually cause dikasts' legitimate envy (ἄξιοι φθονεῖσθαι).

The examples that I have examined in this section indicate that the word *phthonos* is used in contexts revolving around the desert of one's prosperity, i.e. *phthonos* is used by public speakers to designate the emotion that Aristotle calls τὸ νεμεσᾶν. A further piece of evidence from Aristotle's times concerning the use of the label *phthonos* to designate the morally responsive emotion of 'indignation' (τὸ νεμεσᾶν) can be found in the treatise *Rhetorica ad Alexandrum*. The author of this treatise claims that *phthonos* targets the following categories of people (34, 1440a 35–39): "those who have had, are having, or will have *undeserved* (ἀναξίως) good fortune; those who have never been, are not being, or will never be deprived of some good; or those who have never suffered, are not suffering, and will never suffer some misfortune" (transl. E. Sanders).[37] The fact that a treatise providing prospective orators practical advice on effective public speaking employs the label *phthonos* to designate 'indignation' suggests that, by the time of its composition, there was little doubt about the criteria of application of the term and, correlatively, that Aristotle's definition reflects ideological biases rather than his fear that the use of *phthonos* is unequivocally dangerous because it may reflect badly upon speakers who employ it.

---

37 φθόνον δὲ παρασκευάσομεν συλλήβδην πρὸς τούτους, οὓς ἀποφαίνομεν ἀναξίως εὖ πεπραχότας ἢ πράττοντας ἢ πράξοντας, ἢ ἀγαθοῦ μηδέποτε ἐστερημένους ἢ <μὴ> στερομένους ἢ μὴ στερησομένους, ἢ κακοῦ μηδέποτε τετυχηκότας ἢ μὴ τυγχάνοντας ἢ μὴ τευξομένους.

## 4.4 Meidias' lifestyle: spectacles of luxuriousness and legitimate envy

In this section, I turn my attention to Demosthenes' *Against Meidias* 158–159. In a recent publication (2017b), I discussed the importance of *enargeia* in Demosthenes' presentation of Meidias' excessive lifestyle in this passage. In the remaining pages of this chapter, I recapitulate my discussion, but I offer a more contextualized reading of it and focus my attention on the evaluative appraisals of legitimate envy in 4th century Athens.

Although in his personal attack on Meidias, laying stress on the hybristic character of his opponent, Demosthenes relies heavily on scripts of anger, legitimate envy is vital to his argument. As I suggest, because of its emphasis on social inequalities, especially their repercussions upon civic life and Demosthenes' understanding of the law's enforcement as a medium through which the *hybris* of the rich and powerful is constrained, the speech puts together enhanced scripts of legitimate envy, even in cases were the emotion, i.e. *phthonos* is not named. *Against Meidias* is heuristically useful and, as I suggest, supports my Skinnerian interpretation of the ideological uses of *phthonos* in democratic Athens.

One of the most distinctive characteristics of the speech is the extent to which it thematizes the social implications of wealth. The qualification οἱ πλούσιοι ('the wealthy'), to which Demosthenes contrasts 'middling' Athenians represented by the dikasts (112, 209, 212–213), recurs in the speech. The pejorative uses of οἱ πλούσιοι are ideologically charged, in so far as they convey condemnable traits and behaviours. In most of the cases, οἱ πλούσιοι is employed as a derogatory term indicating a deeply antidemocratic ethos. Note for example that Demosthenes combines the word 'wealthy' with the qualification θρασύς ('bold', 'arrogant'), while in another passage wealthy Meidias is presented as being 'full of himself', loud, and shameless (66 and 201). Furthermore, οἱ πλούσιοι in general and Meidias in particular are portrayed as being fully aware of their superiority which they display obnoxiously, as the following tricolon with the emphatic use of anaphora shows: ἡμεῖς οἱ λητουργοῦντες, ἡμεῖς οἱ προεισφέροντες ὑμῖν, ἡμεῖς οἱ πλούσιοί ἐσμεν: WE, WE, WE (153). In the eyes of Meidias, those who do not belong to the πλούσιοι are just social scum, 'beggars' (πτωχοὺς ἀποκαλεῖ, 211). In line with this negative presentation of the wealthy, Demosthenes presents the haves' wealth as the main cause of hybristc behaviour. In a significant passage, for example, he claims that if the dikasts convict Meidias and deprive him of his property they will have succeeded in mitigating his *hybris* (211). In another passage Demosthenes stresses the heartlessness of the rich (209). He thereby asks dikasts to imagine the harsh treatment that they would receive as defendants, if their legal cases were heard by juries manned by prosperous citizens who display Meidias' antisocial behavioural traits. In this imaginary court of law, wealthy citizens such as Meidias and his supporters would be pitiless, because they are irresponsive to the compassionate and moderate ethos of democratic juries (τῶν πολλῶν καὶ δημοτικῶν, 208). The proceedings of this imaginary jury –a dystopian nightmare of mock trials conducted by democracy's enemies– are reminiscent of oligarchic practices (especially summary executions). This passage, therefore, strengthens Demosthenes' presentation of Meidias as a man with oligarchic predilections.

Social inequalities are therefore thematized in the speech only in so far as they are related to key aspects of democratic ideology, especially citizens' equality, sense of honour, and the reciprocal relationship of *charis* that regulated the liturgic system of the polis (on this points, see discussion below). These values, rather than wealth gap, inform the appraisals that primarily determine Demosthenes' deployment of legitimate envy. In this respect, Demosthenes' rhetoric is in pace with other instances in which forensic speakers construct scripts of legitimate envy (see previous section). However, Demosthenes' rhetoric in this speech is ambivalent. At the time of the trial, Demosthenes was politically active and, as the legal case under discussion shows, wealthy enough to undertake a *choregia*. In addition, Demosthenes openly compares his rich liturgic record with that of Meidias. This self-presentation apparently impinges on his recurrent attempts to identify himself with the dikasts, i.e. impersonate an ordinary, 'middling' (*metrios*) citizen who is typically the victim of an arrogant member of the elite. However, as Ober has plausibly suggested (1999), Demosthenes' ambivalent self-presentation is a deliberate choice. For the purposes of my argument, however, it is important to stress that Demosthenes is able to endorse this rhetorical strategy, because the value system to which he appeals, especially by emphasizing his loyalty to the city and his lavish public expenditure, excludes legitimate envy as a possible response to his wealth.

In view of Demosthenes' self-presentation as a 'middling' citizen and a wealthy liturgist, one may argue that the legitimate envy scripts of the speech invite two different types of comparison –comparison being of course an inextricable element of rivalrous emotions. As a victim of Meidias' arrogance, Demosthenes identifies himself with the dikasts and distances himself from the *plousioi*. As a *metrios* citizen, Demosthenes is an ally of his audience and brandishes in front of it the hybristic behaviour of wealthy citizens like Meidias by presenting it as a result of social inequalities. At the same time, as a champion of *metriotes* Demosthenes induces dikasts to become conscious of their power to form majorities and control antidemocratic behaviour. But in the instances where Demosthenes presents himself as a wealthy liturgist, he integrates himself with the demos, by arguing that he is sensitive to the pivotal role of reciprocal *charis* and the privilege of the people to grant honours. As he suggests in the paragraphs indicating healthy and democratic expressions of *philotimia* (62–66), wealthy citizens' competition for honour is regulated by the demos, the only responsible for its outcome.

Demosthenes' contrast between ordinary citizens' democratic *metriotes* with the insolence and arrogance of the wealthy is also directly relevant to the speech's *pathopoiia* resting mainly on the emotions of anger and legitimate envy. When Demosthenes' target is Meidias (and wealthy citizens') *hybris*, he typically appeals to dikasts' anger. One of the most notable examples appears in 34, where Demosthenes claims that his opponent deserves dikasts' 'public anger' (δημοσίας ὀργῆς), because the victim of his *hybris* was the city as a whole. In this connection, it is worthy of our note that most of the occurrences of the label anger in the speech appear in contexts focusing on hybris. Hence, wealth is inextricably interwoven with scripts of anger, in so far as excess is construed as a factor that causes or intensifies hybristc behaviour. Legitimate envy is also closely related to wealth, even if in a more direct way. Because the emotion typically targets uncooperative members of the elite who accumulate private wealth at the cost of the polis' interests, relevant scripts are constructed throughout the speech, even in cases where *phthonos* is not mentioned. One may compare for example the passage describing Meidias' conduct during a military campaign in Euboea to which he participated unwillingly. During the campaign, Demosthenes says, Meidias carried expensive sympotic items and clothes instead of military equipment and rode on a silver mule-chair (133). Furthermore, later in the speech Demosthenes points out, that, when Meidias was cavalry leader, he chose to lead the procession on the horse of Philomelus of Paeania, a renowned liturgist, rather than purchase his own horse (174).

As the passages that I have discussed so far indicate, Demosthenes' comments on Meidias' wealth and the instances in which he openly invites dikasts to compare themselves with the πλούσιοι do not emphasize the unequal distribution of assets among citizens. In other words, nowhere in the speech (or in other relevant sources of evidence discussed by Fisher 2003) do we find Demosthenes asking dikasts to deprive Meidias of his property because he is significantly wealthier than they are. In other words, the scripts of envy in the speech do not revolve around the appraisal 'why not me/we?', an appraisal which is characteristic of bad envy (the *phaulon* emotion that Thatcher projected on her political opponents). Furthermore, as Fisher (2003) usefully reminds us, the successful outcome of the undertakings for which *choregoi* (or liturgists) spent their money required a cooperative mentality in the frame of a value system whose norms were shared by the wealthy leaders and the ordinary people.

In the remaining pages of this chapter, I turn my attention to a significant passage from the speech, which, as I suggested, offers fertile ground for our understanding of the criteria of application involved in the scripts of legitimate envy in democratic Athens. The passage under discussion emphasizes Meidias' luxuriousness, but also includes or appeals to the key concepts of *lamprotes* and *philotimia* which are directly relevant to my discussion of the democratization of envy in the public discourse of the polis. As I suggest, the uses of these concepts in democratic Athens can also be analyzed on the basis of Skinner's theory about the language of ideology. This approach, emphasizing that new ideological schemata commonly modify the meaning of existing concepts, gives scope for a more accurate and contextualized understanding of legitimate envy. For, as Skinner points out, "to recognise the role of our evaluative language in helping to legitimate social action is to recognise the point at which our social vocabulary and our social fabric mutually prop each other up" (2002: 174).

As has been pointed out by scholars, in its early, 5th century uses the term *philotimia* was ambivalent. Fisher, for example, suggests that during the Peloponnesian War "there was more explicit recognition of mass-elite conflict over the liturgies" and that this conflict "raged in particular over contested and changing meanings and use of...*philotimia*" (2003: 191). Furthermore, the negative evaluative function of *philotimia* may be attributed, as Fisher (2003: 191) argues, to the fact that many ambitious liturgists "turned out to be oligarchs or their supporters either in 411–410 or in 405–403". Although it is difficult to pin down the reasons that contributed to the ambiguousness of *philotimia*, one may take into account that even in the heroic world of Homer's poetry, competition and ambitiousness were not without limits. As Cairns (2011b: 38) concludes in a study comparing ancient and modern shame, "[T]he association between honour and morality, identity, and integrity is there already in Homer. Yet, though Homer's heroes are proud and independent, their pursuit of honour implies a community with both the power to judge them and the ability to enlist individuals' honour in support of the security and cohesion of the group. Individual identity is intimately bound up with group membership. Self-esteem depends on the esteem of others".

Cairns' arguments against primitivist views of early Greek ethics, postulating that the struggle for honour was limitless and unregulated and that a clear distinction between cooperative and competitive values is possible, are useful for our understanding of *philotimia* because they indicate that the negative evaluative function of the term has a longer history than we may tend to believe. Furthermore, it disputes approaches, such as Wilson's that 'aristocratic' values were not understood by the masses and that "the fractures in the ideology of *philotimia* are all of a part with the manner in which Athenian democracy was unable or unwilling to operate in a manner quite free from aristocratic principles and practices" (2000: 191). The fact that "the fractures in the ideology of *philotimia*" are already present in 'aristocratic' ethics indicates that since societies, and social groups within them, are hierarchical and competitive they struggle to harness personal honour and distinction by channeling them into common interest.

On my Skinnerian analysis, thus, the evaluative force of negative and positive *philotimia* in the discourse of 4th century democratic Athens has a constitutive function in so far as in its forensic uses it enhances the stigmatization of egotistic types of competitive behaviour and, by facilitating punishment of self-interested members of the elites, it enhances the masses' control over the rich and powerful. Hence, although Wilson (2000: 157) is certainly right when he points out that the dikasts that Demosthenes addresses did not have the means "to engage in the form of high-level *philotimia*" which prompted his dispute with Meidias, in my view he underplays their power to restrain self-serving members of the elite *through* the deployment of the evaluative term *philotimia*. Philotimia, thus, must be viewed as one of the key concepts that constituted the repertoire of norms which contributed to the wide angle perspective of Athenian trials through the deployment of concepts which asserted the polis' shared values.

The use of extra-statutory norms in a speech of prosecution is predictably enlisted in support of the speaker's attempt to secure conviction. Thus, implicit to Demosthenes' emphasis on Meidias' egotistic *philotimia* is his sense of the attitude that the dikasts must endorse in casting their votes. This, I believe, is the message that Demosthenes wants to convey when he compares Meidias and Alcibiades (143–149), who was banished by his fellow-citizens on account of his outrageous *hybris*. Although one does not need to side with Demosthenes' presentation of Alcibiades as a positive example of cooperative *philotimia*, Meidias' comparison with Alcibiades is so designed as to suggest the limits of ambitiousness in democracy. This, no doubt, is Demosthenes' point, when he emphasizes that the 'aristocratic' qualities of birth, wealth, and power (for which Alcibiades boasts in his speech in Thucydides that we saw earlier) were of little help to Alcibiades. In the glorious past of the city (κατὰ τὴν παλαιὰν ἐκείνην εὐδαιμονίαν, 143), *hybris* was just unacceptable.

Throughout the speech, Demosthenes exploits the evaluative ambivalence of *philotimia*. By identifying Meidias with negative *philotimia* and presenting himself as incorporating positive ambitiousness, Demosthenes enhances the speech's contradistinctive characterization. At 67–68, for example Demosthenes claims that, if Meidias engaged willingly in a *choregia*, he would have indicated his *philotimia* in a positive and lawful manner. This passage reveals clearly, in my view, the reciprocal nature of public *philotimia* and the norms that surrounded elite competition. For, as Demosthenes says, engaging in public *philotimia*, i.e. spending for the city, is an indication that a wealthy citizen honours the demos (ἐτίμησεν, 69). Rather than being a "palliative fiction", as Wislon would suggest, with which Demosthenes seeks to dodge harsh social realities, especially the fact that most of the dikasts would be unable to engage in public spending, the use of ἐτίμησεν in this context reveals the decisive role of the demos in the frame of the reciprocal *philotimia*. The demos' *time* lies in its members' ability to control the dispensation of honours in the city. This becomes evident from the fact that Meidias displays his deviant, private *philotimia* through antagonistic (and, indeed, illegal) activities which are not regulated by the demos. In paragraphs 62–65, for example, Demosthenes presents instances of illustrious and *philotimoi*, albeit occasionally unsuccessful *choregoi*, who accepted the demos' judgment ungrudgingly. This may be an idealized representation of these ambitious citizens' response to personal failure, but it reveals the type of behaviour which is compatible with the reciprocal nature of gratitude.

Another important concept that appears in the passage which I further discuss at the end of this section is *lamprotes*. As Wilson has shown (2000: 139–140), the term is closely related to choregic activity, in so far as it conveys the spectacular nature of the choruses, the very object of *theoria*, along with the brilliance of the *choregos* himself. Despite its close relationship with *choregia*, however, *lamprotes* is sometimes used to describe the illustriousness of public spending, thereby granting with visibility activities typically associated with public *philotimia* which grant their undertakers with distinction. In this sense, *lamprotes* may be taken to indicate the visual aspects of *megaloprepeia*. According to Aristotle, it is a characteristic of the μεγαλοπρεπής to make public spending the appropriate object of his ambition (εὐφιλοτίμητα [sc. δαπανήματα] πρὸς τὸ κοινόν, *EN.* 1122b 21–22). Notably, among the examples of *megaloprepeia* that Aristotle adduces is splendid *choregic* expenditures (χορηγεῖν λαμπρῶς).

In *Against Meidias*, the word *lampros* is used sarcastically to describe Meidias' poor liturgic record (133, 153, 174), his criminal activity, which, according to Demosthenes' sarcastic locution, his opponent does not deem brilliant enough, if it is not sufficiently outrageous (131), and his private *philotimia* which I discuss below (158). The uses of *lamprotes* in the speech indicate that the term primarily conveys the visual aspects of *philotimia*. As a leader of the cavalry, Meidias was 'brilliant' enough, Demosthenes says ironically, to lead a procession on the horse of another citizen (174). Similarly, Meidias is described as 'brilliant' in a context where Demosthenes emphasizes his opponent's loud, unbearable displays of his liturgies in the assembly (153). However, the visual qualities of *lamprotes* acquire significant prominence in paragraphs 158-159, where Demosthenes invites his audience to an unusual *theoria*. The relevant passage runs as follows:

> τίς οὖν ἡ λαμπρότης, ἢ τίνες αἱ λητουργίαι καὶ τὰ σέμν' ἀναλώματα τούτου; ἐγὼ μὲν γὰρ οὐχ ὁρῶ, πλὴν εἰ ταῦτά τις θεωρεῖ· οἰκίαν ᾠκοδόμηκεν Ἐλευσῖνι τοσαύτην ὥστε πᾶσιν ἐπισκοτεῖν τοῖς ἐν τῷ τόπῳ, καὶ εἰς μυστήρια τὴν γυναῖκ' ἄγει, κἂν ἄλλοσέ ποι βούληται, ἐπὶ τοῦ λευκοῦ ζεύγους τοῦ ἐκ Σικυῶνος, καὶ τρεῖς ἀκολούθους ἢ τέτταρας αὐτὸς ἔχων διὰ τῆς ἀγορᾶς σοβεῖ, κυμβία καὶ ῥυτὰ καὶ φιάλας ὀνομάζων οὕτως ὥστε τοὺς παριόντας ἀκούειν. ἐγὼ δ' ὅσα μὲν τῆς ἰδίας τρυφῆς εἵνεκα Μειδίας καὶ περιουσίας κτᾶται, οὐκ οἶδ' ὅ τι τοὺς πολλοὺς ὑμῶν ὠφελεῖ· ἃ δ' ἐπαιρόμενος τούτοις ὑβρίζει, ἐπὶ πολλοὺς καὶ τοὺς τυχόντας ἡμῶν ἀφικνούμεν' ὁρῶ. οὐ δεῖ δὴ τὰ τοιαῦθ' ἑκάστοτε τιμᾶν οὐδὲ θαυμάζειν ὑμᾶς, οὐδὲ τὴν φιλοτιμίαν ἐκ τούτων κρίνειν, εἴ τις οἰκοδομεῖ λαμπρῶς ἢ θεραπαίνας κέκτηται πολλὰς ἢ σκεύη καλά, ἀλλ' ὃς ἂν ἐν τούτοις λαμπρὸς καὶ φιλότιμος ᾖ, ὧν ἅπασι μέτεστι τοῖς πολλοῖς ὑμῶν· ὧν οὐδὲν εὑρήσετε τούτῳ προσόν (158-159).

> So what is his distinction? What are his liturgies, and his impressive expenditures? I can't see any – unless these are the items that one considers: he has built a house at Eleusis so big that it overshadows everyone in the neighbourhood; he takes his wife to celebrations of mysteries, and anywhere else he wishes, in a carriage drawn by the pair of white horses that he got from Sikyon; and he clears a way for himself through the Agora with an escort of three or four slaves, talking about 'cups' and 'drinking-horns' and 'chalices' loudly enough for the passers by to hear. Well, when Meidias acquires possessions for the sake of his persona luxury and advantage, I don't know what use they are to the majority of you; but when he's impelled by them to behave insolently, I can see that does affect many ordinary people among us. That surely isn't the kind of conduct you should honour and admire when it occurs; nor should you judge aspirations to honour by these criteria– whether a man builds a distinguished house or possesses a lot of maidservants or fine furniture: you should look for a man whose distinction and aspiration to honour are in things of which the majority of you all have a share. You'll find that none of this applies to Meidias
>
> (transl. D.M. MacDowell).

The use of the verbs ὁρῶ and θεωρεῖ at the beginning of the passage prepares the ground for a spectacle. In view of the two questions that follow and the ensuing description, the question "What is his distinction?", or better "In what consists his brilliance", *lamprotes* not only reflects the visual aspects of Demosthenes' account, but also emphasizes that Meidias' *philotimia* is egotistic and self-serving. That Demosthenes prepares the ground for the description of a spectacle is also brought out when he ingeniously anticipates the possibility that the jurors may be awed by Meidias' possessions (θαυμάζειν).³⁸ The verb θεωρῶ in particular introduces an invitation to a peculiar *theoria*, i.e. a visit to a spectacle, which, in the present case, is Meidias' privately accumulated wealth at the cost of the polis' interests. Furthermore, it points to the markedly theatrical aspects of loud-mouthed Meidias' obnoxious and antisocial behaviour.³⁹ If Demosthenes is a habitual liturgist, who undertakes the task of offering money for a public spectacle, i.e. a costly dithyrambic chorus in the frame of the Great Dionysia, Meidias' private 'brilliance' –a 'brilliance' that deprives the polis of his money– is so great that it can be the object of an awe-inspiring spectacle of ostentation.

Meidias' spectacular wealth, the object of the extraordinary *theoria* to which Demosthenes invites the jurors through his vivid account, is carefully described. The first item that Demosthenes refers to is Meidias' house at Eleusis. Notably, Demosthenes emphasizes the size of his opponent's house by indicating that it was so big that it covered the surrounding houses in darkness. Through the use of the verb ἐπισκοτεῖν ('overshadow'), no doubt a rhetorical exaggeration, Demosthenes not only stresses the size of Meidias' house, but also highlights the repercussions of its owner's selfishness upon his neighbours' daily lives. Furthermore, the present reference to 'darkness' is symptomatic of Demosthenes' rich imagery in a context full of visual and acoustic images, which highlights the sparkling surfaces of Meidias' possessions and his loud public displays. Meidias' private 'brilliance' (*lamprotes*) deprives his neighbours of sunlight.⁴⁰ The next detail that Demosthenes 'reveals' is Meidias' use of a carriage led by two horses from Sikyon to take his wife to public festivals and elsewhere.

Demosthenes' reference to Meidias' horses and use of a carriage are socially significant –status symbols rather than just commodities. By presenting his opponent as a *hippotrophos*, Demosthenes not only implies that his poor liturgic record facilitated an excessive private life, but also insinuates that Meidias is a possible enemy of democracy. In his discussion of the present passage, Wilson has pointed out that Demosthenes' portrayal of Meidias relies on stereotypes surrounding tyrants' lifestyle.⁴¹ Wilson's point, emphasizing Meidias' antidemocratic conduct, gains further significance if we take into account the ideological implications of material culture.

---

**38** On the interconnections between *thauma* and *theoria*, see Nightingale 2004: 256–257.
**39** Worman 2008 *passim* emphasizes the interconnections between loud speakers, shamelessness, and violence.
**40** On the visual aspects of *choregic lamprotes*, see Wilson 2000: 139–140. On evidence concerning the ideological implications of luxurious houses in classical Athens, see Millet 1998: 209–212.
**41** See Wilson 1991: 182–184.

According to a well-known and much debated incident described by Herodotus (1.60), Peisistratus returned to the city of Athens on a chariot, on which he had placed a beautiful girl, Phye, dressed as Athena.[42] Regardless of the individual details of this public display or the historical accuracy of Herodotus' account, the description indicates that carriages or chariots were used in 'aristocratic' contexts as a symbol of power. As Sinos (1998) shows, chariots blur the limits between human and divine nature and serve as a vehicle for displaying one's heroic status. Standing higher than the rest of the citizens, charioteers attracted the attention of passers-by and thus advertised their superiority over the rest of the *demos*. Furthermore, it is particularly significant that Meidias used a 'posse', as MacDowell rightly understands the word ἀκολούθους, when he swaggered in the agora. This image is also in pace with Meidias' portrayal as an enemy of the city with tyrannical predilections. As our sources make clear, tyrants relied on bodyguards either to establish or maintain their power.[43] Demosthenes' reference to Meidias' attendants, therefore, highlights his opponent's contempt for the rest of the citizens who are forced by a bunch of bodyguards to get out of his way, but also indicates an outrageous excessiveness, which is in breach with the democratic ethos of the polis.

Before I proceed to discuss Meidias' sympotic possessions, it would be appropriate to comment briefly on the implications of the civic space of the agora for the presentation of Meidias' displays of wealth and power. As Shear argues, (2011: 199–222), "[I]n the context of the years after 411...the construction projects in the Agora allowed the *demos* to gain control of this contested space and to stamp its possession visibly on the square. These structures displayed the democratic system in operation and reinforced the dynamics which we have observed with the inscribed documents. Together, buildings and texts identified the Agora as a space now particularly associated with the rule of the *dēmos*" (222). Shear's comments on the ideological implications of the agora's architecture offer a key to our understanding of why Demosthenes chose to 'stage' the instances of Meidias' ostentation in this ideologically significant public space. Meidias' displays of excessiveness, with all their performative qualities, are set in a civic space that represents the polis' democratic ethos.

According to Demosthenes, Meidias swaggers in the agora and talks loudly about his 'cups', his 'drinking-horns', and his 'chalices'. The audience at these performances of sympotic luxuriousness is his fellow-citizens, in other words

---

[42] On Herodotus' narrative about Phye, see Connor 1987 and Bell 2004: 71–72; for a detailed discussion, see Lavelle 2005: 99–107.
[43] On tyrants' use of bodyguards, see Lavelle 1992.

common people who, just like most of the dikasts, had a frugal lifestyle. However, it is important to bear in mind that the agora was also the place of the Tholos, the public building that served as a meeting place for the *prytaneis*. The Tholos was also the place where the *prytaneis* were fed at public expense. The circular rather than rectangular shape of this building, in which the *prytaneis* dined seated rather than reclined, has been interpreted by scholars as an indication of the democratic polis' ideological distancing from the aristocratic symposium. As Cooper and Morris claim, the Tholos was "perhaps the first politically designed building in Western culture" (1990, 79).[44] Furthermore, several examples of ordinary pottery with the indication ΔΕ, standing for the word δημόσιον, have been taken to indicate the moderation of the democratic *syssitia*.

Even if, as Fisher (2000) has argued, in the course of the late 5th and 4th centuries the symposium, along with other activities of the so-called 'leisure class', became accessible to less powerful and less wealthy citizens, our evidence from the orators indicates that the symposium remained in Athenian civic imagination an 'aristocratic' privilege of the most affluent citizens. Furthermore, orators frequently associate the symposium and heavy drinking with hybristic misconduct. Note for example that in Demosthenes' *Against Conon* (discussed in chapter 3) Ariston, the young prosecutor, claims that before Conon and his sons attacked him in the agora, they were dining in a symposium, while during their military service at Panacton, Conon's sons exhibited the sympotic *hybris* that they habitually practised in the city.[45] In Demosthenes' narrative, Meidias employs his public display of his luxurious sympotic objects as an indication of his superiority in a self-dramatized performance of ostentation.

The fact that Demosthenes places Meidias' loud public displays of private wealth in the agora, the civic centre of Athens which, as we saw, symbolized the rule of the demos, is significant. Meidias' sympotic ostentation contravenes the norms that regulate democratic dining at the Tholos, a building exemplifying the decorousness of modest democratic commensalities. Meidias uses his wealth to obnoxiously advertise his superiority in an environment that symbolizes in every possible way the keystone of democratic ideology, i.e. citizens' equality.

If, as I argued, legitimate envy was democracy's response to elites' projective uses of dispositional envy, their response was both dramatic and confrontational.

---

[44] See also Rotroff/Oakley 1992: 39–50; Steiner 2002: 348–351. On the public nature of dining, see Schmitt-Pantel 1992: 176–177. Luke 1994: 25–32 discusses the democratic features of the *syssition*, including the absence of a 'mixing-bowl' (*krater*).

[45] Cp. Dem. 54. 3–4. For other instances of hybristic behaviour in sympotic contexts, see, for example, Lysias 3; 4; and fr. 279 (Carey), *Agianst Teisis*, also analysed in chapter 3.

Elites' deployment of projective envy as an explanation of the masses' motives relies on the notion that the emotion is 'shamefaced', to use La Rochefoucauld's maxim.[46] Explaining egalitarian claims as motivated by envy is thus a strategy that intimidates its targets and reduces them to silence, in so far as their attempts to explain their real motives are arbitrarily interpreted as transmutations of their base sentiments and, thereby, confirm rather than dispute top-down projective uses of the emotion. The democratic response to these uses through the concept of legitimate envy would not, of course, suffice to eliminate the effectiveness of the elites' projective deployment of envy. But the uses of *phthonos* in democratic contexts to describe the sentiment that uncooperative members of the elites deserved was an effective response to top-down projective envy. In other words, democratic ideology picked up the gauntlet and, by modifying the criteria of application of *phthonos*, directed the sentiment against its ideological opponents.

If the Athenian masses heard Margaret Thatcher comparing them with the Lilliputians who pin Gulliver down, they would certainly get extremely angry. Their natural response would be to invite her to read the following lines from Sophocles' *Ajax* (157–161):

πρὸς γὰρ τὸν ἔχονθ' ὁ φθόνος ἕρπει.
καίτοι σμικροὶ μεγάλων χωρὶς
σφαλερὸν πύργου ῥῦμα πέλονται·
μετὰ γὰρ μεγάλων βαιὸς ἄριστ' ἂν
καὶ μέγας ὀρθοῖθ' ὑπὸ μικροτέρων.

It is against the man who *has* that envy creeps. And yet small men without the great are a treacherous defensive tower; for with the great to help him a humble man might best be kept upright, and a great man too if served by smaller men. (transl. A.F. Garvie)

But if she failed to take their point, she would surely cause their legitimate φθόνος.

---

46 La Rochefoucauld 2007: 10–11.

# 5 Self-praise and envy in rhetoric and the Athenian courts

## 5.1 Introduction

In his article under the title "Ego-Bama Swallow Some of That Pride" (*New York Post*, July 13, 2008), Jonah Goldberg, the author of the book *Liberal Fascism*, called Barack Obama an 'adulation junkie' and commented on his decision to give the acceptance speech at Mile High in Denver with the following words: "Only a man with an Olympian's sense of entitlement to mass worship could describe such a choreographed descent upon a place called 'Mile High' as an effort to bond with the common man. A demigod, it seems, is never so tall as when he stoops to bask in the adoration of the little people." Although I suspect that Goldberg would have been less sarcastic with Isocrates,[1] a strong candidate for the title of 'adulation junkie' in antiquity, his acrimonious language illustrates saliently –note his statement's rich imagery– the dangers involved in self-gratulatory rhetoric.

Ancient authorities seem to have an unfavourable view of self-praise (*periautologia*).[2] Rhetorical treatises and the speeches of the orators include a great range of words –or rather metaphors and metonymies– to designate the psychological *pressures* placed upon listeners of self-eulogizing speakers. As is typically the case with emotion metaphors, the sentiments experienced by listeners of self-eulogizing speakers are conceptualized as embodied feelings, most typically as a heavy burden.[3] Self-praise is thus described in rhetorical practice and theory as ἐπαχθής, φορτικόν, λυπηρόν, and, more importantly for the purposes of the present study, ἐπίφθονον. However, these terms of condemnation concerning the *decorum* of public speaking reflect only the surface appearance of the problem.[4] For pejorative terms such as 'repulsive', 'tasteless' or 'intolerable', along with the embodied metaphors that we saw, may, on a cognitive or cultural level, be viewed

---

1 On envy in the work of Isocrates, see Saïd 2003 and section 3 below.
2 Pernot 1998: 102 n. 2 shows that the first attested occurrence of the term appears in Philodemus; Pernot also provides a full list of sources employing it.
3 On conceptual metaphors and emotions, see Kövecses 2003. For a brief presentation of conceptual metaphors and their implications for ancient emotions, see Cairns' introductory remarks in his chapter on ancient metaphors for hope (2016).
4 These terms are discussed meticulously by Pernot 1998: 107–108. Although Pernot's treatment of the topic is exhaustive, in my view his formalistic approach –focusing on literary rather than cultural criticism– does not pay due attention to the social implications of envy.

as ways of rationalizing and therefore masking a 'shamefaced' emotion (La Rochefoucauld 2007: 11) rarely admitted even to oneself, but still an emotion that figures in every rhetorical treatment of self-praise, namely envy. As Plutarch suggests (see section 2), self-praise compromises listeners' self-esteem.

In the previous chapter, I argued that in the public discourse of classical Athens, and especially in forensic contexts, 'legitimate envy' is sometimes used as the equivalent of Aristotle's 'indignation' (*to nemesan*), i.e. a negative sentiment targeting people who prosper undeservedly, and that these uses reflect instances in which speakers' targets are portrayed as self-interested citizens. In this chapter, my aim is to discuss the rhetoric of self-praise and especially the discursive or other ways that speakers employ or are advised to employ, in order to forestall the (existing, perceived, or projected) envy of their listeners. I also suggest that *periautologia* can give scope for a deeper understanding of envy in the political environment of classical Athens and may therefore be used as a test case about the emotion's function in its uses in arguments.

## 5.2 Self-praise and envy

In his work *How to praise oneself inoffensively*, Plutarch (539D–E) points out that *periautologia* entraps listeners in an embarrassing situation, because to respond with silence to a self-praising speaker may be interpreted as a sign of envy, while enthusiastic approval of boasting indicates servile flattery and therefore compromises listeners' honour (τιμή):[5]

> τρίτον ἢ σιωπῶντες ἄχθεσθαι καὶ φθονεῖν δοκοῦμεν, ἢ τοῦτο δεδοικότες ἀναγκαζόμεθα συνεφάπτεσθαι παρὰ γνώμην τῶν ἐπαίνων καὶ συνεπιμαρτυρεῖν, πρᾶγμα κολακείᾳ μᾶλλον ἀνελευθέρῳ προσῆκον ἢ τιμῇ τὸ ἐπαινεῖν παρόντας ὑπομένοντες.

> [A]nd in the third place if we listen in silence we appear disgruntled and envious, while if we shy at this we are forced to join in the eulogies and confirm them against our better judgment, thus submitting to a thing more in keeping with unmanly flattery than with the showing of esteem –the praise of a man to his face (Loeb transl.).

---

**5** It is therefore always advisable to have others praise you; on this point see Ar. *Rh.* 1418b 23–27 adducing the example of Isocrates' 'friend' in the *Antidosis* (Isocr. 15.141–146). In this connection it is worth noting that Plutarch attributes the pseudonymous publication of Xenophon's *Anabasis* to self-referentiality of the work, which would jeopardize the author's good reputation (*Mor.* 345E). On self-praise and historiography, see Marincola 1997: 175–181.

As Aristotle says, envy is a painful emotion arising from the prosperity of a person who is 'similar' to us; envy therefore requires an unfavourable comparison with someone who seems to possess something that we lack.[6] For this reason, public expression of feelings of envy is commensurate with recognition of one's own inferiority. As Plutarch says, "among the disorders of human mind, envy is the only unmentionable" (ἀπόρρητον, *Mor.* 537E).[7]

In an article that appeared in 1989, Glenn Most concluded that in pre-Hellenistic literature, all the passages including self-presentation in front of strangers relate a story of misfortune or mistreatment. This, according to Most, is a way of mitigating the consequences of psychological imposition upon listeners, especially in a culture where individuals "were preoccupied with preserving their integrity" (127). As we shall see, modern anthropological material from various cultures shows that appeals to misfortunes are commonly employed by people who fear and, thus, wish to forestall the envy of others.

Forensic speeches offer the first instances of non-fictional autobiographical discourse in antiquity.[8] Because ancient litigants supported their cases in person (or by assigning them to supporting speakers, *synegoroi*)[9] and because the arguments that they produced frequently emphasized their conduct in the social and

---

**6** On Aristotle's definition of envy, see ch. 4.

**7** The full passage from Plutarch runs us follows: "For it is a kind of baseness to be hateful to the best of men. But men deny that they envy as well; and if you show that they do, they allege any number of excuses and say they are angry with the fellow or fear or hate him, cloaking and concealing their envy with whatever other name occurs to them for their passion, implying that among the disorders of the soul it is alone unmentionable'[transl. Loeb.]; cp. also *De invidia*, 537E. For the view that envy is an emotion never admitted to oneself or to others and that enviers commonly transmute expressions of their sentiments, see Foster 1972: 165–166 and Elster 1999: 164, 167–169, 183, 351–353 and cp. François La Rochefoucauld 2007: 11: "We often pride ourselves on our passions, even the most criminal ones; but envy is a timid, shamefaced passion, which we never dare to acknowledge". Contrast, however, the careful comments of Cairns 2003: 237–238, who rightly observes that there are cases in which 'transmuted' envy is the righteous indignation of the masses appropriately manipulated by the elites. On envy and inferiority, see Ben Ze'ev 1992.

**8** By non-fictional I do not, of course, mean that ancient litigants' self-referential accounts reflect their 'real' lives. Just like forensic narratives in general, speakers' stories about their past are well calculated tales which, as is argued here, revolve around public concerns. On the orators and autobiography, see Momigliano 1971: 57–58 and Most 1989: 124, who also explains in detail why the use of 'I' in other literary genres, such as lyric poetry or historiography, cannot be interpreted as autobiographical. Antiphon's speech in his own defence was composed for delivery in a real courtroom, but as Gagarin argues, its rhetoric gravitates towards a defence of his entire life (2002: 164).

**9** Rubinstein (2000) offers the most detailed treatment of *synegoria*.

civic life of Athens, forensic speeches are unique in that speakers' autobiographical 'I' is identified with the speaking person rather than a singing chorus, as is the case with, say, Pindar's uses of first person singular. Arisophanes' 'I' in the *parabases* of his plays, self-adulatory as it may be, is impersonated by an actor rather than the poet himself (and note that the poet's praise of his own art is conveyed amid complaints about undeserved ill-treatment in previous *agones* or assertions that his comedy serves the polis' interests).[10] In addition, forensic speakers' 'autobiographical' accounts are shaped decisively by the commonplaces that inform the 'wide angle' perspective of Athenian trials. As we saw in chapter 3, this 'wide angle' contextualization of cases, largely facilitated by the cohesive and relatively uninterrupted narratives that litigants presented in Athenian courts, revolves around what Lanni (2009) describes as 'extra-statutory' social norms that transcend the limits of factual evidence. Hence, forensic speakers' 'autobiographical' points construct an objectivist 'I' on which they project communal concerns, mainstream ideological assumptions, and the shared values of the city.[11]

Forensic speakers' manipulation of listeners' possible sentiments of envy in contexts of self-praising rhetoric is salient in the passages that I discuss briefly in the following pages of this section.

In Gorgias' *Defence of Palamedes* (28), a speech that, as far as I can see, offers the earliest surviving piece of self-praise in Greek rhetoric,[12] Palamedes claims that it was the false accusation brought against him by Odysseus that forced him to display his benefactions to humanity even at the cost of triggering off his listeners' envy. In this speech, the mythical hero Palamedes defends himself against Odysseus' false-accusation that betrayed the Greeks to the barbarians. Not unlike prominent political figures of 4th century Athenian civic life presenting their contributions to the city in forensic contexts or less prominent litigants' speeches in private cases, Palamedes displays his contributions to the community and, hence, highlights a righteous and altruistic version of wisdom which

---

**10** On self-praise in Aristophanes' *parabases*, see Most 1989: 121, emphasizing the deployment of the poet's appeals to previous misfortunes. E.g. in the *Peace* (734–738), comic playwrights who praise-themselves in anapests are presented as deserving corporeal punishment. This rhetorical exaggeration, however, which is underpinned by a solemn oath in the following lines, paves the ground for the chorus' statement that the playwright is worthy of 'great praise' (εὐλογίας μεγάλης).
**11** On the 'objective-participant' conception of the self, see Gill 1996.
**12** The date of *Palamedes* cannot be determined with certainty, but it is possible that it antedates Antiphon's *apologia pro vita sua*.

caused Odysseus' sentiments of envy.[13] The false allegations brought against him, the hero complains, are the product of Odysseus' resentment:

> πρὸς δ' ὑμᾶς ὦ ἄνδρες κριταὶ περὶ ἐμοῦ βούλομαι εἰπεῖν ἐπίφθονον μὲν ἀληθὲς δέ, <μὴ> κατηγορημένῳ μὲν οὐκ ἀνεκτά, κατηγορουμένῳ δὲ προσήκοντα. νῦν γὰρ ἐν ὑμῖν εὐθύνας καὶ λόγον ὑπέχω τοῦ παροιχομένου βίου. δέομαι οὖν ὑμῶν, ἂν ὑμᾶς ὑπομνήσω τῶν τι ἐμοὶ πεπραγμένων καλῶν, μηδένα φθονῆσαι τοῖς λεγομένοις, ἀλλ' ἀναγκαῖον ἡγήσασθαι κατηγορημένον δεινὰ καὶ ψευδῆ καί τι τῶν ἀληθῶν ἀγαθῶν εἰπεῖν ἐν εἰδόσιν ὑμῖν.

> As for you judges, I wish to say something invidious, but true about myself; this would be intolerable for someone not accused but is fitting for an accused man. I am now before you undergoing a scrutiny and giving an account of my past life. So I ask this of you: if I remind you some of the fine things I have done, do not resent what I say. Please understand that since I am falsely accused of terrible crimes, it is necessary for me to mention some good things [about me] to you who already know the truth (transl. Gagarin-Woodruff).

For lack of a real opponent, elderly Isocrates invents one in order to make his self-eulogizing *Antidosis*, a speech in which he defends his *philosophia* and his long career as a teacher, palatable. The fictional legal dispute in which Isocrates defends himself against Lysimachus, an invented prosecutor portrayed as a *sycophant*, concerns, as the title suggests, an *antidosis* case, i.e. a case in which a citizen who failed to challenge an allegedly wealthier citizen to undertake a liturgy in his place was obliged to exchange his property with the latter. As Isocrates says (15.8):

> εἰ μὲν οὖν ἐπαινεῖν ἐμαυτὸν ἐπιχειροίην, ἑώρων οὔτε περιλαβεῖν ἅπαντα περὶ ὧν διελθεῖν προῃρούμην οἷός τε γενησόμενος, οὔτ' ἐπιχαρίτως οὐδ' ἀνεπιφθόνως εἰπεῖν περὶ αὐτῶν δυνησόμενος· εἰ δ' ὑποθείμην ἀγῶνα μὲν καὶ κίνδυνόν τινα περὶ ἐμὲ γιγνόμενον [...] ἐμαυτὸν δ' ἐν ἀπολογίας σχήματι τοὺς λόγους ποιούμενον, οὕτως ἂν ἐκγενέσθαι μοι μάλιστα διαλεχθῆναι περὶ ἁπάντων ὧν τυγχάνω βουλόμενος.

> I saw that, if I were to attempt a eulogy of myself, I would not be able to include everything I chose to cover or speak in an acceptable manner without arousing envy. But I saw that I could treat all the topics I wanted if I invented a lawsuit that threatened me, a sykophant who had brought this charge to cause me problems and who had invoked the slanders employed in the exchange suit, and then composed my arguments after the fashion of a legal defense (transl. Mirhady-Too).

---

[13] Note, however, that even in this model speech concerning the dispute of mythical persons, the speaker refrains from attributing sentiments of envy to his opponent openly: Palamedes presents his opponent's envy as a *possible* motive (εἰ δὲ φθόνῳ, 3).

Finally, in his *On the crown*,¹⁴ a speech delivered by Demosthenes in the summer of 330 in support of Ctesiphon, a citizen prosecuted by Aeschines with a *graphe paranomon* on account of his decree proposing the award of a crown to Demosthenes in public recognition of his services to the city, Demosthenes puts the blame for embarking on a detailed account of his own career and achievements to his opponent (ἀναγκασθήσομαι, ἀναγκάζῃ, 4) and reiterates in the speech, albeit with extreme circumspection, that his words may cause feelings of envy (Dem. 18.4).¹⁵ In this speech, Demosthenes provides a powerful defence of his political career and, if we may judge from dikasts' decision –Aeschines failed to secure one fifth of their votes and was therefore exiled– the speech made a great impression on the audience at the time of its delivery, but also on later rhetoricians. The prominence of self-praise in the speech is thus explained by the very nature of the case, essentially Demosthenes' apologia *pro vita sua*, but it is notable how carefully the speaker prepares the ground for a speech that emphasizes his achievements from its outset. As he says,

> ἐὰν δ' ἐφ' ἃ καὶ πεποίηκα καὶ πεπολίτευμαι βαδίζω, πολλάκις λέγειν ἀναγκασθήσομαι περὶ ἐμαυτοῦ. πειράσομαι μὲν οὖν ὡς μετριώτατα τοῦτο ποιεῖν· ὅ τι δ' ἂν τὸ πρᾶγμα αὔτ' ἀναγκάζῃ, τούτου τὴν αἰτίαν οὗτός ἐστι δίκαιος ἔχειν ὁ τοιοῦτον ἀγῶν' ἐνστησάμενος.

> [While] if I embark on an account of my political achievements, I shall be forced to make many references to myself. Therefore I shall try to do this as modestly as I can; but what I am forced to do by the case itself is fairly to be blamed upon the person who set this prosecution in train –my opponent (transl. Usher).

Notably, in his speech of prosecution, Aeschines had attempted to prejudice the dikasts against Demosthenes, by comparing the psychological effects of his opponent's insufferable boastfulness with nothing less than the distress caused by the defeat of the city at Chaeronea (Aeschin. 3.241). Indeed, given the consequences of this battle on Athens, a battle that essentially marked the end of its independence, the comparison is extremely powerful and, thereby, indicates the dangers involved in aggressive uses of self-praise:¹⁶

---

**14** Yunis 2001: 109 claims that "Demosthenes' mastery of this [sc. self-praise] rhetorical problem became a touchstone for later rhetorical criticism in which self-praise was understood as a problem of decorum'.

**15** Other instances of envy in the speech occur in paragraphs 13, 279, 305, 315.

**16** Note that in the first part of this *a fortiori argument* Aeschines takes it for granted that self-praise is intolerable, even in cases where a speaker's devotion to the city's well-being is beyond doubt. Furthermore, it is worthy of our attention that Aeschines emphasizes the consequences

Οὗτος δ' ἀναβὰς [sc. Δημοσθένης] ἑαυτὸν ἐγκωμιάσει, βαρύτερον τῶν ἔργων ὧν πεπόνθαμεν τὸ ἀκρόαμα γίγνεται. ὅπου γὰρ τοὺς μὲν ὄντως ἄνδρας ἀγαθοὺς οἷς πολλὰ καὶ καλὰ σύνισμεν ἔργα, τοὺς καθ' ἑαυτῶν ἐπαίνους οὐ φέρομεν· ὅταν δὲ ἄνθρωπος αἰσχύνη τῆς πόλεως γεγονὼς ἑαυτὸν ἐγκωμιάζῃ, τίς ἂν τὰ τοιαῦτα καρτερήσειεν ἀκούων;

[If] Demosthenes has the nerve to take the stand and speak in praise of himself, listening to him is more infuriating than our actual misfortunes. For we refuse to accept it when men of real worth, whose many fine achievements we know, speak in their own praise; so when a person who has been a disgrace to the city speaks in praise of himself, who could endure listening to this kind of thing? (transl. Carey).

The passages cited so far anticipate some of the discursive strategies that self-praising speakers deploy in order to avoid listeners' envy. In later rhetorical theory, *periautologia* receives due attention. Plutarch's moralizing treatise on *How to praise oneself inoffensively* offers the most exhaustive treatment of the topic, supported by numerous examples.[17] Plutarch's tone in this admittedly poorly written treatise emphasizing the repercussions of *periautologia* is unusually combative. This may be due to the fact that his examples derive from oratory, a genre in which exaggeration is not uncommon, but also reflects his concern about unrestrained uses of self-praise.[18]

Plutarch provides prospective self-praising speakers no fewer than nine discursive devices that enable them to forestall listeners' envy and most of these devices recur in other treatments of the topic.[19] In what follows, I examine these devices in comparison with modern anthropological material that I draw from Foster's work on envy. This comparison shows that the rhetoric of *periautologia* can give scope for a better understanding of the role of envy in the frame of democratic Athens.

---

of self-praise upon listeners through an embodied metaphor which we commonly find in later rhetorical treatises (see Introduction to this chapter).
17 Other treatments of the topic include Quintilian (11.1.15–26) and Hermogenes, *Meth.* 25, pp. 441–442 Rabe. On Pliny and self-praise, see Gibson 2003 and Whitton 2013. On Aelius Aristides, see n. 19 below.
18 On the addressee of the treatise, possibly C. Julius Eurycles Herculanus L. Vibullius Pius, see Cartledge/Spawforth 2002: 110–116.
19 Aelius Aristides' *Concerning a Remark in Passing*, a work composed to justify an earlier self-gratulatory point made by its author, abounds with examples from earlier literature that also appear in Plutarch's treatise on self-praise. According to Rutherford 1995: 201, these similarities may suggest a common source.

## 5.3 Self-praise and envy avoidance strategies

Foster gathers together anthropological material from various cultures to show that people who fear the envy of others employ four different strategies to forestall it. These strategies are (a) concealment, (b) denial, (c) sop (that is 'symbolic sharing') and (d) true sharing.[20] Concealment means that someone who fears the envy of others will never be boastful nor will she attempt to display enviable possessions. "Denial of reason to be envied takes the forms of both verbal protestations and symbolic acts" (Foster 1972: 176) and commonly consists in highlighting –verbally or in other socially significant manners– one's own sufferings or exaggerating a misfortune. 'Sop', that is symbolic sharing or *offers* to share, is a device that aims to buy off the envy of others, as is the case when drinks or food are offered to celebrate a success. Finally, true sharing is "significant sharing going well beyond symbolic sop levels" (Foster 1972: 179), associated particularly with institutions such as taxation.

Foster's system is exclusive, in that the four forms of action that he isolates are the only available. Furthermore, as Foster says, these cultural forms "fall along a continuum of preferred choices, in the order that I cite them" (175). This means that a possible target will employ denial only when concealment is impossible and so on. Foster's classification of preemptive strategies appeared before the emergence of cognitive analysis of emotions and, therefore, does not take into account appraisal-oriented approaches. In Foster's analysis, concealment, denial, sop and true sharing are viewed as 'mechanisms' rather than as behavioural strategies directly relevant to the cognitive structure of envy. However, the four types of strategies that he proposes are directly relevant to the appraisals that give rise to the emotion. Concealment makes it impossible for possible agents of envy to compare themselves with their target, in so far as enviable possessions are hidden from them. Denial invites modification of the (possible) agent's appraisals concerning the *desert* of the target's enviable possession. Notably, many of Foster's examples involve manipulation of possible agents' appraisals through the construction of pity scripts, i.e. scripts that revolve around targets' misfortunes. Despite Aristotle's view that desert is not enlisted in the appraisals that are characteristic of envy, ancient sources construe pity as the opposite of envy, because they focus on targets' fortunes rather than desert.[21]

---

20 For a different typology of envy avoidance behaviour, see Elster 1999: 178–179.
21 On this point, see previous chapter.

Foster's 'sop sharing', the third preemptive strategy that he found in the cultures that he examined, may also be interpreted as a type of behaviour which diverts agents' attention from targets' possessions. But as Foster points out, symbolic sharing may sometimes increase rather than diminish a possible agent's envious sentiments. For 'sop' may operate as a reminder of existing inequalities. In so far as existing or perceived inequalities prompt agents' thought 'Why not me?', symbolic sharing can do very little to assuage or buy off their envy (I discuss the rhetoric of 'sop' sharing in more detail below).

A close examination of Plutarch's treatment of *periautologia* indicates that the devices suggested to self-praising speakers in ancient authorities fall within one or more of Foster's pre-emptive strategies. Before I proceed to classify them according to Foster, it is important to note that in Plutarch's times rhetoric did not serve the purposes that it served in the polis of classical Athens. As Fields (2008) points out, Plutarch's treatment of self-praise is determined by the political and cultural environment in which he produced the treatise under review. Elites' self-praise under Roman domination was dangerous and politically erosive, because it jeopardized *homonoia*. Hence, if for Athenian speakers self-praise impinged on political equality and was thus self-harming, the *periautologia* of prominent members of the Greek elites in the political context in which Plutarch composed his treatise could result in Roman intervention. In addition, Plutarch's approach to self-praise reflects his own priorities as a moralizer. Note for example that in his treatise *On envy and hatred* he postulates, following Aristotle, that envy targets the prosperous (τοῖς εὖ πράττειν δοκοῦσιν, 537A), while in the second half of the work envy chases the virtuous (τοῖς μᾶλλον ἐπ' ἀρετῇ προϊέναι δοκοῦσι, 537F).[22]

I now proceed to classify Plutarch's suggestions into Foster's scheme.

(a) *Concealment*. All ancient authorities agree that self-praise should be avoided, even as they accept that opportune use may sometimes be necessary or helpful.[23] Since *periautologia* is by definition a public display of one's own merits, concealment is *prima facie* loosely related to it. However, Plutarch allows for the possibility that the display of supreme fortune forestalls envy as effectively as a

---

[22] Desert is a recurring theme in recent discussions of envy; most notably Ben Ze'ev 1992: 563 postulates that envy presupposes undeserved inferiority. On envy and desert in Greece, see Konstan 2006: 120–121.
[23] For an inclusive discussion of the moral restrictions surrounding *periautologia* in ancient rhetorical treatises, see Pernot 1998: 117–120.

great misfortune (538A).[24] This assumption depends on the 'neighborhood theory' that underlies Aristotle's discussion of envy.[25] According to this theory, envy targets those similar to us and, therefore, when the distance between the envier and the envied increases, envy is removed from the agent of this emotion. This, Plutarch says, explains why many people hated, but did not envy Alexander (538B).[26] Consequently, Plutarch suggests that self-praise, or rather aggressive uses of self-praise, is a useful tool in the hands of distinguished speakers who aim to humble headstrong listeners (544F; cp. also 540D).

(b) *Denial* takes the forms of verbal protestations or symbolic acts. As Foster's examples show, this device commonly involves appeals to or exaggeration of a misfortune[27] and responding to compliments with expressions of modesty. As we already saw, as early as Gorgias self-praising speakers extenuate self-gratulatory accounts through appeals to unwarranted accusations. Plutarch, who makes opportune occasion (*kairos*) conditional for embarking on *periautologia*, emphasizes the appropriate *état d'être* of self-praising speakers. He thus claims that *periautologia* is advisable only when one defends oneself against false accusations (ἀπολογούμενος, 540C)[28] or is the victim of a misfortune (δυστυχοῦσι, 541A) or of a wrongdoing (ἀδικουμένῳ, 541C).[29] As is clear, the headings 'false accusation' and 'injustice' can be classified under 'misfortune'. The reason why misfortunes

---

**24** The same line of argument is also taken by Isocrates, when he suggests that envy is never at work in monarchies, because of the great distance separating the ruler from his subjects (Isocr. 3.18); on this point, see Saïd 2003: 223. Cairns 2003: 239, though, shows convincingly that envy can also be a top-down emotion (cp. Ar. *Rh.* 1387b 29; *Pol.* 1295b 21–3; and Hdt. 3.80 with Elster 1999: 186–187).
**25** On Aristotle and the neighbourhood theory, see Elster 1999: 170.
**26** As far as I can see, Foster does not discuss this type of aggressive exploitation of envy. On Isocrates' aggressive rhetoric of envy in the *Antidosis* (cp. esp. Isocr.15.13), see Saïd 2003: 225.
**27** On the importance of misfortunes in autobiographical accounts, see Most 1989.
**28** For similar views, see Quintilian, *I.O.* 11.1.16; 11.1.22 (on Demosthenes' *On the crown*); Ps.-Dionysius (*On Figured Speeches* 1.8) on Plato's *Apology*; Ps.-Aristides, *On Political Language* (2.506.8–20); Ps.-Hermogenes, *On the method of power* 442.6ff.
**29** Cp. Dionysius' hostile criticism of Pericles' speech in Thucydides (2.45): "it would be remarkable if Pericles, the greatest orator of his day, did not know what every man of average intelligence must have known, that while in all orations speakers who praise their own virtues without restraint invariably exasperate their audiences (οἱ μὴ τεταμιευμένως ἐπαινοῦντες τὰς ἑαυτῶν ἀρετὰς ἐπαχθεῖς τοῖς ἀκούουσι φαίνονται), this is especially so when they are on trial in the lawcourts or in the assembly, where they face the prospect not of loss of prestige but of actual punishment. In such circumstances they not only annoy others but also bring misfortune upon themselves by evoking the hatred of the populace (ἐκκαλούμενοι τὸν παρὰ τῶν πολλῶν φθόνον)" (Loeb. transl.). Plutarch cites the same passage approvingly (540C), because, as he claims, Pericles defends himself against wrongful accusations.

assuage envy is revealed in a context where Plutarch seems to draw on peripatetic sources.[30] 'Misfortunes' he says, 'put an end to envy' and 'those who envy take the greatest delight in pitying' (538B–C). Appeals to misfortune mitigate envy, or even transform it into pity, because the appropriate feeling towards undeserved suffering is pity, not envy.[31] It is therefore the case that, comforted by speakers' misfortunes, listeners who are prone to envy are much likelier to lend a favourable ear to self-praise. Consequently, appeals to misfortunes enable self-praisers to have their cake and eat it too, especially in the context of Athenian courts of law, where appeals to pity indicate speakers' respectful recognition of the power handed over to the dikasts by the *demos*.[32] But more importantly, defendants' identification of the lawsuit to which they have been dragged with an unwarranted 'misfortune' is in pace with Athenian' defendants' unequivocal self-presentation as victims of their opponents' false-accusations.

In addition to considerations of opportunity, rhetorical theory proposes discursive devices corresponding to 'denial'. Plutarch suggests that references to unimportant shortcomings or mistakes can effectively mitigate the splendour of excessive glorification (543F). Furthermore, he advises speakers to shift the load of their glory to God or chance, given that good fortune dispels concerns of undeserved inferiority (542E).[33] By pretending to be equal with their listeners, speakers make their audiences loose sight of their inferiority.

(c) Sop-sharing. What Foster calls 'sop-sharing' has received much scholarly discussion recently, especially in studies focusing on the significance of envy in the social tension between the elites and the masses in classical Athens. Symbolic sharing is prominent in theoretical discussions of *periautologia*. 'Sop' in the relevant literature most commonly takes the forms of either mingling self-praise with praise of the listeners[34] or, most importantly, stressing one's own commitment to co-operative values and one's services to the city (543A–B), thereby avoiding to appear self-important. As Plutarch says, when people praise you for your wealth or power, it is advisable that you employ *correctio* (ἐπανόρθωσις) and protest that you should rather be praised for being 'virtuous' (χρηστός) or 'harmless' (ἀβλαβής), or 'useful' (ὠφέλιμος). Although Plutarch's advice is offered to elites

---

30 See Spatharas 2013.
31 On pity and envy in Aristotle, see Ben Ze'ev 2003 and Konstan 2006: 128.
32 On the implications of pity in Athenian courtrooms, see Johnstone 1999: 122–125. On pity and Athenian politics, see Konstan 2005.
33 On luck and desert, see Ben Ze'ev 2003: 110.
34 Plutarch praises Demosthenes for his masterful use of this technique in *De corona*; for an illustrating example from this speech, cp. Dem. 18. 304–305.

that operated in a significantly different political environment from that of classical Athens, it is compatible with the line of thought endorsed by the authors of treatises composed during the classical period and forensic speakers' rhetorical strategies.[35] As a matter of fact, the identification of one's own achievements with the polis' interests is one of the most recognizable ways in which speakers preempt their isolation from the body of citizens.

As we saw, Foster understands 'sop sharing' as a means of 'buying off' possible agents' envy. This understanding of 'sop' is sometimes used in modern discussions of the social tensions between the elites and the masses in classical Athens, especially in discussions centering on the rhetoric of liturgies and therefore invites our attention. In a paper about the politics of envy in classical Athens, Douglas Cairns (2003) argued that readings taking the masses' envy for granted and elite expenditure as a means of assuaging the masses' emotion are ill-founded. As we saw in the previous chapter, these readings are biased by elite writers' essentialist conceptualization of envy as a dispositional characteristic of the masses. Furthermore, when we take the masses' envy for granted, we do not pay due attention to the nature and the purposes of our sources. Because emotions involve evaluative appraisals, our task is to pin down how *projecting* feelings of envy on the masses enhances relevant ideological uses of the emotion.

In the rhetoric of self-praise, 'sop' sharing must be understood as the product of Athens' egalitarian ideology and, correlatively, of the tensions caused by the prominence of citizens, such as Demosthenes or Aeschines, who professed to possess the knowledge and skills that enabled them to have a leading role in the city's politics. As Sanders rightly points out (2014: 87), "accusing someone of envy directly is highly antagonistic, and when that 'someone' is the *dêmos*, politically potentially suicidal". This explains why dispositional envy is attributed to the masses only by elite *writers*, such as Isocrates or Aristotle, rather than public speakers addressing audiences of citizens.

---

[35] Cp. also Anaximenes, *Rhetorica ad Alexandrum* 1442a 6–16: δεῖ δὲ αὐτοὺς ἐκ τούτων ἐπαινεῖν, ὧν μάλιστα μέτεστι τοῖς ἀκούουσι, λέγω δὲ φιλόπολιν φιλέταιρον ‹εὐχάριστον› ἐλεήμονα τὰ τοιαῦτα, τὸν δ' ἐναντίον κακολογεῖν ἐκ τούτων, ἐφ' οἷς οἱ ἀκούοντες ὀργιοῦνται, ταῦτα δέ ἐστι μισόπολιν μισόφιλον ἀχάριστον ἀνελεήμονα τὰ τοιαῦτα; Alexander, *De figuris* 16.6 (discussing a specific type of *correctio*); Ps.-Aristides, *On Political Language* 2.506.8–20. Examples from the orators include Dem. 18.299 and *Ep.* 2.24, stressing that his loyalty to the city is enough to remove envy from his audience. On cooperative values, and especially *eunoia*, see Whitehead 1993; Ober 2005: 138–141; on the relationship between the ideology of the middling citizen (*metrios*), a pivotal notion in Demosthenes' *On the crown*, and these values, see Morris 1996.

In my view, however, the 'potentially suicidal' projection of envy on the masses are better explained if we emphasize the social tensions between the *demos* and elite speakers, especially so because in classical Athens these social tensions were negotiated in an environment that favoured a distinctively egalitarian ideology (see previous chapter). The predominance of political equality in the ideological discourse of classical Athens is directly relevant to the rhetorical uses of envy in the frame of *periautologia*: to emphasize self-assertively your superiority in front of your fellow-citizens was commensurate with counter-intuitive misrecognition of the friction between your status as a privileged and *philotimos* speaker and the status of the masses which controlled the granting of honours by forming majorities.

It is noteworthy that audiences' 'envy' is *explicitly* expressed as a possible outcome of self-eulogizing discourse only in forensic speeches dealing with major political issues. Because these speeches deal with speakers' contribution to the polis' public affairs, audiences' envy is cautiously treated as an avoidable possibility which necessitates integrative rhetorical strategies. In these instances, 'sharing' is predictably the most appropriate tool through which speakers avoid isolation from the community of equals. But at the same time, speakers' circumspect references to audiences' possible sentiments of envy in major political trials are also symptomatic of their deployment of the emotion as a way of indicating their merits and personal achievements. Hence, the desired goal of speakers' circumspectly expressed anticipation of possible, albeit unwarranted sentiments of envy is no different from the purposes served by Isocrates' aggressive uses of the emotion in his *Antidosis*. Even as no public speaker would identify his audiences' (dispositional) envy with a disease (Isocr. 15.13), public speakers' pleas for favourable, unresentful responses to their elaborate accounts of their achievements –accounts made necessary by their opponents' malicious accusations– are essentially an enhanced way of self-advertisement. What distinguishes privately writing and, therefore, overtly boasting Isocrates from public speakers is chiefly that the latter present their achievements either as the result of their cooperation with the demos or by providing evidence of how the demos recognized their services. Hence, the rhetorical manipulation of envy by speakers who address real audiences encourages the demos, represented by the dikasts, to respond with sentiments of legitimate envy (or what Aristotle describes as *to nemesan*) to all those who, unlike them, isolate themselves from the citizenry of equals.

In the next section, I discuss passages from the orators illustrating how self-praising speakers appeal to cooperative values[36] or emphasize their concern for

---

36 On the forensic uses of cooperative, 'extra-statutory' values, see Lanni 2009.

the common good to pre-empt the consequences of their isolation from the body of the citizens.

## 5.4 Self-praise and cooperation in classical Athens

The discussion so far has shown that rhetorical manipulation of *periautologia* goes hand in hand with envy avoidance devices. However, as I suggested, the projection of sentiments of envy upon one's opponents or audience sometimes enhances self-laudatory discourse for reasons which are directly relevant to the cognitions that give rise to the emotion. To claim that others may envy you implies that you have an enviable possession, quality, or skill. As the Chorus puts it in Sophocles' *Ajax* (157) "it is on the powerful that envy creeps" (transl. Jebb).[37] It is therefore a common practice of self-praising speakers to extol their merits by claiming that legal action against them was ignited by their opponents' maliciousness. Demosthenes, for instance, describes Aeschines' legal attempt to deprive him of the crown as a *dike phthonou* (Dem. 18.121).

In Gorgias' *Defence of Palamedes* that we saw earlier, the mythical hero displays his benefactions to humanity in a context that alludes to *euthyna*. Gorgias thus invests Palamedes with the qualities of an Athenian litigant who presents his services to the state.[38] The emphasis that Palamedes places on his benefactions not only draws a clear line of distinction between his own altruistic resourcefulness and Odysseus' self-serving type of wisdom, but also prepares the ground for his declaration of commitment to such cooperative values as those that we find in Gorgias' *Funeral Oration*, thereby underscoring the importance of his inventiveness for the common good. Palamedes is compassionate (οἰκτίρμων, 32), he incorporates the ideal of a 'middling' citizen (15), he is 'useful' to the community (οὐκ ἀνωφελής, 32). Indeed, envy is one of the motives that according to

---

**37** Note that the Chorus, depicted throughout the play as dependent on Ajax, projects envy on the hero's enemies (on tragic envy, see Goldhill 2003). The assumption that envy targets men of distinction makes envy a prominent theme in encomiastic contexts, and especially in the funeral speeches and epinician poetry. On the emotion's delicate deployment in epinician poetry, see Eitrem 1951–1953; Kirkwood 1984; Vallozza 1989; Bulman 1992; Most 2003. Examples from the funeral speeches include Gorgias (fr. 6); Pl. *Menex.* 242a; Dem. 60.23. Cp. also Isocr. 9.39; 10.30.
**38** Gorgias' passage is the following (32): "I cause no pain to the old, am not unhelpful to the young, do not envy the fortunate, and have compassion for the unfortunate. I neither scorn poverty nor honor wealth above *arete*, but *arete* above wealth. I am not useless in councils or lazy in battles but carry out my assignment and obey those in charge. It is not my business to praise myself, but the present situation and the accusations made against me have compelled me to defend myself in every way" (transl. Gagarin-Woodruff).

Palamedes may have induced Odysseus to bring against him a charge of treason (3). In the context of the present speech, the projection of envy onto Odysseus serves both the purpose of denigrating a knavish opponent, but also indicates the superiority of Palamedes' resourcefulness and wisdom, qualities which are beneficial for the whole community.[39]

Like Palamedes in Gorgias' model speech (note that the phrase παροιχόμενος βίος appears three times in the text, 15, 22, 29) real defendants in Athenian courtrooms frequently appeal to their past lives (πίστεις ἐκ τοῦ βίου) in order to convince jurors about their innocence or warn them about the repercussions of a possible conviction. As is expected, the effectiveness of these accounts depends upon the appropriate presentation of the speaker's *ethos*, a presentation that commonly highlights one's adherence to the norms favoured by the community. These accounts are essentially arguments from probability (*eikos*), because they seek to establish on a conceptual level that it is not possible for a man who has lived an exemplary life to have committed the crimes that he is accused of.[40] The stories about speakers' personal achievements vary in length according to the nature of each individual case,[41] but in a good deal of speeches (especially those composed for *dokimasiai*, 'scrutinies') we find some quite extensive accounts. In the self-eulogizing sections, defendants highlight their services to the city, thereby suggesting not only that a possible conviction would harm the city's interests and well-being, but also that the jurors, who are commonly taken to represent the body of citizens as whole, must express their gratitude (*charis*) in exchange for their public services.

In a speech by Lysias concerning a case of bribery (Lys. 21),[42] the speaker offers an extensive description of his past life. He thus advertises the liturgies that he undertook for the state and offers a long list of the victories that he won in athletic games and choral contests. The presentation of his liturgies reaches a climax when he says, indeed, very cautiously, that during an expedition, Alcibiades, who was fussy about his own safety (and, just like the speaker, a very generous liturgist), chose to travel on a trireme that the speaker had lavishly equipped

---

**39** On 'sophistic' types of wisdom, see Worman 2008 *passim*.
**40** See Lanni 2006: 60–61, who rightly points out that the persuasiveness of these arguments depends on the assumption that character is "stable and unchanging" (60). See also Johnstone 1999: 97–97.
**41** As is expected, these accounts appear more frequently in speeches of defence; on this point see Lanni 2006: 63 with further literature.
**42** This is the earliest extant example of a speaker presenting his liturgies; Lysias' client defends himself in an *euthyna* (a public official's account of his conduct); for a convenient presentation of the speech, see Usher 1999: 72–74.

(21.7). Although it is the case that the defendant seems to be unapologetic for presenting his achievements in length, it is important to bear in mind that he faces a charge of bribery and therefore he has every reason to exaggerate his expensive liturgies, thereby suggesting that he had no need to take bribes.[43] At the same time, his self-praise is so designed as to stress his commitment to such democratic values as decency and self-restraint (*kosmios* and *sophron*, 21.19)[44] and his concern for the common good which, as he says, he values ahead of his personal well-being and the safety of his family (21.23–24). Furthermore, when at some point he attempts to neutralize the opponents' attempt to arouse dikasts' feelings of envy, he warns them that a possible conviction would be equally harmful to them insofar as they will cease to have a share in his wealth. As he puts it in an elaborate reversal of the accusation that he is facing (21.16),

> ἡγοῦμαι δ', ὦ ἄνδρες δικασταί (καὶ μηδεὶς ὑμῶν ἀχθεσθῇ), πολὺ ἂν δικαιότερον ὑμᾶς ὑπὸ τῶν ζητητῶν ἀπογραφῆναι τὰ ἐμὰ ἔχειν, ἢ ἐμὲ νυνὶ κινδυνεύειν ὡς τοῦ δημοσίου χρήματα ἔχοντα.
>
> In my view, gentlemen of the jury,– please do not be annoyed at this suggestion– it would be far more just for you to face an *apographe* ('writ of confiscation') in front of the commission of investigators (*zetetai*) on a charge of possessing my property than for me now to be prosecuted for possessing property belonging to the Treasury (transl. Todd).

In another speech by Lysias (Lys. 16), the young speaker, a certain Mantitheus, defends himself in a *dokimasia* against the allegation that he served in the cavalry under the Thirty. The nature of this procedure, involving examination of a person's right to hold a public office or entitlement to a privilege, made it necessary for scrutinized speakers to provide jurors with rather elaborate accounts of their civic lives. Following a rhetorical *topos*, Mantitheus expresses his gratitude to his accusers for giving him the opportunity to defend the whole of his life. In doing so, Mantitheus implies that his references to his own civic merits and achievements were necessitated by the accuser's groundless allegations. Since Mantitheus is a young aristocrat and indeed one who, despite the amnesty of 403/2,

---

[43] Davies 1971: 592–593 suggests that the speaker's father was involved in the oligarchy of the Four Hundred; consequently, his unusually expensive liturgies were intended to restore his name.

[44] According to the speaker's own words, to live with self-restraint and decency is the most painstaking liturgy; cp. also the words of a client of Isaeus (fr. 131 Sauppe), according to whom the most important liturgy is to live decently and with self-restraint. On *kosmos*, see Cartledge 1998; on *sophrosyne* as a cooperative value see Whitehead 1993; on the uses of *sophrosyne* by the orators see Rademaker 2005: 233–247 and Lanni 2006: 26.

is now accused of oligarchic predilections, he delivers a speech that seeks to establish that he is a man loyal to democracy and also a middling citizen (μετρίως βεβιωκώς, 3).⁴⁵

After some brief comments on his exemplary family life (16.10–11), that corroborate his self-presentation as a *metrios* citizen who was brought up in a democratic environment, Mantitheus refers to his bravery in the military campaigns and his readiness to sacrifice his personal safety: he preferred, out of free choice, as he says, to fight with the hoplites rather than the cavalry. In this context (16.14), Mantitheus also mentions in passing that before the battle at Haliartus he gave thirty drachmas each to two soldiers. This gesture, he says, was meant to serve as an example for other wealthy citizens, not as a display of his wealth. This is a clear instance in which 'symbolic' sharing is deployed to indicate a wealthy citizens' adherence to the collaborative values of the city and, thereby, forestall dikasts' possible prejudices against his origin.

Having sketched his ethos in such democratic colours, towards the end of the speech Mantitheus feels no hesitation to claim that he is politically ambitious (φιλοτίμως καὶ κοσμίως πολιτευομένους, 16.18) and invites jurors to avoid interpreting his appearance as a sign of antidemocratic feelings.⁴⁶ Mantitheus thus expresses his commitment to democratic *philotimia*, according to which the community bestowed honours to ambitious individuals in return for their pursuit of common good, but at the same time he emphasizes that his personal ambition is controlled by his sense of decency towards his fellow-citizens.⁴⁷ *For Mantitheus* is a speech whose rhetoric is directly relevant to current political concerns and shows the extent to which forensic storytelling may be viewed as a barometer of such issues. However, it is particularly important for the purposes of the present study that in his account of his life, no doubt the product of Lysias' careful selection of appropriate narrative material, emphasizes Mantitheus' concern for the public interest.

Although one may argue that Lysias' speech for this wealthy client, a client who tactfully endorses a low-profile, and, thereby, does not advertise openly his achievements, is primarily designed to address dikasts' possible sentiments of anger on account of the speaker's political predilections, it is equally important

---

**45** On the ideological assumptions surrounding the middling citizen, see Morris 1996.
**46** The majority of scholars adopt Hamaker's ingenious emendation of τολμᾷ to κομᾷ ('wearing long hair') at 18. This habit was associated with the Spartans and could thus be interpreted as a sign of oligarchic sentiments.
**47** On *philotimia*, see Whitehead 1983; Wilson 2000: 171–197 and my discussion of the term in the previous chapter. On *philotimia* in this passage, see Fisher 2003: 192–193.

that, as we saw, the speech, through its narrative specificity, frames Manitheus' case by addressing issues related to social inequality. Mantitheus' life is exemplary because loyalty to the democratic ethos of the polis means that one is ready to help, i.e. share his property, with the masses' less privileged members.

Although by virtue of their nature the *dokimasia* speeches that I discussed emphasize scrutinized citizens' past life, in none of these speeches does the label 'envy' appear. As I pointed out earlier, *phthonos* is salient in self-eulogizing contexts of speeches dealing with major political disputes, where prominent citizens defend their political actions. Envy, however, looms large in the least suspected place, namely a *dokimasia* speech (Lys. 24), where an unnamed man, described as an old cripple, defends himself against his opponent's allegations that he does not deserve the humble pension that he receives from the state on account of his inability to work.

Lysias' speech is characterized by *pathos*, humour, and possibly irony. Scholarly views concerning the speaker's arguments are divided: Usher's verdict is that the proofs are untidy and unconvincing, while Carey supported the view that Lysias employs 'guerilla tactics' –mainly humorous digressions– by way of trivializing the case: the small amount that the invalid receives from the city does not even deserve a scrutiny from the Boule.[48] Admittedly, it is extremely difficult to determine the nature of the speech and analyse the persuasive strategies that the speaker employs here. If the speaker is a poor man who is on the dole, how did he secure the money to pay a logographer of Lysias' caliber? And does, as Harding points out (1994: 203), the speech's ambiguous title (if, of course, the title belongs to Lysias) reveal its intentionality? *peri*, instead of *hyper*, and *adynaton* (neuter, '*the* impossible') rather than *adynatos* (masc. 'the invalid'), i.e. *On the impossible*. In other words, is this speech an exercise in making the worse argument into the better on the basis of an indefensible case?

The speech for the invalid, I would suggest, offers a particularly interesting test case for my discussion of envy and *periautologia*. From the outset of the speech, the invalid employs *reductio ad absurdum* to conclude that his opponent was motivated by envy, because, as he boastfully claims, his entire life is praiseworthy. Enmity, the speaker says, was not a possible motive for the prosecution, because, on account of his opponent's moral baseness, he had no relationship with him in the past. More importantly perhaps, he excludes monetary gain through a strong aposiopesis (εἰ μὲν γὰρ ἕνεκα χρημάτων με συκοφαντεῖ –, 24.2)

The cause of his opponent's envy invites our attention: his envy, he says, was ignited by the fact that *he* (the invalid) was a better citizen than the accuser. This

---

[48] Usher 1985; Carey 1990.

is a pugnacious use of the emotion which establishes that the speaker is morally superior to his opponent (as a matter of fact, the speaker would be unwilling to befriend the opponent because of the latter's 'villainy', πονηρίαν 24.2) Notably, this boastful declaration is expressed in a context identifying, as is typically the case with *dokimasia* proems, the present legal procedure with an opportunity for the speaker to present his entire civic life in public. In view of the fact that in the extant speeches envy is expressly presented as a possible outcome of self-praise only in trials concerning major political disputes, delivered by prominent citizens defending their public conduct and careers, the invalid's unabashed attribution of sentiments of envy to his opponent gains further significance.

In his discussion of envy in this speech, Ed Sanders points out that the invalid foists on his opponent dispositional envy to deal with his use of "*to nemesan*-type emotion, or rather 'good *phthonos*,' since it relates to a putative abuse of money— even though very little money is actually at stake" (2014: 85). Yet, the use of *to nemesan*-type emotion (discussed in chapter 4), which, as Sanders rightly maintains, was sometimes also expressed with the word *phthonos*, would not do much to support the invalid's *opponent's* argument. As far as we can see, indignation (*nemesan*) is employed in the frame of attacks directed against people with substantial wealth who indulge in ostentatious lifestyle and refuse to serve the polis' interests, say a wealthy man of Meidias' calibre. Even if the invalid's property was more than three *minae*, as his opponent alleges, this amount of money would not, in my view, suffice to substantiate a scenario of indignation or what I call 'legitimate envy' (chapter 4). Indeed, the *nemesan* scenario *is* envisaged by the speaker, albeit sarcastically, when he addresses the possibility that his opponent brought him to the court out of *phthonos* for his money (2).

As I suggest in the following paragraphs, 'indignation' is useful to the *speaker* rather than his opponent. By assuming that the prosecutor was motivated by sentiments of 'legitimate envy' in the frame of a *reductio ad absurdum*, the speaker enhances significantly the irony of the speech. Conversely, to claim, along with Sanders' line of interpretation, that the opponent's prosecution *relied* on *to nemesan*-type emotion and that the speaker seeks to refute it would be commensurate with believing that the prosecutor *really* argued that the invalid was fortunate enough to use two crutches, while others used only one or that in his speech of prosecution he presented the disabled man as a 'wealthy heiress'. If he did so, he would have very little chance to win the case –this allegation would indeed cause the audience's laughter. Dikasts' laughter, I suggest, is more suitable for the invalid's argumentative purposes.

As Wohl points out (forthcoming), comic irony in this speech highlights the invalid's opponent's 'deliberate deception'.[49] Hence, even as Sanders is right that *to nemesan*-type emotion, an emotion that targets people who prosper undeservedly, plays a significant role in the invalid's argumentation, I would suggest that its deployment in the present speech is due to the fact that Lysias saw fit to project it onto his client's opponent in an attempt to 'interpret' his motives for taking legal action against the invalid. By doing so, the invalid emphasizes in a markedly ironic fashion the incongruity of a prosecution that does not even deserve a scrutiny. In other words, the invalid's serious tone about his opponent's alleged motives, the very fact that his opponent proposes seriously that the defendant is worthy of 'indignation' (or, 'legitimate envy'), an emotion revolving around unwarranted, but significant prosperity, enhances the irony of a speech delivered for a mere obol and, thereby, trivializes the case. To put it differently, because the projection of 'legitimate envy' onto the invalid's opponent requires the impossible assumption that the crippled man who speaks in front of the Boule belongs to the elite of wealth, it contributes to the *reductio ad absurdum* (and the irony) that determines the rhetoric of the speech. Thus, the subsersive use of 'legitimate envy' is analogous to the invalid's ironic point that he is a wealthy heiress or the outrageous hypothesis that he might undertake the funding and supervision of a dramatic production as a *choregos*. Through the use of irony the invalid indicates the absurdity of his opponent's legal action against him, possibly motivated, as he says, by his insolently playful capriciousness (ἀλλ' ἐμὲ κωμῳδεῖν βουλόμενος, 18), an aspect of his hybristic character.

But if the projection of the morally and socially responsive emotion of 'legitimate envy' onto the opponent contributes to the speaker's attempt to throw into relief the prosecutor's deceitful falsifications, how should we understand his statement that the prosecutor envies him because he is a better citizen (3) and because his conduct throughout his life has been praiseworthy (ἐπαίνου μᾶλλον ἄξιον ἢ φθόνου, 1)? And what are the distinctive characteristics of the *periautologia* of a man who, on account of his disability and poverty cannot include in his account of his past life his services to the city?

---

**49** V. Wohl "Irony, suspicion, and the temporality of legal narrative in Lysias 1 *On the Murder of Eratosthenes,*" in M. Edwards/D. Spatharas (eds.), *Forensic narratives in Athenian courts* (London). In the *Rhetoric* (1415b 36–38), Aristotle points out that in some cases it is impractical to make hearer's attentive and that laughter is a good tool to divert their attention from serious points highlighted by one's opponent. On the use of humour in the speech, see Carey 1990.

The *periautologia* that Lysias composed for the invalid invests, in my view, in the incongruity between the social and civic invisibility of his client and his unexpected appearance in the proceedings of a public scrutiny. Despite the idiosyncrasies of the speech, the invalid's aggressive use of envy –embedded in a markedly self-praising speech– is comparable with the emotion's uses in speeches dealing with high-stakes. What invites our full attention in discussing Lysias' present speech is the emphasis that the invalid places on potent civic considerations. For example, when he says that his opponent envies rather than pities him, thereby construing pity as the opposite of envy, he does more than just substantiate his unfortunate condition: he accuses his prosecutor of anti-social behaviour and violation of typical Athenian attitudes towards misfortune and poverty.

As has been noted, in the idealized conceptualizations of Athenian identity that we find in our sources, and especially in the funeral speeches, compassion plays a predominant role.[50] In his speech *Against Androtion*, Demosthenes points out that pity, a merit of free men, is a characteristic of the laws ('Contained in them, on the contrary, are pity, forgiveness, all the qualities free men ought to possess' 22.57, transl. E. Harris),[51] and elsewhere, he identifies it as a distinctive characteristic of Athenian *ethos* (24.171).[52] Furthermore, as we noted earlier, in his speech of defence Palamedes emphasizes his compassionate nature and thereby highlights the altruistic nature of his benefactions, while wealthy Mantitheus indicates his generosity by offering an amount of money to his fellow-soldiers during a military campaing. At paragraph 7, the invalid appeals to jurors' compassionate nature (ἐλεημονέστατοι) in an attempt to involve them emotionally in his case *and* emphasize his opponent's insensitivity to the *polis'* values. In fact, the speaker insinuates that his opponent's legal action against him is commensurate with *hybris* (16), a typical characteristic of wealthy citizens who are sufficiently confident that their humiliating displays of superiority will remain unpunished.

The invalid's identification of the prosecutor's legal action against him with *hybris* not only underscores the latter's self-indulgent sense of superiority which he showcases by dragging the crippled man to the court out of a reckless playfulness, but also, or rather correlatively, indicates his antidemocratic feelings. Note

---

[50] On this point, see Loraux 1986: 67; Tzanetou 2005; on non-tragic pity in Athens, see Sternberg 2006.
[51] ἀλλ' οὐ ταῦτα λέγουσιν οἱ νόμοι, οὐδὲ τὰ τῆς πολιτείας ἔθη, ἃ φυλακτέον ὑμῖν. ἀλλ' ἔνεστ' ἔλεος, συγγνώμη, πάνθ' ἃ προσήκει τοῖς ἐλευθέροις.
[52] τοὺς ἀσθενεῖς ἐλεεῖν, τοῖς ἰσχυροῖς καὶ δυναμένοις μὴ ἐπιτρέπειν ὑβρίζειν, οὐ τοὺς μὲν πολλοὺς ὠμῶς μεταχειρίζεσθαι, κολακεύειν δὲ τὸν ἀεί τι δύνασθαι δοκοῦντα.

also that towards the end of the speech, the invalid addresses his opponent's allegation that he is a violent hybrist by emphasizing that he did not collaborate with the Thirty (25). In view of the oligarch's elitism –i.e. the audience would not believe that the oligarchs enlisted a man like the speaker in their forces–, this is another instance in which the speaker endorses subversive irony to defend himself. The irony is notably underpinned by the fact that accusations about oligarchic predilections are common in *dokimasiai* (cp. for example the case of Mantitheus that I discussed earlier).

I would therefore conclude –even as sweeping answers are impossible– that Carey (1990: 49) is right when he says that the rhetoric of this speech reflects the idiosyncratic characteristics of the case at hand and that "[T]he logographer's technique ... may reasonably be described as verbal guerilla tactics, a regular sequence of attacks on his subject followed by retreats into entertaining or emotive irrelevance". The use of legitimate envy (*to nemesan*) enhances the speaker's 'guerilla tactics'. Its projection onto the opponent as a possible motive for the prosecution that he brought against the invalid is in pace with the speech's irony. The effectiveness of the projective use of *to nemesan*, an emotion that, as we saw, is directed against wealthy individuals, is brought out by the invalid's emphasis on the insignificant stake of this case in the concluding paragraphs, where he asks dikasts to bear in mind that his defence concerns a mere obol:

> τὴν αὐτὴν ψῆφον θέσθε περὶ ἐμοῦ ταῖς ἄλλαις βουλαῖς, ἀναμνησθέντες ὅτι οὔτε χρήματα διαχειρίσας τῆς πόλεως δίδωμι λόγον αὐτῶν, οὔτε ἀρχὴν ἄρξας οὐδεμίαν εὐθύνας ὑπέχω νῦν αὐτῆς, ἀλλὰ περὶ ὀβολοῦ μόνον ποιοῦμαι τοὺς λόγους (26).

> Cast the same vote for me as your predecessors have done. Remember that I am not giving an account after administering public funds, and I have not held any public office for which I am now undergoing the audit of my accounts (*eutunai*); but instead I am making this speech simply for a simple obol (transl. Todd).

The subversive deployment of 'legitimate envy' in the speech, underscores the invalid's admittedly bold allegation that the prosecutor envies him for being a better citizen. The invalid may be poor and unable to advertise his services to the city, but, unlike his opponent, he is not an insolent member of the elite who takes advantage of his power to display his social superiority. Depite his disability, his ethos is more akin to the ideals shared by the dikasts. Notably, as he points out at the very end of the speech, their vote will put an end to his opponent's insolent attempts "to plot against those who are weaker thank himself" (26, transl. Todd). As his life indicates, the invalid is a champion of Athenian democratic values and, thereby, the victim of anti-democratic *hybris*.

In the rest of this chapter I discuss instances of *periautologia* that we find in the speeches of major Athenian figures. In his speech on the *False embassy*, Demosthenes provides a denigrating description of Aeschines' conduct, in the context of which he sarcastically calls his opponent a 'splendid soldier' (113). In his speech of defence under the same title, Aeschines replies to this heavy sarcasm by offering a rather extensive list of his military services, including details about the expeditions in which he participated when he was still an *ephebos* and a list of the military campaigns on which he served. Aeschines also stresses that on one occasion the Athenians awarded him a crown for his bravery (167–171).

In introducing the list of his military achievements, Aeschines expresses his awareness, albeit circumspectly through a plea for a favourable hearing (ἀνεπίφθονον), that his self-gratulatory account may kindle listeners' envy and excuses himself for his self-praise by appealing to the gravity of the accusations that he is facing (167):

> ἐμνήσθη δέ που περὶ στρατείας, καὶ καλὸν στρατιώτην ἐμὲ ὠνόμασεν. ἐγὼ δὲ οὐχ ἕνεκα τῆς τούτου βλασφημίας, ἀλλὰ τοῦ παρόντος κινδύνου προνοούμενος, καὶ περὶ τούτων ἀνεπίφθονον λέγειν εἶναί μοι νομίζω. ποῦ γὰρ ἢ πότε αὐτῶν ἢ πρὸς τίνας, παραλιπὼν τήνδε τὴν ἡμέραν, μνησθήσομαι;

> He also spoke about military service and called me "that noble soldier." And I think I may speak on this subject as well without giving offense; my concern is for the danger that now faces me rather than for his insults. For where or when or to whom shall I speak on this subject, if I do not mention them today? (transl. Carey)

Instead of praising himself directly, in the following paragraphs Aeschines mentions several occasions on which his fellow-citizens sang his praise for his courage:[53] he draws dikasts' attention to his military distinction by brandishing in front of them the decree according to which the city offered him a crown in recognition of his bravery and also invites witnesses to testify that after his first experience in the battlefield he won the officers' praise. Thus, Demosthenes' sarcastic point in the speech of prosecution offered Aeschines the appropriate pretext to include in his defence an account of his military achievements on the basis of which he emphasizes his bravery and devotion to the safety of the city –notably, of course, in a speech of defence against allegations of bribery and treason. This allows him to reach the conclusion that he is not an enemy of democracy, as Demosthenes spitefully alleges (171), but an enemy of the wicked.

---

53 The same method of self-praise is also followed by a speaker in Isaeus who mentions two times in his speech (2. 18, 36) that his fellow demesmen commended him on the accomplishment of his duties to his family.

Aeschines' account of his achievements and his defence of his civic conduct is thus placed, as rhetorical theory advises, in a wider contextual frame indicating his concern for the public interest, the demos' recognition of his contributions to the city, and, above all, an explicit reference to his present unfortunate situation (τοῦ παρόντος κινδύνου προνοούμενος), which provides him a fitting opportunity to describe in public his career as a citizen.

As I suggested earlier, the most representative examples of *periautologia* in the orators are provided in Isocrates' *Antidosis* and Demosthenes' *On the crown*. Despite their differences, these speeches are elaborate accounts of their authors' careers. But because Isocrates composed the *Antidosis* for readers rather than for a real forensic audience, his treatment of self-praise is characterized by distinctive self-consciousness.[54]

At the beginning of his speech, Isocrates claims that his composition is an 'image' (εἰκών) of his thoughts and his life as a whole (an image which is finer than statues, 7). As we saw earlier, Isocrates informs his readers that he chose to give to his *apologia pro vita sua*, a particularly ambitious undertaking, the form of a forensic speech in order to make it more palatable and avoid his readers' envy (Isocr. 15.8). By anticipating that his speech may cause feelings of envy, Isocrates not only reveals his awareness that self-praise jeopardizes a favourable reception of his arguments, but also capitalizes on his imaginary audiences' sensitivity in order to enhance his own encomiastic purposes. At 4, for instance, Isocrates says explicitly that his talent inflicts feelings of envy, while at 13 he provides a programmatic statement according to which his text aims to restore his reputation, even as he knows that his defence of his educational career will intensify the envy of those who are prone to this emotion. Indeed, in this context Isocrates assimilates dispositional envy with a disease and expresses openly his prediction that his speech will make those who suffer from it experience intense pain (ἔτι μᾶλλον ὑπὸ τῆς νόσου ταύτης λυπεῖσθαι).

Isocrates however does not employ this type of aggressive rhetoric throughout the speech. By contrast, a number of passages are so designed as to mitigate (legitimate) envy. These sections resonate with Isocrates' attempt to grant his speech with the characteristics of a forensic defence composed for delivery. He therefore claims that no sophist made a great fortune out of his teaching (155), while in the course of his speech he stresses his willingness to undertake liturgies for the state (Isocr. 15.5, 145, 150, 158). In a significant passage that appears to-

---

[54] See Saïd 2003; on Isocrates' treatment of the tension between public speakers and mass audiences in the *Antidosis*, see Ober 2001: 264–268.

wards the end of the speech, Isocrates advises his (imaginary) audience to abstain from envy and thus refrain from stripping distinguished rhetoricians of their prestige, because, as he claims, Athens owes her renown to them, not to ephemeral athletic achievements (15.302–303). In doing so, Isocrates stresses that the mass's envy is self-harming, thereby implying that his own talent promotes the city's reputation and therefore that it is to the interest of the *hoi polloi* to realize that they have a share in his distinction.

Isocrates' uses of envy in the *Antidosis* are symptomatic of the idiosyncracies of this speech. Intended for private reading, the *Antidosis* embeds many of the *topoi* of orally delivered forensic speeches by means of which Isocrates invests his text with an air of extemporaneousness. But because the *Antidosis* is not intended for delivery in a real courtroom, the author takes the liberty to deploy envy in an aggressive way by way of indicating his prominence among current intellectuals. At the same time, the open deployment of listeners' envy may be explained from Isocrates' elitist criticism of democracy and the implications of majorities' civic deliberation for the institutions of the polis. Yet, in those cases where Isocrates' uses of envy are resonant with real speakers' rhetorical strategies, his deployment of self-praise incorporates the preemptive strategies that we find in the corpus of forensic speeches composed for oral delivery. As we saw, Isocrates emphasizes the wrongful accusation against which he purportedly defends himself in order to introduce the account of his achievements. Furthermore, later in the speech, he informs his listeners that one of his friends warned him that on account of their dispositional envy, *hoi polloi* foster negative sentiments, including hatred and envy, towards those who distinguish themselves and, what is more, their envy makes them want to destroy those who excel. The presentation of his friend's warning is introduced by Isocrates' explicit statement that Lysimachus' prosecution gave him the opportunity to think "about these very issues, as each of you might, and I examined my life and my accomplishments, spending the most time on what I thought I ought to receive praise for" (141). Isocrates' explicit qualification of his speech as a self-eulogy has no parallel in the forensic speeches delivered by major political figures. Hence, it underscores the projective uses of envy as a means of indicating one's superiority (comparisons between Isocrates and the *hoi polloi* are too many to quote) in a context that, on the basis of his friend's condescending points about Athenian civic bodies, castigates the masses' intolerance to excellence.

In his much admired speech *On the crown*, Demosthenes is perhaps no less boastful than Isocrates, but, as I argue in the following paragraphs, his subtle manipulation of envy indicates the limits of *periautologia* in real courtroom practice. The speech under discussion gave Demosthenes the opportunity to offer an account of his political career and propound his loyalty to the city. As we saw at the beginning of this chapter, Demosthenes expresses his fear that his *apologia pro vita sua* may cause feelings of envy and therefore attempts to secure the goodwill of the dikasts from the outset of his speech (4). He thus explains that the accusations that he is facing make *periautologia* inevitable and attempts to mitigate the effects of his self-praise by promising that he will speak as moderately as he can (μετριώτατα).

*Metriotes* is pivotal to a passage from the speech where envy is referred to explicitly. Demosthenes claims that the signs of a *metrios* ('middling') citizen are his loyalty to the city and maintaining the polis' primacy (18.320–321).[55] Laying claim to these qualities, he says, is least invidious (ἀνεπιφθονώτατον). Interestingly enough, this passage comes immediately after a dismissive reference to Aeschines' horse-breeding, which caps the contradistinctive characterisation of his own patriotic feelings and Aeschines' primacy in the world of Athenian traitors. The notion of 'loyalty' (εὔνοια),[56] which appears no less than 14 times in the speech, encapsulates Demosthenes' attempt to consolidate the belief that his political career was one of a patriot who, despite the unfortunate defeat at Chaeronea, a defeat that he constantly attributes to chance (τύχη), struggled by all possible means to maintain the city's greatness.

Demosthenes' handling of the possible consequences of self-praise in this speech is obvious in a much discussed passage where he describes with distinctive vividness (*enargeia*) the turmoil and panic caused by the news that Philip had captured Elateia (Dem. 18.173–174). In this passage Demosthenes does not employ the word 'envy', but, on account of the powerful rhetoric that he endorses in the description of his self-presentation as a 'deus ex machina' at a critical moment for the polis' survival it deserves detailed discussion. I cite the relevant passage in full:

ἀλλ', ὡς ἔοικεν, ἐκεῖνος ὁ καιρὸς καὶ ἡ ἡμέρα 'κείνη οὐ μόνον εὔνουν καὶ πλούσιον ἄνδρ' ἐκάλει, ἀλλὰ καὶ παρηκολουθηκότα τοῖς πράγμασιν ἐξ ἀρχῆς, καὶ συλλελογισμένον ὀρθῶς τίνος εἵνεκα ταῦτ' ἔπραττεν ὁ Φίλιππος καὶ τί βουλόμενος· ὁ γὰρ μὴ ταῦτ' εἰδὼς μηδ'

---

**55** The relevant passage (Dem. 18.321) runs as follows: "the responsible citizen (τὸν φύσει μέτριον πολίτην), men of Athens, should have two characteristics (for I may so describe myself as to give the least offence); when in power, the constant aim of his policy should be to preserve the dignity and primacy of his state (τὴν τοῦ γενναίου καὶ τοῦ πρωτείου τῇ πόλει προαίρεσιν διαφυλάττειν), and on every occasion and in every action, his own loyalty (τὴν εὔνοιαν). His nature controls this purpose, but his power and strength to implement it depend on other considerations" (transl. Usher). For a detailed commentary, see Wankel 1976 and Yunis 2001 *ad loc.*
**56** On *eunoia* in this context, see Whitehead 1993: 52–54, esp. 53.

ἐξητακὼς πόρρωθεν, οὔτ' εἰ εὔνους ἦν οὔτ' εἰ πλούσιος, οὐδὲν μᾶλλον ἔμελλ' ὅ τι χρὴ ποιεῖν εἴσεσθαι οὐδ' ὑμῖν ἕξειν συμβουλεύειν. ἐφάνην τοίνυν οὗτος ἐν ἐκείνῃ τῇ ἡμέρᾳ ἐγὼ καὶ παρελθὼν εἶπον εἰς ὑμᾶς, ἅ μου δυοῖν εἵνεκ' ἀκούσατε προσσχόντες τὸν νοῦν, ἑνὸς μέν, ἵν' εἰδῆθ' ὅτι μόνος τῶν λεγόντων καὶ πολιτευομένων ἐγὼ τὴν τῆς εὐνοίας τάξιν ἐν τοῖς δεινοῖς οὐκ ἔλιπον, ἀλλὰ καὶ λέγων καὶ γράφων ἐξηταζόμην τὰ δέονθ' ὑπὲρ ὑμῶν ἐν αὐτοῖς τοῖς φοβεροῖς, ἑτέρου δέ, ὅτι μικρὸν ἀναλώσαντες χρόνον πολλῷ πρὸς τὰ λοιπὰ τῆς πάσης πολιτείας ἔσεσθ' ἐμπειρότεροι.

But it seems that that moment and that day called for a man who not only was devoted and wealthy but had also followed events from the beginning and figured out correctly what Philip was aiming at and what his intentions were in taking the action he did. Someone who did not know these things and had not studied the situation for a long time, even if he was devoted and even if he was wealthy, would not be better informed about what had to be done or be able to advise you. The one who emerged as the right man on that day was I. I stepped forward and addressed you, and for two reasons listen carefully to what I said. First, you should know that I alone of the speakers and politicians did not abandon my post of civic concern at the moment of danger but rather proved to be the one who in the very midst of the horrors both advised and proposed the necessary measures for your sake. (transl. Yunis)

Demosthenes' rhetoric in this context is particularly relevant to my argument, because it reflects an instance in which an individual contrasts himself to the whole body of citizens –and no doubt when Demosthenes says πᾶς ὁ δῆμος (169), he emphasizes that each and every citizen followed his lead. As Slater (1998) has pointed out, Demosthenes' description resembles that of a divine epiphany.[57] His double and emphatic use of οὗτος ... ἐγώ contrasts the οὐδείς at 170 and emphasizes the determination with which he intervened at that critical moment. The strong deictic οὗτος also attracts the audience's gazes to the speaker and bridges the spatial and temporal gap between the urgent meeting of the Assembly and the legal space and time of the courtroom. In addition, μόνος, commonly employed in third-person encomiastic contexts, is embedded in a battle metaphor (μόνος ἐγώ...τὴν τῆς εὐνοίας **τάξιν** ἐν τοῖς δεινοῖς οὐκ **ἔλιπον**) which stresses Demosthenes' resilience and courage. In the following lines (173–178), Demosthenes gives an account of the speech that he delivered at the time of his epiphanic emergence whose "stress on Athens' honor is fully integrated with the real speech that circumscribes it" (Yunis 2001: 208). On that critical moment, the whole

---

57 Petridou (2015: 130 n. 111) points out that the speech "contains stereotypical elements of divine speeches delivered in epiphanies that take place in the course of a battle or a siege, and not, as Slater has assumed, in parodies of epiphanies as found in comedies". If this is so, Demosthenes' epiphanic self-fashioning resonates with the military metaphor through which he portrays himself as the only citizen who had the strength to fight the battle of *eunoia* for the city.

Atheinian demos (πάντων notably recurs here, 179) praised him for his advice (συνεπαινεσάντων). As Yunis (2001: 210) points out, Demosthenes' "claim of utter dominance surpasses the mastery which Thucydides attributes to Pericles" (at 2.65.8–10),[58] but it is important to stress that he cautiously places the self-adulatory presentation of his epiphanic appearance in front of the demos within a frame emphasizing Athenian citizens' unanimous praise of his initiative. Hence, Demosthenes' self-praise in this context is indirect, in so far as his merit is implicit to citizens' collective response.

The description of the turmoil experienced by Athenians is characterized by *enargeia*. The vivid description emphasizes the sentiments of panic which seized Athenians by laying stress on specific details of their response to the news. The description of citizens' fear and tumult serves as the appropriate background on which Demosthenes portrays his overtly theatrical self-presentation as a savior of the polis. Although envy is not named in this context, Demosthenes' epiphanic appearance on the empty rostrum explains more than any other passage from this speech his emphasis on ἀνάγκη at the proem. Even as it is not necessary to believe him when he says that the whole polis praised his speech at that critical moment, citizens' unanimous response conveyed by συνεπαινεσάντων indicates that although *he* was the only Athenian who had the nerve to break the unsettling silence, his words represented the sentiments of each and every patriotic citizen. Furthermore, Demosthenes is extremely cautious to prepare the ground for the description of his 'epiphany' at the Assembly in the paragraphs that precede it (esp. 171–172), by stressing the loyalty of all Athenian citizens to the city. In an obvious attempt to integrate himself into the demos, he claims that if the only requirement for efficient public speaking at that perilous moment was citizens' willingness to save the polis, then the whole citizenry –including the dikasts– would have wanted to give a speech. But Demosthenes was entitled to speak not only because he had the political experience, but also because *he* (along with other citizens) was both loyal to the city and sufficiently rich (but not excessively rich, like the Three hundred) to spend money as a liturgist immediately after Chaeronea.

From my analysis of Demosthenes' speech on the crown, it becomes clear that even the most spectacular and overtly theatrical example of *periautologia* in our extant sources deriving from a defence with far-reaching implications for both the prosecutor and the polis as a whole embeds the self-protective discursive

---

[58] For a detailed analysis of this passage, see Yunis 1996: 268–277, who shows that it presents interesting similarities with Pericles' (self-referential) speech at Thucydides 2.60.5–6.

strategies that characterize the rhetoric of self-praise. Demosthenes praises himself indirectly in a defence speech which he delivered in response to an accusation which, as he says, was prompted by his opponent's envy. Furthermore, as has been noted, Demosthenes constructs an objective self by constructing an 'autobiography' which reflects the polis' glorious past and key concepts of its ideology. The speech thus offers the most eloquent example of how Athenian speakers advertised their achievements without isolating themselves from the demos. Demosthenes lays stress on his public expenditure and the unanimous willingness of his fellow-citizens to defend the polis' interests thereby suggesting that he put his experience and his privileged knowledge of the appropriate course of action, and, hence, his prominence as a *sumboulos*, to the service of the city. But more importantly his *apologia pro vita sua* was *necessitated* by his opponent's wrongful accusations.

## 5.5 Conclusion

Greek rhetorical treatises and the speeches of the orators indicate that the major problem involved in self-praise concerns listeners' *phthonos*. The envy that springs from self-glorification harms speakers' ethos because it isolates them from the deliberating masses that they seek to manipulate. In the egalitarian environment of classical Athens, speakers often, if not always, pre-empt the repercussions of this individualisation by emphasising their adherence to cooperative values and their concern for the well-being of the city on the basis of which they seek to reintegrate themselves into the community of equals. The rhetoric of *periautologia* seems to corroborate recent scholarly work showing that 'legitimate envy' is a socially responsive, egalitarian emotion rather than an unspeakable psychic disease targeting those who distinguish themselves indiscriminately. In the light of my arguments concerning 'legitimate envy' in the previous chapter, the rhetorical strategies by means of which speakers mitigate the emotional effects of self-praise, i.e. scripts of *phthonos* in contexts of *periautologia*, involve morally responsive appraisals revolving around social tensions including the domains in which prominent citizens prevailed over the demos, especially wealth and expert knowledge. Self-praise is useful, but it cannot be without limits, because one's honour and personal distinction impinge on democtaric audiences' sense of self–esteem. To put it simply, unlike Demosthenes (or even less significant speakers), privetely writing Isocrates was able to advertise his achievements by projecting envy on the masses and, thereby, by intimidating them, because his career and his distinction did not depend on their votes. The fact that circumspect appeals to audiences' *phthonos* appear in major public speeches indicates that self-adulatory accounts of one's public conduct were thought to be suitable for types of public deliberation revolving around the polis' interests and prominent figures' actions in support of its citizens' well-being.

# Afterword

Classicists' interdisciplinary approaches to ancient emotions in recent years have provided analytical tools which enable us to explore the well-established importance of emotions for persuasion on a more solid basis. As the treatment of individual authors in this book suggest, however, we can hope to get a better grasp of ancient emotions only if we pay due attention to the ways in which the cultures that we attempt to understand viewed and expressed their sentiments. One of the major problems involved in our attempt to pursue a culturally oriented study of ancient emotions is quite common in other areas of literary criticism: the literary pieces that we want to interpret by taking into account their wider cultural contexts are also the main sources of evidence about the cultures which produced them. But oratory is heuristically useful in a way which distinguishes it from other literary texts. Courtroom speakers, for example, wanted to persuade their audiences about their innocence or about the guilt of their opponents. It is therefore the case that the elaborate and highly fabricated emotion scripts that they put together appeal to mainstream rather than peripheral ideological understandings. For this reason the ways in which they deploy emotions in support of their arguments reflect cognitions which are in concert with cardinal social values. Emotional persuasion in the orators is therefore good to think with.

Appraisal-oriented approaches to emotions do not provide an all-encompassing understanding of the category EMOTION, but they help us enhance our knowledge about the ideological concerns, beliefs or mentalities favoured by the societies that we study. I hope that my discussion of emotions in the chapters that constitute this book will contribute to scholarly work on the implications of social norms for Athenian courtroom practice. A more technical, but very important issue, concerns the importance of emotions' forensic uses for the notion of 'relevance'. This is not the place to discuss this thorny issue in detail. But my discussion of individual emotions in this book suggests that approaches relying on 'statistics' of emotion labels is the least appropriate method in our attempt to assess the function of *pathe* in courtroom practice. My discussion of emotion scripts indicates the elaborate ways in which forensic narratives contribute to audiences' psychological manipulation.

As I suggested, modern interdisciplinary approaches should not induce us to neglect the fact that the ancient cultures that we study had their own understandings about the phenomenology of emotions –even before systematic definitions of sentiments emerged. But even systematic approaches to emotions in antiquity are characterized by bi-disciplinarity. As Aristotle avers (*De an.* 403a29–b1), philosophers' analysis of emotions emphasize appraisals, whereas physical scientists focus on the body's physiological changes. The situation is no different today. In the study of emotions, the body and the mind remain irreconcilable categories. My investigation of vision's implications for emotions and persuasion, a recurring topic in this book, indicates the limitations of exploring ancient emotions through commonsensical, culturally biased categories of description or on the basis of systematic definitions such as Aristotle's. Cultural variations define the ways in which emotions are felt, expressed or suppressed in modern and ancient societies alike. The fact that vision, conceived as a haptic sense, is integral to the phenomenology of certain ancient emotions –and is thereby commonly identified as the cause of their onset– suggests that the bipolar mind/body dichotomy can do very little to explain ancient emotions or, for that matter, ancient conceptualizations of persuasion. In the emotion scripts that we find in genres ranging from lyric poetry to the novel, vision, persuasion, and emotions are concurrent experiential categories which involve the physical body. These ancient understandings of emotive persuasion may serve as a warning against our logocentric predilections. We commonly analyze the speeches –and their deployment of emotions– as written texts. Their performative, extralinguistic aspects, however, which have recently attracted scholars' attention, are also pivotal to the rich emotion scripts included in ancient oratory. Clothes, movements, physical characteristics, wounds, the pitch of speakers' voices are only some of the elements which, in concert with arguments, contributed to psychological manipulation.

Another topic that I hope emerges from my analysis concerns the interfaces between emotions and ideology. Although in recent years classicists (or perhaps cultural and literary critics in general) seem to be uncomfortable with the term ideology, my discussion of emotions' place in the civic context of classical Athens emphasizes the implications of emotions for the polis' public discourse. It is my contention that such analytical categories as 'persuasive strategies', 'public conduct', 'morality' and 'appeals to emotion', commonly employed in treatments of ancient rhetorical practice, are both heuristically and conceptually subordinate to *ideology*. Viewing ideology as the product of persisting social tensions, I read the concepts which inform speakers' arguments as performative (on the basis of Quentin Skinner's theory which I outline in chapter 4). Emotions, on my view, play a predominant role in ancient ideologies in ways that transcend the limits of my investigation in this book. This is partly due to the fact that the cognitions which give rise to (social) emotions are directly relevant to social frictions. In spite of Aristotle's (ideologically) biased stance towards democracy, his treatment of emotions in the *Politics*, a topic which remains under-explored, indicates the limitations of attempting to understand ancient emotions in purely 'ethical' (or, indeed, lexical) terms. The understanding of rhetorical uses of emotions, or for that matter values in general, is a task that invites our full attention to speakers' uses of concepts in arguments.

More work has to be done on persuasion and emotions. We live in turbulent times. The public discourse of our societies is dominated by emotions. Indeed, dubious uses of emotions are pivotal to the rhetoric of hatred and intolerance which in some cases leads to social violence. These uses are directly relevant to social realities. For example, in a televised address Donald Trump responded to his opponents' unwillingness to pass a spending bill that would "defend the borders" with the following words: "Some have suggested a barrier is immoral. Then why do wealthy politicians build walls, fences, and gates around their homes? They don't build walls because they hate the people on the outside, but because they love the people on the inside". One can say much about President Trump's oversimplification of the issues involved in migration, but his understanding of the wall as a protective device indicating his love for those "on the inside" speaks volumes about the implications of emotions for *populist* rhetoric. The deployment of emotions in ancient oratory, i.e. in speeches delivered in front of decision-making civic bodies, is good to think with. But as I have tried to show in the chapters that constitute this book, thinking with ancient *pathe* about the public discourse of our times is a task that invites us to (re-)consider the 'logic' of emotions.

# Bibliography

Alexiou, E. 2010. *Der Euagoras des Isokrates: Ein Kommentar*. Berlin/New York.
Allen, D.S. 2000. *The World of Prometheus: The Politics of Punishing in Democratic Athens*. Princeton.
Allison, J.W. 1989. *Power and Preparedness in Thucydides*. Baltimore/London.
Alwine, A.T. 2015. *Enmity and Feuding in Classical Athens*. Austin, Texas.
Amsterdam, A.G./Bruner, S.J. (eds.) 2000. *Minding the Law*. Cambridge Mass./London.
Apostolakis, K. 2009. *[Δημοσθένους]* Πρὸς Φαίνιππον, Περὶ ἀντιδόσεως, Athens.
Apostolakis, K. 2017. "Pitiable Dramas on the Podium of the Athenian Law Courts." In: S. Papaioannou/A. Serafim/B. Da Vela (eds.), *The Theatre of Justice: Aspects of Performance in Greco-Roman Oratory and Rhetoric*, 133–156. Leiden/Boston.
Arrowsmith, W. 1973. "Aristophanes' *Birds*: The Fantasy Politics of Eros." *Arion* 1: 119–167.
Azoulay, V. 2004. *Xénophon et les grâces du pouvoir : De la charis au charisme*. Paris.
Balla, Ch. 2004. "Από την εικασία στην διαλεκτική: μια απάντηση στον Παύλο Καλλιγά." *Δευκαλίων* 22.1: 127–142.
Balla, Ch. (ed.) 2008. *Φιλοσοφία και ρητορική στην κλασική Αθήνα*. Herakleion.
Barringer, J.M./Hurwit, J.M. (eds.) 2005. *Periklean Athens and Its Legacy*. Austin, Texas.
Bandes, S.A./Blumenthal, J.A. 2012. "Emotion and the Law." *The Annual Review of Law and Social Science* 8: 161–181.
Bandini, M./Dorion, L.-A. (eds.) 2011. *Xénophon : Mémorables*, v. ii. Paris.
Bassi, K. 1995. "Male Nudity and Disguise in the Discourse of Greek Histrionics." *Helios* 22: 3–22.
Bell, A. 2004. *Spectacular Power in the Greek and Roman City*. Oxford.
Ben-Ze'ev, A. 1992. "Envy and Inequality." *Journal of Philosophy* 89: 551–581.
Ben-Ze'ev, A. 2003. "Aristotle on Emotions Towards the Fortune of Others." In: D. Konstan/N.K. Rutter (eds.), *Envy, Spite and Jealousy: The Rivalrous Emotions in Ancient Greece*, 99–121. Edinburgh.
Bers, V. 1985. "Dikastic Thorubos." In: P.A. Cartledge/F.D. Harvey (eds.), *Crux: Essays in Greek History Presented to G.E.M. de Ste. Croix on his 75th Birthday*, 1–15. London.
Bers, V. 1994. "Tragedy and Rhetoric." In: I. Worthington (ed.), *Greek Rhetoric in Action*, Persuasion, 176–195. London/New York.
Bertrand, J.-M. (ed.) 2005. *La violence dans les mondes grec et romain: actes du colloque international (Paris, 24 Mai 2002)*. Paris.
Bettini, M. 1999. *The Portrait of the Lover* [transl. Laura Gibbs]. Berkeley.
Blundell, S. *et al.* 2013. "Introduction." *Helios* 40: 3–37.
Bobonich, C. 1991. "Persuasion, Compulsion, and Freedom in Plato's *Laws*." *CQ* 41: 365–388.
Boegehold, A.L./Scafuro, A.C. (eds.) 2002. *Athenian Identity and Civic Ideology*. Baltimore, MD.
Bornstein, B.H./Wiener, R.L. (eds.) 2010. *Emotion and the Law: Psychological Perspectives*. New York.
Borthwick, E.K. 1993. "*Autolekythos* and *Lekythion* in Demosthenes and Aristophanes." *LCM* 18: 34–37.
Bourdieu, P. 1984. *Distinction: A Social Critique of the Judgment of Taste* [Engl. transl. R. Nice]. Cambridge, Mass.
Brancacci, A. 1995. "*Ethos* e *pathos* nella teoria delle arti. Una poetica socratica della pittura e de la scultura." *Elenchos* 16: 101–127.

Brancacci, A./Morel, P.-M. (eds.) 2007. *Democritus: Science, the Arts, and the Care of the Soul: Proceedings of the International Colloquium on Democritus (Paris, 18–20 September 2003).* Leiden/Boston.
Braund, S./Most, G.W. (eds.) 2003. *Ancient Anger: Perspectives from Homer to Galen* [Yale Classical Studies 32]. Cambridge.
Brock, R. 1991. "The Emergence of Democratic Ideology." *Historia: Zeitschrift für Alte Geschichte.* 40: 160–169.
Brock, R. 2013. *Greek Political Imagery from Homer to Aristotle.* London/New York.
Brooks, P. 2002. "Narrativity of the Law." *Law and Literature* 14: 1–10.
Brooks, P. 2005. "Narrative in and of the Law." In: J. Phelan/P.J. Rabinowitz (eds.), *A Companion to Narrative Theory*, 415–426. Oxford.
Brooks, P./Gewirtz, P. (eds.) 1996. *Narrative and the Rhetoric in the Law.* Yale.
Buchheim, T. 1985. "Maler, Sprachbildner. Zur Verwandtschaft des Gorgias mit Empedokles." *Hermes* 113: 417–429.
Bulman, P. 1989. *Gorgias von Leontinoi: Reden, Fragmente und Testimonien.* Hamburg.
Bulman, P. 1992. *Phthonos in Pindar.* Berkeley, CA/Los Angeles/Oxford.
Burns, R.P. 2001. *A Theory of the Trial.* Princeton.
Buxton, R. 1982. *Persuasion in Greek tragedy: A study of Peitho.* Cambridge.
Cairns, D.L. 1996. "Hybris, Dishonour and 'Thinking Big.'" *JHS* 116: 1–32.
Cairns, D.L. 2003. "The Politics of Envy: Envy and Equality in Ancient Greece." In: D. Konstan/N.K. Rutter (eds.), *Envy, Spite and Jealousy: The Rivalrous Emotions in Ancient Greece*, 232–252. Edinburgh.
Cairns, D.L. 2008. "Look Both Ways: Studying Emotion in Ancient Greek." *Critical Quarterly* 50: 43–62.
Cairns, D.L. 2011. "Looks of Love and Loathing: Cultural Models of Vision and Emotion in Ancient Greek Culture." *Mètis* 9: 37–50.
Cairns, D.L. 2011a. "Honour and Shame: Modern Controversies and Ancient Values." *Critical Quarterly* 53: 22–41.
Cairns, D.L. 2012. "Atê in the Homeric Poems." *Papers of the Langford Latin Seminar* 15: 1–52.
Cairns, D.L. 2013. "The Imagery of *Erôs* in Plato's *Phaedrus*." In: E. Sanders et al. (ed.), *Erôs in ancient Greece*, 233–250. Oxford.
Cairns, D.L. 2015. "Revenge, Punishment, and Justice in Athenian Homicide Law." *Journal of Value Inquiry* 49: 645–665.
Cairns, D.L. 2016. "Metaphors for Hope in Archaic and Classical Greek Poetry." In: R.R. Caston/R.A. Kaster (eds.), *Hope, Joy, and Affection in the Classical World*, 13–44. Oxford/New York.
Calame, C. 1999. *The Poetics of Eros in Ancient Greece* [Trans. J. Lloyd]. Princeton.
Canevaro, M. 2016. *Demostene, "Contro Leptine": Introduzione, traduzione e commento storico.* Berlin/New York.
Carey, C. 1989. *Lysias: Selected speeches.* Cambridge.
Carey, C. 1990. "Structure and Strategy in Lysias 24." *G&R* 37: 44–51.
Carey, C. 1994. "Rhetorical Means of Persuasion." In: I. Worthington (ed.), *Persuasion: Greek Rhetoric in Action*, 26–45. London.
Carey, C. 1995. "Rape and Adultery in Athenian Law." *CQ* 45: 407–417.
Carey, C. 2000. *Aeschines.* Austin, Texas.
Carey, C. 2017. "Style, Persona, and Performance in Aeschines' Prosecution of Timarchus." In: S. Papaioannou/A. Serafim/B. Da Vela (eds.), *The Theatre of Justice: Aspects of Performance in Greco-Roman Oratory and Rhetoric*, 265–282. Leiden/Boston.

Carey, C./Reid, R.A. 1985. *Demosthenes: Selected Private Speeches*. Cambridge.
Carney, E. 2007. "Symposia and the Macedonian Elite: The Unmixed Life." *Syllecta Classica* 18: 129–180.
Cartledge, P. 1996. "Comparatively Equal." In: J. Ober/C. Hedrick (eds.), *Demokratia: A Conversation on Democracies, Ancient and Modern*, 175–185. Princeton.
Cartledge, P. 1998. "Introduction: Defining a *Kosmos*." In: P. Cartledge/P. Millett/S. von Reden (eds.), *Kosmos: Essays in Order, Conflict and Community in Classical Athens*, 1–12. Cambridge.
Cartledge, P./Millett, P./Todd, S.C. (eds.) 1990. *Nomos: Essays in Athenian Law, Politics and Society*. Cambridge.
Cartledge, P./Millet, P./von Reden, S. (eds.) 1998. *Kosmos: Essays in Order, Conflict and Community in Classical Athens*. Cambridge.
Cartledge, P./Spawforth, A. 2002. *Hellenisitc and Roman Sparta: A Tale of Two Cities*. London/New York.
Chapman, H.A/Kim, D.A/Susskind, J.M./Anderson, A.K. 2009. "In Bad Taste: Evidence for the Oral Origins of Moral Disgust." *Science* 323: 1222–1226.
Christ, M. 1998. *The Litigious Athenian*. Baltimore/London.
Christ, M. 2012. *The Limits of Altruism in Democratic Athens*. Cambridge.
Cohen, D. 1991. *Law, Sexuality, and Society: The Enforcement of Morals in Classical Athens*. Cambridge.
Cohen, D. 1995. *Law, Violence and Community in Classical Athens*. Cambridge.
Cohen, D. 1999. *Law, Sexuality, and Society: The Enforcement of Morals in Classical Athens*. Cambridge.
Cohen, D. 2005. 'Introduction." In: D. Cohen/M. Gagarin (eds.), *Cambridge Companion to Greek Law*, 1–26. Cambridge.
Cohen, D./Gagarin, M. (eds.) 2005. *Cambridge Companion to Greek Law*. Cambridge.
Cole, T. 1991. *The Origins of Rhetoric in Ancient Greece*. Princeton.
Connor, W.R. 1984. *Thucydides*. Princeton.
Connor, W.R. 1987. "Tribes, Festivals and Possessions: Civic Ceremonial and Political Manipulation in Archaic Greece." *JHS* 107: 40–50.
Cooper, F./Morris, S. 1990. "Dining in Round Buildings." In: O. Murray (ed.), *Sympotica: A Symposium on the Symposion*, 66–85. Oxford.
Cover, R. 1983. "The Supreme Court 1982 Term–Foreword: *Nomos and Narrative*." *Harvard Law Review* 97: 4–68.
Croally, N.T. 1994. *Euripidean Polemic*. Cambridge.
Csapo, E. 1993. "Deep Ambivalence: Notes on a Greek Cockfight." *Phoenix* 47: 1–27, 115–124.
Csapo, E. 2006. "Cockfights, Contradictions, and the Mythopoetics of Ancient Greek Culture." *Arts: The Journal of the Sydney University Arts Association* 28: 9–41.
Dalby, A. 1993. *Siren Feasts: A History of Food and Gastronomy in Greece*. London/New York.
D' Angour, A. 2011. *The Greeks and the New: Novelty in Ancient Greek Experience and Imagination*. Cambridge.
Damasio, A. 1994. *Descartes' Error: Emotion, Reason and the Human Brain*. New York.
Davidson, D. 2000. "*Gnesippus Paigniagraphos*: The Comic Poets and the Erotic Mime." In: J. Wilkins/D. Harvey (eds.), *The Rivals of Aristophanes: Studies in Athenian Old Comedy*, 41–64. London.
Davidson, D. 2007. *The Greeks and Greek Love*. London.
Davies, J.K. 1971. *Athenian Propertied Families, 600–300 B.C.* Oxford.

Davies, J.K. 1981. *Wealth and the Power of Wealth in Classical Athens*. New York.
Davies, M. 1986. "Symbolism and Imagery in the Poetry of Ibycus." *Hermes* 114: 399–405.
Davies, M. 2011. "Hegesippos of Sounion: An Underrated Politician." In: S. Lambert (ed.), *Sociable Man: Essays on Ancient Greek Social Behaviour in Honour of Nick Fisher*, 11–24. Swansea.
Deigh, J. 2008. *Emotions, Values and the Law*. Oxford.
de La Rochefoucauld, F. 2007. *La Rouchefoucauld: Collected Essays and Other Reflections* [English. transl. by E.H. and A.M. Blackmore and F. Giguère]. Oxford.
de Romilly, J. 1975. *Magic and Rhetoric in Ancient Greece*. Cambridge, Mass.
Dickie, M.W. 1991. "Heliodorus and Plutarch on the Evil Eye." *CP* 86: 17–29.
Dodds, E.R. 1951. *The Greeks and the Irrational*. Berkeley/Los Angeles.
Donadi, D. 2002. "Gorgia e il kairos." *Institutio* 2: 201–215.
Donlan, W. 1980. *The Aristocratic Ideal in Ancient Greece: Attitudes of Superiority form Homer to the End of the Fifth Century B.C. Lawrence*, Kansas.
Dougherty, C. 1996. "Democratic Contradictions and the Synoptic Illusion of Euripides' *Ion*." In: J. Ober/C. Hedrick (eds.), *Demokratia: A Conversation on Democracies, Ancient and Modern*, 249–270. Princeton.
Dougherty, C./Kurke, L. (eds.) 1998. *Cultural Poetics in Archaic Greece: Cult, Performance, Politics*. Oxford.
Dover, K.J. 1974. *Greek Popular Morality in the Time of Plato and Aristotle*. Oxford.
Dover, K.J. 1978. *Greek Homosexuality*. Cambridge, Mass.
Dow, J. 2015. *Passions and Persuasion in Aristotle's Rhetoric*. Cambridge.
Eden, K. 1986. *Poetic and Legal Fiction in the Aristotelian Tradition*. Princeton.
Edwards, M.J. 2004. "Antiphon." In: I.J.F. De Jong/R. Nünlist/A.M. Bowie (eds.), *Narrators, Narratees, and Narratives in Ancient Greek Literature: Studies in Ancient Greek Narrative*, 317–324. Leiden.
Edwards, M.J. 2004a. "Andocides." In: I.J.F. De Jong/R. Nünlist/A.M. Bowie (eds.), *Narrators, Narratees, and Narratives in Ancient Greek Literature: Studies in Ancient Greek Narrative*, 325–332. Leiden.
Edwards, M.J. 2004b. "Lysias." In: I.J.F. De Jong/R. Nünlist/A.M. Bowie, (eds.), *Narrators, Narratees, and Narratives in Ancient Greek Literature: Studies in Ancient Greek Narrative*, 333–336. Leiden.
Edwards, M.J. 2004c. "Isocrates." In: I.J.F. De Jong/R. Nünlist/A.M. Bowie (eds.), *Narrators, Narratees, and Narratives in Ancient Greek Literature: Studies in Ancient Greek Narrative*, 337–342. Leiden.
Edwards, M.J. 2004d. "Demosthenes." In: I.J.F. De Jong/R. Nünlist/A.M. Bowie (eds.), *Narrators, Narratees, and Narratives in Ancient Greek Literature: Studies in Ancient Greek Narrative*, 343–348. Leiden.
Edwards, M.J. 2004e. "Aeschines". In: I.J.F. De Jong/R. Nünlist/A.M. Bowie (eds.), *Narrators, Narratees, and Narratives in Ancient Greek Literature: Studies in Ancient Greek Narrative*, 349–353. Leiden.
Edwards, M./Spatharas, D. (eds.) forthcoming. *Forensic Narratives in Athenian courts*. London.
Efstathiou, A. 2014. "Το ιδιωτικό και το δημόσιο στην *δοκιμασίαν ρητόρων* στην Αθήνα των κλασσικών χρόνων." In: L. Athanassaki/T. Nikolaidis/D. Spatharas (eds.), *Ιδιωτικός βίος και δημόσιος λόγος στην ελληνική αρχαιότητα και στον διαφωτισμό*, 231–254. Herakleion.
Eidinow, E. 2016. *Envy, Poison, and Death: Women on Trial in Classical Athens*. Cambridge.
Elsner, J. 2007. *Roman Eyes. Visuality and Subjectivity in Art and Text*. Princeton.

Elster, J. 1999. *Alchemies of the Mind: Rationality and the Emotions*. Cambridge.
Eitrem, S. 1951–1953. "The Pindaric *Pthonos*." In: G.E. Mylonas (ed.), *Studies Presented to D.M. Robinson*, 531–536. St Louis.
Elster, J. 1999. *Alchemies of the Mind: Rationality and the Emotions*. Cambridge.
Fantham, E. 2002. "Orator and/et Actor." In: P.E. Easterling/E. Hall (eds.), *Greek and Roman Actors: Aspects of an Ancient Profession*, 362–376. Cambridge.
Farenga, V. 2006. *Citizen and Self in Ancient Greece: Individuals Performing Justice and the Law*. Cambridge.
Ferrucci, S. 2013. "L'ambigua virtù: *Philotimia* nell'Atene degli oratori." *Studi Ellenistici* 27: 123–135.
Fields, D. 2008. "Aristides and Plutarch on Self-praise." In: W.V. Harris/B. Holmes (eds.), *Aelius Aristides between Greece, Rome, and the Gods*, 151–172. Leiden.
Fisher, N. 1990. "The Law of *hubris* in Athens." In: P.A. Cartledge/P.C. Millett/S. Todd (eds.), *Nomos: Essays in Athenian law, politics and society*, 123–138. Cambridge.
Fisher, N. 1992. *Hybris: A Study in the Values of Honour and Shame in Ancient Greece*. Warminster.
Fisher, N. 1994. "Sparta Re(de)valued: Some Athenian Public Attitudes to Sparta between Leuctra and the Lamian War." In: S. Hodkinson/A. Powell (eds.),*The Shadow of Sparta*, 347–400, London/New York.
Fisher, N. 1998. "Gymnasia and the Democratic Values of Leisure." In: P.A. Cartledge/P.C. Millet/S. von Reden (eds.), *Kosmos: Essays in Order, Conflict and Community in Classical Athens*, 84–104. Cambridge.
Fisher, N. 2001. Aeschines, Against Timarchos. Oxford.
Fisher, N. 2003. "'Let Envy Be Absent': Envy, Liturgies and Reciprocity in Athens." In: D. Konstan/N.K. Rutter (eds.), *Envy, Spite and Jealousy: The Rivalrous Emotions in Ancient Greece*, 181–215. Edinburgh.
Fisher, N. 2005. "Body-abuse: The Rhetoric of Hybris in Aeschines' *Against Timarchos*." In: J.-M. Bertrand (ed.), *La violence dans les mondes grec et romain: actes du colloque international (Paris, 24 Mai 2002)*, 67–90. Paris.
Fisher, N. 2006. "The Pleasures of Reciprocity: *Charis* and the Athletic Body in Pindar." In: F. Prost/J. Wilgaux (eds.), *Penser et représenter le corps dans l'Antiquité*, 227–245. Rennes.
Fisher, N. 2008. "The Bad Boyfriend, the Flatterer and the Sycophant: Related Forms of the 'Kakos' in Democratic Athens." In: I. Sluiter/R.M. Rosen (eds.), *Kakos: Badness and Antivalue in Classical Antiquity*, 185–232. Leiden.
Fisher, N. 2010. "Kharis, *Kharites*, Festivals, and Social Peace in the Classical Greek City." In: R. Rosen/I. Sluiter (eds.), *Valuing Others in Classical Antiquity*, 71–112. Leiden.
Fisher, N. 2013. "Erotic *charis*: What Sorts of Reciprocity?" In: E. Sanders (ed.), *Erôs and the polis: Love in Context, BICS Supplement* 119, 39–66. London.
Fisher, N. 2017. "Demosthenes and the Use of Disgust." In: D. Lateiner/D. Spatharas (eds.), *The Ancient Emotion of Disgust*, 103–124. Oxford/New York.
Fisher, N. 2017a "Socialisation, Identity and Violence in Classical Greek Cities." In: I.K. Xydopoulos/K. Vlassopoulos/E. Tounta (eds.), *Violence and Community: Law, Space and Identity in the Ancient Eastern Mediterranean World*, 99–141. London.
Fisher, N./Van Wees H. (eds.) 2015. *Aristocracy in Antiquity: Redefining Greek and Roman Elites*. Swansea.

Fisher, N./Van Wees, H. 2015. "The Trouble with 'Aristocracy'" In: N. Fisher/H. Van Wees (eds.), *Aristocracy in Antiquity: Redefining Greek and Roman Elites*, 1–58. Swansea.

Flower, M.A./Toher, M. (eds.) 1991. *Georgica: Greek Studies in Honour of George Cawkwell*. London.

Ford, A. 1999. "Reading Homer from the Rostrum: Poems and Laws in Aeschines' *Against Timarchus*." In: S. Goldhill/R. Osborne (eds.), *Performance Culture and Athenian Democracy*, 231–256. Cambridge.

Ford, A. 2002. *The Origins of Criticism: Literary Culture and Poetic Theory in Classical Greece*. Princeton.

Fortenbaugh, W.W. 2006. *Aristotle's Practical Side: On His Psychology, Ethics, Politics and Rhetoric*. Leiden.

Foster, E. 2010. *Thucydides, Pericles, and Periclean Imperialism*. Cambridge.

Foster, G.M. 1972. "The Anatomy of Envy: A Study in Symbolic Behaviour." *Current Anthropology* 13: 165–202.

Foxhall, L./Lewis, A.D.E. (eds.) 1996. *Greek Law in Its Political Setting: Justifications not Justice*. Oxford.

Frank, R. 1988. *Passions Within Reason: The Strategic Role of the Emotions*. New York.

Frijda, N.H./Manstead, A.S.R./Bem, S. (eds.) 2000. *Emotions and Beliefs: How Feelings Influence Thoughts*. Cambridge.

Frontisi-Ducroux. F. 1995. *Du masque au visage: Aspects de l'identité en Grèce anciennne*. Paris.

Fulkerson, L. 2004. "*Metameleia* and Friends: Remorse and Repentance in Fifth- and Fourth-Century Athenian Oratory." *Phoenix* 58: 241–259.

Gagarin, M. 1994. "Probability and Persuasion: Plato and Early Greek Rhetoric." In: I.Worthington (ed.), *Persuasion: Greek Rhetoric in Action*, 46–68. London.

Gagarin, M. 1996. "The Torture of Slaves in Athenian Law." *CP* 91: 1–18.

Gagarin, M. 1997. *Anrtiphon: The Speeches*. Cambridge.

Gagarin, M. 2001. "Did the Sophists Aim to Persuade?" *Rhetorica* 19: 275–291.

Gagarin, M. 2001a. "Women's Voices in Attic Oratory." In: A.P.M.H. Lardinois/L. McClure (eds.), *Making Silence Speak: Women's Voices in Greek Literature and Society*, 161–176. Princeton.

Gagarin, M. 2002. *Antiphon the Athenian: Oratory, Law, and Justice in the Age of the Sophists*. Austin, Texas.

Gagarin, M. 2003. "Telling Stories in Athenian Law." *TAPA* 133: 197–207.

Gagarin, M./Woodruff, P. (eds.) 1995. *Early Greek Political Thought from Homer to the Sophists*. Cambridge.

Gewirtz, P. 1996. "Victims and Voyeurs: Two Narrative Problems at the Criminal Trial." In: P. Brooks/P. Gewirtz (eds.), *Narrative and the Rhetoric in the Law*, 135–165. Yale.

Gibson, R. 2003. "Pliny and the Art of (In)offensive Self-Praise." *Arethusa* 36: 235–254.

Gill, C. 1996. *Personality in Greek Epic, Tragedy, and Philosophy: The Self in Dialogue*. Oxford/New York.

Gill, C. 2003. "Is Rivalry a Virtue or a Vice?" In: D. Konstan/N.K. Rutter (eds.), *Envy, Spite and Jealousy: The Rivalrous Emotions in Ancient Greece*, 29–51. Edinburgh.

Gilhuly, K. 2009. *The Feminine Matrix of Sex and Gender in Classical Athens*. Cambridge.

Goldhill, S. 1998. "The Seductions of the Gaze: Socrates and his Girlfriends." In: P. Cartledge/P. Millett/S. von Reden (eds.), *Kosmos: Essays in Athenian Politics, Law and Society*, 105–124. Cambridge.

Goldhill, S. (ed.) 2001. *Being Greek Under Rome: Cultural Identity, the Second Sophistic and the Development of Empire*. Cambridge.
Goldhill, S. 2001. "The Erotic Eye: Visual Stimulation and Cultural Conflict." In: S. Goldhill (ed.), *Being Greek Under Rome: Cultural Identity, the Second Sophistic and the Development of Empire*, 154–194. Cambridge.
Goldhill, S. 2003. "Tragic Emotions: The Pettiness of Envy and the Politics of Pitilessness." In: D. Konstan/K. Rutter (eds.), *Envy, Spite and Jealousy: The Rivalrous Emotions in Ancient Greece*, 165–180. Edinburgh.
Goldie, P. 2000. *The Emotions: A Philosophical Exploration*. Cambridge.
Goldie, P. 2012. *The Mess Inside: Narrative, Emotion, and the Mind*. Cambridge.
Gribble, D. 1999. *Alcibiades and Athens: A Study in Literary Presentation*. Oxford.
Gribble, D. 2012. "Alcibiades at the Olympics: Performance, Politics, and Civic Ideology." *CQ* 62: 45–71.
Griffith, M. 1990. "Contest and Contradiction in Early Greek Poetry." In: M. Griffith./D. Mastronarde (eds.), *Cabinet of the Muses: essays on Classical and Comparative Literature in Honor of Thomas G. Rosenmayer*, 185–207. Atlanta.
Griffith, M. 1995. "Brilliant Dynasts: Power and Politics in the 'Oresteia'." *CA* 14: 62–129.
Griffith, M./Mastronarde, D. (eds.) 1990. *Cabinet of the Muses: essays on Classical and Comparative Literature in Honor of Thomas G. Rosenmayer*. Atlanta.
Guthrie, W.K.C. 1965. *A History of Greek Philosophy*, vol. II. Cambridge.
Hall, E. 1995. "Law court Dramas: The Power of Performance in Greek Forensic Oratory." *BICS* 40: 39–58.
Halliwell, S. 2000. "Plato and Painting." In: K. Rutter/B.A. Sparkes (eds.), *Word and Image in Ancient Greece*, 99–116. Edinburgh.
Halliwell, S. 2002. *The Aesthetics of Mimesis: Ancient Texts and Modern Problems*. Princeton.
Halliwell, S. 2008. *Greek Laughter: A Study of Cultural Psychology from Homer to Early Christianity*. Cambridge.
Halliwell, S. 2011. *Between Ecstasy and Truth: Interpretations of Greek Poetics from Homer to Longinus*. Oxford.
Halperin, D.M./Winkler, J.J./Zeitlin, F.I. (eds.) 1990. *Before Sexuality: The Construction of Erotic Experience in the Greek World*. Princeton.
Hammond, M./Rhodes, P.J. 2009. *Thucydides: The Peloponnesian War*. Oxford.
Hansen, M.H. 1991. *The Athenian Democracy in the Age of Demosthenes: Structure, Principles and Ideology*. Oxford.
Harding, P. 1994. "Comedy and Rhetoric," In: I. Worthington (ed.), *Persuasion: Greek Rhetoric in Action*, 196–221. London.
Harper, K. 2013. *From Shame to Sin: The Christian Transformation of Sexual Morality in Late Antiquity*. Cambridge, Mass.
Harris, E.M. 1995. *Aeschines and Athenian Politics*. Oxford.
Harris, E.M. 2000. "Open Texture in Athenian Law." *Dike* 3: 27–79.
Harris, E.M. 2006. *Law and Society in Ancient Athens*. Cambridge.
Harris, E.M. 2008. *Demosthenes, Speeches* 20–22. Texas.
Harris, E.M. 2009/10. "Review of Lanni (2006)." *Dike* 12/13: 323–331.
Harris, E.M. 2013. *The Rule of Law in Action in Democratic Athens*. Oxford.
Harris, E.M. 2017. "How to 'Act' in an Athenian Court: Emotions and Forensic Performance," In: S. Papaioannou/A. Serafim/B. Da Vela (eds.), *The Theatre of Justice: Aspects of Performance in Greco-Roman Oratory and Rhetoric*, 223–242. Leiden/Boston.

Harris, W.V. 2001. *Restraining Rage: The Ideology of Anger Control in Classical Antiquity*. Cambridge, Mass.
Harris, W.V./Holmes, B. (eds.) 2008. *Aelius Aristides between Greece, Rome, and the Gods*, Leiden.
Harvey, D. 2005. *A Brief History of Neoliberalism*. Oxford.
Heath, M. 1987. *The Poetics of Greek Tragedy*. Stanford.
Herman, G. 1987. *Ritualised Friendship and the Greek City*. Cambridge.
Hersey, G.L. 2009. *Falling in Love with Statues: Artificial Humans from Pygmalion to the Present*. Chicago/London.
Hobden, F. 2009. "Symposion and the Rhetorics of Commensality in Demosthenes 19." In: M. Christian/M. Haake/R. von den Hoff (eds.), *Rollenbilder in der athenischen Demokratie: Medien, Gruppen, Räume im politischen und sozialen System*, 71–87. Wiesbaden.
Hobden, F. 2013. *The Symposion in Ancient Greek Society and Thought*. Cambridge.
Holmes, B. 2010. *The Symptom and the Subject: The Emergence of the Physical Body in Ancient Greece*. Princeton.
Hornblower, S. 1987. *Thucydides*. London.
Hornblower, S. 1991. *A Commentary on Thucydides*, vol.1: Books I–III. Oxford.
Huart, P. 1968. *Le vocabulaire de l'analyse psychologique dans l'oeuvre de Thucydide*. Paris.
Humphreys, S. 1985. "Social Relations on Stage: Witnesses in Classical Athens." *History and Anthropology* 1: 313–369.
Hunter, V. 1973. *Thucydides: The Artful Reporter*. Toronto.
Hunter, V. 1986. "Thucydides, Gorgias and Mass Psychology." *Hermes* 114: 412–429.
Hunter, V. 1990. "Gossip and the Politics of Reputation in Classical Athens." *Phoenix* 44: 299–325.
Hunter, V. 1994. *Policing Athens: Social control in Athenian lawsuits, 420–320 B.C.* Princeton.
Hunter, R. 2009. *Critical Moments in Classical Literature: Studies in the Ancient View of Literature and its Uses*. Cambridge.
Hurwit, J. 1994. "Peitho." *LIMC* 7: 242–250.
Ierodiakonou, K. 2005. "Empedocles on Colour and Colour Vision." *Oxford Studies in Ancient Philosophy* 29: 1–37.
Innes, D./Hine, H.M./Pelling, C.B.R (eds.) 1995. *Ethics and Rhetoric: Classical Essays for Donald Russell on His Seventy-Fifth Birthday*. Oxford.
Johnson-Laird, P.N./Oatley, K. 2016. "Emotions in Music, Literature, and Film." In: L.F. Barrett/M. Lewis/J.M. Haviland-Jones (eds.), *Handbook of Emotions* (4th edition), 82–97. New York.
Johnson, M./Tarrant, H. (eds.) 2012. *Alcibiades and the Socratic Lover-Educator*. Bristol
Johnstone, S. 1999. *Disputes and Democracy: The Consequences of Litigation in Classical Athens*. Austin, Texas
Jouanna, J. 2012. *Greek Medicine from Hippocrates to Galen: Collected essays* [edited by P. van der Eijk]. Leiden.
Jordan, B. 2000. "The Sicilian Expedition Was a Potemkin Fleet." *CQ* 50: 63–79.
Kahan, D.M. 1998. "The Anatomy of Disgust in Criminal Law." *Faculty Scholarship Series*, Paper 112 (available at http://digitalcommons.law.yale.edu/fss_papers/112, accessed June 2 2017).
Kahan, D.M./Nussbaum, M.C. 1996. "Two Conceptions of Emotion in Criminal Law." *Columbia Law Review* 96: 269–374.
Kallet, L. 2001. *Money and the Corrosion of Power in Thucydides*. California.

Kallet, L. 2003. "Dēmos Tyrannos: Wealth, Power, and Economic Patronage." In: K. Morgan (ed.), *Popular Tyranny: Sovereignty and its Discontents in Ancient Greece*, 117–153. Austin, Texas.
Kalligas, P. 2003. "Από την εικασία στη διαλεκτική: η σοφιστική κληρονομιά του Πλάτωνα." *Deukalion* 21.2: 141–169.
Kampen, N.B. (ed.) 1996. *Sexuality in Ancient Art*. Cambridge.
Kapparis, K. 1999. *Apollodoros, Against Neaira*. Berlin/New York.
Kapparis, K. 2017. "Narrative and Performance in the Speeches of Apollodorus." In: S. Papaioannou/A. Serafim/B. Da Vela et al. (eds.), *The Theatre of Justice: Aspects of Performance in Greco-Roman Oratory and Rhetoric*, 283–303. Leiden/Boston.
Kaster, R.A. 2005. *Emotion, Restraint, and Community in Ancient Rome*. Oxford/New York.
Kennedy, G. 1991. *On Rhetoric. A Theory of Civic Discourse*. Oxford.
Kerferd, G.B. (ed.) 1981. *The Sophists and Their Legacy* [Hermes Einzelschriften 44]. Wiesbaden.
Kirkwood, G.M. 1984. "Blame and Envy in the Pindaric Epinician." In: D.E. Gerber (ed.), *Greek Poetry and Philosophy: Studies in Honour of L. Woodbury*, 169–183. Chico, CA.
Konstan, D. 2001. *Pity Transformed*. London.
Konstan, D. 2003. "Aristotle on Anger and the Emotions: the Strategies of Status." In: S. Braund/G.W. Most (eds.), *Ancient Anger: Perspectives from Homer to Galen Yale Classical Studies* 32], 99–120. Cambridge.
Konstan, D. 2005. "Pity and Politics." In: R.H. Sternberg (ed.), *Pity and Power in Ancient Athens*, 48–66. Cambridge.
Konstan, D. 2006. *The Emotions of the Ancient Greeks: Studies in Aristotle and Classical Literature*. Toronto.
Konstan, D./Rutter, N.K. (eds.) 2003. *Envy, Spite and Jealousy: The Rivalrous Emotions in Ancient Greece*. Edinburgh.
Kövecses, Z. 2000. *Metaphor and Emotion : Language, Culture, and Body in Human Feeling*. Cambridge.
Kremmydas, C. 2012. *Commentary on Demosthenes' Against Leptines*. Oxford.
Krier, T.M. 1990. *Gazing on Secret Sites: Spencer, Classical Imitation, and the Decorums of Vision*. Ithaca/London.
Kurke, L. 1991. *The Traffic in Praise: Pindar and the Poetics of Social Economy*. Ithaca.
LaCourse Munteanu, D. 2012. *Tragic Pathos: Pity and Fear in Greek Philosophy and Tragedy*. Cambridge.
Lanni, A. 1997. "Spectator Sport or Serious Politics? Οἱ περιεστηκότες and the Athenian Lawcourts." *JHS* 117: 183–189.
Lanni, A. 2005. "Relevance in Athenian Courts." In: M. Gagarin/D. Cohen (eds.), *The Cambridge Companion to Ancient Greek Law*, 112–128. Cambridge.
Lanni, A. 2006. *Law and Justice in the Courts of Classical Athens*, Cambridge.
Lanni, A. 2009. "Social Norms in the Courts of Ancient Athens." *Journal of Legal Analysis* 1: 691–736.
Lanni, A. 2016. *Law and Order in Ancient Athens*. Cambridge.
Lardinois, A.P.M.H./McClure, L. (eds.) 2001. *Making Silence Speak: Women's Voices in Greek Literature and Society*. Princeton.
Lateiner, D. 2018. "*Elpis* as Emotion and Reason (Hope and Expectation) in Fifth-century Greek Historians." In: G. Kazantzidis/D. Spatharas (eds.), *Hope in Ancient Literature, History, and Art*, 131–149. Berlin.
Lateiner, D./Spatharas, D. (eds.) 2017. *The Ancient Emotion of Disgust*. Oxford/New York.

Lavelle, B.M. 1992. "Herodotos, Skythian Archers, and the *doryphoroi* of the Peisistratids." *Klio* 74: 78–97.
Lavelle, B.M. 2005. *Fame, Money, and Power: The Rise of Peisistratos and 'Democratic' Tyranny at Athens*. Ann Arbor.
Lazarus, R. 2001. "Relational Meaning and Discrete Emotions." In: K.R. Scherer/A. Schorr/ T. Johnstone (eds.), *Appraisal Processes in Emotion: Theory, Methods, Research*, 37–67. Oxford.
Leighton, S.R. 1982. "Aristotle and the Emotions." *Phronesis* 27: 144–174.
Lintott, A. 1992. "Aristotle and Democracy." *CQ* 42: 114–128.
Lloyd, G.E.R. 1979. *Magic, Reason and Experience: Studies in the Origins and Development of Greek Science*. Cambridge.
Lloyd, G.E.R. 1987. *The Revolutions of Wisdom: Studies in the Claims and Practice of Ancient Greek Science*. Berkeley.
Long, A.A. 1966. "Thinking and Sense-Perception in Empedocles: Mysticism or Materialism." *CQ* 16: 256–276.
Loraux, N. 2006. *The Invention of Athens: The Funeral Oration in the Classical City*. New York.
Lovatt, H. 2013. *The Epic Gaze: Vision, Gender and Narrative in Ancient Epic*. Cambridge.
Ludwig, P.W. 2002. *Eros and Polis: Desire and Community in Greek Political Theory*. Cambridge.
Luke, J. 1994. "'Kratos' and the 'Polis.'" *G&R*: 23–32.
MacDowell, D.M. 1976. "*Hybris* in Athens." *G&R* 23: 14–31.
MacDowell, D.M. 1982. *Gorgias: Encomium of Helen*. Bristol.
MacDowell, D.M. 1990. *Demosthenes*, Against Meidias. Oxford.
MacDowell, D.M. 2000. *Demosthenes*, On the False Embassy (Or. 19). Oxford.
MacDowell, D.M. 2000a. "Athenian Laws about Homosexuality." *RIDA* 47: 13–27.
Macleod, C. 1983. *Collected Essays*. Oxford.
Mann, J.E. 2012. *Hippocrates*, On the Art of Medicine [Studies in ancient medicine, 39], Leiden.
Marincola, J. 1997. *Authority and Tradition in Ancient Historiography*. Cambridge.
Macleod, C. 1983. *Collected Essays*. Oxford.
Meijering, R. 1987. *Literary and Rhetorical Theories in Greek Scholia*. Groningen.
Miller, H.W. 1952. "*Dynamis* and *Physis* in On Ancient Medicine." *TAPA* 83: 184–197.
Millett, P. 1998. "Encounters in the Agora." In: P. Cartledge/P. Millet/S. von Reden (eds.), *Kosmos: Essays in Order, Conflict and Community in Classical Athens*, 203–228. Cambridge.
Mirhady, D./Too, Y.L. 2000. *Isocrates I*. Austin, Texas.
Mitchell, A.G. 2009. *Greek Vase-Painting and the Origins of Visual Humour*. Cambridge.
Mitchell, L.G. 1997. *Greeks Bearing Gifts: The Public Use of Private Relationships in the Greek World 435–323 BC*. Cambridge.
Momigliano, A. 1971. *The Development of Greek Biography*. Cambridge, Mass.
Monoson, S. 2000. *Plato's Democratic Entanglements: Athenian Politics and the Practice of Philosophy*. Princeton.
Montiglio, S. 2000. *Silence in the Land of Logos*. Princeton.
Morris, I. 1996. "The Strong Principle of Equality and the Archaic Origins of Greek Democracy." In: J. Ober/C. Hedrick (eds.), *DĒMOKRATIA: A Conversation on Democracies, Ancient and Modern*, 19–48. Princeton.
Morales, H. 2004. *Vision and Narrative in Achilles Tatius' Leucippe and Clitophon*. Cambridge.
Morel, P.-M. 1996. *Démocrite et la recherche des causes*. Paris.

Morgan, K. 1994. "Socrates and Gorgias at Delphi and Olympia: *Phaedrus* 235d6–236b4." *CQ* 44: 375–386.
Mossé, C. 1987. «Égalité démocratique et inegalités sociales: le débat à Athènes au IVème siècle.» *Mètis* 2: 165–176, 195–206.
Most, G.W. 1989. "Self-Disclosure and Self-Sufficiency in Greek Culture." *JHS* 109: 114–133.
Most, G.W. 2003. "Epinician Envies." In: D. Konstan/N.K. Rutter (eds.), *Envy, Spite and Jealousy: The Rivalrous Emotions in Ancient Greece*, 123–142. Edinburgh.
Mourelatos, A.P.D. 1987. "Gorgias on the Function of Language." *Philosophical Topics* 15: 135–170.
Murray, O. 1990. "The Affair of the Mysteries: Democracy and the Drinking Group." In: O. Murray (ed.), *Sympotica: A Symposium on the Symposion*, 149–161. Oxford.
Murray, O. 2016. "Violence at the *Symposion*." In: W. Riess/G.G. Fagan (eds.), *The Topography of Violence in the Greco-Roman World*, 195–206. Michigan, Ann Arbor.
Mylonas, G.E. (ed.) 1951–1953. *Studies Presented to D.M. Robinson*. St Louis.
Nicolai, R. 2004. *Studi su Isocrate. La comunicazione letteraria nel IV secolo a.C. e i nuovi generi della prosa*. Rome.
Nightingale, A.W. 2004. *Spectacles of Truth in Classical Greek Philosophy: Theoria in its Cultural Context*. Cambridge.
Nussbaum, M.C. 1994. *The Therapy of Desire: Theory and Practice in Hellenistic Ethics*. Princeton.
Nussbaum, M.C. 1996. "Aristotle on Emotions and Rational Persuasion." In: A.O. Rorty (ed.), *Essays on Aristotle's* Rhetoric, 303–321. California.
Nussbaum, M.C. 2001. *Upheavals of Thought: The intelligence of emotions*. Cambridge.
Nussbaum, M.C. 2003. "Compassion & Terror." *Daedalus* 132: 10–26.
Ober, J. 1989. *Mass and elite in Democratic Athens: Rhetoric, Ideology, and the Power of the People*. Princeton.
Ober, J. 1998. *Political Dissent in Democratic Athens: Intellectual Critics of Popular Rule*. Princeton.
Ober, J. 1999. *The Athenian Revolution: Essays on Ancient Democracy and Political Theory*. Princeton.
Ober, J. 2005. *Athenian Legacies : Essays on the Politics of Going on Together*. Princeton.
Ober, J./Hedrick, C. (eds.) 1996. *Demokratia: A Conversation on Democracies, Ancient and Modern*, Princeton.
O'Brien, D. 1970. "The Effects of a Simile: Empedocles' Theories of Seeing and Breathing." *JHS* 90: 140–179.
O'Connell, P.A. 2017. *The Rhetoric of Seeing in Attic Forensic Oratory*. Austin, Texas.
Papaioannou, S./Serafim, A./Da Vela, B. (eds.) 2017. *The Theatre of Justice: Aspects of Performance in Greco-Roman Oratory and Rhetoric*. Leiden/Boston.
O'Sullivan, N. 1992. *Alcidamas, Aristophanes, and Early Greek Stylistic Theory* [Hermes Einzelschriften 60]. Stuttgart.
Olson, G. 2014. "Narration and Narrative in Legal Discourse." In: P. Hühn/J.C Meister/J. Pier/W. Schmid (eds.), *Handbook of narratology*, 371–384. Leiden, (available at http://www.lhn.uni-hamburg.de/article/narration-and-narrative-legal-discourse, accessed May 30 2017, 13.20).
Omitowoju, R. 2002. *Rape and the Politics of Consent in Classical Athens*. Cambridge.
Osborne, R. 1985. "Law in Action in Classical Athens." *JHS* 105: 40–58.

Osborne, R./Hornblower, S. (eds.) 1994. *Ritual, Finance, Politics: Athenian Democratic Accounts Presented to David Lewis*. Oxford.
Ostwald, M. 1986. *From Popular Sovereignty to the Sovereignty of the Law: Law, Society and Politics in Fifth-Century Athens*. California.
Parry, J./Bloch, M. (eds.) 1989. *Money and the Morality of Exchange*. Cambridge.
Parry, J./Bloch, M. 1989 "Introduction: Money and the Morality of Exchange." In: J. Parry/ M. Bloch (eds.), *Money and the Morality of Exchange*, 1–32. Cambridge.
Patterson, C. 1994. "The Case against Neaira and the Public Ideology of the Athenian Family." In: A.L. Boegehold/A.C. Scafuro (eds.), *Athenian Identity and Civic Ideology*, 199–216. Baltimore, MD.
Padel, R. 1995. *Whom Gods Destroy: Elements of Greek and Tragic Madness*. Princeton.
Parker, R. 1987. "Festivals of the Ancient Demes." In: T. Linders/G. Nordquist (eds.), *Gifts to the Gods. Proceedings of the Uppsala Symposium* 198 [*Boreas* 15], 137–147. Uppsala.
Pelliccia, H. 1992. "Sappho 16, Gorgias' *Helen*, and the Preface to Herodotus' *Histories*." *YCS* 29: 63–84.
Pelling, C.B.R. 1991. "Thucydides' Archidamus and Herodotus' Artabanus." In: M.A. Flower/ M. Toher (eds.), *Georgica: Greek Studies in Honour of George Cawkwell*, 120–142. London.
Pelling, C.B.R. 2000. *Literary Texts and the Greek Historian*. London/New York.
Pendrick, G.J. 2002. *Antiphon the Sophist: The Fragments* [Cambridge Classical Texts and Fragments 39]. Cambridge.
Perlman, D. 1964. "Quotations from Poetry in Attic Orators of the Fourth Century BC." *AJP* 85: 155–172.
Pernot, L. 1998. "*PERIAUTOLOGIA:* Problèmes et méthodes de l'éloge de soi-même dans la tradition éthique et rhétorique Gréco-romaine." *REG* 111: 101–124.
Petridou, G. 2015. *Divine Epiphany in Greek Literature and Culture*. Oxford.
Pirenne-Delforge, V. 1991. "Le culte de la persuasion. Peitho en Grèce ancienne." *RHR* 208: 395–413.
Plant, I.M. 1999. "The Influence of Forensic Oratory on Thucydides' Principles of Method." *CQ* 49: 62–73.
Pollitt, J.J. 1974. *The Ancient View of Greek Art: History, Criticism and Terminology*. Yale.
Porter, J.R. 1997. "Adultery By The Book: Lysias 1 (*On the Murder of Eratosthenes*) and Comic Diegesis." *EMC* 16: 421–453.
Porter, J.I. 1993. "The Seductions of Gorgias." *CA* 12: 267–299.
Porter, J.I. (ed.) 1999. *Constructions of the Classical Body*. Ann Arbor.
Prost, F./Wilgaux, J. (eds.) 2006. *Penser et représenter le corps dans l'Antiquité*. Rennes.
Race, W.H. 1989. "Sappho, fr. 16 L-P. and Alkaios, fr. 42 L-P.: Romantic and Classical Strains in Lesbian Lyric." *CJ* 85: 16–33.
Rademaker, A. 2005. Sophrosyne *and the Rhetoric of Self-restraint*. Leiden/Boston.
Rawls, J. 1999. *A Theory of Justice*. Cambridge, Mass.
Rengakos, A./Tsakmakis, A. (eds.) 2006. *Brill's Companion to Thucydides*. Leiden.
Rhodes, P.J. 1981. *A Commentary on the Aristotelian* Athenaion Politeia. Oxford.
Rhodes, P.J. 2004. "Keeping to the Point." In: E.M. Harris/L. Rubinstein (eds.), *The Law and the Courts in Ancient Athens*, 137–158. London.
Riess, W. 2012. *Performing Interpersonal Violence: Court, Curse, and Comedy in Fourth-century BCE Athens*. Berlin.
Riess, W./Fagan, G.G. (eds.) 2016. *The Topography of Violence in the Greco-Roman World*. Ann Arbor.

Rogkotis, Z. 2006. "Thucydides and Herodotus : Aspects of their Intertextual Relationship." In: A. Rengakos/A. Tsakmakis (eds.), *Brill's Companion to Thucydides*, 57–86. Leiden.
Roisman, J. 2005. *The Rhetoric of Manhood: Masculinity in the Attic Orators*. Berkeley/Los Angeles/London.
Roisman, J. 2006. *The Rhetoric of Conspiracy in Ancient Athens*. Berkeley/Los Angeles/London.
Rorty, A.O. 1996. (ed.), *Essays on Aristotle's Rhetoric*. Berkeley/Los Angeles/London.
Rosen, R.M./Farrell, J. (eds.) 1993. *Nomodeiktes: Greek Studies in Honor of Martin Ostwald*. Ann Arbor.
Rosen, R.M./Sluiter, I. (eds.) 2010. *Valuing Others in Classical Antiquity*. Leiden.
Rosenmeyer, T. 1955. "Gorgias, Aeschylus and *Apatê*." *AJP* 76: 225–260.
Rosivach, V.J. 1987. "*Autochthony* and the Athenians." *CQ* 37: 294–306.
Rothwell, S.K., Jr. 1990. *Politics and Persuasion in Aristophanes'* Ecclesiazusae. Mnemosyne Supplements 111. Leiden/Boston.
Rotroff, S.I./Oakley, J.H. 1992. *Debris from A Public Dining Place in the Athenian Agora*, Hesperia Supplement 25. Princeton, New Jersey.
Rouveret, A. 1989. *Histoire et imaginaire de la peinture Ancienne*. Rome.
Roux, G. 1961. "Le sens de TUPOS." *REG* 63: 5–14.
Rubinstein, L. 2000. *Litigation and Cooperation: Supporting Speakers in the Courts of Classical Athens*, Historia Einzelschriften 147. Stuttgart.
Rubinstein, L. 2013. "Evoking Anger through Pity: Portraits of the Vulnerable and Defenceless in Attic oratory." In: A. Chaniotis/P. Ducrey (eds.), *Unveiling Emotions II. Emotions in Greece and Rome: Texts, Images, Material Culture. Heidelberger althistorische Beiträge und epigraphische Studien (HABES)*, Bd 55, 136–165. Stuttgart.
Rubinstein, L. 2004. "Stirring Up Dicastic Anger." In: D.L. Cairns/R.A. Knox (eds.), *Law, Rhetoric, and Comedy in Classical Athens: Essays in Honour of Douglas M. MacDowell*, 187–204. Swansea.
Rudolph, K. 2011. "Democritus' Perspectival Theory of Vision." *JHS* 131: 67–83.
Rudolph, K. 2016. "Sight and the Presocratics: Approaches to Visual Perception in Early Greek Philosophy." In: M. Squire (ed.), *Sight and the Ancient Senses: The Senses in Antiquity*, 36–53. London/New York.
Rusten, J.S. 1989. *Thucydides: The Peloponnesian War*, Book II. Cambridge.
Rutter, K./Sparkes, B.A. (eds.) 2000. *Word and Image in Ancient Greece*. Edinburgh.
Rutherford, I. 1995. "The Poetics of the *Paraphthegma*: Aelius Aristides and the *Decorum* of Self-Praise." In: D. Innes/H.M. Hine/C.B.R. Pelling (eds.), *Ethics and Rhetoric: Classical Essays for Donald Russell on His Seventy-Fifth Birthday*, 193–205. Oxford.
Saïd, S. 2003. "Envy and Emulation in Isocrates." In: D. Konstan/N.K. Rutter (eds.), *Envy, Spite and Jealousy: The Rivalrous Emotions in Ancient Greece*, 217–234. Edinburgh.
Sanders, E. 2008. "*Pathos phaulon*: Aristotle and the Rhetoric of *Phthonos*." In: I. Sluiter/R.M. Rosen (eds.), *Kakos: Badness and Anti-value in Classical Antiquity*, 255–282. Leiden.
Sanders, E. 2012. "'He is a Liar, a Bounder and a Cad': the Arousal of Hostile Emotions in Attic Forensic Oratory." In: A. Chaniotis (ed.), *Unveiling Emotions. Sources and Methods for the Study of Emotions in the Greek World. Heidelberger althistorische Beiträge und epigraphische Studien* (HABES) 52, 259–287. Stuttgart.
Sanders, E. 2014. *Envy and Jealousy in Classical Athens: A Socio-Psychological Approach*. Oxford/New York.
Sanders, E./Johncock, M. (eds.) 2016. *Emotion and Persuasion in Classical Antiquity*. Stuttgart.

Sawada, N. 2010. "Social Customs and Institutions: Aspects of Macedonian Elite Society." In: J. Roisman/I. Worthington (eds.), *A companion to Ancient Macedonia*, 392–408. West Sussex.
Scafuro, A.C. 1997. *The Forensic Stage: Settling Disputes in Graeco-Roman New Comedy*. Cambridge.
Schaps, D.M. 1977. "The Women Least Mentioned: Etiquette and Women's Names." *CQ* 27: 323–331.
Scheppele, K. 1989. "Foreword: Telling Stories." *Michigan Law Review* 87: 2073, 2083–2098.
Scherer, K.R./Schorr, A./Johnstone, T. (eds.) 2001. *Appraisal Processes in Emotion: Theory, Methods, Research*. Oxford.
Schloemann, J. 2002. "Entertainment and Democratic Distrust: The Audience's Attitudes Towards Oral and Written Oratory in Classical Athens." In: I. Worthington/J.M. Foley (eds.), *Epea and Grammata: Oral and Written Communication in Ancient Greece*, 113–146. Leiden.
Schmit-Pantel, P. 1992. *La cité au banquet: Histoire des repas publiques dans les cités grecques*. Rome.
Schoeck, H. 1987. *Envy: A Theory of Social Behaviour*. Indianapolis.
Schrager, S. 1999. *The Trial Lawyer's Art*. Philadelphia.
Scodel, R. 2007. "Lycurgus and the State Text of Tragedy." In: C. Cooper (ed.), *Politics of Orality (Orality and Literacy in Ancient Greece, vol. 6), Mnemosyne Supplement* 280, 129–154. Leiden.
Scott, L. 2005. *Historical Commentary on Herodotus Book 6*. Leiden.
Sedley, D.N. 1992. "Empedocles' Theory of Vision and Theophrastus' *De sensibus*." In: W.W. Fortenbaugh/D. Gutas (eds.), *Theophrastus: His Psychological, Doxographical and Scientific Writings*, 20–31. New Jersey.
Segal, C. 1962. "Gorgias and the Psychology of the Logos." *HSCP* 66: 99–155.
Shear, K. 2011. *Polis and Revolution: Responding to Oligarchy in Classical Athens*. Cambridge.
Serafim, A. 2017. *Attic Oratory and Performance*. London/New York.
Shapiro, H.A. 2005. "The Judgment of Helen on Athenian Art." In: J.M. Barringer/J.M. Hurwit (eds.), *Periklean Athens and Its Legacy*, 47–62. Austin, Texas.
Sinos, R.H. 1998. "Divine Selections: Epiphany and Politics in Archaic Greece." In: C. Dougherty/L. Kurke (eds.), *Cultural Poetics in Archaic Greece: Cult, Performance, Politics*, 73–91. Oxford.
Sissa, G. 1999. "Sexual Bodybuilding: Aeschines against Timarchus." In: J.I. Porter (ed.), *Constructions of the Classical Body*, 147–168. Ann Arbor.
Skinner, Q. 2002. *Visions of Politics*, vol. 1: *Regarding Method*. Cambridge.
Slater, W.J. 1988. "The Epiphany of Demosthenes." *Phoenix* 42: 126–130.
Smith, A.C. 2011. *Polis and Personification in Classical Athenian Art*. Monumenta Graeca et Romana, 19. Leiden/Boston.
Spatharas, D. 2001. "Patterns of Argumentation in Gorgias." *Mnemosyne* 54: 393–408.
Spatharas, D. 2002. "Gorgias' *Encomium of Helen* and Euripides' *Troades*." *Eranos* 100: 166–174.
Spatharas, D. 2006. "Wounding, Rhetoric, and the Law in Lysias IV." *RIDA* 53: 87–106.
Spatharas, D. 2006a. "Λυσίας, *Κατὰ Τείσιδος* (απ. 17 Gernet – Bizos): μια ερμηνευτική προσέγγιση." *Ariadne* 12: 47–67.
Spatharas, D. 2007. "Gorgias and the Hippocratic Treatise *De arte*." *C&M* 58: 159–163.
Spatharas, D. 2008. "Δόξα, γνώση και απάτη στον Γοργία." In: Ch. Balla (ed.), *Φιλοσοφία και ρητορική στην κλασική Αθήνα*. Herakleion.

Spatharas, D. 2009. "Liaisons dangereuses: Procopius, Lysias, and Apollodorus." *CQ* 62: 846–858.
Spatharas, D. 2009a. "Kinky Stories from the Rostrum: Storytelling in Apollodorus' *Against Neaira*." *Ancient Narrative* 9: 99–119.
Spatharas, D. 2009b. *Ἰσοκράτης, Κατὰ Λοχίτου*. Athens.
Spatharas, D. 2011. "Self-praise and Envy: From Rhetoric to the Athenian Courts." *Arethusa* 44: 199–219.
Spatharas, D. 2013. *"Plutarch's De invidia et odio and Aristotle's Rhetoric."* In: G. Pace/ P.V. Cacciatore (eds.), *Atti del IX Convegno Internazionale della International Plutarch Society*, 411–422. Napoli.
Spatharas, D. 2017. "Sex, Politics, and Disgust in Aeschines' *Against Timarchus*." In: D. Lateiner/ D. Spatharas (eds.), *The Ancient Emotion of Disgust*, 125–139. Oxford/New York.
Spatharas, D. 2017a. "The Mind's Theatre: Envy, Hybris and Enargeia in Demosthenes' *Against Meidias*." In: S. Papaioannou/A. Serafim/Da Vela, B. (eds.), *The Theatre of Justice: Aspects of Performance in Greco-Roman Oratory and Rhetoric*, 201–222. Leiden/Boston.
Spatharas, D. (forthcoming) "The Social Construction of Disgust in Ancient Greece." In: A. Chaniotis (ed.), *Unveiling Emotions III*. Stuttgart.
Sprague Rothwell Jr., K.S. 1990. *Politics and Persuasion in Aristophanes'* Ecclesiazusae. Leiden.
Squire, M. (ed.) 2016. *Sight and the Ancient Senses: The Senses in Antiquity*. London/New York.
Stafford, E.J. 2000. *Worshiping Virtues: Personification and the Divine in Ancient Greece*. Swansea.
Stanford, W.B. 1983. *Greek Tragedy and the Emotions: An Introductory Study*. London.
Steiner, A. 2002. "Private and Public: Links Between Symposion and Syssition in Fifth-Century Athens." *CA* 21: 347–390.
Steiner, D. 2001. *Images in Mind: Statues in Archaic and Classical Greek Literature and Thought*. Princeton.
Sternberg, R.H. 2005. "The Nature of Pity." In: R.H. Sternberg (ed.), *Pity and Power in Classical Athens*, 15–47. Cambridge.
Sternberg, R.H. 2006. *Tragedy Offstage: Suffering and Sympathy in Ancient Athens*. Texas, Austin.
Stevens, M. 2000. "Victim Impact Statements Considered in Sentencing." *California Criminal Law Review* 3 (available at http://scholarship.law.berkeley.edu/bjcl/vol2/iss1/3, accessed on June 2, 2017).
Strauss, B.S. 1993. *Fathers and Sons in Athens*. Princeton.
Suk Gersen, J. 2013. "'The Look in His Eyes': The Story of *State v. Rusk* and Rape Reform." (available at https://ssrn.com/abstract=1546602, accessed on August 2, 2017).
Sutton, R.F. Jr. 1997/1998. "Nuptial Eros: The Visual Discourse of Marriage in Classical Athens." *The Journal of the Walters Art Gallery* 55/56: 26–48.
Tanner, J. 2005. *The Invention of Art History in Ancient Greece: Religion, Society and Artistic Rationalisation*. Cambridge.
Taplin, O. 1978. *Greek Tragedy in Action*. London.
Taylor, C.C.W. 1999. *The Atomists: Leucippus and Democritus*. Toronto.
Thomas, R. 1994. "Law and the Lawgiver in the Athenian Democracy." In: R. Osborne/S. Hornblower (eds.), *Ritual, Finance, Politics: Athenian Democratic Accounts Presented to David Lewis*, 119–133. Oxford.

Thomas, R. 2000. *Herodotus in Context: Ethnography, Science and the Art of Persuasion*. Cambridge.
Thomas, R. 2006. "Thucydides' Intellectual Milieu and the Plague." In: A. Rengakos/ A. Tsakmakis (eds.), *Brill's Companion to Thucydides*, 87–107. Leiden.
Thumiger, C. 2013. "The Early Greek Medical Vocabulary of Insanity." In: W.V. Harris (ed.), *Mental Disorders in the Classical World*, 61–95. Leiden.
Thür, G. 1977. *Beweisführung vor den Schwurgerichtshöfen Athens: die Proklesis zur Basanos*. Vienna.
Todd, S.C. 1990. "The Purpose of Evidence in Athenian Courts." In: P. Cartledge/P. Millett/ S.C. Todd (eds.), *Nomos: Essays in Athenian Law, Politics and Society*, 19–39. Cambridge.
Todd, S.C. 1993. *The Shape of Athenian Law*. Oxford.
Todd, S.C. 1996. "Lysias *Against Nikomachos*: The Fate of the Expert in Athenian Law." In: L. Foxhall/A.D.E. Lewis (eds.), *Greek Law in Its Political Setting: Justifications not Justice*, 101–131. Oxford.
Todd, S.C. 2000. *Lysias*. Texas, Austin.
Tompkins, D.P. 1993. "Archidamus and the Question of Characterization in Thucydides." In: R.M. Rosen/J. Farrell (eds.), *Nomodeiktes: Greek Studies in Honor of Martin Ostwald*, 99–111. Ann Arbor.
Trevett, J. 1990. "History in [Demosthenes] 59." *CQ* 40: 407–420.
Tsakmakis, A. 2006. "Leaders, Crowds, and the Power of the Image: Political Communication in Thucydides." In: A. Rengakos/A. Tsakmakis (eds.), *Brill's Companion to Thucydides*, 161–187. Leiden/Boston.
Tzanetou, A. 2005. "A Generous City: Pity in Athenian Oratory and Tragedy." In: R.H. Sternberg (ed.), *Pity and Power in Classical Athens*, 98–122. Cambridge.
Usher, S. 1993. *Demosthenes, On the crown*. Warminster.
Usher, S. 1999. *Greek Oratory: Tradition and Originality*. Oxford.
Vallozza, M. 1989. "Il motivo dell' invidia in Pindaro." *QUCC* 60–62, n.s. 31–3: 13–30.
Verdenius, W.J. 1981. "Gorgias' Doctrine of Deception." In: G.B. Herferd (ed.), *The Sophists and Their Legacy* [Hermes Einzelschriften 44], 116–129. Wiesbaden.
Vernant, J.P. 1990. *Figures, idoles, masques*. Paris.
Yunis, H. 1996. *Taming Democracy: Models of Political Rhetoric in Classical Athens*. Ithaca/London.
Yunis, H. 2000. "Politics as Literature: Demosthenes and the Burden of the Athenian Past." *Arion* 8: 97–118.
Yunis, H. 2001. *Demosthenes, On the crown*. Cambridge.
Walcot, P. 1978. *Envy and the Greeks: A Study of Human Behaviour*. Warminster.
Walker, A.D. 1993. "Enargeia and the Spectator in Greek Historiography." *TAPA* 123: 353–377.
Wankel, H. 1976. *Demosthenes: Rede für Ktesiphon über den Kranz*. Heidelberg.
Warren, J. 2007. "Democritus on Social and Psychological Harm." In: A. Brancacci/P.-M. Morel (eds.), *Democritus: Science, the Arts, and the Care of the Soul, Proceedings of the International Colloquium on Democritus (Paris, 18–20 September 2003)*, 87–104. Leiden/Boston.
Webb, R. 1997. "Imagination and the Arousal of the Emotions in Greco-Roman Rhetoric." In: S.M. Braund/C. Gill (eds.), *The Passions in Roman Thought and Literature*, 112–127. Cambridge.
Webb, R. 2009. *Ekphrasis, Imagination and Persuasion in Ancient Rhetorical Theory and Practice*. Surray.

Webb, R. 2016. "Sight and Insight: Theorizing Vision, Emotion and Imagination in Ancient Rhetoric." In: M. Squire (ed.), *Sight and the Ancient Senses. The Senses in Antiquity*, 205–219. London/New York.

Westwood, G.A.C.M. 2014. *History and the Making of the Orator in Demosthenes and Aeschines*. PhD Diss. Oxford.

White, J.B. 1985. *Heracles' Bow: Essays on the Rhetoric and Poetics of the Law*. Wisconsin.

Whitehead, D. 1983. "Competitive Outlay and Community Profit: *Philotimia* in Democratic Athens." *C&M* 34: 55–74.

Whitehead, D. 1986. *The Demes of Attica 508-7 - ca.250 BC: A Political and Social Study*. Princeton.

Whitehead, D. 1993. "Cardinal Virtues: The Language of Public Approbation in Democratic Athens." *C&M* 44: 37–75.

Whitmarsh, T. 2011. *Narrative and Identity in the Ancient Greek Novel: Returning Romance. Greek culture in the Roman world*. Cambridge.

Whitton, C. 2013. *Pliny the Younger: Epistles Book II*. Cambridge.

Wilson, P. 1991. "Demosthenes 21 (*Against Meidias*): Democratic Abuse." *PCPS* 37: 164–195.

Wilson, P. 1996. "Rhetoric: The Use of Tragedy and the Tragic in the Fourth Century." In: M.S. Silk (ed.), *Tragedy and the Tragic: Greek Theater and Beyond*, 310–331. Oxford.

Wilson, P. 2000. *The Athenian Institution of the Khoregia: The Chorus, the City and the State*. Cambridge.

Winkler, J.J. 1990. "Laying Down the Law: The Oversight of Men's Sexual Behavior in Classical Athens." In: D.M. Halperin/J.J. Winkler/F.I. Zeitlin (eds.), *Before sexuality: The construction of erotic experience in the Greek world*, 171–210. Princeton.

Winkler, J.J. 1991. *Auctor and Actor: A Narratological Reading of Apuleius's* Golden Ass. Berkeley/Los Angeles/Oxford.

Wohl, V. 2002. *Love Among the Ruins: The Erotics of Democracy in Classical Athens*. Princeton.

Wohl, V. 2010. *Law's Cosmos: Juridical Discourse in Athenian Forensic Oratory*. Cambridge.

Wohl, V. 2012. "The Eye of the Beloved: *Opsis* and *Eros* in Socratic Pedagogy." In: M. Johnson/H. Tarrant (eds.), *Alcibiades and the Socratic Lover-Educator*, 45–60. Bristol.

Worman, N. 2002. *The Cast of Character: Style in Greek Literature*. Austin.

Worman, N. 2008. *Abusive Mouths in Classical Athens*. Cambridge.

Worthington, I. 2003. "The Length of an Athenian Public Trial: A Reply to Professor MacDowell." *Hermes* 131: 364–371.

Xydopoulos, I.K./Vlassopoulos, K./Tounta, E. 2017. *Violence and Community: Law, Space and Identity in the Ancient Eastern Mediterranean World*. London.

Zanker, G. 1981. "*Enargeia* in the Ancient Criticism of Poetry." *RhM* 124: 296–311.

Zanker, G. 2004. *Modes of Viewing in Hellenistic Poetry and Art*. Madison, WI.

Zeitlin, F. (ed.) 1991. *Jean Pierre Vernant, Mortals and Immortals: Collected Essays*. Princeton.

# Index Rerum et Nominum

Acharnae/Acharnians 72–73, 76–77
Acragas 32
adultery 101 n.49
*agora* 102 n.51, 103, 105–106, 107 n.71, 118, 120, 154, 156–157
*aischrologia* 118 n.98
Alcibiades 21, 62 n.19, 65, 68–69, 69 nn.39–40, 70, 70 n.43, 78–79, 87, 87 n.17, 103 n.55, 128, 132–133, 133 n.19, 133 n.21, 134, 139, 152, 173
Alexander 168
*anakrisis* 85, 85 n.9
*ananke* 4 n.14, 30–31, 38 n.35, 186
anger 1, 1–2 n.3, 2, 5 n.18, 9 n.28, 10–11, 14, 14 n.41, 15–16, 16 n.44, 21–22, 38, 40, 57, 59, 59 n.10, 60, 60 n.12, 72–74, 74 n.53, 75–76, 76 n.57, 77–79, 94, 96, 101–102, 102 n.51, 102 n.53, 103, 108, 110, 110 n.74, 114–115, 118 n.95, 122, 124, 133, 142, 145–146, 148, 150, 158, 161 n.7, 175
*antidosis* 120, 146, 163
*apate* 3 n.8
Archidamus 21, 57, 60, 72–73, 73 nn.50–51, 74, 74 n.53, 74 n.55, 75–76, 76 n.57, 77–78, 78 n.60, 79
*aselgeia* 105 n.62
*ate* 27–28 n.14
*ateleia* 143–144
*atimia* 116
Austin, John 44, 138
*autolekythos* 105, 105 n.61

Balinese mourners 19, 20 n.53
*basanos* 100, 100 n.46
*baskania* (evil eye) 34, 36
*bdelyria* 119
*bia* 4 n.14
Bourdieu, Pierre 133
Brooks, Peter 80, 80 n.1, 81 nn.3–4, 82–83

chance (τύχη) 30–31, 36–37, 71 n.48, 130 n.15, 169, 184
chariots 132, 146, 156
*charis* 53, 63–64, 120 n.100, 125, 140, 143, 149–150, 173
*chitoniskos* 115
*choregia/choregos* 117, 142, 149, 151, 153, 155 n.40, 178
cocks (and masculinity/sex) 104–105, 105 n.60, 107, 118, 120
cognitive approach to emotions 1, 2 n.7, 3, 5, 5 n.15, 6, 8, 10–11, 15, 17–19, 21, 23, 25, 37–38, 38 n.37, 40–44, 48, 50–51, 60, 68, 75, 81, 84, 91–92, 95, 95 n.36, 96, 114, 119, 122, 128, 140, 144, 159, 166, 172, 189–190
Cover 84

*deinosis* 108
de La Rochefoucauld, François 158, 158 n.46, 160, 161 n.7
*diabole* 5
*diadikasia* 146
*diaitetes* 85
*diegesis* 87, 97, 103
*dike*
– *aikeias* 94, 97, 103, 107, 107 n.71, 110 n.74, 118 n.97
– *biaion* 118 n.97
– *blabes* 118 n.97
disgust 1, 9, 9 n.30, 14, 19, 19 n.51, 20, 94, 95 n.37, 107, 114, 114 n.86, 119, 123
*dokimasia* 15, 116 n.89, 173–174, 176–177, 180
*doxa* 24, 43, 51, 67, 90
drug(s) (φάρμακον/α) 28 n.17, 49–50, 59 n.11
drunkenness 97, 99, 103, 103 n.55, 109, 112 n.82, 113–114, 117, 157
*dynamis* (δύναμις) 30, 49–50, 50 n.62, 51, 61, 69 n.39, 132
*dyseros* 66, 66 n.33

effluences (ἀπορροαί) 29, 31–33, 33 nn.28–29, 34–35, 56 n.81
eidolon/a 7, 21, 31–32, 34–36, 36 n.34, 37, 41–42, 50–51, 55 n.74, 56 n.81
eikos/eikota 21, 25, 25 n.5, 27, 27 n.12, 37, 47, 52–53, 75–77, 90, 173
ekphrasis 6 n.20, 89
ekplexis 39–40, 55 n.79, 75
elites/masses 18, 18 n.49, 35, 35 n.32, 42, 57–58, 59 n.10, 60, 63, 68–69, 72, 78–79, 97, 107–109, 112, 124, 124 n.2, 125, 125 n.6, 126–128, 130–132, 133 n.19, 133 n.21, 134–137, 137 n.27, 138–140, 143–144, 146, 149–153, 157–159, 161 n.7, 167, 169–171, 176, 178, 180, 182 n.54, 183, 187
emanation/emanationist models of vision 29–30, 33, 41, 54, 56 n.81, 133
emotions
– metaphors for 9, 9 nn.28–29, 74–75, 159, 159 n.3
– scripts of 5, 9 n.30, 10, 12, 12 n.35, 13–14, 16–18, 20–21, 72, 84, 91, 91 n.28, 92, 94, 96, 101–102, 106, 108, 110, 110 n.74, 111, 113, 116, 118 n.95, 122, 127, 128 n.12, 141, 144–151, 166, 187, 189–190
enargeia 2, 2 n.6, 4, 6 n.20, 7 n.23, 8, 22, 57, 57 n.1, 69, 80, 85 n.11, 89–90, 90 n.23, 92–93, 93 n.32, 94, 122, 148, 184, 186
epideixis/epideictic 7, 21, 24, 25, 25 n.6, 26, 27 n.11, 30–32, 32 n.25, 39, 42, 49, 52, 55, 55 n.79, 68 n.36, 73, 143
epieikes/epieikeia 135–137, 143
epiphany 185, 185 n.57, 186
erastes/eromenos 40, 61, 64, 67, 79, 101, 120
ergon 52, 57, 61, 71, 73–74, 76–79, 90, 123, 139 n.31, 142, 165
eros 2, 4, 4 n.12, 7, 21, 27–28, 28 n.14, 30 n.20, 31, 40, 41 n.41, 53–54, 56, 56 n.81, 57, 57 n.3, 60, 62–63, 63 n.22, 64–66, 66 n.31, 67–69, 71, 71 n.48, 78, 101 n.47

ethos 2 n.6, 22, 63, 77 n.59, 124, 143, 148–149, 156, 173, 175–176, 179–180, 187
eukleia (εὔκλεια) 26 n.9
Eumolpus 24, 24 n.1
eunoia 170 n.35, 184, 184 nn.55–56, 185, 185 n.57
euthyna 172, 173 n.42, 180
extromissive/intromissive models of vision 6, 30–31, 33, 55

Foster 69 n.39, 161 n.7, 165–168, 168 n.26, 169–170

gestures 3, 20, 82, 93, 104, 104 n.57, 105, 108–109, 114–115, 121–122, 175
gnome 28, 52, 74
graphe (public prosecution) 16
graphe hybreos 97, 97 n.41, 101, 107, 110 n.74, 118 n.97
graphe paranomon 164
gymnasium 98 n.43

hetairein/hetairesis 107 n.68, 120
hetairos 111
hippotrophia/hipotrophos 146, 155
homoerotic 3, 72, 101 n.47, 121 n.103
homosexual 63 n.22, 104
honour (τιμή) 22–23, 41, 76, 81, 83, 88–89 n.21, 96, 96 n.39, 104 n.56, 108–109, 119, 126, 132, 134, 137 n.29, 140, 141–143, 145, 149–154, 160, 171, 172 n.38, 175, 185, 187
honourary decrees 146 n.36
honorific inscriptions 146
hope (ἐλπίς) 1, 1 n.1, 66, 68–69, 71, 71 nn.47–48, 159 n.3
hybris 16, 16 n.44, 82, 82 n.5, 83, 93, 93 n.32, 94, 96–100, 102, 102 n.53, 103, 103 n.55, 104, 106–109, 110 n.74, 112, 114, 116, 118, 124–125, 131, 131 n.17, 132, 137 n.29, 145–150, 152, 154, 157, 157 n.45, 178–179, 179 n.52, 180
hypocrisis (actio) 2, 2 n.6, 3

internal audiences  20–21, 42 n.42, 101–102, 102 n.52, 105, 121–122
*isotes*  137
*Ithyphalloi*  104–105

John Chrysostom  9 n.30

*kairos*  58, 86, 168, 184
*kalokagathia*  137 n.27
*kinaidos*  20, 104
*kosmos/kosmios*  24 n.2, 28 n.17, 38, 46, 84, 174, 174 n.44, 175
*krater*  157 n.44
*komos*  99

Labour  129–130
*lampros/lamprotes*  62 n.19, 64, 64 nn.25–26, 65, 69–71, 151, 153–155, 155 n.40
laughter  104 n.57, 106, 108, 177, 178 n.49
'Law and literature movement'  80 n.2, 85
Lazarus, Richard  5
leader/leadership  7, 21, 68, 72, 78–79, 150–151, 154
legitimate envy  4, 22, 123, 125, 128, 128 n.12, 129, 133, 137–138, 140–141, 144, 144 n.35, 145–151, 157–158, 160, 171, 177–178, 180, 182, 187
liturgy/liturgist  88, 123–124, 131, 133 n.19, 134, 141, 143, 146–147, 149–151, 153–155, 163, 170, 173, 173 n.42, 174, 174 nn. 43–44, 182, 186
*logos/logoi*  24, 24 n.2, 25 n.6, 27, 27 n.11, 28 n.17, 34, 38 n.35, 43–44, 44 n.46, 46–49, 49 n.61, 50–52, 55 n.79, 57, 58 n.6, 59, 59 n.11, 60–63, 67, 73 n.51, 78, 86, 90, 92–93, 142, 163, 180

Macedonia  111–112, 112 n.82, 113, 113 n.83, 115, 115 n.88
magic  4, 11, 42 n.42, 49, 49 n.60, 50–51, 59, 59 n.11, 119
medicine  25 n.5, 28 n.17, 49, 49 n.60, 50 n.62, 68 n.36
*megaloprepeia*  62 n.19, 69, 153

*metrios/metriotes*  123, 126, 145, 149–150, 170 n.35, 175, 184, 184 n.55
*mimesis/mimetic*  45, 47, 92
Muses  25 n.6
*physis*  28, 30–31, 49–50, 65, 132–133, 133 n.21, 141–142, 144, 184 n.55

*neanikos/neanieuesthai*  107 n.70
neo-liberalism  129 n.13, 130 n.14
Nicias  21, 62 n.19, 65–66, 66 nn.30–31, 67–69, 71, 78–79, 136 n.25

Olynthus  109–111, 113–116
*opsis*  28–29, 31–33, 35, 38, 41–42, 42 n.42, 44, 57 n.3, 66, 70–71, 79, 92, 121

*paignion*  32 n.25, 55 n.79
painting  26 n.9, 34 n.30, 44, 44 n.47, 45, 45 n.49, 45 n.51, 46, 46 n.52, 48, 48 n.58, 54 n.73, 56 n.80, 64 n.24, 121
*palaestra*  98, 98 n.43, 99–100
*parabasis*  162, 162 n.10
*paroinia*  113
*pathopoiia*  2, 5, 5 n.18, 10, 10 n.32, 11, 13, 17–18, 18 n.48, 22, 38, 40, 49 n.61, 102, 122, 127–128, 150, 176, 189, 191
Peisistratus  156
*peitho*  2–3, 3 nn.8–9, 4, 4 nn.11–12, 4 n.14, 7, 7 n.21, 28–29, 48, 67
performance  2 n.6, 6 n.20, 20–21, 24, 24 n.2, 93, 105, 105 n.63, 106–107, 132, 156–157
*periautologia*  22, 159–160, 165, 167, 167 n.23, 168–169, 171–172, 176, 178–179, 181–184, 186–187
Pericles  21, 59, 59 nn.10–11, 60, 60 n.12, 61–62, 62 n.19, 63–65, 65 n. 29, 66–67, 69, 72–74, 74 n.53, 75, 78–79, 168 n.29, 186, 186 n.58
*phallos*  104–105
*phantasia*  7, 7 n.23, 92
*pharmakon/pharmaka*  28 n.17, 49
*phaulon/phaulos*  68, 69 n.39, 135–136, 136 n.25, 150
*philotimia*  22, 68–69, 69 n.40, 70, 70 n.43, 125–127, 131, 133 n.19, 140, 143,

145–146, 146 n.36, 150–154, 171, 175, 175 n.47
Philip II of Macedonia 111–115, 184–185
*phronema* (φρόνημα) 31, 35, 42–43
*phthonos* (φθόνος) 22, 128, 135–136, 138–142, 144–145, 147, 147 n.37, 148, 150, 158, 163 n.13, 168 n.29, 172, 176–178, 187
Phye 156, 156 n.42
pity 1, 1–2 n.3, 2, 5 n.18, 10–11, 14, 16, 22, 38, 44, 58 n.6, 92, 94, 95 n.38, 102, 106, 106 n.64, 107–108, 110 n.74, 112, 114–115, 120–122, 135, 142, 145, 166, 169, 169 nn.31–32, 179, 179 n.50
*plousioi* 148–150, 184–185
*porneia* 120
*pothos* 2, 21, 46, 46 n.53, 47, 47 nn.54–55, 54, 57, 60, 63, 65–66, 71, 78
*priamel* 24 n.2, 28 n.17, 46, 52, 52 n.68, 53
*proklesis* 100
*prytanis* 66 n.31, 68, 157
public expenses 157
Pygmalion 47 n.56

Rawls, John 128
relevance 88, 88 nn.20–21, 189
rumor (*pheme*) 26 n.9, 117, 117 n.92, 126 n.9

sculpture 46, 47 n.57, 48
shame 9, 20, 89 n.21, 94, 96, 105, 108–109, 116, 121, 144, 151
Sicilian expedition 21, 57, 57 n.1, 65–66, 66 nn.30–32, 68–71, 78, 132
Skinner, Quentin 22, 83, 125–128, 138–139, 139 n.31, 145, 148, 151–152, 190
Solon 20, 20 n.55, 88

*sophron/sophrosyne* 119, 174, 174 n.44
*stasis* 26 n.10, 42, 131, 131 n.17, 139 n.31
*status qualitativus* 26 n.10
*symboulos* 20, 114, 187
symposium 97, 103, 103 n.55, 105–107, 107 n.68, 107 n.71, 109–112, 112 n.82, 113–115, 115 n.88, 116–117, 150, 156–157, 157 n.45
*synegoros/synegoria* 97, 125 n.7, 141, 161, 161 n.9
*syssition* 157, 157 n.44

*taxis* (τάξις) 28 n.17, 42 n.42, 50, 185
*teichoscopia* 53–54
Thatcher, Margaret 123, 129, 129 n.13, 130, 130 n.15, 131, 150, 158
*thauma/thaumaston* 54, 54 n.71, 61, 155 n.38
Theodote 7, 63, 63 n.20, 64
*theoria* 66, 69 n.39, 132, 153–155, 155 n.38
Thirty 15, 111–112, 174, 180
Tholos 157
*thorybos* 86 n.13, 110 n.74
*thysia* 113
*timoria* 76 n.57, 96, 96 n.39
*topos/topoi* 55, 62, 94, 97, 127, 143 n.34, 174, 183
*tropoi* (τρόποι) 29 n.18, 42, 42 n.42
*tryphe* 113, 154
*typos* 29 n.18, 34

Victims Impact Statement (VIS) 94, 94 n.34, 95

*xenia* 110–111, 113, 113 n.83, 114

# Index Auctorum Antiquorum et Locorum

**Achilles Tatius**
1.9.4 — 56 n.81

**Aelian**
*Varia Historia*
12.32 — 24 n.2

**Aelius Aristides**
*Concerning a Remark in Passing* 165 n.19

**Aeschines**
*Against Timarchus (Or. 1)* 88 n.21, 94, 109, 112 n.80, 125 n.6, 126 n.9
25–26 — 119
25 — 20
26 — 20
40 — 119
52–53 — 116
53–62 — 116
54 — 117
57–62 — 117
57 — 120
58 — 117
59 — 118
61 — 121
80–84 — 118 n.98
125–131 — 117 n.92
131 — 20
141–154 — 88 n.18
166 — 14 n.41
*On the embassy (Or. 2)*
4 — 111 n.78
153–158 — 110 n.74
158 — 111 n.78
167–171 — 181
167 — 181
171 — 181
*Against Ctesiphon (Or. 3)*
85 — 123 n.1
241 — 164–165

**Aeschylus**
*Agamemnon*
385 — 47 n.55
385 — 4 n.13
742–743 — 54
*Choephori*
726 — 4 n.13
*Supplices*
1003–1005 — 54

**Alcman**
3.6–12 — 54

**Alexander**
*De figuris*
16.6 — 170 n.35

**Anaximenes**
*Rhetorica ad Alexandrum*
1424a 12–26 — 137 n.27
1440a 35–39 — 147
1441b 16–23 — 86
1442a 6–16 — 170 n.35

**Antiphon**
*Against the Stepmother (Or. 1)*
15 — 121 n.104
*On the murder of Herodes (Or. 5)*
57 — 14 n.39
69 — 14 n.39

**Aristophanes**
*Clouds*
547–8 — 27 n.11
*Lysistrata*
155–156 — 4
*Peace*
734–738 — 162 n.10
*Wasps*
705 — 104

**Aristotle**
*Athenaion Politeia*
53 — 85 n.10

## Index Auctorum Antiquorum et Locorum

| | | | |
|---|---|---|---|
| *De Anima* | | 1388a 36 | 135 |
| 1.403a 3–13 | 38 n.36 | 1389a 9–13 | 77 n.59 |
| 1.403a 29–b 1 | 189 | 1404a 13 | 58 n.6 |
| 2.424a 19 | 32 n.24, 35 n.33 | 1410b 33–34 | 9 n.29 |
| 3.425b 23 | 32 n.24, 35 n.33 | 1415b 36–38 | 178 n.49 |
| 3.434a 29 | 32 n.24, 35 n.33 | 1418b 23–27 | 160 n.5 |
| *Eudemian Ethics* | | *De somniis* | |
| 1224a 39 | 4 n.14 | 460b 4–16 | 40, 71 n.45 |
| *Historia animalium* | | | |
| 539a 32 | 104 | **Cicero** | |
| *Metaphysics* | | *De inventione rhetorica* | |
| 985b 13–19 | 50 | 2.1.1 | 44 |
| *Nicomachean Ethics* | 135 | | |
| 1122b 21–22 | 153 | **Comica adespota (Kock)** | |
| 1149a 24–31 | 40 n.40 | 1213 | 104 |
| 1187a 6 | 46 n.53 | | |
| *Poetics* | | **Democritus** | |
| 1451b 5–11 | 24 n.2 | B 3 DK | 50 |
| 1453b 1–12 | 92 | B 7 DK | 50 |
| *Politics* | 131, 190 | B 33 DK | 50 |
| 1282b 23–30 | 134 n.24 | B 228 DK | 29 n.18 |
| 1295b 21–23 | 168 n.24 | | |
| 1301b 2–14 | 131 | **Demosthenes** | |
| 1302b 1–14 | 131 n.17 | *Olynthiac 2 (Or. 2)* | |
| 1304a 33–38 | 131 n.17 | 19 | 115 n.88 |
| 1318b 27–1319a 3 | 136 | *On the crown (Or. 18)* | 22, 87, 88 n.19, |
| *Rhetoric* | 5, 5 n.16, 5 n.18, | | 168 n.28, 170 |
| | 10–11, 17, 38, 75, | | n.35, 182–183 |
| | 138, 145 | 4 | 164, 184 |
| 1354a 16–17 | 5 | 13 | 164 n.15 |
| 1355b 10 | 24 n.2 | 121 | 172 |
| 1377b 20–24 | 38, 38 n.35 | 169 | 185 |
| 1378a 19–21 | 10, 38 | 170 | 185 |
| 1378a 30 | 76 n.57 | 171–172 | 186 |
| 1378a 30–33 | 76 | 173–174 | 184–185 |
| 1378a 33–35 | 76 | 173–178 | 185 |
| 1378b 35–1379a 4 | 76 | 179 | 186 |
| 1379b 4–5 | 76 | 279 | 164 n.15 |
| 1379b 7–10 | 76 | 299 | 170 n.35 |
| 1385b 11–15 | 135 | 304–305 | 169 n.34 |
| 1386a 29–35 | 14 n.40 | 305 | 164 n.15 |
| 1386b 16–20 | 135 | 315 | 164 n.15 |
| 1387a 16 | 130 n.15 | 320–321 | 184 |
| 1387b 28–32 | 131 | 321 | 184 n.55 |
| 1387b 29 | 168 n.24 | *On the false embassy (Or. 19)* | 19, 94, 116 |
| 1388a 1–14 | 137 | | n.90 |
| 1388a 35 | 143 | 75 | 86 n.13 |

| | | | |
|---|---|---|---|
| 113 | 181 | *Against Aristocrates* (*Or.* 23) | |
| 193–195 | 113 | 18–19 | 86 n.13 |
| 195 | 113 n.84 | *Against Timocrates* (*Or.* 24) | |
| 196–199 | 109 | 171 | 179 |
| 196 | 109 | 218 | 14 n.41 |
| 197 | 115 | *Against Spoudias* (*Or.* 41) | |
| 198 | 115–116 | 17 | 86 n.13 |
| 305–306 | 114 | *Against Phaenippus* (*Or.* 42) | |
| 306 | 114 | 22 | 146 |
| 309 | 114 | 24 | 146 |
| *Against Leptines* (*Or.* 20) 22, 127, 141, 143 | | *Against Evergus and Mnesibulus* (*Or.* 47) | |
| 140–142 | 141–142 | 80 | 14 n.41 |
| *Against Meidias* (*Or.* 21) 19, 22, 87, 87 n.17, 110 n.74, 125, 127–129, 141, 144–146, 148–157 | | *Against Timotheus* (*Or.* 49) | |
| | | 63 | 86 n.13 |
| | | *Against Nicostratus* (*Or.* 53) | |
| | | 15–16 | 101 |
| | | *Against Conon* (*Or.* 54) | 83, 94, 98 n.42, 100, 103–109, 110 n.74, 137 n.29, 157 |
| 34 | 150 | | |
| 62–65 | 153 | | |
| 62–66 | 150 | 2 | 106 |
| 66 | 148 | 3–4 | 157 n.45 |
| 67–68 | 153 | 8 | 105 n.62, 106 n.66, 108 |
| 69 | 43 n.45, 153 | | |
| 71–73 | 82 | 9 | 96, 106 |
| 73 | 93 | 11 | 96, 106 |
| 83–96 | 145 | 12 | 106 |
| 112 | 148 | 20 | 106 |
| 123 | 15 | 34 | 107 |
| 131 | 153 | 39 | 107 |
| 133 | 150, 153 | 40 | 109 |
| 143–149 | 152 | 42 | 106, 108 n.73 |
| 143 | 152 | 43 | 96, 108 |
| 153 | 148, 153–154 | *Against Neaera* [*Or.* 59] | 87, 120 n.99, 124 n.3 |
| 154–157 | 145 | | |
| 158–159 | 148, 154 | 5 | 14 n.42 |
| 158 | 154 | 33 | 112 |
| 167 | 123 | 35 | 112 |
| 174 | 150, 153–154 | 37 | 112 |
| 196 | 142 | *Funeral Speech* (*Or.* 60) | |
| 201 | 148 | 23 | 172 n.37 |
| 208 | 149 | *Epistulae* | |
| 209 | 148 | 2.24 | 170 n.35 |
| 211 | 148 | | |
| 212–213 | 148 | **Dialexeis (Dissoi Logoi)** | |
| *Against Androtion* (*Or.* 22) | | 3.10 | 46 n.52 |
| 57 | 179 | | |

## Diodorus Siculus
16.7.2                 123 n.1

## Dionysius of Halicarnassus
[Art of Rhetoric]
8                       168 n.28
Demosthenes
11                    103
13                    103
On Imitation
fr. VI, pp. 203–204, U.–R. 44 n.47
Lysias
7                       85 n.11, 90
Thucydides
2.45               168 n.29

## Empedocles
B 23DK            45 n.49
B 115DK          30 n.21
B 115DK          28 n.16

## Euripides
Andromache
627–630           4
Bacchae
430                 136 n.25
853                 43 n.43
Hippolytus
525–526           54
Ion
834–835           136 n.25
Troades
987–988           56 n.80
991–996           56 n.80

## Gorgias
On not being (frr. 1–5) 24 n.4
Funeral Speech (frr. 5a–6) 172
6                       46, 47 n.54, 172 n.37
Encomium of Helen (fr. 11) 21, 24 n.2, 25, 25 n.5, 26 n.10, 29, 31, 32 n.25, 49, 51, 55, 56 n.80, 72, 72 n.49, 79
1                       26, 46
2                       28 n.16, 52, 58, 68 n.36
3–4                 56 n.80
4                       27 n.11, 30, 30 n.20, 45, 45 n.50, 53, 56 n.80
5                       30–31, 46, 52–53, 62 n.18
6                       30, 52
8–14               27
8                       44, 46–47, 52, 55 n.79
9–10              29, 58 n.6
9–14              43, 47
9                       28, 44, 44 n.46
10                    42 n.42, 50–51, 59 n.11
11                    25 n.6, 47, 51, 90
12                    30, 52
13                    25 n.5, 29, 47–48, 51, 55 n.79, 67, 90
14                    28 n.17, 42 n.42, 48
15–19            24, 27
15                    28, 29 n.18, 30, 42, 52, 55 n.79
16–17           36–37, 52
16–19           29
16                    29, 36, 38, 41, 42 n.42, 75
17–18           36
17                    29, 31, 35, 37, 42 34 n.30, 35–36, 44, 47, 54
18                   
19                    28 n.14, 28 n.16, 30, 41 n.41, 52–53
21                    26, 55 n.79
Defence of Palamedes (fr. 11a) 24–25 n.4, 25 n.5, 51, 90, 162 n.12
3                       163 n.13, 173
15 172–173
22                    173
25                    43, n.45

| | | | |
|---|---|---|---|
| 26 | 27 n.11 | *On the estate of Philoctemon (Or. 6)* | |
| 28 | 162–163 | 60 | 147 |
| 29 | 173 | Fragments | |
| 32 | 172, 172  n.38 | fr. 131 Sauppe | 174 n.44 |
| 33 | 58 n.6 | | |

**Heliodorus**
*Aethiopica*
3.7.5                    56 n.81

**Hermogenes**
*On the method of power*
25                       165 n.17
442.6ff.                 168 n.28

**Herodotus**
1.60                     156
3.80                     168 n.24

**Hesiod**
*Theogony*               51

**Hippias of Elis**
B 16 DK                  140

**Hippocrates & Corpus Hippocraticum**
*De arte*                68 n.36
11.2                     25 n.5
*On ancient medicine*    50 n.62
*On the sacred disease*  3 49

**Homer**
*Iliad*
3.141–160                54
18.247–248               39
22.131–137               39
*Odyssey*
4.261                    27 n.14

**Ibycus**
287.1–4 *PMG*            54

**Isaeus**
*On the estate of Menecles (Or. 2)*
18                       181 n.53
36                       181 n.53

**Isocrates**
*To Demonicus (Or. 1)*
1                        136 n.25
*Nicocles (Or. 3)*
6                        4 n.14
18                       168 n.24
*Panegyricus (Or. 4)*
8                        55 n.77
48                       4 n.14
*Euagoras (Or. 9)*
34                       58 n.5
39                       172 n.37
73–74                    48 n.58
*Encomium of Helen (Or. 10)*
14                       26 n.8
30                       172 n.37
*Antidosis (Or. 15)*     130, 131 n.16,
                         133, 182, 182
                         n.54, 183
4                        182
5                        182
7                        48 n.58, 182
8                        163, 182
13                       168 n.26, 171,
                         182
141–146                  160 n.5
141                      183
145                      182
150                      182
155                      182
158                      182
254                      4 n.14
302–303                  183
*Against Lochites (Or. 20)* 137 n.29

**[Longinus]**
*On the sublime*
9.2                      59
15.8                     91 n.24
15.9                     92

**Lycurgus**
*Against Leocrates (Or. 1)*
58                               14 n.41–42,

**Lysias**
*On the Murder of Eratosthenes (Or. 1)* 85
                                 n.11, 87, 89 n.21,
                                 178 n.49
*Funeral speech (Or. 2)*
19                               4 n.14
*Against Simon (Or. 3)*          98 n.42, 99, 157
                                 n.45
*On a Wound by Premeditation (Or. 4)* 66
                                 n.33, 120, 157
                                 n.45
*Against Theomnestus 1 (Or. 10)*
29                               14 n.41
*Against Eratosthenes (Or. 12)*
58                               14 n.41
80                               14 n.41
90                               14 n.41
*Against Alcibiades 1 (Or. 14)*
8                                14 n.42
*For Mantitheus (Or. 16)*        174–175
3                                175
10–11                            175
18                               175, 175 n.46
*For Polystratus (Or. 20)*
1                                14 n.41
*Defence against a charge of taking bribes*
  *(Or. 21)*                     173
7                                174
16                               174
19                               174
23–24                            174
*On the refusal of a pension (Or. 24)* 176
1                                178
2                                176–177
3                                178
7                                179
16                               179
18                               178
25                               180
26                               180

*Defence against a charge of subverting*
  *the democracy (Or. 25)*
1–5                              14 n.39
5                                15 n.43
*Against Philon (Or. 31)*
11                               14 n.42
*Against Diogeiton (Or. 32)* 87, 87 n.16
*Against Teisis (fr. 279 Carey)* 94, 97–103,
                                 118, 118 n.96, 137
                                 n.29, 157 n.45
5                                99

**Pindar**
*Olympian Odes*
O. 6.16                          47 n.54
*Pythian Odes*
P. 3.47ff.                       49 n.60
P. 4.216–219                     4
*Nemean Odes*
N. 5.1–6                         48 n.58

**Plato**
*Apology*                        168 n.28
*Charmides*
155c–d                           54 n.73
156b                             50
*Cratylus*
419b                             46 n.53
420a9–b4                         56 n.81
*Crito*
49e–51e                          4 n.14
*Gorgias*
456b 1–5                         49
*Hippias Minor*
363c                             24 n.2
*Menexenus*
242a                             172 n.37
*Meno*
76c–e                            32–33
*Phaedrus*                       4 n.12, 35 n.31,
                                 56, 56 n.81, 57
                                 n.3, 101 n.47
267b 1–2                         55
267c                             58 n.6
*Philebus*
39a–b                            32 n.24, 35 n.33

*Protagoras*
317a–b                  24 n.2
*Symposium*
198a                    12
*Theaetetus*
191c–d                  32 n.24, 35 n.33

**Plutarch**
*Moralia*
345E                    160 n.5
419A                    36
537A                    167–168
537E                    161, 161 n.7
537F                    167
538B                    168
538B–C                  169
539D–E                  160
540C                    168, 168 n.29
540D                    168
541A                    168
541C                    168
542E                    169
543A–B                  169
543F                    169
544F                    168
681A–F                  56 n.81
682F–683A               34
734F–735B               35

**Quintilian**
*Institutio oratoria*
6.2.30                  91 n.24
6.2.31                  91 n.24
8.3.62                  92
9.3.65                  139 n.31
11.1.15–26              165 n.17
11.1.16                 168 n.28
11.1.22                 168 n.28

**Sappho**
fr. 1V                  121 n.104
fr. 16                  53 n.69
fr. 31V                 54

**Sextus Empiricus**
*Adversus mathematicos*
9.19                    36

**Sophocles**
*Ajax*
157–161                 158
157                     172
*Antigone*
354f.                   4 n.14
*Philoctetes*
102–103                 4 n.14
*Trachiniae*
1253                    66 n.31

**Theognis**
1283 West               121 n.104

**Theophrastus**
*De sensibus*
7                       33, 33 n.29

**Thucydides**
1                       73 n.51, 77, 78 n.60
1.10                    71 n.46
1.22.1                  58
1.24.6                  76 n.57
1.80ff.                 73 n.51
1.84.3–4                73 n.51
2                       21, 57, 59–60, 72, 72 n.49, 74, 79
2.11.7–8                74
2.11.8                  75
2.16.2                  73 n.51
2.20.2                  76
2.21.2–3                77
2.22.1                  59, 74
2.39.4                  61
2.43.1                  61
2.49                    66 n.31
2.59.1                  59
2.60.5–6                186 n.58
2.64.5                  62 n.19, 64
2.65.8–10               186
2.65.10                 65 n.29
2.72–74                 78
3.37.4                  136 n.25
3.38.4                  60
3.38.24–25              27 n.11
3.45.5                  71 n.48

| | | | |
|---|---|---|---|
| 3.82.4 | 139 n.31 | 6.54.2 | 64 n.25 |
| 6 | 60 | 7 | 60 |
| 6.11.4 | 68 | 7.77.2 | 68, 136 n.25 |
| 6.12.1 | 62 n.19 | | |
| 6.12.2–3 | 62 n.19 | **Tzetzes** | |
| 6.14 | 66 n.31 | *Historiarum variarum Chiliades* | |
| 6.14.1 | 68 | 6.56 | 116 n.90 |
| 6.16 | 128, 132 | | |
| 6.16.1–4 | 69 | **Xenophon** | |
| 6.16.2 | 69 n.39 | *Anabasis* | 160 n.5 |
| 6.16.3 | 65 | *Cyropaedia* | |
| 6.20–23 | 65 | 2.2.24 | 136 n.25 |
| 6.24.2 | 67 | *Memorabilia* | |
| 6.24.3 | 66 | 1.2.10 | 4 n.14 |
| 6.30 | 69 | 2.6.13 | 59 n.11 |
| 6.31.1 | 69–70 | 3.10 | 45 n.48 |
| 6.31.3 | 69 n.39 | 3.11.2–3 | 7, 62 |
| 6.31.4 | 71 | 4.2.31 | 136 n.25 |
| 6.31.6 | 70–71 | 11.1.1 | 63 |
| 6.46 | 71 n.45 | | |

www.ingramcontent.com/pod-product-compliance
Lightning Source LLC
Chambersburg PA
CBHW031812220426
43662CB00007B/610